AUGUSTINE

The Scattered and Gathered Self

AUGUSTINE

The Scattered and Gathered Self

SANDRA LEE DIXON

St. Louis, Missouri

Biblical quotations, unless otherwise noted, are from the *New Revised Standard Version Bible*, copyright 1989, Division of Christian Education of the National Council of Churches of Christ in the USA. Used by permission.

Portions of Augustine's *Confessions* are © Henry Chadwick 1991. Reprinted from *Saint Augustine's Confessions*, translated by Henry Chadwick (1991) by permission of Oxford University Press.

Quotations from Paula Frederiksen Landes, *Augustine on Romans: Propositions from the Epistle to the Romans, Unfinished Commentary on the Epistle to the Romans*, are used with permission of Scholars Press.

Quotations from Augustine, *Confessions*, 3 vols., ed. James J. O'Donnell, are used with permission of James J. O'Donnell.

Cover design: Scott Tjaden
Cover art: "The Arrival of St. Augustine in Milan" by Benozzo Gozzoli.
        By permission of Scala/Art Resource, N.Y.
Interior design: Rhonda Dohack
Art direction: Michael Domínguez

This book is printed on acid-free, recycled paper.

Visit Chalice Press on the World Wide Web at
www.chalicepress.com

10 9 8 7 6 5 4 3 2 1   99 00 01 02 03

Library of Congress Cataloging–in–Publication Data

Dixon, Sandra Lee, 1955-
    Augustine : the scattered and gathered self / by Sandra Lee Dixon.
        p.   cm.
    Includes bibliographical references.
    ISBN 0-8272-0024-2
    1. Augustine, Saint, Bishop of Hippo.   2. Augustine, Saint, Bishop of Hippo—Psychology.   3. Christian saints—Algeria—Hippo (Extinct city) Biography.   I. Title.
    BR1720.A9D58   1999   99–29766
    270.2'092—dc21   C1P
    [B]

Contents

Acknowledgments

I have taken an interpretive approach to social-scientific understanding of Augustine's early life and work in order to explore a marvelous apprehension of meaning, self-expression, collective and individual life, and the intersection of what is written and what may be lived. My hermeneutic approach limits claims to definitive findings and timeless certainty and encourages the use of the subjunctive voice. Bolder declarations sometimes appeal to me as both a writer and a reader, but I remember often that psychological interpretations of historical people cannot produce "knowledge" of the solidity we expect, for instance, regarding birth dates and authorship. I have concluded that the enticement of psychohistory should lead the curious scholar to utterly engaging activity completed by thoroughgoing caution in attempting to open for others the treasures created from discovery.

As I have pursued this fascinating effort, I am fortunate to have had the support of many people, especially my colleagues in the Department of Religious Studies at the University of Denver. Only some of their assistance can be acknowledged if I am not to write another monograph. I am grateful to William B. Gravely and Carl A. Raschke for reading the manuscript and offering salutary suggestions that moved the project forward at crucial moments; to Gregory Allen Robbins for many enlightening conversations on Augustine and early Christianity, not to mention the loan of his valuable copy of James J. O'Donnell's three-volume edition of Augustine's *Confessions*; and to Frederick Greenspahn and Ginette Ishimatsu for various kinds of help in the breach and for their tireless voices, intertwining unbeknownst to each other in the one-word chant called "Book." The students and administrative assistants who have come and gone the last few years have made possible the turning of the "pile of papers" into a finished product. My thanks to all of them: Eric Adams, Margie Arms, John Burke, Natalie Gamboa, Fay Jeys, Luke Johnson, Neil Kromer, Jack Lowe, Tapiwa Mucherera, Arlene Sgoutas, and Kay Gardner Pyle. Fay Jeys inspires particular appreciation for creating, against the odds, an office both friendly and workable. I must make special mention also of Benjamin Bennett-Carpenter, Jeanne Hoeft, and Mark A. Peckler, who read the manuscript and whose comments loosened up my thoughts, refined my prose, and lifted my spirits. In addition, I thank the Ph.D. Colloquium in Religion and Psychological Studies of 1997—Margie Arms, Larry Kent Graham, Jeanne

Hoeft, Byoung Hoon Kim, Joretta L. Marshall, Tapiwa Mucherera, Bernard Spilka, and Kay Gardner Pyle—for reading the first two chapters and offering very helpful suggestions.

I am grateful to our just-retired dean, Roscoe Hill, for his wise support of mini-sabbaticals, even for junior faculty, so that scholars can push forward substantial and demanding projects. I appreciate the Faculty Research Fund grant from the University of Denver that allowed me to delve into the libraries of Northwestern University, the University of Chicago, McCormick Theological Seminary, the Lutheran School of Theology, and Jesuit School of Theology in Chicago. In addition, on this trip I was able to meet with the faculty who first sponsored my work, Don S. Browning, Bernard McGinn, and Marvin Zonis of the University of Chicago. I thank them and Richard A. Shweder, also at the University of Chicago, for making the foray into psychological and cultural study of a historic figure as safe as it could be for a starting scholar.

I am also fortunate to have the support of many people outside of my current and past institutional homes. Jon Berquist's reassurance and clarity as the academic editor at Chalice Press have been invaluable, as were the comments of the Press's reviewer. Terrence Shaw's detailed reading of chapters 1 and 2 yielded marked improvements. Hearty thanks to him for his insights and to Eugene A. Hilliard, David Andrew Mueller, and Julianne Elaine Puckett for spending part of a Saturday helping me with the bibliography. The library of the Iliff School of Theology has been indispensable, as has the encouragement and support of the Iliff faculty, present and past. Friends who usually remain anonymous are also much in my thoughts of gratitude as I finish this work, as are many others, who, undeterred by the potential pitfalls of social scientifically informed biography, have encouraged me as I try to understand Augustine. Remaining problems in the study that follows are undoubtedly mine alone—surely one of these fine people has already pointed them out to me.

This book is dedicated to my nieces and nephews, Michelle Dixon, Jessica Whitcomb-Trance, Jonathan Whitcomb-Dixon, and Caleb Whitcomb-Dixon, with thanks to my parents Sally and Norman Dixon, and to the parents on the front line with the younger generation, especially Michael Dixon and Deborah Whitcomb, for helping us to be who we are.

Abbreviations List

ACI	Robert J. O'Connell, *Art and the Christian Intelligence in St. Augustine*
ACW	*Ancient Christian Writers*
Ad Simp.	*De diversis quaestionibus ad Simplicianum* (*To Simplician—on Various Questions*)
AOH	Peter Brown, *Augustine of Hippo*
AOS	Heinz Kohut, *The Analysis of the Self*
BA	Bibliothèque augustinienne, Oeuvres de saint Augustin
CA	*Contra Academicos* (*Against the Academics*)
CLP	*Contra litteras Petiliani donatistae Cirtensis, episcopi* (*Answer to Letters of Petilian, the Donatist Bishop of Cirta*)
Conf.	*Confessiones* (*Confessions*)
CTh	*Codex Theodosianus*
DBC	*De bono conjugali* (*On the Good of Marriage*)
DBV	*De beata vita* (*The Happy Life*)
DCD	*De civitate dei* (*The City of God*)
DDC	*De doctrina christiana* (*On Christian Doctrine*)
DLA	*De libero arbitrio* (*On Free Will*)
DM	*De magistro* (*The Teacher*)
DME	*De moribus ecclesiae catholicae* (*On the Morals of the Catholic Church*)
DO	*De ordine* (*Divine Providence and the Problem of Evil* or *On Order*)
DUC	*De utilitate credendi* (*The Usefulness of Belief*)
Enn.	Plotinus, *Enneads*
Ep.	Augustine, *Epistolae* (*Letters*)
FOC	*Fathers of the Church*
HDA	Heinz Kohut, *How Does Analysis Cure?*
In Johann	*In epistolam Joannis ad Parthos tractatus X*

Inch. Ex.	*Epistolae ad romanos inchoata expositio* (*Unfinished Commentary on the Epistle to the Romans*)
JSSR	*Journal for the Scientific Study of Religion*
NPNF	*Nicene and Post-Nicene Fathers of the Christian Church*
PL	*Patrologiae Cursus Completus, Series Latina*, ed. J. P. Migne
PCPD	Psalmus contra partem Donati
Propp.	*Expositio quarundam propositionum ex epistola ad romanos* (*Propositions from the Epistle to the Romans*)
ROS	Heinz Kohut, *The Restoration of the Self*
RSV	*Revised Standard Version of the Bible*
S	Augustine, *Sermons*
SAC	Robert J. O'Connell, *Saint Augustine's Confessions*
SAE	Robert J. O'Connell, *Saint Augustine's Early Theory of Man*
SE	*Standard Edition of the Complete Psychological Works of Sigmund Freud*
Sol.	*Soliloquia* (*Soliloquies*)
SFS1	Heinz Kohut, *The Search for the Self*, vol. 1
SFS2	Heinz Kohut, *The Search for the Self*, vol. 2
Vita	*Augustini vita scripta a Possidio episcopo* (*Life of Saint Augustine Written by the Bishop Possidius*)
WLA	Peter Brown, *The World of Late Antiquity*

CHAPTER 1

Augustine for His Time and Ours

Imagine what a Javanese saying proposes—a "water buffalo listening to an orchestra." Does the water buffalo hear a symphony? Does it even notice melody? harmony? dissonance? Could the image apply, as the anthropologist Clifford Geertz suggested, to all of us who sense that "the events through which we live are forever outrunning the power of our ordinary, everyday moral, emotional, and intellectual concepts to construe them"?[1] Do we hear music in our lives—or just incomprehensible sounds? Even if the human intellect can be clumsy, perhaps some of us are less like water buffalo than the rest. Maybe one person or another actually hears a symphony. Can we learn from such a person? Can we break away from plodding in time to an unrecognized rhythm? Can we awaken from unnoticed strains floating incoherently through our senses and come to hear a symphony?

Geertz suggests that religion can make the sounds around us more musical and human listeners more confident of the differences between themselves and their animal kindred. He proposes in other writings that religion can be integrated into ways of comprehending our social and personal lives.[2] This integration can give it power for the human race as well as for individuals.

But how would the integration of religion in life and history work? Even within a religiously oriented life, a person can change how deeply convictions are held and how widely they are applied. That is, their forcefulness and scope can fluctuate.[3] If we turn to experts for help in understanding the integration of religion in life, we find that their descriptions of the processes of religious influence on people and societies proliferate continually. One might resign oneself to working in flooded fields and eating grass like a water buffalo rather than attempt to find the answer to this

1

question. But not if one has studied and reflected on the life and thought of Augustine.

Saint Augustine, as he is widely known, was not a water buffalo. Amidst all the vagaries of epistemology and interpretation in the post-modern world, one can still stake this claim. Even if one disagrees with him, rejects his ideas, or positively excoriates him, one has to admit that he described human life powerfully and inspired many readers with the hope for participation of humans in the love of God. If one has attended long enough to the passion of his thought, one can imagine him saying impatiently, "None of us are water buffalo! We are souls, created in the image of God! We are human beings, fallen away from our heavenly homes, yes, but drawn by God's love to become pilgrims making the journey to our eternal resting place in God. How often must I say this? How shall I find the words to show you what you really are, and what this world is? I will try again, and perhaps God will give me words to speak to you…"

Augustine wrote the powerful symphonic work, his *Confessions*, to speak of his own experience of the integration of religion in life and personal history.[4] His richly patterned answer to the question is one to take seriously, one from which to learn, even 1,600 years after he wrote it. Although we cannot import his answer wholesale into our own lives, Augustine exposed enough of his feelings and thoughts to the scrutiny of other people that we can compose for ourselves an understanding of religion in his emotional and intellectual life. The effort to do so may show us the processes by which religion can shape our own lives.

But why choose Augustine's life and thought as the subject through which to explore religion's influence? The power and longevity of the *Confessions* is the first and most obvious reason. The fullness of metaphors and symbols describing human life on earth and the intersection of grand patterns of thought with the retelling of small incidents provoke reflection and demand our engagement to understand them. More important, the *Confessions* portrays the struggles that ensue on trying to find meaning in life. We might actually be able to see our own lives and perplexities in the struggles of this man to know, as he says elsewhere, God and his soul.[5]

Augustine's legacy, moreover, has permeated European and American culture. For instance, Augustine himself was a psychological thinker. He explored human thought processes and patterns of feeling and cogently expressed his comprehension of them. In addition, modern psychologists in the United States have been influenced by his work. William James in his *Varieties of Religious Experience* mentioned Augustine as a paradigm case of the "divided self."[6] Erik Erikson remarked on Augustine and his identity crisis in the widely read *Young Man Luther*.[7] Erikson's contribution, although often challenged, had to be acknowledged by everyone in psychoanalytic camps and outposts. The influence of Augustine might be lurking in the thought of any scholar of psychology.

Augustine's influence on the beliefs and practices of Christians, even today, is incalculable. His theological arguments undergird key elements of both Protestant and Catholic thought. The story of his conversion in the *Confessions* is often taken as a paradigm for later accounts of conversion and later conversion experiences.[8] The *Confessions* itself has been deemed the earliest introspective autobiography and one of the great examples of the genre.[9]

Lastly, perversely, but crucially, the *Confessions* leaves us at first unsatisfied. Frustration keeps provoking questions about the text and thereby attaches us to it. For instance, why should a volume divided into thirteen relatively short "books" (what we today would call chapters) devote the first nine of them to a man's life story, the last three to theology, philosophy, and biblical interpretation (and a rather odd interpretation at that), and one to—well, what is book 10 devoted to? It may be seen as a meditation on the problems of Augustine's present moment. Yet it exhibits his rather strange concern as a bishop—in a region of great ecclesiastical and political conflict—about his own tendency to be distracted from prayer by a spider trapping flies (X.xxxv.lvii).[10] Do such concerns in book 10 give evidence of a mind a little distorted by religion? Has the author manifested a neurotic response to human curiosity?

The answer in psychological studies of religion in Augustine's life sometimes has been yes, Augustine responded neurotically to normal human life. Some authors, drawn by the many expressions of emotion in the text, have concentrated on various hints of neurosis. They find in Augustine's words much evidence to confirm that his life fit the theory of psychopathology of their choice.

But others have argued that such inquiries have taken the wrong tack and ought to pursue a different course.[11] Such is my strategy. Although I have been instructed by psychological studies of Augustine as abnormal or as arrested in development, I am turning the inquiry in a different direction.

My interpretation of Augustine's life and work holds that the conscious and unconscious currents that probably formed in his life in response to cultural and social influences led him to struggle with the best ideas that his culture had to offer him, and that he lived out his conscious and unconscious struggles until they resolved themselves sufficiently for him to take up lay and clerical social roles of a dedicated Christian. In these roles he continued to express and to salve emotional stresses about his own worth and the reliability of his ideals while he developed tremendously persuasive and powerful intellectual lines of thought. One of his especially revealing lines of thought reverts to the idea of earthly life as subject to many, many stimuli, and heavenly life, toward which people strive, as focused on the one God. The ideas and images that cluster around the notions of the many and the One turn them into symbols that connect intelligibly many other ideas and images available in Augustine's culture. They helped him discover an intelligent perception of his life and world that a water buffalo could never glimpse. Moreover, they seem to have allowed him expression of unconscious personal distresses about what self psychology will call grandiosity and idealizing as well as expression of imagined resolution of his residual sorrows. Resounding through conscious and unconscious aspects of his being, the symbols "the many" and "the One" carried Christianity, as he discovered it and refashioned it, through the harmonies and discords of his life.

What were the influences and experiences that combined and recombined to lead Augustine to Christianity as a source for his powerful and complex descriptions of human life? How did Christianity and his understanding of human life help him cope with the many challenges that confronted him? How did they become so deeply integrated in his way of life, his writings, his actions?

These questions encourage the exploration of Augustine's past and the many startling inquiries it provokes. What shall we make of his youthful enjoyment of the racy atmosphere of Carthage during his advanced studies in the 370s of the Common Era? Can we make sense of why, in his late teens, he decided to be a Manichean heretic, then stayed with that legally proscribed and intellectually unsatisfying sect? What can we comprehend of his life with a woman, to whom he was not married, from the time he was about seventeen until he was well advanced in his profession as a teacher and a city's rhetorician shortly after he reached age thirty? How shall we comprehend his separation from her to marry up the social ladder after he had traveled to Milan to advance his career, his liaison with another woman as he waited for the marriage date, and his renunciation of all sex at thirty-one in 386 C.E. when he committed himself to Christian baptism? What happened then to the ambitions that led him from North Africa, where he was born and raised, to Rome and then Milan, the seat of the Western Roman Empire at the time?

The question about the influences on Augustine also requires some attention to the development of his thought in the years not discussed in the *Confessions*. What can we know about the years after his mother Monica's death in 387 in Ostia and his return from Italy to North Africa? What insight can we gain into his respite as a layman devoted to Christian life in community with others like himself? What was he like as a priest after his ordination in 391? What sort of life did he have as a bishop after his predecessor's death in 396?

These points of inquiry turn attention away from a narrow focus on Augustine's conversion experience as presented in the *Confessions*. His conversion has claimed much of the spotlight in psychological interpretations of Augustine thus far, and it is important to the story he tells. Yet in light of the attention to other sources of information about Augustine and his life and thought, the conversion scene in book 8 of the *Confessions* need not take center stage. Some scholars argue that, while vivid and memorable, it is not the linchpin of the *Confessions* in any case.[12] For the moment I would raise the simple question, Who would care about Augustine's conversion if he had not gone on to write his many volumes and to remain an imposing figure in history as a bishop, a pastor of souls, and an advocate in the great debates of the church and the state in his era? The image of dramatic conversion is not what is at stake in the psychological understanding of Augustine. How his acceptance of Christianity permeated his life so completely and orchestrated his views of himself and his world is instead my interest for this study.

Preparing a New Approach to Studying Augustine

As I explore the answers to my questions, I depart significantly from previous studies of Augustine that have employed the social sciences and especially psychology. Although their usefulness to my inquiry will be evident to readers who know them, I am answering the call, made many times, for a more complex and sensitive interpretive framework. A brief review will help readers see why a departure is necessary and how the way has been prepared for an advance in psychological interpretation of Augustine's life and writings.

From the early beginnings of modern psychological studies of Augustine, prior to 1960, we have a few scattered essays, two of which became very influential. The longest, *Augustinus: Eine Psychographie* by Bernhard Legewie, has had the least impact, perhaps because it is the only one not published in English. Moreover, Legewie's theoretical concerns with the whole personality and character of the adult Augustine fell outside the then developing Freudianism that would inform later studies.[13] Shortly after Legewie's book appeared, E. R. Dodds wrote the much more widely cited article, "Augustine's Confessions: A Study of Spiritual Maladjustment." He set the tone for two major themes of the first collection of psychological studies of Augustine: Freudianism and psychopathologizing. Although Dodds sidesteps direct reliance on Freud, the key Freudian notions of the importance of relationships of parents and children and of their enduring influence on the psyche are clear: "One need not have studied Freud to recognise in this exceptional relationship to his mother one of the determining factors in Augustine's life story." This "determining factor" of Augustine's relationship to his mother Monica does not assure psychological well-being from Dodds's point of view: "From this springs his inability to find happiness in the love of women; from this his desperate pursuit—in philosophy, in friendship, at last in religion—of an elusive substitute for that happiness."[14] Ultimately, Freudianism and psychopathologizing will prove to be too narrow a foundation for understanding Augustine.

The first fully Freudian article on Augustine came from Charles Kligerman in 1957. The Freudian influence added to Dodds's psychopathologizing the tendencies to infantilize the person studied and to reduce many aspects of the subject's life and culture to the results of psychological processes. Kligerman notes the aspects of the *Confessions* most likely to fit in his Freudian framework of interpretation, like the "spontaneous quality" of the text, the important role of Augustine's mother in the story, and Augustine's discussions of his adolescent and young adult sexuality.[15] Kligerman uses specific Freudian strategies, like reliance on details that might seem tangential to the main point, interpretation of stories of significance to the analysand, and more general psychoanalytic or even psychiatric considerations, such as a profile (from the 1950s) of a relationship between spouses.[16] The possibility that the Freudian strategies, lifted from psychoanalytic practice and overlaid on the *Confessions*, might be anachronistic, and therefore obfuscating, does not appear to have troubled Kligerman.

A similar confidence in psychoanalytic approaches and a continued tendency to pathologize Augustine continued in the first major collection of articles, which appeared six years after Kligerman's essay. The symposium, entitled "St. Augustine's Confessions: Perspectives and Inquiries,"[17] set an agenda for most of the psychological studies of Augustine.

The tendency, found in Dodds's and Kligerman's articles, toward pathologizing Augustine's life story is easily inferred from the title of editor Paul Pruyser's contribution to the symposium: "Psychological Examination: Augustine." Pruyser presents his study as a clinical report covering various areas of Augustine's life that would be of psychiatric interest, such as "Perception," "Thought Processes," and "Emotion."[18] The pathologizing approach extended into the studies more broadly named and conceived. In a scathing article, innocuously titled "Some Thoughts on Reading Augustine's *Confessions*," David Bakan accuses Augustine of "compulsive sexuality."[19] Amidst Bakan's other harsh claims ("Augustine falls very short"; "Augustine was one of the vainest of men because he so sought to concern himself only with himself"[20]) the charge of compulsive sexuality implies a severe disorder. Exemplifying the tendency to infantilize Augustine, Bakan is almost refreshingly blunt. He holds that Augustine's "severe distinction of lust from affective involvement is in itself indicative of immaturity."[21] Bakan here exposes his ignorance of how very widely spread that "immaturity," if it may be called such, was in Augustine's culture.[22]

Philip Woollcott attempted to surpass such pathologizing in his article "Some Considerations of Creativity and Religious Experience in St. Augustine of Hippo." Woollcott keeps in mind the idea that "Augustine… *used* his conflicts."[23] He opens: "To determine from his life a great man's psychopathology is easy—it is usually glaring. To determine the development of his genius, there is the rub. Psychological studies of great men suggest that they achieve their greatness both because of and in spite of intense conflict."[24] He concludes: "Like other great historical figures, he seemed to have had the uncanny ability to play out his problem solving on a cosmic scale."[25] Nonetheless, Woollcott feels at liberty to point out ways in which Augustine did not reach psychoanalytic par. For instance, he claims: "It is questionable whether Augustine ever successfully integrated his own masculine strivings."[26] But most of the criticisms that infantilize Augustine spring from the oedipal analyses of his life.

The oedipally based infantilizations of Augustine may be more or less explicit. The less explicit refer obliquely to some aspect of the oedipal conflict as formulated by Freud. For instance, Pruyser introduces the notion of the oedipal conflict through a reference to the superego. The superego, according to Freud, emerges from a boy's oedipal conflict. In this conflict, he is sexually attracted to his mother and frightened of his father's power to retaliate for his desire to take his father's place. Rather than risk punishment by his father and the loss of his father's love, argued Freud, the boy gives up his sexual attachment to his mother, allies himself with his father, and takes on his father's moral values. His anger about his father's favored status with the mother turns into the unconscious power of conscience. The superego is the part of the personality, Freud said, that retains the father's values and exercises the function of conscience.[27] Although Pruyser does not carefully analyze Augustine's oedipal conflict,[28] he does suggest that Augustine never fully renounced his attachment to his mother and never completely identified with his father: "His lengthy description of his resistances to becoming a Christian and peculiar absence of true remorse (indeed, very little guilt feeling is expressed directly) once more suggest the ambivalence of feeling for his parents and the subsequent inconsistencies within the superego."[29]

James E. Dittes' "Continuities between the Life and Thought of Augustine" highlights Augustine's oedipal conflict: "Perhaps the conflict is best characterized as an uncertainty as to whether he is to be a father or a son."[30] Dittes draws a conclusion about its eventual outcome after Augustine's conversion and acknowledges the power of ongoing psychological conflict in Augustine's life:

> Augustine submitted. He surrendered to his mother, and to her church and to her wishes. He abandoned masculine sexuality. He abandoned all active personal striving, including his vocational roles and aspirations. He abandoned those things which his father particularly endorsed and represented. He abandoned, in short, the effort to be a father. Instead he became an obedient son.[31]

Observing that Augustine went on to become "one of the most noted *fathers* of the church, an authority and dominant leader," Dittes remains true to Freud's view of life as beset throughout by psychic conflict: "This is not an irony. It is a reminder that Augustine was still endowed with conflicting tendencies within himself."[32]

Woollcott analyzes the oedipal situation more fully and concludes that the *Confessions* provide evidence "that Augustine did not succeed in resolving his 'oedipal complex' satisfactorily."[33] Although interest in Augustine's creative contributions to his culture allows Woollcott to see this continuing childhood tension from the oedipal conflict as a force in Augustine's creativity, he demonstrates a residual reductionism that characterizes the early studies already discussed. Woollcott's values clearly privilege his view of psychological health. For instance, the importance of Augustine's view of personal wholeness is not reflected in Woollcott's summary: "It is important also to remember that Augustine's conflict with his mother, although apparently not fully resolved and no doubt a personal emotional handicap, may have driven his creative effort to a more penetrating view of God."[34] Woollcott suggests as a plus "a more penetrating view of God" on Augustine's balance sheet, contrasted with the minus of "a personal emotional handicap." For Augustine, personal emotional deficits could never count for as much as an opportunity for "a more penetrating view of God." Moreover, Augustine would have believed that the view of God would provide at least the start of a process of correction for any personal emotional handicap. Much more explication of Augustine's points and response to them in our era weaves itself into the present study. For now let us note that Woollcott's article exemplifies how even the broadly conceived earlier efforts betray a need for a model of understanding that gives fuller weight to Augustine's point of view without ignoring our own psychological insights.

Other studies in the 1965 and 1966 symposium were even more reductionistic than Woollcott's. Dittes calls Augustine's worldview not only monistic, but "mom-istic," as he sees in it traces of Augustine's relationship to Monica.[35] Just a few years later, Robert J. O'Connell would show how much richer the maternal aspects of Augustine's concept of God were.[36] While O'Connell's book would not have been available to Dittes, the play on words about monism and "mom-ism" follows well from the reductionism inherent in the psychological framework Dittes adopted. Bakan introduces a reduction not just of Augustine's religiosity, but of the whole world's, to psychological immaturity: "It is perhaps one of the unfortunate things of the history of Western culture, that this particular immaturity [Augustine's separation of physical desire and 'affective involvement'] should have been made one of the foundation tenets of the world's religiosity."[37] Joseph Havens' modestly titled "Notes on Augustine's *Confessions*" defends the reductionistic convictions of psychological approaches from a justifiable scientific point of view. Yet he glimpses no opening for an integrated reading that allows religious appreciation, although such a reading is what Augustine's life and work require.[38]

Fortunately, articles that followed on the 1965–1966 symposium often addressed the problems noted above. They appeared in a variety of books and journals and were written by scholars from several fields. They challenged the previous articles as offering too narrow a reading of Augustine's

Confessions philosophically, theologically, rhetorically, historically, and psychologically.

David Burrell, in the first of these articles, set the interpretation of the *Confessions* in the context of larger questions of hermeneutics, or interpretation.[39] Burrell pointed out possibilities and problems of speaking across differences of time and culture.[40] He noted the connectedness of language and ways of life. He argued that coming to understand Augustine involves learning more and more about their linkages in Augustine's milieu.[41] The challenge of understanding Augustine also leads to the task of reflecting on our own language and way of life, especially the terms we use in studying him and their theoretical foundations. Burrell welcomed the psychoanalytic approach as a test case of interpreting Augustine's writings for our age's comprehension of him and for the examination of our own modes of understanding.[42] My attention to explicating theory in this book owes much to the cautions that Burrell first so wisely advanced.

Paula Fredriksen criticized the symposium because it ignored too much of the historical context of Augustine's writings, often because of inattention to the text, but sometimes because of sheer ignorance of the historical circumstances.[43] In addition, although she is primarily a historian and historical theologian, she astutely suggested an alternate psychological reading that would concentrate on theories emphasizing the earliest years of childhood, the years before the oedipal conflict. This suggestion would soon be pursued beyond Fredriksen's admirable opening effort,[44] but not before Lawrence J. Daly launched criticisms similar to Fredriksen's and broadened the field of secondary sources that supported their critiques.[45] He in turn proposed a reading of Augustine's life based on Erik Erikson's notion of the identity crisis.[46] In addition, Margaret R. Miles introduced psychoanalytic theory into her close, historical reading of Augustine's adult thought about the body.[47] A few years later she offered a sophisticated psychoanalytic interpretation of Augustine's account of his conversion experience. She shows how psychology can serve the historical and theological interests of scholars of Augustine and helps us see that these other interests may deserve, on the whole, to remain the dominant forces in understanding Augustine.[48]

Donald Capps developed an idea like Fredriksen's that scholars should interpret the themes of the pre-oedipal years in Augustine's *Confessions*. In an earlier piece, Capps took unusually seriously the rhetorical strategies Augustine used, highlighted episodes of the *Confessions* as parables, refocused discussions concerned with guilt and the oedipal conflict, drew the reader's attention instead to shame and the pre-oedipal phases of development, and referred to Helen Merrell Lynd's psychology of shame and its relationship to Erikson's ideas about early childhood development.[49] In a 1985 article, he replied to a hermeneutically driven argument by Paul Rigby. Rigby had recast the psychological study of Augustine as an instance of the "constructive dialogue between Freudianism and religion" proposed by Paul Ricoeur.[50] Rigby tried to overcome the reductionism of the articles in the first symposium by looking at reductionism as a "moment" of interpretation.[51] I will follow him in this. Yet a pathologizing tendency remains in Rigby's article.[52] The identification of psychological struggles and conflicts will become for me, in the light of Ricoeur's hermeneutics, part of an understanding of how people make meaning rather than primarily a species of diagnosis.

Capps, in his 1985 response to Rigby, not only explicitly pursues Fredriksen's suggestion that psychological analyses turn to the pre-oedipal years in addition, he introduces further resources for the discussion of narcissism, identified by Freud and some of his followers as a dominant theme of the first years of life. Capps invokes Heinz Kohut, a psychoanalyst whose understanding of narcissism gives the word a technical definition with morally positive connotations. According to Kohut, narcissism is the underlying sense of wholeness that sustains a person through the trials and successes that confront everyone from time to time. The joining of Ricoeur's and Kohut's ideas through the articles by Capps and Rigby has proven extraordinarily valuable in studying Augustine.[53] Kohut's theory, known as self psychology, will undergird the analysis in this book.

These scattered articles were not to remain small lights in a dark universe. A second symposium in the *Journal for the Scientific Study of Religion*, marking the twentieth anniversary of the first,[54] kept scholarly activity on the psychological interpretation of Augustine's life and work alive. This collection, much more savvy about the problems of reductionism than the first, includes a sensitively corrective article by a noted scholar of Augustine, the theologian Eugene TeSelle,[55] philosophical and cultural ruminations by Lonnie D. Kliever,[56] and analysis of ritual, adding ideas from social sciences other than psychology, by Richard Fenn.[57] The drawback of the collection is that even the new article contributed by Dittes, with its reading strongly influenced by psychology, does not specify the powers and limitations of its theory.[58] The authors depend heavily on insight and intuition and often fail to discipline their interpretations by adherence to theory. Volney Gay, who concentrates most on carefully delineated theory, is the one who is able to advance the interpretation of Augustine's life through pre-oedipal themes, beyond Fredriksen's and Capps's earlier important efforts. He holds himself to Kohut's texts while grounding them in relationship to their inspiration, the writings of Freud. Moreover, he attends carefully to the text of the *Confessions* and avoids the mistakes about events, sequence, characters, and voice that dog many other studies.[59]

Several articles, again widely scattered, followed the second symposium. In 1988, Lynn Poland added a salutary familiarity with Latin and Augustine's literary genres and pushed the Freudian reading of Augustine's work into an interpretation of actual passages of his *On Christian Doctrine*.

She thereby broadened the scope of application of psychoanalytic readings and grounded them more firmly in Augustine's language and rhetorical tradition than previous articles had.[60] W. Paul Elledge also reverts to Freudian theory[61] and introduces an interesting focus on a motif of "embrace" along with some insights into closeness and distance of relationship in Augustine's portrayals. In the long run, however, he relies so heavily on earlier flawed studies and draws in enough anachronistic assumptions that his reading does not advance the psychological study of Augustine.[62] In the same year, Charles Melman and Jean-Marc Lamarre each contributed an analysis using the ideas of Jacques Lacan to speak to the opposition between the psychoanalytic and Augustinian points of view.[63] While Lacanian interpretive strategies lie outside the range of this book, despite their interest, Poland's attention to language and text is extended here in later chapters.

Several articles appeared in 1990. Paul J. Archambault critiqued some earlier psychobiographical studies of Augustine and defended the need for more sophisticated psychoanalytic works.[64] He completed his contribution with a brief reading of the story of the adolescent Augustine's theft of pears and suggested its interpretation both in Freudian and Lacanian frameworks.[65] William B. Parsons thoroughly reviewed earlier articles and complemented them by his own strong thesis that Augustine's development could be better understood through the "object relations" school of psychoanalysis. Using this psychological theory, he spells out more specifically what might have happened to allow Augustine to "use his conflicts," as Woollcott had suggested.[66] Parsons advocates looking for the way Augustine's life incorporated earlier stages as he developed and transformed earlier conflicts into adult strengths. One of the most important of these, points out Parsons, is Augustine's mystical insights.[67] Andrès G. Niño advanced a reading of personal change understood through self psychology and through Augustine's *Confessions*. Niño does not elaborate the full range of issues raised by previous studies but does underscore how sympathetic readings of Augustine and self psychology can enhance appreciation of both Augustine's life and the transformative processes of psychotherapy.[68] Don S. Browning offered a hermeneutically sophisticated reading of Augustine's *Confessions*. He used Ricoeur's philosophy and raised the question of how the psychological study of Augustine might affect the philosophy of religion.[69] Quite usefully for this book, he also proposed a complementary reading of Augustine from the psychoanalytic point of view advanced by Freud and the self psychology developed by Kohut.[70]

Meanwhile, Capps and Dittes, key players in the earlier symposia, had undertaken the collection of a variety of articles into a book, *The Hunger of the Heart: Reflections on the "Confessions" of Augustine*.[71] The book-length format allowed a fuller representation of approaches to the psychological study of Augustine. The book provides the invaluable service of bringing many issues to the attention of psychologically oriented students of Augustine. For instance, the noted historian Karl Weintraub's discussion of Augustine with an eye to the history of self-representation in autobiography provides a wealth of historical and cultural context.[72] One article massively revised for *The Hunger of the Heart*, Capps's own "Augustine's *Confessions*: The Scourge of Shame and the Silencing of Adeodatus," extends the idea of the reflexive relationship between reader and text and moves toward amending the positivist approach to Augustine's writing that dominated the earliest articles in the field.[73]

Despite all the variety of perspectives in *The Hunger of the Heart*, Diane Jonte-Pace rightly pointed out that attention to Augustine's rhetoric and cultural setting were still largely neglected, as were consideration of the "subject of psychohistory…and the problem of hermeneutics."[74] Taking her criticism of the studies up to 1990 seriously and developing more the strategy for psychological analyses of the depth and sources of meaning in human life, I set out in the pages that follow both a model for integrating thought about culture and the psyche in the life of a religious person and an analysis of Augustine's life and writings through the *Confessions* in those terms.

One unsurprising problem with *The Hunger of the Heart* is that, as an edited collection, it cannot advance a coherent view of Augustine's life and writings. While it comes closer to comprehensiveness than single articles can, it cannot draw the evidence together persuasively. The guiding question the editors pose to unify their presentation of the individual selections will not bear much scrutiny. The question "Who is Augustine?"[75] loses its power in the light of interpretive theory. Interpretive theory holds that no matter the strategies of analysis used, interpretations will always be only partial. They can only be more or less adequate to the phenomenon they seek to elucidate and more or less intelligible to the audience to whom they are addressed. None of them reveals the phenomenon in question fully.[76] So the question posed by the editors of *The Hunger of the Heart* begins to dissolve before it has a chance to unify the work.[77]

I will use the metaphor of the symphony, and its contrast to the tuneless water buffalo, as a reminder of the challenge to bring together hermeneutics, historical studies, literary considerations, and social sciences in the effort to understand how Augustine's Christianity helped him discover and compose, from elements of culture and experience, a meaningful view of his crowded and disparate life.[78] Greater knowledge of Augustine's language, wider familiarity with his writings, and more extensive research into his times set my study of Augustine apart from the efforts reviewed above. Book-length exposition is most obviously the step to be taken to encompass so many aspects of the subject. In drawing together these approaches to Augustine, I supplement the metaphor of the water buffalo and the symphony with three conceptual categories from social science:

society, culture, and the person. They establish the structure of each of the biographical chapters that follow chronologically (chapters 3 through 8).

The categories of society, culture, and person will give shape to this study of Augustine and the integration of religion in life. The composition of an understanding of Augustine requires consultation with sociological explanations of the movements of social forces and concomitant smaller social pressures and possibilities so that we can discern his opportunities and the boundaries set on his capabilities and their fruition. It also begs for the resources of psychological anthropology and cultural psychology, explicit approaches to the interactions of culture and psyche. Because of the resources of our time that have shaped our intellects, we can profit by thoughtful engagement with ideas derived from psychoanalysis. Particularly, we will see symbols as a crosscutting phenomenon and category drawing together culture and person in analysis of Augustine's thought.

A Preview of Interpretation and the Use of Theory

Our comprehension of Augustine and his writings depends on the clarity of our own thought about social, cultural, and personal factors. This clarity expands with the conceptual sharpness and coherence of the theories we bring to bear on the evidence from Augustine's writings and on the intellectual and physical monuments left by his contemporaries. This tall order sets an ideal toward which to strive, not an easily attainable goal. Yet a particular conceptualization of symbols, that of Paul Ricoeur in *Freud and Philosophy*, will help. Ricoeur holds that symbols have two major aspects. One is their participation in a cultural legacy. The other is their representation of the conscious and unconscious psychological currents of the people who created them.[79] Hence the concept of the symbol allows an examination of the interaction of culture and person, neither of which survives without society. Much of the analysis of Augustine's situation and writings will turn on this broad understanding of symbols, described more fully below, after the exploration of the categories society, culture, and person.

The words "society," "culture," and "person" name the social scientific categories repeated throughout my analysis of Augustine's life and expression. These three categories have given form, like a skeleton hidden under skin, muscle, and fat, to social science in the U.S. since the middle of the century. Talcott Parsons is the name most associated with the systematic exploration of these categories. The words existed long before Parsons appropriated them, but the appearance of this threefold scheme in either the foreground or background of writing in sociology, anthropology, and psychology, as well as in political science and economics, owes its prevalence to work by Parsons and often his collaborator Edward Shils.

The categories society, culture, and person were always intended as tools of analysis, not definitions of fixed truths. Parsons and his colleagues believed that if the distinctions could be drawn reasonably clearly, the interactions and mutual influences of these aspects of human life could be better understood. The greater understanding that did result has led to serious modification in the accepted use of the categories, although nothing like unanimity exists in defining them. The need therefore arises to explain, at least in outline, what these terms will mean as I use them. Although these categories were not Augustine's primary modes of analysis, they can help us understand what he tells us, as brief examples from the *Confessions* will show.

The word "society" evokes many related theoretical terms. It is an umbrella term, emphasizing patterns of people's interaction.[80] In the extensive patterning of human interactions that is a society, people hold social roles. That is, they are expected to carry out more or less specifiable tasks for a noticeable duration. The person in the role is held responsible for having the requisite knowledge and skills for its tasks, as well as for acquiring more knowledge and skill as needed.[81] A role is not the same as the person who fills it, and any one person can, and often does, fulfill more than one social role.[82] Another closely allied term, "institution," means a pattern of human interaction of considerable stability. The patterns are well established and reasonably well known to the people involved and sometimes to outsiders as well. For purposes of analysis, one can understand an institution as an interlocking set of social roles that endure well beyond any one person's tenure in them.[83] Institutions can also interact with each other and contribute to the complete set of patterns of interaction that form a society.

At the beginning of *Confessions* book 10, Augustine reorients himself and the reader to the themes of confession to, and praise of, God with which he started telling his story at the very beginning of the whole work. He sets himself and the reader in the present in which he was writing. We see immediately a social aspect to his composition: "What I now am at this time when I am writing my confessions many wish to know, both those who know me and those who do not but have heard something from me or about me..."(X.iii.4).[84]

In this passage, Augustine touches on much of the range of the concept of society. First, we have a pattern of human interaction. People want to know about Augustine. Some know him personally and some do not, but they communicate with each other, so that those who have heard of Augustine have a desire to know more about him, and their desire can reach his awareness. He in turn responds, not haphazardly, but by writing a book that he knew would be circulated among literate people, certainly in North Africa, where he resided at the time, and probably in Rome and Milan where he had lived a decade earlier. Quite possibly it would make its way all around the Mediterranean to Jerusalem as well as to Gaul and Spain. The pattern of interaction of reading a book and passing it to one's associates, or having it copied and sending it on, was already established. Augustine's social role as a confessing Christian also implies the existence of an institution, the church. This inference is readily made by readers who know that, in the late fourth century, individuals would often confess publicly in church.

The appeal to a wide range of readers leads Augustine to a distinction of what we might now call culture. I will use the much-discussed term "culture" to mean the accumulated guidance available for people's lives. Some of this guidance develops intentionally and explicitly, and some emerges without anyone's immediate notice. Some of it relates to knowledge, some to aesthetics, and some to legal or moral standards for good conduct. Knowledge includes both practical and theoretical comprehension. Aesthetics encompasses standards and judgments of beauty and ugliness. It also highlights frequent styles of expression. These guide people's perceptions of the world around them and the ways they express themselves. Even the creative urge to find a new mode of expression depends on what kinds of expression prevail in a society at the time, in addition to what practical knowledge allows. Legal and moral standards of conduct guide, but do not necessarily force, all kinds of choices about social and personal life.[85]

Some debates about culture speak to issues of how this guidance occurs and what it makes possible. For instance, archaeologists may be concerned with material culture and spend much more time studying physical artifacts than do historians of culture, who instead occupy themselves more often with written records and the ideas and views contained therein. Yet physical artifacts, and especially ideas recorded in writing, can provide guides for human life. Some culture is passed on primarily orally and does not depend much on physical artifacts or texts at all. Other parts of culture, even in artifacts and texts, are essentially dead, although available to shape the lives of individuals and societies.[86] For instance, while a musical score may have little influence unless someone performs it, even an unplayed score can communicate to the trained eye and mind. Like discarded artifacts and unread texts, it can be rediscovered and reinterpreted. Thence it can guide people's aesthetics, thoughts, and feelings. Hence elements of culture can persist, even if they do not actively guide people's lives at a given moment.

As book 10 of the *Confessions* proceeds, we see the working of culture in Augustine's self-expression:

> To such sympathetic readers, I will indeed reveal myself...A brotherly mind will love in me what you [God] teach to be lovable, and will regret in me what you teach to be regrettable. This is a mark of a Christian brother's mind, not an outsider's—not that of "the sons of aliens whose mouth speaks vanity, and their right hand is a right hand of iniquity" (Ps. 144:7f.). A brotherly person rejoices on my account when he approves me, but when he disapproves, he grieves on my behalf. (X.iv.5)[87]

Augustine's opening words expose some of his culture's conceptions, for example, the idea that the self has an inner aspect that other people cannot perceive directly and that the person may choose to obscure or conceal. He also transmits moral norms about what to do when one approves or disapproves another person's behavior. Moreover, we notice that the norms to which Augustine adheres, and on which he desires his readers to rely, are different from other norms that might influence people in the diverse society of late antiquity. The influence of written culture on Augustine appears in his quotations from the Psalms. Even in other rather short quotations from the *Confessions* many aspects of culture can be identified.

The third category of analysis, the person, has been described in many ways. Most simply stated, the category of the person in this theoretical scheme includes the psyche (the mind and emotions) and the body. Parsons relied heavily on Freud's understanding of the person, which certainly included mind, emotions, and body. Of course, Freud's models have been disputed ever since he proposed them, but one can still use the notion of person-as-mind, -emotions, and -body as a heuristic. The later developments of psychoanalysis are also highly contested, so one has to delimit a range of conceptualization in which to examine the material. To do so, I accept the following ideas.

First, physical and psychological distress can rather easily overwhelm a tiny infant's ability to cope. These experiences, which seem so small to the adults who relieve the problem (change the diapers, give the feeding, apply the cool washcloth), are sufficient to start an involuntary process that psychoanalytic schools call "repression." It means that distressing feelings that go with an experience, and some of the knowledge that might derive from it, become unavailable to conscious thought, although they have left traces in the infant's psyche. As life goes on, repression continues to keep them unconscious and to render other painful or overwhelming experiences unconscious. Introduction to a wider world and to more complex social interactions allows greater sophistication in human interactions and in the sorrows, pains, and repression occasioned thereby.

We would never know about these unconscious sorrows and pains unless they revealed themselves in some form. Their conscious form turns out to be a recalcitrant disguise of unconscious thoughts and feelings. Freud formulated the basic rules for dispelling the disguise and interpreting the appearance of unconscious material. These rules have proven useful for the interpretation of Augustine's life. One is that unconscious ideas and feelings can spontaneously recombine, so that a whole complex of ideas and feelings can slip into consciousness in one unrecognizable conglomeration. This is called "condensation" of ideas and feelings.[88] Another is that the intensity of an idea in consciousness is not a good clue to the intensity of the unconscious material associated with it. Rather, one of the best disguises of unconscious material is a shift in its intensity so that the unconscious pain remains hidden by a passing thought like, "Oh, that's not important. Let's pay attention to something else." This process is known as "displacement."[89] Finally, the disguised unconscious material will refer to repressed childhood memories.[90] Freud often writes as though these childhood memories are the only ones that are repressed, or are the only repressed memories that matter, and that they are all fundamentally sexual, in a broad definition of that word.[91] Yet any moderately careful reading of Freud's case studies and dream analyses will show that he finds repressed memories from the years after early childhood crucial to his interpretations,[92] so I have no qualms about attending to intimations of such memories in Augustine's writings. Moreover, many analysts have elucidated cases by attending to material that is not primarily sexual, but has been hidden from a person's awareness and, once brought to light, helped to clarify the person's problems and eased the person's life.[93] Such successes lead me to believe that sexuality and society's responses to it are not the major source of repression. Nonetheless, they are among the sources, especially because the younger the child, the more bound to and by the body the child's experience is, the more easily he or she is overwhelmed, and the fewer mental and emotional resources he or she has to cope with distress. Repression of wordless physical experience could not escape sexual tinges.

Augustine clearly takes seriously the person and not just his or her social sphere or cultural resources. Although he had no concept of a repressed unconscious, we see that his personal focus is intense: "But you Lord...'have pity on me according to your mercy for your name's sake' (Ps. 51:1). You never abandon what you have begun. Make perfect my imperfections" (X.iv.5).[94] He continues, remarking on the profoundly personal side of his effort: "When I am confessing not what I was but what I am now, the benefit lies in this: I am making this confession not only before you with a secret exaltation and fear and with a secret grief touched by hope, but also in the ears of believing sons of men,...For my part, I carry out your command by actions and words; but I discharge it under the protection of your wings (Ps. 17:8; 36:7)...I am a child. But my Father ever lives and my protector is sufficient to guard me" (X.iv.6).[95]

The hints of the unconscious in the passage from *Confessions* book 10 cannot be explored here because too much of Augustine's childhood is, as yet, obscure. Nonetheless, the classic Freudian critique of religion seems at first glance to apply to his prayer: "My weakness is known to you. I am a child. But my Father ever lives and my protector is sufficient to guard me" (X.iv.6). Freud's key idea about religion is that it functions as a consolation for the loss of the father's protection as a child grows into adulthood. As a child grows up, said Freud, his or her repressed longing for the father in childhood is projected from the unconscious into the figure of God in religion.[96] He could not have hoped for more pithy phrasing than Augustine's for the conscious thoughts that psychoanalytic theory identifies as rooted deeply in unconscious childhood experiences of fear and longing.

The Fates of These Categories upon Further Reflection

Parsons did not intend the separations between the categories society, culture, and person to be absolute. Once they begin to facilitate an analysis of a phenomenon, their overlaps and mutual influence become obvious.

Schools of thought have arisen to explore the interactions between these aspects of human life. As the evidence of them in the previous short quotations from the *Confessions* suggests, they intermingle in Augustine's texts. Therefore, developing an understanding of some of their modes of interaction is crucial for the interpretation of Augustine's life and work. From his ability to orchestrate their influences comes the impression that he heard in them a symphony. Three influential elaborations of the categories' interconnectedness will help build the model of interpretation to be used throughout this book.

Erik Erikson devised a theory of eight developmental stages that he thought described the "psychosocial" course of people in all societies. His interactive view of development requires attention because his books, *Young Man Luther* and *Gandhi's Truth*,[97] set the pattern for psychological studies of historical figures that stands in the background of later efforts. [98] Erikson's term "psychosocial," describing the stages, signals a hybrid of two of the three categories introduced thus far. Erikson tended to subsume the category of culture under the rubric of "society," thus suggesting one way of reducing the complexity of managing three categories.

Erikson based his stage schema on the idea that individuals start life with a wide array of potential capacities. Which of those capacities will develop, he observed, depends heavily on what society calls for.[99] Yet he believed that the unfolding of human capabilities and personality traits falls under the constraint of biological maturation. Biology limits the extent to which societies can control individual development. For instance, every society has to have a method of weaning infants. Studies of different groups of people reveal many approaches to this aspect of a child's growth, but all children have to free themselves from mother's milk (or its substitute from nurses or bottles). Children's modes of coping with weaning are also multitudinous, but neither the children nor their society can escape some effect of weaning on a child's physical and psychological development. In fact, Augustine's own comments on infants' nursing in his society (I.vi.7) will suggest one source of psychological strength for him and alert us also to psychological injury. Erikson's concern with early childhood development and the relatedness of psychological development to physical development came from his training in psychoanalysis, a debt to Freud that he openly acknowledged. Yet from the vantage point Erikson elaborated, acceptance of a more reductionistic mode of psychological analysis, such as Freud's *Leonardo Da Vinci and a Memory of His Childhood*, becomes impossible.

A major article by Anne Parsons, Talcott Parsons' daughter and a psychoanalytically trained anthropologist in her own right, demonstrates attention to interactions of society, culture, and individual in a framework more adequate to this study of Augustine. Her exposition has the advantage over Erikson's work of starting with fewer assumptions about human development and allowing the data she gathered in the field to shape her theoretical conclusions. Parsons takes up the debate between Freud's loyal follower, Ernest Jones, and the anthropologist Bronislaw Malinowski about whether Freud's key theoretical construct, the oedipal conflict, applies universally. Jones said yes and Malinowski, reporting on fieldwork in the Trobriand Islands, said no. Parsons adduced evidence from her own field work in a south Italian village to argue that an oedipal complex as described by Freud is not universal but that some form of "nuclear conflict" involving sexuality and affection, social roles, and cultural norms within the family and society would be.[100]

Erikson's and Anne Parsons' approaches differ in the ways they might direct the study of Augustine. Erikson suggests that Augustine went through a period of "moratorium similar to Martin Luther's." The young Luther's years in the monastery in his late teens and his twenties gave him a quiet time between the beginning of formulating an identity as a person in an accepted social role (tasks of stage 4 of Erikson's scheme) and the fruition of that identity in a capacity for committed sexual and emotional intimacy (stage 5), followed by a concern with establishing and nurturing the next generations (stage 6). According to Erikson, Augustine went through a similar period as a Manichean heretic before he came to speak with his fully developed Christian voice. Both men, he implies, took on a "negative identity," a denial of their real identity, until they could find a way to form the identity that they truly could live.[101] This thought provoking comment seems illuminating of Augustine's years as a heretic, who would later describe himself also as having been bound by sexual desire (VIII.v.10, VII.xi.25–26), which he could control when he had committed himself to Catholicism (VIII.xii.29). But within Erikson's own framework this brief interpretation is hard to sustain. During this so-called moratorium, Augustine lived faithfully in a physically intimate relationship. In addition, Augustine had assumed a place in society as a teacher of rhetoric and supported himself, his concubine, and his son. His life at this time reflects a "negative identity" only from the perspective that the winner writes history—that is, the later and longer identity was the real one. But perhaps that is not true—perhaps the person, and certainly the person's identity, shifts so that each identity would have been equally the real Augustine.[102]

Anne Parsons' work would propose that social and cultural and familial influences might produce their own typical constellation of the developmental schema appropriate to Augustine's society and its cultural norms. Her idea that the psyche in its typical form would vary across cultures and societies has found a more radical expression in the recent exposition by Richard Shweder of what he calls "cultural psychology." His dictum "culture and psyche make each other up"[103] sounds like Parsons' ideas and may in some ways be indebted to them. He and the psychological anthropologists who have expounded the ideas that inform cultural psychology, however, highlight some implications of the dictum that Parsons did not.

For instance, Michelle Rosaldo makes a persuasive case that emotions quite different from hers as an American manifest themselves in the lives of the Ilingot people she lived with and studied in the Philippines. The events that trigger emotion as well as the emotions themselves and their mode of expression may have very little, if anything, in common.[104] Shweder's own studies of moral thought in an orthodox Hindu area of Bhubanewsar, Orissa, India, argue strongly that most of mid-twentieth-century moral thinking in the U.S. seems to lack points of agreement or even contact with much of the moral thought of these orthodox Hindus.[105]

Ideally, cultural psychology would lead to a formulation of the psyche and culture peculiar to Augustine's time and place. Unfortunately, this discipline can only attain a sketchy beginning here.[106] As Augustine was psychologically astute and expressive, he does give us some clues to the interaction of culture and psyche in his time. Nonetheless, the data that would help validate a description of the cultural psyche of fourth-century Roman North Africa leave many gaps. Cultural psychology does teach us, however, to attend to the possibility that aspects of thought and behavior that seem to us sure signs of a psychological condition described in this century in Europe or the U.S. can take on completely different significance in the context in which they occurred. For instance, many scholars have commented on Augustine's emotionality. Descriptions of the emotional volatility of people at that time suggest that the emotionality of Augustine's expressions made him close to the statistical norm, the most frequent mode of behavior. The historians' invocations of a sensitive and expressive North African temperament[107] explicate the idea of "temperament" so little that almost nothing can be learned from their use of the term. Augustine, therefore, was not necessarily, as the more reductive psychological interpretations cited earlier suggest, psychologically abnormal or in need of better adjustment. After all, he had to "adjust," if one favors that term, to his world and not any other, including ours and its own psychological predilections.[108] Hence, neither Sigmund Freud's nor Talcott Parsons' view of psychology can explain Augustine for us in advance of a study of his life.

One way to trace the attunement of Augustine to his social and cultural world and his influence on its harmonies and discords is to look at symbols as examples of the interaction of culture and psyche. This interaction is outlined by Ricoeur in *Freud and Philosophy* and played out in another cultural setting by the anthropologist Gananath Obeyesekere.[109] For my purposes, a symbol will be understood as something that represents something else and evokes more than one meaning. This definition should distinguish it from a sign, something that stands for something else, but perhaps for only one other thing.[110] It should allow that the way a symbol stands for something may be arbitrary or clearly connected to the meanings it conveys. It should also allow that a symbol may be created for a particular reason or occasion, or may crop up unexpectedly or eventuate from an unforeseen event.

Symbols are widely seen as elements of culture. They embody meanings that people attribute to them, embed in them, append to them. They can be manipulated, redefined, and appropriated for various uses intentionally on a conscious level.

Symbols also provide excellent cover for unconscious thoughts and feelings to come to expression. In fact, the unconscious processes of condensation and displacement described earlier can create conscious symbols with hidden unconscious content. The conscious symbols can be polished and adjusted to fit into culture without losing their links to their unconscious sources.

The dynamic interactions of cultural symbols and psychological processes will be explained more fully as Augustine's life and writings require. But further abstract explanation will not help as much as the exploration of an example, such as the verbal symbols of "the many" and "the One" sketched in the next chapter.

Focusing on Augustine

Augustine as a late adolescent searched long and hard for meaning in his life and found neither the conviction of a mature person nor the contentment of a water buffalo. In his early thirties, just as his secular career was blossoming, he triumphed in his struggle for a convinced mode of thought. He left his occupation and its many strains and distractions for what he saw as a way of life that would allow him a more unified, if less glamorous, existence.

This feeling of being distracted by many things and hope for greater unity through devotion to one right thing—ultimately God—characterizes much of Augustine's thought. A sense of such a tension was expressed in late antiquity by the philosopher Plotinus and was transmitted to Augustine by Bishop Ambrose's preaching in Milan. The tension between distraction and unified devotion became symbolic for Augustine of the predicament of the soul. In addition, it had correlates in practices in his society, such as advancement in the imperial civil service contrasted with a life of prayer and meditation. Augustine eventually took the guidance of Plotinus and Ambrose for his thinking and living. He went on to mold it in his writings, which in turn shaped much of the culture to follow in the Middle Ages. This theme of Augustine's life and thought will serve as the main symbol drawing together my analysis.

Relationships between Augustine's cultural resources, personal revelations, and the social norms and patterns of his time unfold throughout this book. An instance of the overall pattern of dispersal and unification and more elucidation of the theoretical approach will appear in chapter 2. The developmental base of psychoanalytically oriented theories of the person will provide the framework for the later chapters. Chapters 3 and 4 cover in sequence two processes that Kohut identifies in the very young child's psyche: a sense of grandiosity, or one's own wonderfulness, and a joy and comfort in seeing other people as omnipotent ideals. The symbolic forms in Augustine's writings intimate that both of these aspects of the deeper person suffered some traumatic shocks in his very early childhood. Some of these shocks can be seen as fairly predictable in his social and cultural setting, but social and cultural norms cannot efface all psychological distresses. The fifth chapter will suggest how Augustine's choices in adolescence (which in the Roman parlance could last until one's late twenties) responded to social opportunities and cultural norms, at the same time that they allowed expression and comfort of his unconscious psychological sorrows (which would have persisted from the experiences illuminated in chapters 3 and 4).

The sixth chapter elucidates how the continuing unconscious vulnerabilities could have intersected in new ways with Augustine's social and cultural resources after he moved to Milan. These opportunities made way for a shift in the expression of and comfort for his unconscious difficulties. This shift, I will argue, was manifested in the story of his conversion in the *Confessions*. The seventh chapter will take up the process by which the shift in expression and comfort kept unfolding through his retreat to a villa outside Milan, his baptism by Ambrose, his mystical experience at Ostia with his mother, and his return to North Africa. How the themes implied here persisted in his sophisticated theological thought as he acceded to the episcopal chair and its duties will occupy chapter 8. The themes of "the many" and "the One" seem to have achieved some resolution of his psychological stresses, but in other ways to have kept his psychological upheavals active. No one should be surprised at the ongoing stresses in his life, for he lived in an era of considerable social strife and competing cultural influences. What should surprise us is that he found such rich and powerful ways of orchestrating them, using them for his apprehension of a view of life, perceiving them as parts of a comprehensible whole. They took on historical and cosmic significance in his treatments of them. This is no water buffalo we have encountered, but a person whose life is also a call to appreciating a view of living that is instructive, even if it is not applicable wholesale to our own lives and thoughts.

What about God?

Now and then a scholar of religious studies might ask this question. It is nearly inescapable for a student of Augustine. What about God?

Clearly a central premise of the *Confessions* is that the story of Augustine's life, like the understanding of time and the depiction of creation in the last three books, reflects the work of God. The parts that Augustine played in it were mostly sinful, he confesses. The outcome was not, to his mind, explicable by social science or literary criticism or theories of symbols or any other human conceptualization, but by acknowledgment of the work of God. Am I then immediately misunderstanding both Augustine and his *Confessions* by attempting to look at his creative interaction with society, culture, and his personal history in the pattern of meaning in his life?.

One answer comes from a careful reading of the text, in which one sees that Augustine believes that society and culture helped lead him astray and also provided the occasions for God's recalling him to the sure path back to God. Augustine himself engaged in social and cultural analysis. He dissected his own motives. For him these reflections were extremely important, although the presence of God meant that they were not complete. In fact, from Augustine's point of view, if they are not understood with God in the picture they will hide the real story.

I, too, will undertake social, cultural, and individual analysis of Augustine's life events. I, however, will not attempt to judge where the work of God fits in his story. The most I can do is report what Augustine believed and insist that it must remain in view, bearing with it all his testimony to God.

The idea that social, scientific, and humanistic modes of understanding can help us engage a text or a life or historical events does not entail that we agree that those modes of analysis have exhausted the meaning of what we study. Of course, many social scientists have insisted that their analyses do deprive religious experiences, lives, and events of any remainder of religious meaning or divine intervention. This is a separate question. If I can introduce you to a sufficiently Augustinian understanding of Augustine's life and thought, you, too, may imagine that God could work in ways as complex as those we are about to encounter. I have come to hear more of a symphony by listening to these voices, including especially Augustine's, than I heard before. I chew cud less and imagine divine harmonies more. But when I go back to work, I want always to understand as best I can. Understanding makes even rumination more satisfying.

CHAPTER 2

The Many and the One, Person and World

The terms "the many" and "the One" cover a whole series of concepts, feelings, and concerns for Augustine. They fit my working definition of symbols: they are representations that evoke more than one meaning. Augustine magnifies them as symbols by the multitudinous manifestations of a broad view of the world that he attaches to them.

Augustine did not originate attention to the themes of the many and the One. He would have read them in the writings of the third century philosopher Plotinus, who reworked ideas of Plato. Augustine called Plotinus one of the Platonists, although later scholars tag him a "Neoplatonist." When Augustine heard Bishop Ambrose preach, he learned how the Bible might be comprehensible in the categories of Plotinus' thought. The parallel of the Christian God to Plotinus' notion of a One toward whom to look, existing in a more divine realm, above all things, easily suggested itself to Augustine and others at the time. He could have found the conceptualization of the many and the One both in Plotinus and in the Bible.[1]

As we look back toward the time when Augustine lived, with the tools of our three categories of analysis, the social and cultural forces confirm a contrast of actual *many-ness* with a much-desired *one-ness*. Augustine certainly saw the contrast in instances in the social world. He may not have recognized all the examples I will note, but they form the background in the social and cultural world for a personal elaboration of meaning and may well have pervaded Augustine's thought patterns and perceptions as he developed his views. In addition, his unintentional clues to disguised expressions of unconscious thoughts and feelings seem to allude to an extensive experience of personal division and longing for unity.

A Brief Look at the Social World of Late Antiquity

Augustine's social world gave evidence of the many—of division and of sources of distraction and confusion—in its social institutions and its customary ways of life. Examples of many kinds abound.

For instance, the political geography of the Roman Empire shifted frequently during the fourth and fifth centuries. It permitted as many as four Caesars, their bases of power in the east, west, a mid-region spreading out from Italy, with what is now Greece sometimes standing as a fourth unit.[2] This division allowed considerable divisiveness in transitions of power. Intrigue could arise for every change of power, multiplied by two or three. Several emperors were murdered. Their successors were to be elected, although chosen might more aptly describe their accession to highest leadership because elections could degenerate into military acclaim or conniving in highly placed social circles.[3] Some ascended the throne in childhood to head off a genuine election and keep the imperial purple in a particular family.[4] The orderly handover of power, ensuring a single framework for rule, rarely eventuated from the process.

What have become known as the barbarian invasions had started long before Augustine lived. These assaults caused all kinds of disunity, from the division of lands and the fluctuation of borders, to the disruption of families by the military service of their men, to the need for flight by the unprotected. The invasions also left gaps in the experiences of the peoples of the empire: North Africans along the Mediterranean coast escaped incursions until the fifth century, while the natives of Gaul, Germanic lands, northern Italy, Greece, and Asia Minor suffered destruction, famine, and other devastation a century and more earlier.[5] Moreover, various invading peoples made peace with the empire. The invaders of one year might well be a common sight in the ordinary life of a town in another. Their presence increased the variety of nationalities, languages, and customs in evidence in the major cities.[6] Some were imperial soldiers, others advisors. Some achieved prominence as wealthy residents in principal towns, while others, stuck at the lower end of the economic scale, served as slaves to the rich or as politically free labor bound by poverty to a household.

The fate of the invaders has suggested another aspect of social life full of divisions in the late empire: social class. Class may be a more fluid, or at least more ill-defined, category than either social institutions or social roles as defined in the previous chapter. It can lack the clarity of demarcations expected in institutions and social roles, and apparently it did in the fourth century. Generally, it depends on economic well-being, or lack thereof, and the access to, and use of, power that commonly follow on the degree of one's wealth and the social status related to it.[7] Sometimes it can change fairly substantially for a person or family in response to individual initiative. Late antiquity was a time when it could shift within a life span.[8]

By definition, the very wealthy were the highest social class. They frequently came from families that had wielded considerable political power and were related by blood to emperors and governors of provinces and other high officials.[9] They would have had estates in more than one place, servants at each, amenities at all times, entertainment whenever they wanted. They might travel substantial distances around the Mediterranean. They had public monuments built.[10] They extended lavish hospitality to friends and relatives and funded schools or teachers, theater, spectacles, and circuses for the masses.[11] They also supported less-well-to-do but talented citizens, like Augustine in his early years.

Patronage and supervision of their property might bring the upper classes into contact with the lower classes, but social mobility rarely allowed for someone of the lower classes to become one of the very wealthy. Individuals from the lower classes might, however, associate with such well-heeled people, or might marry into one of the families, and the lower-class parent might raise well-to-do offspring.[12]

Other approaches to success presented themselves. The army certainly was one. It comprised an extensive hierarchy in which valor could be proven against invaders and internal uprisings. While many officers hailed from the upper-class families, others rose by their skill and wits to high ranks.[13]

A parallel hierarchy matched the military from the civilian side. The prefects, the major divisions of the empire, were divided into dioceses (political, not ecclesiastical, divisions in this sense) and dignitaries headed each of these. Provinces together made up each diocese, and each of the fifty-nine provinces had its own governor, who administered all civil affairs and also made sure that the army had access to supplies if it campaigned or traveled in the province.[14] These levels of officialdom were open to talented young men who could find their way into them. A provincial governorship might have come to Augustine one day. Ambrose, the bishop of Milan, having been born into a very wealthy family, had served for a short time as a provincial governor before he undertook his ecclesiastical role. These upper levels of government allowed for the mixing of the extremely rich and the rising stars from the middle class, the old Roman families and the colonials.

Below the governors in the provinces, still more local officials functioned. Curials and decurials, as they were called, administered the affairs of cities and towns. They had to possess a certain amount of property and wealth to hold office. A position that had brought them honor in previous generations began to cost them dearly in Augustine's lifetime. They collected taxes and had to make up the difference between the assessments made by the imperial officials and what they could in fact extract from the people. Their own taxes burdened them, too, and many began to try to avoid the curial duties although they wanted the wealth that could accompany the rank.[15]

Patricius, Augustine's father, and Monica, his mother, were "of curial rank."[16] A report to this effect from Augustine's younger contemporary and friend should put to rest comments that Augustine's family was poor.

When Augustine remarks in a sermon that his family was poor, he speaks in relation to the higher classes.[17] Clearly they lacked the resources of the fabulously wealthy. They did have trouble funding all of Augustine's education (II.iii.6). Yet they could gain the attention of their very wealthy fellow citizen of Tagaste, Romanianus, and obtain the money they needed, as well as entree into Romanianus' splendid lifestyle, for their son. Monica had money to grant an allowance to her son (III.iv.7) after Patricius died in about 371. Inheritance continued to assist the children and grandchildren into the fifth century.[18]

The poor, by contrast, barely survived. As tenant farmers, they always lived at the overseer's mercy. Or as servants they endured hard work, fits of temper, and corporal punishment in the homes of people as modest in the middle classes as Patricius and Monica or as rich as Romanianus. Augustine's family may have felt financial stress in their worldly ambitions, but they did not wear hunger on their faces, and they wielded power at home instead of cowering under it (IX.ix.20).

Both unity and division also marked the middle-and upper-class families of the time. Unity becomes evident in various indicators of family life. For instance, husbands expected complete sexual fidelity from their wives, monuments announce the love of parents for children, children for parents, spouses or siblings for each other. Augustine records in his *Confessions* that his brother had come to Milan, as had his mother, and that both he and his brother attended their mother in her last illness (IX.xi.27). Other families traveled great distances together and often shared ascetic practices or increased devotion to their faith.[19]

By contrast, wives could not expect sexual fidelity from their husbands, not even within their own household, where the husband might with impunity take the servants to bed. Women from respectable families had to remain indoors much of the time, often without looking out the windows lest they would be suspected of courting other men's favors.[20] They tended to be much younger than their husbands, and their education would often have stopped after basic schooling in the three R's, although learned women, tutored at home, certainly existed in the upper classes.[21] Their educational level notwithstanding, women wielded considerable power within the household, but experienced almost none of their husbands' world outside the home. Nor could wives or children count on freedom from corporal punishment.[22] For instance, where religious division entered the family, it could bring on beatings as one or another member attempted to enforce a unified faith.[23]

Families could develop in one of several different forms. Legal marriage served as a social bond and an economic arrangement, although it could incorporate love, respect, and emotional and intellectual intimacy in some instances. People who felt constrained by social class to avoid marriage and urged by love or desire to persist in a liaison could establish a long-lasting relationship of concubinage. This was in no way comparable to a harem or a promiscuous love life. Instead, it was a well-recognized alternative to marrying, although it would not secure the social and economic lineage dear to the hearts of the upper classes.[24]

Several fine career paths lay open to Augustine, provided he acquired the right education to move him forward from his respectable, if not glamorous, beginnings. His parents exerted themselves so that he could advance his education past the basic schooling available in their hometown to the higher education of grammar in the larger town of Madaura, and then rhetoric in Carthage. Each educational step divided him from a number of other youngsters who would not go on with him. Each prepared him to join a smaller segment of society.[25] Still, his training in rhetoric served as a sufficiently general credential that he could plan to practice law or to teach or to move into civil service (III.iii.6; VI.vii.12–viii.13; VI.x.16).[26] First he taught grammar in his hometown. Then he moved to Carthage to teach rhetoric. A further move to Rome allowed him not only to continue instructing upper-level students, but also to use his rhetorical skills in government service closer to its center of power. Each move also took him into increasingly diversified settings and let him experience aspects of society that previously had been unfamiliar to him.

A transition from these brief glimpses of the social world of Augustine's time to the cultural world or worlds with all their *many-nesses* comes from Robert A. Kaster's discussion of the role of the grammarian, or teacher of the lower school, in late antiquity:

> The grammarian's instruction was shaped at least as much by social as by intellectual considerations, and the grammarian himself was embedded in a social system where what mattered were wealth, distinction, and eloquence amid a population vastly poor, anonymous, and illiterate; where among the wealthy, distinguished, and eloquent, fine hierarchical discriminations came as naturally as breathing and were every bit as important; where competence was defined largely by personal and social, not technical, criteria, and one's conception of *humanitas* was so circumscribed as to embrace only those who shared one's own attainments. Whatever its other shortcomings, the grammarian's school did one thing superbly, providing the language and *mores* through which a social and political elite recognized its members.[27]

This suggestive summation prompts the realization that even in a highly divided society, various formulae for social glue become effective in different strata at least at some times. If wealth or heredity or place of birth or religion would not hold a social world together, perhaps language and the ways of life that accompany it would bind some of its ill-fitting segments.

The Cultures of the Many

A wide variety of cultural influences have already proposed themselves in the discussion of the social world: traditions of the Greek-speaking east, the Latin-speaking west, the invaders, the military, and more than one religion. Guidance for life, as culture is defined here, came from many histories, customs, languages, and systems of thought. Yet too wide a choice can result in little reliable guidance at all.

Once one understands that Rome had colonized North Africa centuries before Augustine's birth, the influences of ancient Greece and Rome become obvious. Educated people still read Plato. Plotinus and his students and expositors attracted devoted followers as they developed Plato's ideas, first in Alexandria and then in Rome. This following had to have read Greek well into the third century, when Plotinus wrote. (Marius Victorinus translated Plotinus' *Enneads* into Latin only in the fourth century.[28]) Some works of Aristotle also remained extant and entered into the discussions of advanced scholars (IV.xvi.28). Meanwhile, Roman philosophers like the Stoics, the skeptics, and the Epicureans found their way into the curriculum, although not in the study of philosophy per se. They were read in classes on rhetoric (III.iv.7).

The ancient Roman games and theater also survived, as did secular Latin literature. Augustine read not only the philosophical writings, but also plays and poetry, as his quotations from Terence and Vergil demonstrate. Much of the theater he attended would have had nothing to do with plays of enduring value, and instead included farces and obscenities of various explicit sorts. The games themselves shed much blood, both animal and human, and appealed to the less thoughtful, lustier side of the audience (III.ii.2; VI.viii.13).

The stories and characters of the plays proved that pagan ideas and narratives still lived in the people's imaginations.[29] The Christianized emperors took away the state privileges of the Roman cults but did not deliver the coup de grace to rites in the pagan temples until the early 390s. In fact, something of a pagan revival occurred toward the end of the fourth century and the beginning of the fifth. Augustine began to write *The City of God* after the sack of Rome in August 410,[30] to argue that the pagan gods would have protected the city no better than had the Christian one, and that a wholesale return to their worship would miss the point of the Christian God's working in history. His treatise would have had no place in a world where paganism had no adherents.

Particulars of non-Christian practice also survived, even when the links that bound them to a larger system of belief had weakened. Augustine speaks of his own fascination with astrology (IV.iii.4–6). His sermons and writings from his years as bishop attest the continued use of charms and fortune tellers, even among people who saw themselves as Christians.[31] In the *Confessions* he remarks that a "soothsayer" asked him to name a price for a guarantee of victory in a poetry competition. Augustine had not sought and did not accept this reassurance but specifies for the reader that it would have included animal sacrifice (IV.ii.3). Some non-Christian practices had their roots in indigenous North African traditions. Images of ancient

Egyptian gods have turned up in excavations in North Africa and may have been at least a small part of the urban landscape Augustine knew.[32]

Some cultural influences spread through religious movements. Persian traditions appeared in North Africa and Rome through the arrival of disciples of Mani, known as Manichees. Strains of Buddhism and Zoroastrianism could be discovered in Mani's writings.[33]

Heresies contended with each other and the Catholic church in late antiquity. Not even Christianity succeeded in turning all of the many into one. The strongest competitor to orthodox Catholic doctrine in Augustine's lifetime was Arianism. Like Manichees and, by definition, all heretics, the Arians claimed that they were the true Christians, but the church councils that hashed out the questions of orthodox faith and practice overruled that claim. The Arians held that Jesus was not the equal of the Father of the Christian Trinity. His greatness could not prove his equality with the head of the Trinity, and his life on earth spoke against it. How could someone who suffered so and lived in human flesh be the fully equal substance of God as worshiped in heaven? This view, appealing to normal human logic, had proponents in the imperial court, especially in the mid-fourth century. The western empress Justina flaunted her Arian beliefs and intended them to overcome the orthodox Christianity of Ambrose, bishop in the capital. A decisive stage of their conflict (of which more later) occurred while Augustine resided in Milan, and influenced his later practice of Christianity. The Arians did not have a wide following in North Africa, but in the first few years of his episcopate Augustine had encountered their writings in the hands of a different brand of dissident, the Donatists, who shared his homeland.[34] Donatism was a fourth-century schism in Christianity. It was formally designated a heresy in the early fifth century. It sprang from contention about who had lapsed and who had remained faithful during the persecution of Christians by the emperor Diocletian from 303–305 and how the lapsed might rejoin the Christian community after the persecution ceased. In the long run the Donatists thrived in North Africa but survived in very few other places, although they did muster sufficient numbers in Rome to require a bishop. In North Africa, however, they had as many bishops and cathedrals as the Catholics did, frequently one for each side of the schism in each town. The Christianity Augustine knew as a boy and in early adulthood came primarily from his Catholic mother, but all around him in the province at large a competing Christian force made itself known. Donatism had been persecuted in its turn in the mid-fourth century, but it flourished nonetheless and nurtured its new heroic identity of a martyred faith.[35] Although Augustine never adopted Donatism as his religion, and fought it from the 390s onward, it was a constant sign of division in his homeland throughout most of his life.

Finally, one might note that guidance for life certainly comes from other sources, especially norms of everyday life, proverbs, and well-tried or at least well-publicized strategies for economic, social, and physical survival. Recognition of the variety and number of sources leads to sifting carefully through information from the late ancient world to discover what currents might have affected Augustine. The theoretical framework linking psyche and culture requires attention to specific points of intersection. For instance, Patricius' and Monica's decision to send Augustine for advanced education depended in part on the social institutions of schools of grammar and rhetoric, but also on the conventional wisdom that the benefits of such an education merited familial sacrifices.

Christian practice covered a wide spectrum even within non-heretical Catholic circles.[36] Monica's full-blown life of piety, after her husband died and Augustine struck out on his own as a teacher of rhetoric, represents one form of ordinary Christian practice. But many people did not apply Christian teachings rigorously throughout their lives, as can be seen by the comments of preachers against certain behaviors in their flocks. Some people adopted Christianity as a concession to social pressure, as when the peasants converted with their lord, or someone wanted to advance at court under a Catholic emperor. These people did not wear their faith very deeply or very broadly. Others urged themselves onward, but seem to have fallen short of exemplary faith because they lacked the intellectual training to resolve the problems that arose for people trying to reconcile the teachings of Christianity with an abundance of other modes of thought. Augustine pictures himself and Monica as instances of this difficulty before they came under the sway of Ambrose's preaching. Augustine had to discover a way to understand the scriptures, although he had found them foolish before he heard Ambrose discourse on them, and Monica had to give up a desire to be buried by her husband, although the cultural norms of her birthplace would have encouraged that arrangement.[37] The many influences within Christianity itself probably constrained some people to feel as perceptive as water buffalo, despite the richness of the young tradition and the wider culture.

Personal Responses to the Many and the Hope for the One

Three angles of vision can help in the interpretation of personal responses to the many. The first arises from reflection on the intersections of the many in Augustine's social and cultural world and some hypotheses about their effect on him. The second comes from Augustine himself and his synthesis of the cultural resources available to him. The third opens up when possibilities of interpretation by depth psychologies come into view. A particularly inviting theoretical perspective is the self psychology developed by Heinz Kohut from Freudian psychoanalysis because it emphasizes the conception of an unconscious self susceptible, metaphorically speaking, to fragmentation and unification, that is, to its own kind of *many-ness* and *one-ness*.

Augustine does not suffer in these interpretations from the imposition of alien ideas on his thought. Rather, we see passages in which he brings up the same themes. For instance, Augustine describes himself between ages eighteen and twenty-seven as subject to "various desires." He shows the pull of many aspects of social and cultural life in Carthage:

> we were being seduced and seducing, being deceived and deceiving (2 Tim. 3:13) in various desires, publicly through the teachings which they call liberal, privately through a false name of "religion" [Manichaeism]—in the former arrogant, in the latter superstitious, in everything vain. On the one side we pursued the emptiness of popular glory, including applause at the theatre and poetry competitions and contests for crowns of straw, and mere trifles of spectacles and intemperate lusts. On the other side, we sought to purge ourselves of those dirty things when we brought food to those who were called "Elect" and "Holy," from which they could manufacture for us in the workshop of their stomach angels and gods through which we would be liberated (IV.i.1).[38] [Augustine refers to the Manichees' belief that their Elect, by chewing their food and belching, could liberate particles of the kingdom of light caught in the material world of plants (e.g., III.x.18).]

The influence of many forces suggested by this passage is greater than may at first be apparent. Clearly Augustine asserts that he was living a divided life—publicly he taught liberal arts and privately he adhered to the Manichaean religion. What he does not state is that the verse competitions and the practice of Manichaeism could lead him in incompatible directions. The verse competitions could advance his career by demonstrating his mastery of the arts of public speaking and making him appealing as a prospective lawyer or teacher. The practice of Manichaeism could make him an outlaw. Admittedly some Manichees survived as highly placed officials and prominent citizens, but laws prohibited the religion.[39]

When Augustine was thirty and living in Milan, he looked back over the last decade and more and realized that he had long ago felt delighted by philosophy as expounded by Cicero and had decided to pursue its wisdom, "planning, once it was found, to abandon all the empty hopes and mendacious follies of hollow desires." Yet he was torn, not only by philosophical uncertainty and possible forms of guidance for his life, but also by his social situation:

> There is no time for reading…Our pupils occupy our mornings; what should we do with the remaining hours? Why do we not investigate our problem? But then when should we go to pay respects to our more influential friends, whose patronage we need? When are we to prepare what our students are paying for? When are we to refresh ourselves by allowing the mind to relax from the tension of anxieties? (VI.xi.18)[40]

Yet another lifestyle attracted him and his friends also. They could re-
tire to live a communal, contemplative life. It had parallels in other non-
Christian groups and in monasteries, but Augustine did not know about
these at the time (VIII.vi.15).[41] The plan never bore fruit because of the men's
concerns about the reactions of their wives or future wives (VI.xiv.24).

From the vantage point of the late twentieth century, Augustine's indecision in his late teens and twenties may evoke more tolerance than he
himself manifested for it. Some of our social psychologists have more or
less radically argued that the self always forms out of its interactions with
other people. Perhaps it even should be understood as "nuclei of relationships." Note, not "a nucleus of relationships," but "nuclei," many nodes of
relationship making up one person.[42] George Herbert Mead, as early as the
1930s, conceptualized the person as a product of social interactions. That
person he saw less as a single personality than an ever-labile product of a
particular body, a specific constellation of memories and a set of experiences of interpersonal interaction in a social setting that influenced body,
memories, and experiences.[43] If Augustine in Carthage in his early twenties lived as a teacher of liberal arts based on his prior educational experiences and relationships and as a Manichee based on his new friendships
and experience of the wider cultural world, why be surprised?

The late-twentieth-century conceptions that seem even more radical
reflect the situation of post-modernity as showing us that the human being
is ever vulnerable to shifts in self-understanding, behavior, allegiance, and
so on. The late modern or post-modern world contributes to this condition
by multiplying the number of social influences on people. This sounds reminiscent of Augustine's own situation. Before he went to Carthage, he knew
a variety of people of different social classes, pagans, and Christians. In
Carthage, in 371 at age seventeen, if not before, he learned about sexual
promiscuity as a norm for young men his age and had friends to urge him
on with it (III.i.1). Later he met there the Manichees. The same social world
introduced him to Cicero's *Hortensius* and instilled in him a love of philosophy. In 383, when he, now a teacher in Carthage instead of a student,
realized that his pupils were obstructing rather than supporting his genuine interest in education, he moved to Rome. There the Manichaean community introduced him to yet other people, and his students to yet other
vices, which they practiced on him by cheating him of their fees for his
teaching. He moved to Milan in 384. He encountered the imperial court
and its charms and dangers; he made other friends; he entered a social
world that included Ambrose's eloquence, Christianity, Neoplatonism, and
political skill; his mother joined him there and reinstated by her presence
the recollections of his childhood and early beliefs. From the social psychological viewpoints mentioned above, how could Augustine be anything
but undecided during such jumbled years? No individual remained a constant presence in his life from the time he first went away to school in

childhood until his acceptance of Catholic Christianity in Milan, August 386, at age 31. Of course he hesitated and wavered, unsure of what to do.

But Augustine himself did not interpret the situation thus. By the time he wrote the *Confessions* he saw a certain fixity of the person as an important quality in a happy life. And happiness could not simply mean the pleasure of the moment. He sought, and believed he found, more stability. His new conception included a strikingly different view of the person from that of our social psychologists.

Oneness as Augustine's Aspiration

Augustine did see oneness as a possibility (XI.xxix.39). He did not see it as a human actuality, because he recognized the tendency of the person to adjust to the influence of other people, to change as interpersonal interactions change. The sharp distinction of his view from that of the social psychologists of the late-twentieth century lies in his conclusion that the fluctuation of the person is a result of sin. That willingness indicates that he propounds a normative, as well as descriptive, psychology: He makes prescriptions for how people should live based on his descriptions of how they are. And his conception of how they are, the description, depends on his understanding of how anything is. That is, his description of human nature depends on the ontology to which he subscribed.

Augustine expands on Plotinus' claim that human souls have emanated from the One and lost touch with it by turning away from it and becoming involved in the world of the senses: "wherever the human soul turns itself, other than to you [God], it is fixed in sorrows, even if it is fixed upon beautiful things external to you and external to itself, which would nevertheless be nothing if they did not have their being from you." Here Augustine shifts from a description of the soul to an ontological claim, that all things have their being from God. Then he elucidates the condition of these things, and why they lead the soul to fixation in sorrow: "Things rise and set: in their emerging they begin, as it were, to be and grow to perfection; having reached perfection, they grow old and die." This is the best case scenario. In other cases, "not everything grows old, but everything dies." This brief reference to early death merely alludes to a subset of the larger case: "So when things rise and emerge into existence, the faster they grow to be, the quicker they rush towards non-being. That is the law limiting their being" (IV.x.15).[44] Why does Augustine see this pattern of life as pernicious?

Augustine argues that nothing is wrong with transient things as long as they are properly loved: "Let these transient things be the ground on which my soul praises you (Ps. 146:2), 'God creator of all.'" Love of external things can make the soul work well if it leads to praising God. But if people love things, or even other people, improperly, trouble will result: "But let it [the soul] not become stuck in them and glued to them with love through the physical senses. For these things pass along the path of things that move towards nonexistence. They rend the soul with pestilential desires, for the soul loves to be in them and take its repose among the objects of its love." So the soul is attracted by external things, but falls apart because of them. It becomes many. Despite the relaxation glimpsed in the objects of love, they prove ineffective for rest for the soul: "In those things no such place exists because they don't stand still: they flee" (IV.x.15).[45] Even other people have these grievous limitations: "If souls please you, let them be loved in God; for they also are mutable and acquire stability by being established in him. Otherwise they go their way and perish" (IV.xii.18).[46]

If the delights of this world, even genuine beauty and other people's souls, cannot give contentment to the person, why should one look to a normative view of psychology that requires the person to focus on the One? Augustine returns to ontology to persuade his reader: "All that you experience through it [the flesh] is only partial; you are ignorant of the whole to which the parts belong. Yet they delight you. But if your physical perception were capable of comprehending the whole…you would wish everything at present in being to pass away, so that the totality of things could provide you with greater pleasure." He clarifies the point with an example from daily human experience: "The words we speak you hear by the same physical perception, and you have no wish that the speaker stop at each syllable. You want him to hurry on so that other syllables may come, and you may hear the whole." The conclusion follows naturally enough: "That is always how it is with the sum of the elements out of which a unity is constituted, and the elements out of which it is constituted never exist all at the same moment." Unsurprising perhaps in the writing of a bishop is the move from ontology and perception to theology: "But far superior to these things is he who made all things, and he is our God. He does not pass away; nothing succeeds him" (IV.xi.17).[47] God's superiority and perdurance establish the possibility of "the place of undisturbed quietness where love is not deserted, if it does not itself depart" (IV.xi.16).[48] Augustine's concerns with rest and stability indicate why his psychology is grounded in ontology and theology: he is concerned with the main question of classical ethics, what is the happy life? "You seek the happy life in the region of death…" That is, you seek happiness at best among beauties that will pass away. The conclusion is obvious: "It is not there" (IV.xii.18).[49]

The theological framework and its base in the Bible emerge more clearly from the Neoplatonic picture as Augustine talks about the One that is not transient and unreliable. He begins a coda on the incarnation of God in Jesus: "He who for us is life itself descended here and endured our death and slew it by the abundance of his life" (IV.xii.19).[50] Previously in Augustine's discussion, each mention of the antidote to the fragmentation of the soul also refers to the Bible: "O God of hosts, turn us and show us your face, and we shall be safe (Ps. 80:7)" (IV.x.15);[51] "All that is ebbing away from you will be given fresh form and renewed, bound tightly to you. They will not put you down in the place to which they descend, but will stand with you and will remain in the presence of the God who stands fast and abides (Ps. 102:13, 27; 1 Pet. 1:23)" (IV.xi.16);[52] "He did not create and then depart; the things derived from him have their being in him. Look where he is...He is very close to the heart; but the heart has wandered from him. 'Return, sinners, to your heart' (Isa. 46:8 LXX), and adhere to him who made you" (IV.xii.18).[53]

The whole view of ontology, perception, psychology, and theology propounded by Augustine implies that while his cultural and social circumstances may have encouraged disunity and psychological distraction by the many influences that surged around him, unity of the self through adherence to the one God is possible, if unlikely, in this world. He could not satisfy himself with the description of the person as divided and constantly susceptible to fluctuating influences. According to his thought after his acceptance of Catholicism, the individual can seek God, try to stay focused on God, cherish closeness with God, and so find some stability and rest in even a very divided social and cultural world.[54]

A Depth Psychology of Many and One

The conception of the self in terms of *many-ness* and *one-ness* appears again in the self psychology of Heinz Kohut. No serious reflection could conclude that Kohut's descriptions of the fragmented or cohesive self, to use his terms, are completely independent of Augustine's view. Kohut certainly makes no big deal of Augustine, but Augustine's legacy has permeated European and American culture, where Kohut received his education. Yet Kohut's understanding of the self is not the same as Augustine's. It does not specify a normative stand as clearly, or trace a relationship to ontology or theology.[55] In fact, Kohut emphasizes the operational and provisional nature of his thought: "that reality *per se*, whether extrospective or introspective, is unknowable, and that we can only describe what we see within the framework of what we have done to see it."[56]

Kohut's more narrowly psychological discussions borrow the starting point for human development traditional in psychoanalytically derived modes of thought: a child is thought to start life with a sense of perfection, usually called primary narcissism. The child cannot distinguish between herself and other people. For her everything is herself—or perhaps herself and her mother, with whom she forms a symbiotic bond. According to Kohut, a person's life takes shape from the unconscious memory of this primary narcissistic wholeness or perfection and the various psychological strategies for replicating it in a more mature form.[57]

Primary narcissism does not last, as Kohut and others who agree with him understand it, because of the inevitable course of events. The parents or other caretakers cannot attend to the child every minute and the child then endures times when the bond to them loses its physical reality, for example, the child is alone and crying. Or the bond can take the physical form of holding and hugging, but teething still hurts, and the world seems less than perfect despite the parent's presence. Kohut describes the ensuing events by drawing from Freud's short work *On Narcissism*. Both Freud and Kohut notice the infant's joy in himself and delight in his own accomplishments.[58] Kohut calls this "grandiosity," a term that applies to every child's spontaneous psychological response to her or his own abilities and accomplishments and to the ways other people approach him or her. Both Freud and Kohut also hold that disrupted narcissism redirects itself into the formation of an internalized ideal.[59] Idealization, as Kohut elaborates the concept, manifests itself most obviously in children's responses to their parents. Mommy and Daddy can do anything, take away hurts, put on clothes, pick up and carry babies, and use lots of big words. To emphasize that idealization is a psychological process, internal to the child and not an accurate reflection of the parents' demonstrated capabilities, Kohut terms the parents (or other such adults) "idealized parent imagoes." The imago, the psychological image the child has of the parents, allows the child to assuage the sorrows of the end of primary narcissism, as does the grandiose part of the child's self.

Of course, both grandiosity and idealizing fail to make up completely for the loss of primary narcissism. The child encounters often the limits of his own powers and the constraints on his grandiosity. Moreover, the parents fail to know all and do all. They get frustrated with broken devices, may find themselves embarrassed publicly, or stand helplessly by when a beloved animal dies. The idealized parent imago looks less glorious and the world again less perfect.

The result, according to Kohut, of such limitations of grandiosity and failures of idealized parent imagoes is that the child builds a psychological structure. If the child is learning to walk and falls down, the bump as she falls may injure her grandiosity, but the feeling of standing and trying to step seems to stay with her and gives her a taste of the power she knows she can exercise. Moreover, one of the important psychological functions that Kohut points out in parents and other grownups is their willingness to delight in the child's progress and accomplishments. He calls this their "mirroring" of the child, their reflection to her of her own strength and goodness.[60] So the rough bump of the floor may distress the child, but the bigger people all around applaud the standing and the attempt to walk and thereby restore a bit of the grandiosity and mitigate the injury of the fall. They help her, thereby, to begin to develop realistic self-appraisal and ambition.[61] The loss of the image of the parent's perfection can lead to a small process of mourning in which the external manifestation of goodness becomes internal, as a sort of a representation of what was wanted but did not happen. Something like an internal shrine to the desired outcome becomes part of the child's psyche. It records both the lack of the outcome and the recollection of what was hoped.[62]

These results, however, depend on the strength of the shock to the child's system by the failure of grandiosity or idealization. If the falls really hurt, especially if they occur extremely often, or if the older people in the area do not comfort the little one and encourage more progress, the results can accumulate traumatically. Some of the worst hurts probably come from an accumulation of lack of caring about the child's accomplishments and delights.[63] A steady coldness,[64] or worse yet, regular belittling,[65] can wound the child's grandiosity to the extent that it remains a sore spot in the psyche for life.[66] The child grows up without a sense of being good enough or capable enough and somehow has to compensate for the pain caused by this lack.[67]

Similarly, if the parents regularly fail to meet the child's expectations of power and protection and capability, the idealized parent imagoes may suffer lasting damage. The sense that one has somewhere to turn when things go wrong, or that one could try to absorb the parents' strength and use it oneself when necessary, is weak. If the disappointment comes in a large shocking blow, such as a parent being terribly humiliated in front of the child, then a traumatic feeling may overwhelm the child and attach itself to the features of that event. The psyche will automatically repress recollection of the event in order to avoid the pain of the memory.[68] In such cases, the child will probably grow up looking always for someone to idealize or will reach adulthood emotionally closed to the hope of help or improvement in a situation.[69]

Kohut and other self psychologists contend that people grow up sustaining a mixture of these experiences. Everyone experiences some reflection of her own grandiosity and an ability to enjoy it. Each encounters some setbacks and doubts her own powers and abilities. All suffer some small and some large disappointments in people who seem more able; all gain some confidence that someone can comfort one's own losses, as well as some hope that someone will help.[70]

Kohut expects that the self, which depends on grandiosity and its reflection back to the child and on the idealized parent imagoes, will begin to cohere more clearly by age five or so. Grandiosity becomes more realistic as a form of manageable ambition and striving toward goals that match the child's talents and interests. The idealized parent imagoes fade while the ideals for which they stood become the guides for the child's view of the good. Kohut thought of the self as a "tension arc" between the poles of modified grandiosity and ideals made more realistic. That is, the differences between these two aspects of the self allow for energy in the person's psyche to flow between striving for the self and following ideals.[71]

The lack of a cohesive self became Kohut's way of talking about various kinds of sorrow, hostility, or coldness.[72] The feelings the patients brought with them to psychotherapeutic sessions did not directly reflect the sort of problem that Kohut thought gave rise to them. Here he follows the old

Freudian saw, that psychological experiences that upset the individual sufficiently undergo repression and become unconscious. The person has no choice in this, nor in the continued existence of these memories outside of conscious awareness, nor in the tendency of these memories to find expression in some distorted form, which makes them less painful and, therefore, able to escape repression and enter consciousness.[73] The disguises may be very clever, especially when the trauma shocks the system very strongly and requires extensive covering not to disrupt consciousness. Clues to a weakened self in Kohut's patients came under the guise of some other sort of psychological distress, such as depression,[74] listlessness, lack of reasonable success in a career,[75] fits of rage,[76] and even voyeurism and exhibitionism.[77]

So Kohut's theory of self psychology offers a way of understanding the individual by using techniques from psychoanalysis for interpreting psychological difficulties. It serves notice of the potential for a psyche to seem incoherent and to manifest the divided self in various disguised forms. It also offers some clear parallels to Augustine's thought about the person. Both writers believed that a person would be divided internally and could find help toward the restoration of wholeness. Both saw the lack of unity as undesirable and likely to precipitate unhappiness. Both saw the extent of division and the possibilities for cohesion as relative during this life to the experiences that people have, to their self-knowledge, and to the help they receive. Neither division nor unity would be complete in anyone we might know or become.

These parallels, however, can be taken as competitive views. The expected form of reflection on them is then some form of reductionism: the psychological depth is reduced to a problem of religion, or the religious interpretation is seen as an artifact left from psychological processes. For instance, someone defending Augustine might argue that Kohut's view is inadequate because it fails to acknowledge the power of God to heal psychological distress. Someone defending Kohut might argue that all the talk about the unity of God and the fall of the soul into the distractions of earthly life is nothing but a disguise for the unconscious fragmentation of Augustine's own psyche. People influenced by clinical views in psychology can dismiss the theological view as antiquated, and theologians—or historians—can ignore the psychological views as theologically or historically unsophisticated. A measure of truth might lie on both sides. Unfortunately, these bits of truth may interfere with appreciation of the possibility for understanding the emergence of meaning from resources like religion in our lives.

An Interpretive Alternative to Both Forms of Reductionism

An alternate that respects analysis of both the conscious and the unconscious construction of meaning can assist a richer understanding of Augustine's text and our own potentials for comprehension of our lives and our worlds. It comes from Ricoeur's proposal that symbols face in two directions: toward the unconscious and the past of individuals and cultures and toward the conscious effort to shape and guide the future. This view meshes with psychological anthropology, as elaborated by scholars like Sudhir Kakar and Gananath Obeyesekere.

Simply restated, Ricoeur's conclusion holds that symbols may allow disguised expressions of unconscious wishes to come to consciousness in distorted form. Simultaneously, as people record and reshape these symbols consciously, they may fit them into already established cultural resources for the guidance of human life. Or the cultural resources may be reformulated by the creative work of individuals with symbolic material. Ricoeur further proposes that a complete interpretation of symbols must include both these directions of interpretation. Symbols then begin to be understood as remnants of repressed experience, sorrow, and hope, and also like multifaceted forms of meaning that play into systems of thought and intentional modes of expression.[78]

Ricoeur's conception of symbols, based in part on an intensive study of Freud, shares with a school of psychological anthropology the Freudian notion that certain cultural forms allow the expression of unconscious wishes.[79] Culture has ready to hand, so to speak, symbols in stories and visual arts and the rules governing social institutions that invite the disguised expression of unconscious wishes. Freud pointed to the worship of gods as such a symbolic expression of longing for a father's love and protection, as well as fear of his wrath.[80]

Psychological anthropologists have found ample justification in Freud's work for the additional thesis that culture shapes the unconscious. This would be so because culture guides people's intentional lives and teaches what people should do and not do. Whatever is forbidden is likely to become repressed to a greater or lesser extent. Therefore the boundaries of the unconscious would be shaped by the experience of desires that can be expressed without incurring psychological pain and of those that have not survived in consciousness. For instance, if a boy were rebuffed sharply for responding to a threat by running to his father, then the desire for the father's protection would undergo repression. The rebuff would be prescribed by some cultures and some philosophies,[81] so one would expect that men in that culture would tend to be unaware of a desire for the protection of their fathers.

Yet, according to the Freudian view, the repressed experiences remain and retain the force of desire, the urge to reach some goal. If the desire for the father's protection could not come to consciousness, then perhaps the upsetting experience would spend its energy in changing to a form that seems less threatening. Maybe it would take the form of desire for protection from another older man in the vicinity. Perhaps that would still recall too much pain for consciousness to accept it. If so, it might become desire for the protection of a head of state or for the approval of someone of higher rank in the profession that the boy, grown to a man, had chosen. The man bearing this unconscious trace of childhood may find another expression of it, if his culture already says that one may worship a god. Then the unconscious desire can find a form to express itself that surely will not meet with rebuff but will be sufficiently like the desire to represent it in disguise. Here we meet half of Shweder's dictum at work—"Culture and the psyche make each other up"[82]—as culture makes up psyche.

Ricoeur also advances a notion of how psyche makes up culture. The energy that Freud noted in unconscious ideas and feelings leads to unusual expressions, "compromise formations," to use the technical term. They compromise between the desired end, which appears in the symbolic formation, and the unsatisfied desire. They require creative activity in the psyche, even if that activity escapes intentional direction. They may pop into dreams, or occur outside an artist's awareness in a work of art.[83] But beyond this unconscious impulse and unexpected combination of ideas and images, psyche makes up culture by shaping it through intentional effort, contemplation, reflection, and efforts to meet the norms that culture has perpetuated in genre, technique, education, and taste. The unconscious may intrude into the production, but the conscious has opportunities to rework the unrecognized unconscious intrusions into something more acceptable to the standards of right or good in the society in which and for which the artist works.[84]

An example will clarify my approach to interpretation and the way it counters reductionism. Augustine wrote:

> "Your right hand upheld me" (Ps. 18:35; 63:8) in my Lord, the Son of Man who is mediator between you, the One, and us, the many, who live in a multiplicity of distractions by many things; so "I might apprehend him in whom also I am apprehended" (Phil. 3:12–14), and leaving behind the old days I might be gathered to follow the One, "forgetting the past" and not moving towards those future things which are transitory but to "the things which are before" me, not stretched out in distraction but extended in reach, not by being pulled apart but by concentration. (XI.xxix.39)[85]

This passage immediately shows the influence of culture and the working of Augustine's intentionality. It includes the cultural influence of the Bible in the quotes from Psalms and Philippians. He knew of debates about the nature of the Christ and took a small and not too controversial stand in this passage by calling Christ the mediator. But by the time he notes between whom the Christ mediates, he has already drawn on his blend of Neoplatonism and Christianity: "between you, the One, and us, the many." Then he invokes again his adoption of Plotinus' normative psychology: "who live in a multiplicity of distractions by many things."

Yet the self psychologist might easily hear in these words the sounds of a child's repressed need to idealize his parents, who somehow failed him. Why suspect that they failed him? Because he expresses a wish that is not yet fulfilled and envisions the fulfillment of it. From this point of view one might say Augustine writes compromise formations. He does not use a phrase like "embarrassment of riches." Clearly he wants to escape the multiplicity of distractions. The sound of desire for an idealized parent rings in the phrase, "I might be gathered to follow the One…" The passive voice implies help from someone outside myself, who is stronger than I.

But the theologians and historians might answer that Augustine soon returns to discussing time and then to the theme of what listening to words tells us about the passage of time and the nature of parts and wholes. The answer to them is the same as to the self psychologists: Yes. One can say yes to both because the two approaches are not mutually exclusive but are interlocked from the outset. Why might his parents have fallen short as ideals? Perhaps because of the problems in ideals that their culture offered them to guide their lives. Why might he seek ideals later? Because of his early disappointments. And why seek the ideals in God and discussions of time and eternity? Perhaps because they were what his culture offered as problems and solutions, biblical riddles, and philosophical guideposts. The interpenetration of culture and psyche could run very deep. What causes blows to a sense of wonderfulness in oneself? The passage of time, when things do not work out as desired. What restores the sense of wholeness and goodness about oneself? In part, affectionate acceptance by someone who seems less battered by the vicissitudes of time. Later we discover that all people are governed by time and its workings, but then we can turn our thoughts and desires to greater questions: What is eternity? Who am I in it? How shall I live in time? What sense do my experiences of time and in the passage of time make? To follow these ideas through as more than intuitions will take several more chapters. We will start them at the beginning of Augustine's life and narrative in the *Confessions*.

CHAPTER 3

Early Childhood Grandiosity and Injury

Augustine's comments about his infancy and childhood appear in book 1 of the *Confessions*, which sets the tone for the whole of the work. Book 1 emphasizes God's greatness and the human being's smallness relative to God. It points to evidence of sinfulness in children and in babies and looks for God's activity in people's lives from their earliest hours. Because his theological goals guide Augustine's portrayal of his early life in this book, our precious source of information about Augustine's earliest years is also a tricky text to assess. For instance, Augustine's reports of his infancy and early childhood are short and sketchy at best. Even if they were more complete, a problem for historical inquiry would still arise, because a forty-year-old's memories of childhood would not survive accurately.[1] When we turn to the self psychological reading of the text, which addresses early childhood and elucidates division and unity in the psyche, we have to remember that, by definition, the indicators of unconscious aspects of the self disguise psychological patterns at the same time that they allow the unconscious access to consciousness.

To handle these challenges, I will proceed carefully, establishing the facts we can glean from the story, putting them into social context, filling in the cultural background, and disentangling the evidence of psychological development from the theological and historical arguments and allusions. First, we will see something of Augustine's family and home life and the beginning of his schooling. The depictions of those aspects of his life fit well with the discoveries of scholars about the family in late antiquity. Research on the cultural context of Augustine's life shows the influence of both Christian and non-Christian elements of culture on the guidance for his youngest days. Finally, looking back at his youth, Augustine's language as a bishop supports the proposition that many aspects of his society and culture encouraged his grandiosity and its development, at the same time that social interaction dealt youngsters quite a few blows to their sense of their own worth. These apparently contradictory dealings of his environment with his mind and feelings seem to have left him with considerable injury to his grandiosity. He also appears to have discovered a means of compensating for that injury by drawing out grandiosity in other endeavors and escapades. The possibilities, which Kohut would expect of idealizing as a compensation for grandiosity, are the subject of the next chapter.

Augustine was born in November 354 C.E. to a twenty-three-year-old mother (IX.xi.28), Monica, who also had at least two other children, a son and a daughter, who grew to adulthood.[2] Augustine may have been the oldest, as some people infer from a story he tells of his adolescence. In his "sixteenth year," when he was fifteen, his father Patricius saw him at the baths and came home rejoicing about the possibility of having grandchildren because he had noticed Augustine's pubescent maturation (II.iii.6). Presumably, if Augustine's brother Navigius had been the elder, Patricius would already have accustomed himself to this prospect. This recital constitutes our only evidence of the birth order of the children, however, and asking it to uphold a strong claim about the effect of birth order on Augustine's relationships with his parents is ill advised.[3]

Augustine had nurses, as well as the attention of his mother in his infancy (I.vi.7). In his older childhood, his family could afford to send him to the local school of letters, where children received a basic education in reading, writing, and arithmetic (I.xiii.20). Later they found the money to send him to Madauros to a grammar school (II.iii.5), the formal educational entry into the professions and the passport to the upper classes.[4]

Augustine excelled in school, where he learned the Latin classics, especially Vergil and within his corpus particularly the *Aeneid*.[5] He also had to study Greek literature (I.xiii.20). Just how much Greek he mastered has caused considerable scholarly debate,[6] but his brilliance lay elsewhere. He had to participate in public speaking competitions and distinguished himself quickly (I.xvii.27). But he also enjoyed playing with the other boys, with whom he had his share of disputes and rivalries. The urge to play sometimes got him in trouble with his schoolmasters, and they beat him and the other children for inattentiveness, tardiness, or truancy, as well as for errors in their schoolwork (I.ix.14, I.xiv.23, I.xvi.26, I.xix.30).

Social Context of the School and the Family in Childhood

Historical studies of the social context of the family and schooling in late antiquity sometimes affirm that Augustine lived in a fairly normal environment.[7] Their argument risks being circular, because Augustine's report of his childhood and family life is often the source for historians' inferences about the family in the wider society of late antiquity. Yet one can probably fairly conclude that he struggled with the same familial problems and social institutions as many other middle-class children of his era.

Augustine did not vary from the most frequent forms of behavior, experience, and emotional response in his age group and society—at least not if he reports accurately. For instance, he found company in other children's desires to play and in the sorrows that followed, if they played during school hours and received a beating when discovered. Moreover, his parents' responses to his troubles at school appear to have matched those that the other children met at home: "our parents would laugh at the torments with which we boys were crushed by the teachers..." (I.ix.15).[8] Augustine's use of the first person plural ("our parents," "we boys") indicates that the same misfortune affected other children also. Other sources confirm the normality of his response in his social context. James J. O'Donnell comments: "Such punishment was common and disdain for it conventional."[9]

Another historian, Brent Shaw, argues that the conditions of family life in late antiquity also supported the enactment of violence.[10] The oft recollected fact of Roman family life, *patria potestas*, the senior male's right to correct physically any member of the family, included capital as well as corporal punishment. Yet both Shaw and Richard Saller adduce factors that limited the actual use of *patria potestas*. Shaw mentions the middle-class or lower-class father's dependence on his sons for support in his old age and for help with farming or a trade. Saller discusses the evidence for an operative distinction between corporal punishment, appropriate for slaves, and forms of discipline appropriate for sons, born as free people and not to be treated as slaves.[11] Augustine never mentions being punished physically, or at all, for that matter, by his own father. In fact, as he writes about later years in the *Confessions* he chides Patricius for *not* trying to control his adolescent son's lusts (II.iii.6). Nor did Patricius take out his anger physically on Monica, although many wives in Tagaste suffered such treatment (IX.ix.19). He did, however, whip servant girls who gossiped maliciously about his new bride to his mother (IX.ix.20). Yet we see that Augustine in adulthood often illustrates commonplace points in sermons and other writings by the image of corporal punishment by one's father.[12]

Augustine enjoyed the good fortune of having talents for other people to admire and, moreover, abilities that fit very well in the larger social context. As he said, people encouraged him to work hard so that he could succeed in the world. The move to grammarian's classes signals that Augustine could aspire to greater social status than most of the children in the village school. Some of his classmates in the grammar school would have been tutored at home instead of attending the village school before they entered the grammar school, so we can conclude that they would have come from families with more money than his. But as he could succeed in this educational setting, he could gain access to the cultured and moneyed elite of his time.[13]

Augustine's educational progress reflects the social status of his family. His biographer Possidius reports that Patricius and Monica were of the subdecurial class.[14] This level of Roman society hung precariously in the balance of events. A decurial family's inheritance could easily vanish because of the duties accompanying the family's role.[15] Patricius apparently succeeded in shouldering the load. He managed to use his pivotal social position to advance his son in the world.

The Guidance of Culture

Augustine comments in book 1 about the cultural influences on him. His mother's pious Christianity reverberated through his childhood, and his father's pagan mores seem to have insinuated themselves at home. Moreover, Augustine himself recognized that his schooling introduced him to culture in several ways. It brought him into contact with the classic literature of the pagan tradition, and it also introduced him to more people in the world to emulate.

Two main instances in book 1 of the *Confessions* indicate some influence of Monica's Christianity on Augustine in his childhood. He mentions that he "was already signed with the sign of the cross and seasoned with salt from the time I came from my mother's womb."[16] These rituals marked him at birth as a Christian catechumen, although not as a baptized Christian.[17] He adds, however, that his baptism did not occur in childhood, "as if it were necessary that I would dirty myself if I were to live, since it seemed that after that washing [of baptism] the guilt in the dirtiness of faults would be greater and more dangerous."[18] These comments form part of Augustine's discussion of the second instance of Monica's Christianity influencing Augustine's life. He speaks of a time when he took ill and nearly died. He recalls,

> When I was still a boy, I had heard about eternal life promised to us through the humility of our Lord God...You saw, my God, because you were already my guardian, with what fervour of mind and with what faith I then begged for the baptism of your Christ, my God and Lord, urging it on the devotion of my mother and of the mother of us all, your Church. My physical mother was distraught. With a pure heart and faith in you she even more lovingly travailed in labour for my eternal salvation. She hastily made arrangements for me to be initiated and washed in the sacraments of salvation, confessing you, Lord Jesus, for the remission of sins. But suddenly I recovered. My cleansing was deferred...[19]

The influence of Monica's faith on him finds confirmation in his claim, "So I already believed, as did she and the whole household, except for my father only. He, nevertheless, did not overcome in me the rights of my mother's piety, so that I would not believe in Christ as he did not yet believe." Augustine says that while she was "better" than her husband, she "served him, for in this she was, at least, obeying you who commanded it" (I.xi.17).[20]

Monica in her context offered Augustine a partial ideal. She showed him the Christian faith and demonstrated the humility it preached (whether we admire her style as Augustine did when he wrote the *Confessions* [IX.ix.19] is a different issue). She could only represent this to him, however, as part of the domestic life. Social convention would not have permitted her to go outside the home much or to spend time in public,[21] except perhaps in church or the women's baths. She could not make clear to him, as he developed his image of a man, what direction his abilities and powers should take if he would follow her Christian example in the larger social world.

Naturally, Patricius would exemplify a man's elevated social rank and his greater freedom to express his sense of his own worth. Monica even reinforced Patricius' ways, although she probably did not think of her conduct as doing so and perhaps realistically could not have done otherwise. Far from exercising the gentleness and self-control that the letters of the apostle Paul praise as the fruits of the Spirit of God,[22] Patricius had a hot temper. He might not make sense, and could lose the rational thread of an argument, but Monica did not interfere with his rage and waited until he cooled off to make her case and win his approval of her plans (IX.ix.19). Augustine would have learned from their behavior that a man could, with impunity, display an awful temper.

Furthermore, the classics in which famous characters engaged in similar behavior reinforced Patricius' anger as being acceptable. Augustine was assigned to enact Juno's rage when her will was thwarted (I.xvii.27). He also read Homer, as well as Vergil's *Aeneid*, full of the glories of men in the Trojan War and their shame and rage in their defeats. He read of Jupiter's rape of Danaë, which recalls for us at the end of the twentieth century a man's power over a woman as an enhancement to his self-image. Augustine attests to the influence of this tale on people's conduct by censuring it as he looked back on it from the bishop's chair (I.xvi.26).

Augustine notes elsewhere in book 1 that people in the social milieu provide by their actions, as well as their instruction, the guidance for life that people need from culture. He concludes that this meant for him a particular direction in his childhood: "When one considers the men proposed to me as models for my imitation, it is no wonder that in this way I was swept along by vanities and travelled right away from you, my God." Here he refers not simply to men's freedom with their anger and demonstrations of power, but points more specifically to the foibles of the well-educated and the scholars: "They would be covered in embarrassment if, in describing their own actions in which they had not behaved badly, they were caught using a barbarism or a solecism in speech" (I.xviii.28).[23] He absorbed this direction for his own efforts: "I was more afraid of committing a barbarism than, if I did commit one, on my guard against feeling

envy towards those who did not. I declare and confess this to you, my
God. These were the qualities for which I was praised by people whose
approval was, at that time, my criterion of a good life" (I.xix.30).[24]

Yet one should also realize that ancient pagan philosophies discussed
at length the advantages of self-control, praised by the Epicureans and Stoics
alike. Asceticism supported many philosophical ways of life; philosophy
meant practice of self-control and reason, as well as systematic reflection
about them. Greater display of one's capacities for anger or shame would
not, by itself, lead to the happy life philosophers described. But Augustine
seems not to have caught on to this train of thought until he read Cicero's
Hortensius (III.iv.7) when he was eighteen. He may have heard of the ancients' restraint, but it did not draw him in until well after his grammar
school years.

We need not deem the more emotional outbursts to which Augustine
attests alien, because we see similar responses in our own society and culture. They may be very widespread across lands and eras. The human impulse to become embarrassed when one makes mistakes and angry when
one cannot carry out one's plans may be familiar in our own experience.
Nonetheless, we note also that a society, family, or culture can instead promote a more matter-of-fact, or even easygoing, recognition of mistakes.
Concentration on learning from errors and disappointments could replace,
or at least mitigate, the emphasis we see on embarrassment and rage as
responses to difficulties. Or sometimes one laughs at mistakes and feels
impelled by thwarted plans to try a new approach. But these responses to
personal insult seem to have not been promoted in the social interactions
that Augustine witnessed, and anger and shame became part of his approach to life as he grew up. The self psychological exploration of book 1
and the circumstances of Augustine's childhood will show more social
patterns and cultural norms that could have entered into his own life's
events, whether they provoked rage or led to pride and pleasure.

Indications of the Fate of Grandiosity in Augustine's Boyhood

Discovering the self psychological themes of Augustine's early childhood will require close examination of his descriptions of his early life.
Psychoanalytic sessions with living people provide the analogical base for
this approach. According to Ricoeur, analogy offers a defensible foundation for psychoanalytic study of people who no longer live.[25] The issues in
psychoanalytic therapy present themselves not simply from the facts of a
person's life or interactions, but from the way the person talks about experiences. While the events and interactions function as part of the person's
subjective experience, the key to understanding its psychological depth
lies in deciphering how the unconscious thoughts, feelings, and processes
have transformed themselves through condensation, displacement, or
other unconscious processes and, thereby, escaped from repression into
expression.

Frequently the clues to the transformations of unconscious thoughts and feelings into conscious symbols reveal themselves in small hints, not in reports of *beaux gestes* or dramatic encounters. In fact, the term "displacement" designates this shifting of the energy associated with a repressed subject from its content to something related, but much less emotionally charged. Inasmuch as displacement occurs, the hints of the unconscious will crop up in asides, juxtapositions, the occasional adjective, and so on, much as Freud expected to find them in the slip of the tongue. The reason for trusting inferences based on these little clues is that they form a pattern. The interpretation of major psychological aspects of Augustine's life does not depend on a single instance on which every other aspect of the interpretation hangs. If Freud's view of overdetermination, widely accepted in psychoanalytically oriented hermeneutics, holds, then an interpretation should move toward the same underlying factors from many different bits of conscious thought and feeling, just as the same underlying thoughts and feelings can give off many conscious but disguised signals.[26] For now, the task before us is that of a sleuth: seeking clues about the possible development and formation of Augustine's unconscious life.

Hints and Conjectures about Infancy

Augustine's descriptions of infancy inadvertently reflect what Kohut would call the baby's grandiosity, the child's apparent belief in his or her own omnipotence, marvelous worth, and centrality in the world. Speaking of the time right after birth, Augustine asserts that as a baby he was welcome, and, we might infer, probably a pleasure, a joy, a cause for delight, and certainly an occasion for loving care: "So I was welcomed by the consolations of human milk." A hint of primary narcissism would be seen by some readers in his description of nursing: "You also granted me not to wish for more than you [God through nurses and mother] were giving, and to my nurses the desire to give me what you gave them." This same intuition of bliss appears in the words: "At that time I knew nothing more than how to suck and to be quietened by bodily delights..." But the next phrase sounds the warning that any sense of early perfection could readily be spoiled: "and to weep when I was physically uncomfortable" (I.vi.7).[27]

Augustine signals that he was the center of attention, as most infants were at that time.[28] He notes in passing that, even when he was not weeping from physical discomfort, grownups focused on him: "The consolations of your mercies (cf. Ps. 51:3; 94:19) upheld me, as I have heard from the parents of my flesh..." (I.vi.7);[29] "Afterwards I began to smile, first in my sleep, then when awake. That at least is what I was told..." (I.vi.8).[30] He adds, "This period of my life, Lord, I do not remember having lived, but I have believed what others told me" (I.vii.12).[31] These passages suggest that people continued to talk to Augustine, perhaps as they spoke to other children, about what he had been like as a baby. Such behavior can confirm to growing children the idea that they as babies were valued, precious to their caretakers, capable of making grown-ups smile, or at least of creating memories that would later make them stop their hustle and bustle long enough to speak of years gone by. Kohut conceives of this sort of experience as reassuring grandiosity and fostering a sense of continuity, of cohesion of the unconscious core of the self over time: "We search for the continuity. 'How was I when I was a little boy?' 'How were you when you were a little girl?' 'What did you do?' 'Tell me about me,' we ask. 'Did I really say clever things? Was I bad sometimes?' It doesn't matter what the questions are exactly…" Then he turns to vocabulary pertaining to grandiosity: "The excitement is the knowledge of me, me, me. You saw me, you held me. Tell me about it. It's the me that's the important issue, that I was important to you and that you remember that and that you can tell me about it."[32]

Anyone who knows the passages about infancy in the *Confessions* might well object that the quotations thus far are simply musings on the earthly side of life, while the passage on the whole concentrates on God's power and goodness in creation.[33] In book 1 the theme of creation does not emphasize grandiosity, but, to the contrary, Augustine's smallness vis-à-vis God. For instance, Augustine opens book 1, chapter vi.7, saying, "Nevertheless allow me to speak before your mercy, though I am but dust and ashes (Gen. 18:27)." After musing on human milk as a gift of God, he concludes: "Indeed all good things come from you, O God, and 'from my God is all my salvation' (2 Sam. 23:5). I became aware of this only later when you cried aloud to me through the gifts which you bestow both inwardly in mind and outwardly in body" (I.vi.7).[34] Augustine's culture, through the norms for his social role as a bishop writing his life's story, allowed him to address the topic of God's greatness, but would not permit him to concentrate with approval on grandiosity, as his reference to Genesis 18:27 regarding human beings as dust and ashes implies. Using our wits, theories, and the text, however, we discover more clues.

One clue to our discovery of empathic conditions for the development of grandiosity comes in a surprising passage in which Augustine dwells on the sin of infants, a passage that has undoubtedly cost him admiration in our century. Augustine's language suggests that social and cultural norms allowed parents to respond empathically to a child's grandiose demands to be the center of attention, but he refuses intellectual assent to the implications of the parents' behavior: "The feebleness of infant limbs is innocent, not the infant's mind." Augustine illustrates his point: "I have personally watched and studied a jealous baby. He could not yet speak and, pale with jealousy and bitterness, glared at his brother sharing his mother's milk. Who is unaware of this fact of experience?" Then comes the hint of the norms that promoted what we could now call an empathic environment: "Mothers and nurses claim to charm it away by their own private remedies." In other words, he lets us see that they do not condemn, but respond gently. Augustine still seems uncomfortable with the manifestation of grandiosity: "But it can hardly be innocence, when the source of milk is flowing richly and abundantly, not to endure a share going to one's blood brother, who is in profound need, dependent for life exclusively on that one food." Nonetheless, common wisdom of the time seems to have governed his elders' actions toward him: "But people smilingly tolerate this behaviour, not because it is nothing or only a trivial matter, but because with coming of age it will pass away. You can prove this to be the case from the fact that the same behaviour cannot be borne without irritation when encountered in someone of more mature years" (I.vii.11).[35]

The caretakers' adjustment to the infant's level of comprehension and ability is very much what Kohut means by an empathic environment: "For a long, long time, the empathic adult environment of a child—correctly empathic, if it is a feelingful, understanding environment—will not insist on object love from the child, but will take for granted that the environment is being used in a narcissistic sense by the child, because it fits his developmental capacities."[36] Kohut contrasts this empathic environment with one in which the grown-ups ask the child for "object love," love for another person understood as separate from oneself.[37] An infant cannot appreciate the separateness and independence of one physical entity, like the mother's milk, from another, like the baby's own body. Infants' cognitive and emotional capacities are so near the beginning of development that they cannot consistently demonstrate the concern for other people that Augustine wanted to see in the jealous baby. We will see later in chapter 7 that he specifies active concern for one's neighbor's welfare as one of the two primary moral norms, based on the two great commandments found in the gospels. But he demonstrates in his example in book 1 no sense of the child's needs and little comprehension of an empathic environment, even though he describes one. Instead, he seems to insist on what Kohut in the psychoanalytic jargon calls "object love," or at least object recognition. Just what might have happened to his intuitive sensitivity to a child's needs can be explored in the next section when we look at Augustine's school years.

If an "object" can be understood as another person, seen as separate from the self, then a selfobject, one of Kohut's key concepts, comes into view by contrast. The selfobject is first and foremost the psychological representation of someone who functions in the psyche as a support for one's own self, despite the fact that he or she actually is a separate human being. Kohut gives a sense of the selfobject for the maintenance of grandiosity when he discusses "the kind of expansion of the self in which one feels great but needs somebody else to be part and parcel and servant to this greatness." He elaborates:

> One assumes one's self is all powerful and fantastically big, except somebody else is needed to maintain this image of self. The baby, having this kind of conviction, could not maintain it very long unless adults were playing their role and helping him to maintain

this. The child does not know that others are doing something out of their goodwill and out of their maternal and paternal instincts. It is done because he is he, and he wants it, and this is part of his greatness.[38]

The selfobject is, as Kohut says elsewhere, the representation of someone who seems more like a part of one's own body than a fully separate person with a life of his or her own.[39] The selfobject for the grandiose self gets about as much respect as one might imagine from the infant whom Freud, in his discussion of narcissism, called "His Majesty the Baby."[40]

Even in Augustine's apparently cold and harsh remarks about what he believed to be the sin of infants, then, we see evidence of the ability of people in Augustine's society to respond empathically to babies and small children with their grandiose demands of the world and other people. The women could allow themselves to be treated by the baby as food supplies, entertainers, and personal attendants. They displayed a certain wisdom, which relied on their experience of children growing out of demanding behaviors. Such wisdom, or a sense of humor about the children's fussing, would indicate, according to Kohut, mature narcissism, transformed from childish grandiosity and indiscriminate idealizing into ready tendencies to cope with the world's difficulties.[41] Admittedly, Augustine himself seems to have lost empathy, another transformation of narcissism according to Kohut, when he condemns infants' imperious wants and neglects to comment on children's generous impulses. This lack of empathy would, according to Kohut, indicate damage to Augustine's own potential for mature narcissism. While Augustine's home in his childhood seems to have supported his infantile grandiosity and given it scope to develop until it could moderate, the world outside home, and his parents' responses to it, seem to have had a damaging effect that may have diminished his ability to let his ethics rest while he watched a jealous baby.

School Years

The empathic environment seems to have changed when Augustine reached the age at which he left the family confines every day for school. Some disjunction between the atmosphere of the home for an infant and the school for a young boy may readily make sense from our own experience. Europeans and North Americans would not regard nursery school and kindergarten as advantageous if the rules and behaviors of the home could transfer simply to school. They do not, and so we give children time to learn how to conform to social life in a group with its expectations about regular time for certain events, quiet when the teacher or another child is talking, cooperation, sharing, and so forth. The extent of the difference for Augustine may be more comprehensible still when one learns that some cultures include a remarkable break in attitudes toward the child at different points in the life cycle. Sudhir Kakar, for instance, describes the psychological dynamics involved in what he calls the "second birth" of the

Hindu boy. A traditional saying, which strongly influences actual child rearing practice, encourages the treatment of sons like kings until they are five,
like slaves from five to fifteen years, and like friends thereafter. Kakar interprets this pattern as allowing a relatively long period of narcissistic sustenance from the outside, then introducing a strong narcissistic blow, so
that the child's self tends to retain a stronger interconnection with other
people as selfobjects than it would if it had gradually separated from them
and internalized the functions they performed for the child.[42] One of many
other examples is Hildred Geertz's description of child rearing in Java.
Geertz observed Javanese fathers having one period of warm closeness to
their children, from the end of the children's first through their fifth year.
After that the father became more like an "outsider" to the children rather
than a familial "insider," and his offspring had to treat the father with the
deference shown to people of higher social rank outside the family. Geertz
does not pursue a psychoanalytically based interpretation very far, but she
does infer that the shifts in the child's relationship with the father fit a
pattern of Javanese emotional control.[43]

What was the change when Augustine went to school? Some affirmation of his desire to shine, as Kohut would speak about maturing grandiosity, remained. For instance, Augustine admits that he *"was said to be* a boy
of high promise" (I.xvi.26).[44] He also says that his potential received confirmation when adults exhorted him "with the purpose that I should succeed
in this world, and should excel in the arts of using my tongue to gain access to human honours and to acquire deceitful riches" (I.ix.14).[45] People
believed in his talents and affirmed them, even if he in his later life saw
their words as directing him toward the wrong ends (most obviously, "deceitful riches," *falsas divitias*). But he paid a price on this road to success. We
see the combination of real acceptance of his strengths and the hint of
wounded grandiosity in one snippet of his years in school:

> Permit me, my God, to say something also about my intelligence,
> your gift, and the ways in which it was wasted on absurdities. A
> task was set, disquieting enough to my soul, with a prize of praise
> and fear of shame or lashes, that I should say the words of Juno,
> angry and sorrowing because she could not keep the king of the
> Trojans out of Italy... (I.xvii.27)[46]

By the time he could accomplish a task of competitive public speaking,
he responded to the challenge with a disquieted soul, because he was afraid
of "shame or lashes" which might result from failure, although he knew
his efforts could also bring "a prize of praise." His fear had a strong element of realism, as he has made clear by his reference to the beating that he
and other children received in school, apparently fairly often. He states
clearly, "This method was approved by adults..." (I.ix.14).[47] Despite his
fears, in the case of the recital of Juno's woes, he won the competition,
evidently handily.

Augustine's language here allows the self psychological interpretation that his grandiosity had not grown into secure confidence in his realistic claims to being a wonderful center of attention, even in a restricted situation designed to show off his abilities. Something had happened to disrupt the admiration of the grown-ups, once the schoolteacher appeared in the circle of adults.[48] This theme of Augustine's sufferings in school bears more attention, partly because it has already entered into psychological interpretations of the *Confessions*, and partly because it leads to further elucidation of Kohut's ideas about narcissism, especially grandiosity.

Augustine tells us that empathy was not the order of the day for him when he suffered a beating at school. The schoolteacher's harshness seems to have elicited an unempathic response from the formerly doting elders: "adult people, including even my parents, who wished no evil to come upon me, used to laugh at my stripes, which were at that time a great and painful evil to me" (I.ix.14).[49] Their behavior could introduce an injury to narcissism that could impede Augustine's transition from childhood grandiosity to mature narcissism that would support his empathy for others when he reached adulthood.

Kohut offers an example very similar to Augustine's experience:

> When a child comes home with a poor grade, he is upset and does not want reproaches on how lazy he has been. He may have been lazy, but at that time he is upset about the poor grade. The first thing is not to blame him; insecure parents tend to respond by blaming the child. But at such a time, it is important to find assets, including the capacity to tolerate a misfortune. One can say, "I guess it was a bad thing that happened to you, but I know you're a strong person. You'll snap back"...The child is upset, but at the same time he is trying to absorb the blow, and one tries to help him with that effort. So in that sense he is beginning to display strength. You are a magnifying mirror for an asset at that particular moment.[50]

Whatever else might be said, one would infer that Augustine's parents were not "a magnifying mirror for an asset at that particular moment" when he came home from school bearing lash marks. They did not try to help him "absorb the blow." Instead, they seem to have magnified the blow itself by laughing at his sorrows.

The prior interpretation may benefit from a note of moderation. Kohut's inference about parents' insecurity might be a culture-bound observation. If the norm in their society was to laugh at those old childhood beatings, they could have adopted that norm without themselves being insecure. On the other hand, like Augustine's adult attitude itself, their laughter might exhibit conformity to culture, as well as expression and relief of repressed personal sadness about their own experience at school and perhaps a similar lack of empathic response from their own parents. At the very least his father would not have been exempt from similar treatment in school: "Many people living long before me had constructed the laborious courses which we were compelled to follow by an increase of the toil and sorrow (Gen. 3:16) of Adam's children" (I.ix.14).[51] Whether the treatment of girls at school was the same or not, and what effect their memories of correction would have on his mother, is hard to say. Widespread emotional distress related to this treatment in school would have been possible, however, and might have played into adults' responses to the children's pains.

The passages from the literature of the time that betray great anger over slights to a person's honor or group suggest just such a broadly based psychological tendency. Augustine himself recalls in these same passages people preoccupied with admiration and highly sensitive to shame. These are the signs of continuing struggle with grandiosity in adult life: "A man enjoying a reputation for eloquence takes his position before a human judge with a crowd of men standing round and attacks his opponent with ferocious animosity. He is extremely vigilant in precautions against some error in language, but is indifferent to the possibility that the emotional force of his mind may bring about a man's execution" (I.xvii.29).[52] Robert Kaster cites *Attic Nights* by Aulus Gellius in which two grammatici, teachers of the younger grades in late antiquity, argue about the declension of an adjective. Their heated scholarly debate degenerates into the ridiculous, but as Kaster points out, it portrays the personal stake that the grammatici had in being recognized by their peers as correct.[53] While social status would have been vulnerable in such an encounter, it also offers grandiosity a moment to assert itself loudly, and the interchange would suggest that ambitions had not integrated themselves manageably into the psyche.

Augustine offers a summation to book 1 of his *Confessions* that repeats clues to some development of grandiosity into confidence and self-awareness that help him as he looks back from midlife to childhood; the summation discloses as well the indicators of pain from incomprehensible thwarting of his self-assertion. He certainly could take initiative, as he implies when he says he would tell "innumerable lies with which I deceived the slave who took me to school and my teachers and parents because of my love of games, my passion for frivolous spectacles, and my restless urge to imitate comic scenes."[54] He could implement his projects and proceed toward his goals, although he did so by complementing dishonesty with enterprise: "I also used to steal from my parents' cellar and to pocket food from their table either to satisfy the demands of gluttony or to have something to give to boys who, of course, loved playing a game as much as I, and who would sell me their playthings in return." He loved to strut for others' admiration, as an infant caught up in grandiosity does (although the infant would lack the devious turn apparently taken by Augustine's desire for mirroring): "Even in this game I was overcome by a vain desire to win and was often guilty of cheating. Any breach of the rules I would not tolerate and, if I detected it, would fiercely denounce it, though it was exactly what I was doing to others." Yet this grandiosity seems already to lack integration, because of its exaggerated quality, the lengths to which Augustine went in order to capture praise, and the shame and rage that awaited breaches of his self-presentation: "And if I was caught and denounced, I used to prefer to let my rage have free rein rather than to give ground" (I.xix.30).[55]

Nonetheless, some of the benefits of grandiosity seem to have come his way more straightforwardly. Augustine reminisces in a philosophical vein that even as a child he "took care for my self-preservation..." (I.xx.31).[56] Although he probably did not think in those terms as a child, apparently he avoided some of the self-destructive behaviors, possible even in childhood, which have turned up in patients in self psychological analysis. Kohut mentions most often childhood depression, not evident in Augustine's reports of his early years.[57]

Augustine phrases his own more healthy behavior thus: "An inward instinct told me to take care of the integrity of my senses and even in my little thoughts about little matters I took delight in the truth." He also was able to use his abilities: "I developed a good memory, I acquired the armoury of being skilled with words, friendship softened me, I avoided pain, despondency, ignorance." Capacities like these Kohut conceived of as an important part of the self, which links grandiosity's ambition and desire to stand out with one's ideals and guiding values. Not only did Augustine develop these qualities, he as a grown-up can be seen mirroring them back to himself: "In such a person what was not worthy of admiration and praise?" (I.xx.31).[58]

Augustine's Self in Culture and Society

Even though understanding Augustine and his unconscious currents must build incrementally, we can try to locate Augustine and his grandiosity in its glories and sorrows in the more complete view of his social circumstances and especially his cultural resources. This will permit a glimpse of what Ricoeur calls teleology, the direction or guidance for life, which inheres in every symbol along with its unconscious undercurrents. It also takes us back to Shweder's ideas about culture and psyche interactively making each other up. Having seen social influences, cultural resources, and developments of the self somewhat independently, we need to note them, if briefly, in interaction.

Augustine himself unknowingly tips us off to an intersection of cultural interpretations with the view advanced so far as self psychological. When he recalls his childhood he remembers hating to learn Greek and contrasts that experience with learning Latin at home. He paints a tender picture of what we might see as a grandiose paradise, full of mirroring and pleasure, and under reasonable control:

> At one time in my infancy I also knew no Latin, and yet by listen-
> ing I learnt it with no fear or pain at all from my nurses caressing

me, from people laughing over jokes, and from those who played games and were enjoying them. I learnt Latin without the threat of punishment from anyone forcing me to learn it. My own heart constrained me to bring its concepts to birth, which I could not have done unless I had learnt some words, not from formal teaching but by listening to people talking; and they, in turn, were the audience for my thoughts.

But as Augustine continues, we see again subtle evidence for the interpretation that, by the time he entered school, the mirroring, admiring environment had changed:

> This experience sufficiently illuminates the truth that free curiosity has greater power to stimulate learning than rigorous coercion. Nevertheless, the free-ranging flux of curiosity is channeled by discipline under your laws, God. By your laws we are disciplined, from the canes of schoolmasters to the ordeals of martyrs. Your laws have the power to temper bitter experiences in a constructive way, recalling us to yourself from the pestilential life of easy comforts which have taken us away from you. (I.xiv.23)[59]

He recalls both "the canes of schoolmasters" and "bitter experiences." This recollection brings no return to narcissistic joy and contentment. But reflection on it does what we may look to culture to do, it sets experience in a context where we at least hope to find meaning. As Geertz puts it, a religious worldview will teach us not so much how to avoid suffering but how to go on with unavoidable suffering.[60] Augustine's religious reflection here offers a kind of conscious consolation to the depth of his remembered sorrow. The sorrow has not disappeared. In fact, the emotion he conveys about his sufferings in school and his parents' inability to respond empathically to his distress draws readers' attention even today.[61] But his philosophy and theology allow him to hope that it will lead him from the many "easy comforts which have taken us away from you [God]," back to God, the one true delight. In the next paragraph, he requests that God sustain him under God's discipline, "so that you might become sweet to me above all the seductions which I pursued" (I.xv.24).[62] Here again he articulates a hope that suffering will return him from the many, "all the seductive delights," to the One, the sweetness that is God in the divine self.

But all these themes dispose themselves to carry the meanings of injured grandiosity, without returning Augustine to the fullest depths of the repressed aspects of it. The narcissistic injury of being beaten can escape repression, as theory would have it, because it comes out in a compromise of painful memory with symbolic expression of happiness restored. Augustine's unconscious could well be saying, "the wonderfulness of my powers of learning sustained injury when my schoolmaster beat me for my mistakes in learning Greek, but real wonderfulness will be shown back to me by a forgiving God."[63] The theory of self psychology would lead us to believe, based on Augustine's writings, that he had trouble acknowledging his own wonderfulness: it got out of hand in his cheating in games, and it did not survive the rigors of school unscathed. But despite the pain that followed on its expression in childhood outside the home, his sense of his own goodness could find expression in symbolic form if it could come to expression in a larger view of life in which everything good came from God and could return to God with help from God: "The talents you have given will increase and be perfected, and I will be with you since it was your gift to me that I exist" (I.xx.31).[64]

The interpretation thus far suggests a further point to keep in mind. Hearing a symphony in the cacophony of one's rapidly moving life does not guarantee that the music is without discord. The unresolved chords sound through in the early telling, despite the rhetorical resolution at the end of book 1. Augustine's churning feelings still assert themselves when he recalls,

> we loved to play, and punishments were imposed on us by those who were engaged in adult games. For "the amusement of adults is called business." But when boys play such games they are punished by adults, and no one feels sorry either for the children or for the adults or indeed for both of them. Perhaps some refined arbiter of things might approve of my being beaten. As a boy, I played ball games, and that play slowed down the speed at which I learnt letters with which, as an adult, I might play a less creditable game. The schoolmaster who caned me was behaving no better than I when, after being refuted by a fellow teacher in some pedantic question, he was more tormented by jealousy and envy than I when my opponent overcame me in a ballgame. (I.ix.15)[65]

Often in these pages Augustine seems to see the goodness in God to whom he can turn, rather than in God's assurance of the increase and perfection of Augustine's own human talents. We might suspect, therefore, that idealizing could be seen from a self psychological point of view as a complement to the consolations for wounded grandiosity. Given the high aspirations of Augustine's philosophical and theological forebears to reach a truth greater than normal earthly life and its struggles, idealizing will be warranted as worthy of attention from the conscious and cultural points of view, as well as from the depths of the psychological.

CHAPTER 4

Childhood, Ideals, and Disillusionment

Augustine's early years extended past his grammar school in Madaura into at least a year spent at home when he was fifteen (II.iii.6). Not long afterward, Augustine again left Tagaste, this time for the highest level of education in Carthage, one of the great educational centers of the Roman empire. The variety of ideals he embraced over these years implies that he was open to a wide range of cultural resources.

This chapter's extension of the study of his life in its cultural context will also expand our understanding of Kohut's view of the unconscious self. The idealizing to be studied in this chapter forms a second main pole of the unconscious coherence of the self. Yet one should note that idealizing begins its development in infancy, so its sequence in development does not limit it to the context of Augustine's school years.[1] Some incidents already described will have to reenter the discussion. Conversely, some suggestive tidbits about grandiosity appear in the episodes I will discuss for the first time in this chapter. But these divisions of early childhood from the later school years and of grandiosity from idealizing will chart what appears to be a shift in Augustine's own psychological life.

The patterns of Augustine's idealizations changed over time. From a self psychological point of view the shifting suggests that idealizing did not establish itself firmly as part of his deepest self in his earliest years. The idea behind this inference is that the deepest parts of what Kohut saw as our self function smoothly, so that we do not usually notice them.[2] All the shifts in Augustine's ideals, however, made them very evident and clearly disjointed aspects of his life and, hence, we may infer, of his unconscious.

Yet one need not conclude that the discords in Augustine's thoughts and feelings reveal only a personal pathology or strictly internal struggle.

To the contrary, the discords echo the tones of an unsettled, even chaotic, social world, guided by a range of conflicting cultural sources. Previous psychological discussions have seen his parents' divided values, which reflect two different cultural traditions, as evidence for an unresolved oedipal conflict.[3] According to Freud's theory, the oedipal conflict results in the formation of ideals. They can be seen as part of the establishment of the superego when a young boy gives up the sexual tinge to his affection for his mother and identifies instead with his father and his father's ideals.[4] Unfortunately, these earlier discussions of Augustine's oedipal conflict[5] do little to account for the actual flow of his life, his early acceptance of cultural norms, the pressures of his social life as he grew up, or the limitations of his cultural resources.

Set in the broader context of Augustine's society and culture, the *Confessions* suggests instead that Monica's influence in Augustine's early childhood offered him a pattern of reliance on Christian guides to action, but that until Augustine reached his late teens he gravitated toward his father's ideals with the support of the world of school and other youngsters. Then the struggle began. It appears in Augustine's text as the echo of a multitude of sounds from his social and cultural milieu. In addition, it continued because Augustine needed to hear strains of thought that did not sound above the din of North Africa where he went to school and started his career.

Most briefly stated, the situation seems to have led Augustine to ideals in his school years that favored behaviors, attitudes, and accomplishments that could easily represent grandiosity to consciousness. The themes he was taught to admire emphasized pride in one's abilities, the importance of ambition, the glamour of glory and praise, concern with one's feeling of inner perfection, and sensitivity to the ways that people reflected agreement with that self-perception. The problem would be that this persistent pattern, idealizing the representations of grandiosity, leaves the weight of the unity of the self, at its deepest psychological foundation, on one pole of the personality, the grandiose self.[6] If anything were to upset this pole, idealizing would also crumble. The person affected would have to scramble unconsciously for another source of cohesion while the grandiose self recovered.

Several more chapters will unfold before all the relevant elements of Augustine's life can come into a psychological interpretation. For now, we will concentrate on the differences in his parents' ideals as they might have affected Augustine's idealizing. A discussion of the oedipal conflict will address concerns remaining for readers aware of the literature to date. But, as always, the self psychological interpretation has to return to the data of Augustine's telling of his life. And our first source of data for Augustine's life is his *Confessions*.

Augustine recounts a few more life events that we must consider as we move toward describing the strengths and weaknesses we can discern from the clues to patterns of his unconscious self. Two pieces of evidence from his childhood, his severe illness and the literature he read in school, will come back into focus later as we try to understand what might have happened to his early childhood tendency to idealize. But for now, we look toward two later incidents. First is the episode at the baths and second the theft of pears.

Augustine tells near the beginning of book 2 that he had to come home from his studies in Madaura. His father was trying to collect enough money to send him to Carthage for advanced study, and Augustine lived at home "on holiday from all schooling" (II.iii.6).[7] He notes that puberty had arrived, and he had begun to take an interest in sexual love. Then, as mentioned in the previous chapter, his father noticed at the baths that Augustine showed signs of sexual maturity. Proudly counting on grandchildren, Patricius told Monica about his observation. Augustine says that Monica later spoke to her son and "warned with great concern that I should not indulge in fornication and, most importantly, that I should not commit adultery with anyone's wife." Augustine did not grant much credence to her point: "These warnings seemed to me womanish; I would have blushed to submit to them." He tells us that his age mates engaged in debauchery and that he felt ashamed if he did not behave as badly as they (II.iii.7).[8]

This same theme, embarrassment about the possibility of not keeping up with his friends in their transgressions, reappears in the story of the theft of pears. During that same year of time off from school, Augustine and some friends decided to take fruit from a pear tree near Augustine's family's vineyard. He says that they may have eaten a few pears, but threw most to the pigs. The fruit did not have an attractive color, nor did it taste delightful (II.iv.9). The pears were beautiful, or at least as the middle-aged bishop recalled the deed, he deemed them so because they were God's creation. The youthful Augustine knew, however, that he had plenty of better pears without stealing any (II.vi.12). He claims to remember that he would not have stolen them if he had been alone, but that the influence of the group of youngsters led him to enjoy the very act he believed, even when he did it, to be wrong. His motive, he says, lay in the fact that "when it is said, 'let's go, let's do it,' it shames one not to be shameless" (II.ix.17).[9]

Beyond the bare facts of these few events lie a rich social context and many cultural influences. Attention to the setting within which these apparently unimportant events took place will help us understand their importance to Augustine.

Social Factors in Augustine's Late Childhood and Early Adolescence

Most of the factors in Augustine's social setting have already appeared in the rest of the discussion. Some deserve to be highlighted. A few should be added from other sources.

Augustine's schooling in Madaura would have exposed him to a some-what more urbane world than his hometown of Tagaste.[10] The location of a grammar school there would itself signal Madaura's greater importance. Moreover, archeological excavations have shown that it could claim all the accoutrements of a well-established Roman town: a large forum, grand baths, a section of pagan temples, a large basilica, and a remarkably well-preserved theater, revealing the identities of some donors in inscriptions.[11] While Tagaste would have shared many of these features, Augustine would have met better-educated people as he frequented such sites in Madaura. He thus had entered a socially and geographically mobile group by the time he returned to Tagaste and waited for his father to finish raising the funds for his education in Carthage.[12]

One can infer, therefore, that Augustine's return to his hometown com-bined, paradoxically, a comedown and a glorification. He would have lost his regular contact with the scholars and members of the upper classes, present and future, in Madaura. He seems to have discovered no new in-tellectual challenges back in Tagaste. At the same time, his status may well have received a boost from the praise his father garnered for the efforts that he made to send his son next to Carthage for further education (II.iii.5).

Whatever his social status and his perception of it, Augustine seems to have made friends or renewed old acquaintances well. Although his train-ing was preparing him to stand above the crowd, he did not lord it over other youngsters to the point of excluding them from his company on that account. If he had, he would never have gone out that evening to join in the games in the street and, thence, the foray to the pear tree. Yet these boys could not have reached his own intellectual or social standing, for without its own grammarian's school, Tagaste could not have supplied a crowd of youths as educated as he.

Augustine's story of the pear tree also alerts us that at least some of the boys had little supervision. They lingered on the streets late into the night. None seems to have hesitated to take the pears for fear of getting caught. So we have to realize that when Augustine complained as a bishop about the lack of discipline during his year at home, he did not simply rue his private lot, but alluded to a pattern that extended to at least several house-holds in Tagaste.

Cultural Norms

Augustine's interests in carousing may have fallen in line with some of the norms and cultural guidance he encountered. Certainly, inasmuch as social patterns provide guidance, he followed along with what was offered him. He had already struggled to excel in academic competitions; he let the group of boys push him into a theft, albeit a petty one; and he seems to have looked to follow in his father's sexual transgressions (II.iii.7). But we also learn of more formal guidance for life from the incidents he recounts.

First, the incident of the baths, like the story of Augustine's near-fatal childhood illness, shows that Monica made her Christianity felt in his life. Her admonition that he avoid fornication and adultery ran counter to the norms for men at the time. Shaw believes that Monica's warning fit the larger social situation very well, because the women Augustine might likely pursue would be married "for obvious reasons," presumably, although Shaw does not say so, because a married woman's pregnancy could pass as legitimate.[13] Several historians point out that the older Augustine would preach frequently against adultery, and that the very regularity of his censure of his flock's sexual vices suggests that they were widespread.[14] But as Van der Meer states: "The law permitted both divorce and the keeping of concubines. Holy Scripture and the Church strictly forbade both."[15] So the voice of Monica against potential for adultery in her son's life rang with the tones of the church, although he perceived the divine voice only later, as he recalled it to write about it in midlife (II.iii.7).

Augustine's presentation of his studies suggests that even in school he noticed pagan literature's applause for the adulterous life. He confirms the culture's idealization of this behavior by citing a play by Terence in which "a worthless young man" appears "citing Jupiter as a model for his own fornication." Augustine, who knew his rhetorical business, pins the blame squarely on the text: "Notice how he encourages himself to lust as if enjoying celestial authority: '…He strikes the temples of heaven with his immense sound. And am I, poor little fellow, not to do the same as he? Yes indeed, I have done it with pleasure.'"[16] Augustine allows no room for any doubt that he himself noticed these influences of culture: "I learnt this text with pleasure and took delight in it, wretch that I was. For this reason I was said to be a boy of high promise."[17] The voice of the bishop looking back and calling himself a "wretch" does not drown out the indication of a different conception of wretchedness when he was a youngster. Moreover, the social system reinforced his attention to the ideals of the story. He acknowledges the beauty of the words he learned but adds: "the wine of error was poured into them for us by drunken teachers and unless we drank we were caned, nor was appealing to any sober judge permitted" (I.xvi.26).[18]

In addition, we may see some indications of culture already influencing Augustine in the theft of pears. Much of the philosophical material blended into that account would have come to Augustine only a decade and a half later, but some of the notions of classical philosophy may have entered his consciousness by the time of the theft itself. For instance, he might well have known that some ancients believed that wrongdoing results from ignorance of the good. Yet Augustine will not countenance a lack of knowledge as the cause of this sin when he tells the story. Instead, he maintains that the boys knew from the outset that what they did was wrong. If they had thought about a defense of their behavior, a protestation of ignorance could not have served their purpose. Second, the ancient philosophers believed that behavior is always directed toward a goal. The theft of pears, however, was not. It was pointless. He tries out several possible goals and finds them wanting as explanations. Perhaps he did so even as a youth. For instance, one might expect that the act of stealing fruit anticipated the pleasure of taste. But the taste of the pears was mediocre, and Augustine says he had plenty that were better. The theft might have assuaged hunger, except that the boys were not hungry. If the youths had followed the lead of Catiline, the villainous Roman of old, they might have committed the crime to stay in practice and eventually attain illicit power (II.v.11).[19] But they had not taken up a life of banditry, nor did they propose to do so. So Augustine dispenses with these philosophical understandings of the act and claims that his experience shows something else motivated the theft. That more complicated evaluation will be the subject of an example drawing together culture and psychological motives with social circumstances, once we have looked more closely at the psychological factors.

Hints of Problems in the Development of Augustine's Idealizing

The predominance of Monica as an idealized figure in Augustine's early life seems plausible from a reading of book 1 of the *Confessions*, while Patricius' influence emerges more strongly in book 2. This presentation mirrors the social influence typical of a boy's life in North Africa in late antiquity. Augustine's turns of phrase seem to suggest that each parent's strengths tended to undermine the other's. This sort of interaction could lead to the blows to idealizing that Kohut terms traumatic. They may occur in small instances, but they come before the child is ready for them. Or they manifest themselves in events that appear insignificant to adults, but cannot be comprehended and absorbed by children. Some familiar evidence and some passages as yet unexplored will make the case.

A familiar passage concerns the episode of Augustine's illness in childhood. Augustine's request for baptism would demonstrate the work of idealizing. The ritual's connection to his mother, a person who would have constituted an idealizable selfobject, and to her faith and her God, would have strengthened its power in his young unconscious mind. This view of his request makes more sense when we note that Kohut acknowledged that illness can increase a person's narcissistic focus. Rarely does a person feel admirable, proud, and cohesive when sick. Instead one tends to feel pitiful, embarrassed, and vulnerable psychologically as well as physically. In such circumstances, the psyche needs to concentrate its energies on itself. Aid from a person better off can seem especially attractive while one waits for physical health to return and psychological well-being to reemerge.[20] Augustine when ill turned to his mother's ministrations and to her faith. He claims he spoke with both "emotion and...faith" when he asked to be baptized. His desire suggests that he saw the church's sacrament as powerful and important, in short as an ideal. Moreover, Monica received social support in the home for the value of her religion: "So already I believed, as did my mother and the whole household, except for my father alone, who did not prevail over my right to follow my mother's piety in order to induce me to believe less in Christ, just as he himself did not yet believe" (I.xi.17).[21]

Further statements in this passage have been read to confirm Monica as undermining Patricius and bolstering herself and her faith as Augustine's ideal: "She busied herself so that you, my God, would be my father rather than he, and in this you were helping her, so that she overcame her husband." He continues by calling Monica "better than" Patricius (I.xi.17).[22] The interpretation of these lines should attend to the Latin, as well as the author's point of view and his purpose in writing the passage. For instance, Chadwick's translation reads, "She anxiously laboured to convince me that you, my God, were my father rather than he…"[23] The words "to convince me" could suggest that Monica actually said to Augustine when he was a boy that she wanted God rather than Patricius to be Augustine's father. But other translations minimize that implication by translating *"esses"* ("were" or "would have been") without adding the notion "to convince." These other translations thereby emphasize the notion that God would *be* Augustine's father. Moreover, the words "more truly than" replace "rather than" in one translation's rendering of the phrase *potius quam*.[24] If God were Augustine's father "more truly than" Patricius, Patricius would retain some role as father in Augustine's life. Whichever emphasis we put on the translation of *"potius quam,"*[25] we must acknowledge that the point of view in this paragraph most surely comes from Augustine as a man about forty years old writing an account of his life in the Christian faith. Therefore, the language provides no assurance that Monica ever said to him in boyhood that she wanted God rather than Patricius as his father. We cannot tell if this is a construction added by the bishop recasting his whole life in terms of his theology,[26] or if it reflects strategies used by Monica. It might do both. It might even suggest strategies used by Monica of which neither she nor her son were ever fully conscious. We do not know.

We do know that the incident prepares the reader rhetorically for a discussion of further issues. First, Augustine will turn to failings of both parents, which he attempts to mitigate in his account of Monica. He tells us that his baptism was postponed when he took a turn for the better in his illness. Neither parent escapes blame entirely in his adult Christian reasoning: "How much better if I had been quickly cleansed and it had been done, by the diligence of my family and my own diligence, so that the health my soul received was kept safe under the protection which you would have given it" (I.xi.18).[27] Here "the diligence of my family" includes both parents.

He does make allowances, however, for Monica's shortcomings in religious rigor by noting cultural understandings as they shaped social practice:

"But many and great waves of temptations were seen as threatening after boyhood; my mother already knew them and she wanted to commit to them the earth out of which I would later be shaped rather than the image itself already formed" (I.xi.18).[28] The image to which he refers is the soul restored to the image of God.[29]

Augustine addresses a widespread social pattern in this passage. Baptism was believed to settle accounts for all previous sin, but by the fourth century much experience had already shown that the human passions of baptized persons would not always follow the leading of religious judgment. Moreover, the penance for sins committed later would involve more public censure than would the sins forgiven in baptism. Therefore, the logic went, one might as well wait to be baptized. Practice widely followed this reasoning, and many people received baptism either quite late in life or even on their deathbeds, although they may have entered the catechumenate years before.[30]

Augustine turns his discussion to his schooldays, and makes statements that fit the view of his ideals being turned away from his mother's Christian ideals and toward the aspects of life that easily represent grandiosity. He says of his teachers: "They…had regard for…satisfying the insatiable greed for impoverished riches and shameful glory…" (I.xii.19).[31] In addition to economic success and notoriety, pride in sexual prowess figured in the stories Augustine read in school. These texts and values clearly contradicted the Christian standards that Monica wanted Augustine to follow. Augustine's early idealizations of his mother's beliefs and the cultural norms of Christianity, seen in the story of the baptism, received little social or cultural reinforcement once he went to school. Instead, values his father favored as guides to life appeared in works of literary culture that Augustine not only read, but had to memorize.

In sum, neither parent maintained an undisputed position as a representative of worthy ideal. When Patricius returned from the baths and asserted his own value of pride in Augustine's sexual maturity and presumed potency, Monica tried to warn Augustine away from the implied actions. But even her life and her ideals mixed worldly values with her Christian aspirations. When Patricius became a local hero in the gossip mill of Tagaste by seeking a "cultured tongue" for Augustine, Monica's goals for him did not differ entirely from her husband's: "I realized that each parent as much as the other wanted a literary education for me: my father because he thought nearly nothing about you [God], and only silly things about me; my mother because she thought not only that it would do no harm, but she even judged that the usual studies of those teachings later would help to set me on the way to you" (II.iii.8).[32] As he looks back from his later Christian perspective he criticizes the real value of the ideals both his parents tried to inculcate in him. Does this criticism also betray some childhood disillusionment with the undertones of disagreement that might have come to the fore from time to time, or with other difficulties in early childhood's idealizing?

Having stayed this close to the text, one may perhaps indulge a little speculation. A standard psychoanalytic assumption would hold that Augustine's story about the baths and his parents' responses to his appearance is a symbol for other similar experiences, quite likely repressed. That is, if experiences that are painful are repressed, and if the repressed unconscious thoughts and feelings from the experiences tend to be expressed in disguised form, then one conscious recollection can carry a distorted image of an earlier experience that caused too much psychological pain to come to consciousness openly.[33] In this instance, Patricius' pride in his son's sexuality could symbolize other times when Patricius' proud actions had seemed to challenge and undermine Monica's ideals. Similarly, Monica's warning, based on her fears about Augustine's potential to commit adultery, could represent other times when she tarnished the image of Patricius' prized values. A childhood marked by such incidents could, from a self psychological viewpoint, lead to difficulties in feeling secure in idealizing anything. Evidence supporting the inference that Augustine had such troubles will appear more strikingly in the next chapter.

Meanwhile, one might note that when Monica worried aloud to Augustine about his sexual capacity, rather than rejoicing about it as his father did, she not only signaled disparagement of the old Roman ideal of perpetuating the family as a major point of honor, but she also failed to support Augustine's grandiosity. Kohut allows that even maturing and moderated grandiosity and ideals need support as we age.[34] His depth psychology insists on seeing us as highly social and interactive beings. He thinks of puberty as one of life's challenges that can temporarily shake a normally cohesive self. An adolescent needs gentle support for so much personal change, as Kohut would see it.[35] Perhaps an affirming comment would have overstepped cultural taboos of relationships between mother and son. But silence would have fit better with a maturing self's needs. Yet Monica's cultural norm led to a moral injunction that Augustine could not accept. He responded by demeaning her view in his own thoughts: "womanish advice." The urge to demean another is, for the self psychological interpreter, a likely sign of a wounded grandiose self.[36] Yet Augustine had cultural reinforcement for his response as Monica had for hers. So the injury to his grandiosity that might have followed from her comments could be assuaged by the recollection of a cultural ideal approving representations of grandiosity.

The Oedipal Conflict

Freud proclaimed the oedipal conflict as the key to psychoanalytic understanding from the time of the first major psychoanalytic publication, *The Interpretation of Dreams*, near the beginning of 1900. Theorists today usually have to take a stand on the oedipal conflict and its centrality in psychological development, even when they treat primarily pre-oedipal development and its influence on later life. The history of the psychological study of Augustine makes the issue particularly relevant. The Freudian, and heavily oedipal, interpretations of Augustine's life and writings drew fire from historians and theologians, which has kept them in the literature, even though pre-oedipal interpretations have yielded powerful alternative readings.[37]

Kohut believed in his later writings, from the late 1970s and early 1980s, that problems in the pre-oedipal development of grandiosity or idealizing could affect the outcome of the oedipal conflict itself. He argued that a coherent and resilient unconscious self will not have trouble in the oedipal phase, when children express grandiosity with sexual assertion and idealize both parents immoderately. He believed that children can adjust themselves to the realistic limits of childhood sexuality and the dynamics of family relationships if their parents can respond with affectionate and measured mirroring to the children's self-assertion. The parents' capacity to serve confidently as ideals also assists in the resolution of oedipal dynamics, so much so that oedipal urges and feelings may not actually become an oedipal conflict.[38]

Don S. Browning combined Kohut's conceptions of the relationship of pre-oedipal and oedipal development with points made in previous essays that suggested pre-oedipal difficulties in Augustine's childhood.[39] Browning concluded that pre-oedipal conflicts may have distressed Augustine and led to repressed oedipal feelings and thoughts that could, and did, emerge later in symbolic forms in Augustine's works.[40]

Browning also pointed out that psychological interpretations of Augustine's life and thought fit in philosophical as well as psychological discussions.[41] The psychological interpretation of events, images, and ideas does not simply stand on its own. Interpretation requires backing from philosophical defenses of the epistemological value of psychoanalysis and its offshoots. This concern with epistemology is crucial to my interpretations in this book. Responding to the debates about the oedipal conflict may help make the import of this study more salient. We will observe the benefits of multifaceted interpretation through closer study of the pear stealing escapade.

Social Structure in the Reading of the Oedipal Conflict

Social circumstances appear to affect the conditions for the appearance of the oedipal conflict. As mentioned in chapter 2, Anne Parsons demonstrated in her fieldwork in southern Italy that a different nuclear family configuration from the one Freud expected could help draw connections between cultural expressions of familial feelings that also differed from Freud's expectations.[42] Also working from a model indebted to Talcott Parsons' notions of the interrelatedness of culture, society, and the individual, Sudhir Kakar described Indian society as so differently structured and guided by cultural norms that the oedipal explanation of the psychodynamics of most Hindu Indians would miss the mark dramatically.

He sketches the family arrangements to show that theories of pre-oedipal years, especially object relations theories, help account for more behavior and cultural expressions of psychological material than do oedipal constructs.[43] These scholars alert us to investigate family arrangements in Augustine's era and locale and consider what bearing they might have had on the oedipal phase of Augustine's development.

To set the groundwork, we might notice that some aspects of the oedipal situation that Freud described do seem to have been present in Augustine's family and society. Children spent much more time with their mothers than their fathers in early childhood. The man's province was the whole public world, but the mother's arena decidedly was not. She remained fairly closely confined to the home,[44] at least in the social class to which Monica and Patricius belonged, especially during her husband's life. The observations made in chapter 3 about the indulgence of mothers and nurses toward children may signal that a strong bond could develop in these affectionate relations. This arrangement could facilitate close ties to the mother in early childhood. From Freud's point of view, the boy would have to break these ties someday if he were to succeed his father as head of a household and its link to the world. Shaw mentions that people thought of a son as "still a 'mummy's boy' (*filius matris*)"[45] while he was nursing, but as "daddy's boy" ("*filius patris*")[46] after weaning. Even the father, whose "life passes outside of the house," would come home at night and join in the baby talk with his little son.[47] Love for the father would also have an opportunity to develop in this setting. Such love, according to Freud, would make the boy afraid of doing something to lose it, and therefore afraid of both the physical and psychological consequences of punishment by his father.[48]

The last pieces for the possibility of the oedipal conflict as we might know it are put in place by the knowledge that a father would indeed act punitively as he deemed necessary. Fathers of late antiquity in North Africa were not afraid to punish their sons, or to threaten them with taking up the whip. Shaw concludes that fathers had started "a training of the son from birth, a training which inculcated in him a sense of shame such that he would blush to disobey. He would also learn to fear his father as a severe judge..."[49] The outcome, according to Shaw, would be that many sons obeyed their fathers for years into adulthood.

Nonetheless, several features militate against matching the family's social arrangements in late antiquity with those we associate with the oedipal conflict. First, Augustine mentions his nurses. Their presence would mean that a son had some focus for his first loves other than just his mother. The attachment could be all the greater given what Hamman reports about nursing: it seems to have continued for three years. Hamman points out that the nurse might stay with the family, as Augustine said his grandfather's nurse did to raise Monica and her sisters also (IX.viii.17). He adds that children remained attached to their nurses, even after the child was weaned. She would "watch over, spend time with, and educate" her former nursling.[50] Augustine does not speak specifically of such a nurse, but he does mention hearing from his nurses what he had been like as a baby (I.vi.8); so they must have been present and willing to talk to him when he was of an age to remember their words. The presence of grandparents (IX.ix.20) in the home indicates also that the family was not a nuclear family of parents and children as we might expect for the oedipal dynamics to develop. The ties to either parent or both might be weaker than Freud's ideas seem to assume.

Another factor that differs from the twentieth-century North American or northern European family inheres in the more extended years allowed for play in Augustine's society. According to Hamman, boys would start school at age seven. Until then, they could play all day. They started to take on the behaviors of the older men before schooling started: they would find their friends and play outside. They "reappeared in the family when hunger tortured" them.[51] Having both father and son out of the house for much of the day could diminish the chances for them to find themselves in competition for the mother's affections. It also means that the boy could relatively easily loosen his ties to his mother for reasons other than his father's intervention. He could begin to identify with his father in behavior without having to resist his mother's presence and without necessarily entering into oedipal dynamics.

Yet the oedipal conflict need not be seen as a direct outcome of social events. It may be seen as having more to do with currents of feeling, broad social understandings, and cultural expectations than with any precise set of interactions in the family. Enough small interactions might occur in the home for the son to express possessiveness of his mother and the hope of excluding his father, especially if he were used to the father's absence and his own earlier constant presence in the house. The father could then step in to establish who really had possession of the mother's sexual affections. In fact, the father would seem to have been ready to do that in regard to any slightly seductive conduct on the part of wives or a wife's potential lover.[52] Perhaps he would not have to say much to the son if marital possessiveness had vividly asserted itself in response to suspicions about other men's desires.

Moreover, we can note specifically from Augustine's own narrative some family interactions implied in the story of the baths. Patricius told Monica something important about their son. The interchange included some real feeling and discussion of something that could as easily have been left unsaid. But Monica appears not to have felt equally comfortable speaking her mind to Patricius about his observation. Perhaps this fit with a pattern of silence that she developed when he was angry and she thought she might upset him further by speaking to him about the problem that provoked him (IX.ix.19). Monica felt, however, that she could talk to fifteen-year-old Augustine about something as intimate and carefully guarded as sex. But what did not happen was a frank discussion among the threesome about Augustine's mores and sexuality. The pattern of conversation suggests that perhaps Monica did feel closer to her son than to her husband. Might that closeness imply that years earlier she did try to prevent him from resolving his oedipal conflict and identifying with his father?[53]

A modest and defensible interpretation would accept that some of the conditions for an oedipal conflict seem to have been present in Augustine's early life. His own portrayal of the family suggests that he did attach himself profoundly to his mother in his childhood, as the story of his illness and desire for baptism suggests. Moreover, he did seem to ally himself with his father, as he showed years later in his dismissal of Monica's concerns about how he would act on his pubescent sexuality. In this instance his father's pride in Augustine's sexual development dominates his response to his own growth. Further confirmation of the usual oedipal outcome of identification with his father comes from the reports that Augustine adopted sexual behaviors not altogether unlike his father's sexual exploits (III.i.1; IX.ix.19).

If this modest solution bears fruit in interpretation, we should expect to see some oedipal dynamics in Augustine's narrative, imagery, and selection of cultural images. Certainly these hints of oedipal issues seem to exist in his texts. So for example, we have seen the possibility of oedipal dynamics in the story of the baths.[54] Other possible instances will appear more richly disguised in some of Augustine's writings from and about later years.

Oedipal Readings in the Larger Interpretive Scheme

The improbable conclusion to draw from social patterns and textual evidence would be that we can take a further step of seeing oedipal issues as causal on a broad scale in Augustine's life and thought. Earlier debates in religion and psychology would have allowed such causal conclusions, but the hermeneutic approach proposed by Ricoeur does not. Instead it encourages attention to the interactions between the unconscious and culture. As explained in chapter 1 above, neither culture nor psyche can claim full causality. Moreover, Ricoeur notes Freud's concession that psychoanalysis can help with the understanding of many things, but that creativity eludes it.[55] Ricoeur can then emphasize the contribution of culture, its guidance for life from law, art, morals, and literature,[56] to individual creativity. The urges of unconscious feelings and ideas have to interact with something, the products of culture, to attain to conscious representation, even in disguise.[57] So we can describe the kinds of interactions we see, and assume that the unconscious makes some causal contribution, but not attain to the certainty implied in previous discussions of Augustine. If our certainty about causality is weak, our boldness in evaluation must all the more be restrained.

For instance, we should not expect to be able to conclude much about personal pathology within the family.[58] Several of the earlier Freudian studies did this, and received a rap on the knuckles from Paula Fredriksen in the first argument for pre-oedipal approaches and more historical and theological finesse in psychological studies.[59] To be fair to the psychologically trained authors, I should also note that the historian Hamman goes as far as suggesting that Monica was "abusive" toward Augustine because of the lack of attention from her husband and her own confinement at home. He makes the defensible move of grounding this claim in the social patterns of the time: "Night having fallen, as late as possible the husband returns to his own entryway. There, his wife leads a reclusive life, busied with household life and the education of her children, surrounded by servants. Frustrated, the mother places her affection on her sons, to the point of becoming abusive." Interestingly, however, Hamman does not refer to a primary source and continues, again without textual support, to make Monica the target of his critique: "This is what explains the behavior of Monica, the mother of Augustine."[60] His lack of citation tips us off, I think, to a heavily Freudian reading that strikes him as right, but not fully supportable from the specific evidence.

But the historian's excess does not dispense with objections to psychological studies. Instead, historical over-reading only adds to the problems found, for instance, in describing Augustine's conversion as a surrender to his mother, in lieu of taking the role of father.[61] This description ignores social and cultural evidence, such as Augustine's status as a father and his portrayal of himself as one.[62] It also neglects natural factors, such as the fact that Augustine's son died. Cast in the social and psychological setting, and in light of Augustine's own writings,[63] the untimeliness of the death of Adeodatus reminds us that we have no reason to believe that Augustine would have abandoned his paternal role had death not taken his son away from him a few years after his conversion.

Data and theory must speak to each other in a more moderated interchange than those yet published. If they do, some heightening of the oedipal conflict by Monica's insufficiently expressed sexual desires seems possible. Rather than assigning personal responsibility, however, to Monica or her adherence to Christianity, one should note the many social pressures limiting her sexual self-expression as well as the cultural injunctions against any sexual freedom for her.[64] Should these or similar considerations hold, then psychological interpretations of Augustine's theological claims might justifiably note oedipal as well as pre-oedipal feelings in disguise. Maternal images of God and erotic images of truth and philosophy, noted without psychoanalytic interpretation by scholars like Robert J. O'Connell,[65] might represent both unconscious pre-oedipal and oedipal feelings. But the question of evaluating such claims deserves further consideration.

By using these ideas, I am making what Ricoeur calls the hermeneutic wager. By adopting a point of view with less than full certainty, I hope to come to understand better, and to help other people understand better, this man who seems to have opened to us his inner life and still remains puzzling in many ways. Therefore, oedipal interpretations will appear plausible in later interpretations of particular passages of the *Confessions*, but they will not be deemed to have revealed the real causes of Augustine's behavior or thought. Nor will they be read as the real meaning of the text. Instead, they will play into the symphony composed of social and cultural influences and psychological counterpoint.

Augustine's Early Years, the Hermeneutic Wager, and the Pear-Stealing Episode

A test of whether my model of interpretation can help better understand Augustine and his writings emerges in the episode of the pear theft. The characterization that Brown attributes to Oliver Wendell Holmes— "Rum thing to see a man making a mountain out of robbing a peartree in his teens"—has appealed to a number of scholars.[66] Our amusement may derive from recognition of our own feelings in Holmes's judgment. Yet Augustine recounts the pear theft to make several arguments. It does not simply indicate an obsessive concern with wrongdoing or a fanatical moralism.

An important rhetorical feature of the story of the pear theft lies in its demonstration that even the relatively minor events of human lives can become meaningful, if not happy or beautiful, when interpreted in terms of a larger framework of understanding. As has been well suggested by Donald Capps, the incidents Augustine elaborates serve as parables, brief narratives that first puzzle the reader, then lead to a new comprehension based on a sharper vision of some aspect of the world and human life.[67] One might notice a similar rhetorical move in Augustine's mention of his parents' responses to Patricius' discovery about him at the baths.

Augustine weaves together in the "parable" of the pear tree cultural debates from ancient philosophy (already noted earlier in this chapter), Plotinus, and the Bible. He incorporates the ideas of Plotinus about why a soul would ever turn away from the One. Applying Plotinus' focus on lust, curiosity, and pride to the incident allows Augustine to reject two goals he might have been said to attain through the theft. Lust as a desire for the beautiful does not satisfy Augustine as the motive for stealing the pears (II.iv.9). Sexual lust was not the motive, nor was a gustatory lust: "I threw away what I had picked" (II.vi.12).[68] Nor did lust have a source in bodily need because the boys had not tried to sate hunger. Lust appears in these passages primarily as a metaphor for a soul unfaithful to God (II.vi.14; II.vii.16). Curiosity may have played a part as the youths set out to deceive their elders and test their ability to get away with stealing. But it does not satisfy Augustine as an explanation. He asks immediately after mentioning the goal of deception, "Why then did I derive pleasure...?" (II.ix.17).[69] What is pleasing about seeing how one can deceive others? Curiosity about trickery will not solve the case. But pride gets much of his attention.

As Augustine attends to pride as the impetus to the sin of theft, he also draws on images of the story of Adam and Eve in Genesis 2 and 3 to make his point. By so doing, he develops in a more distinctively Christian way ideas taken from Plotinus and allows Plotinus' ideas to fill out the implications of the Genesis story. As we have seen, he says, "It was all done for a giggle, as if our hearts were tickled to think we were deceiving those who would not think us capable of such behaviour and would have profoundly disapproved" (II.ix.17).[70] This reason closely resembles the temptation of Eve by the serpent.[71] The serpent tells her that she can think more cleverly than God. God has told you this, suggests the serpent, but I will tell you more, and you can see for yourself that you will want the fruit once you know the power it will give you.[72] "A giggle" as the reason for action, for someone informed by self psychology, deserves comment. It suggests that some grandiosity surfaced in all the boys and allowed them a sense of triumph over the elders who forbade such practices and restrained the delight they might take in exercising all their powers, especially ones turned to prohibited ends. But Augustine could not have discerned such a reason. Instead, Augustine contributes to his culture by developing Plotinus' idea of pride, or *tolma*. O'Connell says that in this passage "Plotinus' tolma [pride] has since become a stronger thing, a veritable 'rebellion' against God."[73] It has taken on the characteristics of the Genesis story, so that it is not a simple falling away from the One because of too much interest in oneself, but an active choice, like Eve's, to rank one's own desires and reasons higher than God's. Tolma has become love of self so great that it generates contempt for God, as Augustine later states the condition.[74]

By returning to the creation story, Augustine highlights another modification of his cultural inheritance from the philosophical tradition. This story of sin actualized as stealing from a fruit tree demonstrates that sin can have a social dimension. The ancient Greeks had held that the city, civilized society, was the setting in which one could grow into virtue. Augustine would not deny that, as he shows in his later discussion in the *Confessions* of the importance of the church to the growth of Christians. He would hold equally, however, that human society could promote vice. Hence the famous themes of the two cities, seen later in *The City of God*, and hinted at in book 13 of the *Confessions* (XIII.xvii.20–xviii.22). The city founded on love of God to the extent of rendering the self unimportant, except for its relationship to God, can train its inhabitants toward virtue. But the city founded on love of self to the extent of rendering God unimportant trains its inhabitants to vice.[75] Augustine's "city," his hometown of Tagaste with its youngsters carousing after dark, did not promote real virtue in its citizens.[76]

The cultural sources modify each other once more when Augustine evokes Plotinus' description of what happens to the fallen soul. If Augustine spoke only of the Genesis story, one might wonder what happened after Adam and Eve took the forbidden fruit and suffered God's judgment of expulsion from the garden. They had sweat on their brows and pain in their childbearing, and so what? But Augustine makes the consequences much more personal: "My depraved soul leaped down from your firmament to ruin" (II.iv.9).[77] He uses the same language here that he uses in book 11 when he explains that he leaped apart into time. With these words he identifies the outcomes of the pear theft as loss of unity with the One and loss of unity of his own soul. This appears to be the ongoing price of the stolen fruit. It resonates more loudly with pre-oedipal themes identified by Kohut than with oedipal themes.

These cultural resources allow Augustine to explore another point that he had recently argued in a more strictly theological vein, in a commentary on Romans 9:10–29: do human beings have a choice about whether they sin?[78] If his readers knew any of their philosophical tradition, they surely recognized the moral requirement that a person must have a choice about a course of action in order to be responsible for it. Yet Augustine in book 1 has already mentioned that even infants who cannot yet talk can demonstrate greed and jealousy. If sin comes before people have fully developed language and other signs of reason, can they be held responsible for what they do? Perhaps sin is original in the human condition. If so, then it would not be their fault. Augustine uses the incident of the pear tree to convince his readers that by stealing fruit as a sixteen year old, he discovered for himself the experiential knowledge of good and evil, like Adam and Eve did in eating of the forbidden tree in the story of the garden of Eden.[79] He had a choice when he took part in a simple act, like the one in Genesis, which clearly contravened what he had come to know as the will of God. Augustine did not suffer from confusion about what God wanted any more than did Adam and Eve. But like them, he caved in to the urging of another creature instead of following the wishes of the Creator.

Reflection on association with the gang demonstrates fairly clearly the interaction of cultural, social, and personal factors in the understanding of meaning in a life. The gang got together at the time because the culture allowed adolescent boys a certain amount of carousing and lack of close supervision in their late teens. Yet as Augustine reflected on it, he saw it as a challenge to cultural norms beyond the governance of adolescent behavior. It represented the tendency for human society to follow the wrong lead and to shame people for not collaborating in badness, much as the schoolteachers would shame the boys who did not apply themselves to learning fine words for adultery and deceit. It served as a challenge to the ancients' high estimate of society as the place of coming to virtue. And it recalled the social nature of sin suggested by the story of the serpent who tempted Eve, who in turn tempted Adam. So it allows Augustine to launch a cultural critique of philosophy by picking up the elements of a biblical story and retelling them as part of his own life.

At the same time, the gang in Augustine's youth was an outlet for the energies of adolescents. His society did not monitor it too closely. It was a peer group against which he would measure himself, as youngsters do in European and American societies and as age mates do in societies that define sharply an initiation period that sequesters boys on the verge of manhood.

Personally for Augustine, it was an experience of a dizzying approach to shame. What if the other youngsters had laughed at him for not joining in: "It shames one not to be shameless" (II.ix.17)?[80] One may suspect at a deeper level that he would have shied away from such blows to his grandiosity, which had already been beaten up by unempathic schoolmasters. Moreover, the urge to participate in the activity could even have formed a way of living up to an ideal. It is an ideal that Augustine as a middle-aged bishop will negate altogether: "Association with the gang is also a nothing" (II.viii.16).[81] In so doing, he draws the reader's attention from the shame that is our tip-off to dynamics of the unconscious grandiose self. He focuses instead on the question of worthy goals and ideals. This rhetorical shift mirrors the patterns of his own later life. He makes the rhetorical and personal shift from grandiosity to idealizing plain to self psychologically informed readers: "I will love you Lord, and I will give thanks and confession to your name because you have forgiven me such great evils and my nefarious deeds. I attribute to your grace and mercy that you have melted my sins away like ice (Eccl. 3:17). I also attribute to your grace whatever evil acts I have not done" (II.vii.15).[82] Through this one symbolic story, then, Augustine turns the feelings that may have originated in the unconscious self into a critique of and innovation on culture. The tale is not just a morbid preoccupation with youthful peccadilloes, but a rhetorical foreshadowing and an instruction of his readers, as well as himself, in the mystery and dynamics of sin.

CHAPTER 5

Strengths of a Long Adolescence

Augustine's culture continued to stoke his ambitions as he moved through his final school years and into his career as a teacher of rhetoric and a public speaker. His writings help us see how his intellect was able to fuel his success. His engagement in activities and accomplishments that could represent grandiosity resounds in books 3 through 7 of the *Confessions*. Yet his own words announce a counterpoint of discontent with worldly interests. But the counter theme fell short of dominance for a long time. Augustine describes these years as an accelerating fall away from union with God, until in book 7 he explains how his return toward God began.

Quotations from the opening of these books show their thematic unity and the pattern of ambition, physical delight, and departure from God that Augustine emphasizes throughout. Students of the *Confessions* remember the lines that open book 3: "I came to Carthage and all around me hissed a cauldron of illicit loves." The fall from the unity of relationship with God into the multiplicity of things in the world appears a few sentences later: "My soul was in rotten health. In an ulcerous condition it thrust itself to outward things, miserably avid to be scratched by contact with the world of the senses" (III.i.1).[1] In the next chapter, Augustine cites an example, an interesting statement in his own words of the interaction of culture and psyche: "I was captivated by theatrical shows. They were full of representations of my own miseries and fuelled my fire" (III.ii.2).[2] He also notes his accomplishments: "I was already first in the school of the rhetor, and rejoiced proudly and swelled with pride…" (III.iii.6).[3] Then a multi-faceted approach comes back as he talks about the many things to which he was drawn: "This was the society in which at a vulnerable age I was to study the textbooks on eloquence. I wanted to distinguish myself as an orator… Following the usual curriculum I had already come across a book by a certain Cicero..." This book formed an important part of training in rhetoric.[4] Although the people formulating Augustine's intellectual world intended it for one purpose, culture made it available to him for another end: "That book of his contains an exhortation to study philosophy and is entitled *Hortensius*. The book changed my feelings. It altered my prayers, Lord, to be towards you yourself. It gave me different values and priorities. Suddenly every vain hope became empty to me...I began to rise up to return to you" (III.iv.7).[5]

The story might seem to have taken its final turn already, here, in the first third of book 3. But Augustine is only stating the complex theme that will carry through the next several books. He begins the next paragraph by assuring us that this first "conversion," to philosophy, only offered a sounding of the music that would follow: "How I burned, my God, how I burned to fly back from earthly things to you, and I did not know what you would do with me...Nevertheless, in only this did I delight in that exhortation, that not in one or another sect, but in whatever one wisdom might be, I should love and seek and pursue and catch hold and be strongly embraced" (III.iv.8).[6] Yet Augustine could not find it, he concludes, because as he cast around for it, his pride prevented his embrace of Christianity. The themes of his life began to vary: "That explains why I fell in with men proud of their slick talk, very earthly minded and loquacious" (III.vi.10).[7] By the beginning of book 4, when he speaks of slightly later years, we find him saying: "We were being seduced and seducing, being deceived and deceiving (2 Tim. 3:13) in various desires, publicly through the teachings which they call liberal; privately through a false name of 'religion' [Manichaeism]..." (IV.i.1).[8]

At the beginning of book 5, we hear the same notes: "Where was I when I was seeking for you [God]? You were there before me, but I had departed from myself. I could not even find myself, much less you" (V.ii.2).[9] And by the end of that book, he speaks of his career much advanced and his learning in philosophy expanded: "After the manner of the Academics [Skeptics], as popularly understood, I doubted everything, and in the fluctuating state of total suspense of judgement I decided I must leave the Manichees...I therefore decided for the time being to be a catechumen in the Catholic Church, which the precedent of my parents recommended to me, until some clear light should come by which I could direct my course" (V.xiv.25).[10]

He heard the preaching of Ambrose, whose intellect apparently matched his own more closely than those he had encountered before. Yet Augustine found himself confused about how to proceed. The excitement of ambition and success drew him in one direction, and his desire for wisdom pulled him in another: "I myself was exceedingly astonished as I anxiously reflected how long a time had elapsed since the nineteenth year of my life, when I began to burn with a zeal for wisdom...And here I was already thirty, and still mucking about in the same mire in a state of indecision, avid to enjoy present fugitive delights which were dispersing my concentration…" (VI.xi.18).[11] Augustine explains in book 7 that after a further conversion, this time to Neoplatonism, he felt closer to God and God's wisdom, but even this experience could not assure the coordination of his thoughts and emotions: "I was caught up to you by your beauty and quickly torn away from you by my weight. With a groan I crashed into inferior things" (VII.xvii.23).[12] Then in book 8 he draws us further into the struggles between his old ways and his new one. From his point of view, God worked in these trials. In our more earthly terms they show the influences of culture and the realignment of the self when social interactions could assist him in a change of heart and lead him to cultural affirmation for the shifts to come in his ambitions and his friendships.

These books, examined more closely, will help us see how Augustine seems to have directed his energies primarily through the maturing, but still immature, force of grandiosity. But it could not in the long run sustain the coordination of his mind and emotions without a much more enticing focus for his idealizations. The outlines of Augustine's life in these years should appear more clearly in brief before the social background and cultural influences affecting him in those years is filled in. Then the psychological interpretation can proceed with the appropriate cautions about the setting in which he lived and the form in which he later retold his life.

Retelling the Adolescent's Life

We have already seen particular incidents from Augustine's adolescence, but have to realign them as a story. The pieces that one can lay out to assemble his life for psychological inquiry and social and cultural contextualization turn up here and there in the *Confessions*. Frustratingly jumbled, they become clearer when matched with comments in his other writings. Drawing the events of his life out of these sources and arranging them chronologically will clear the way for further reflection.

Augustine had a wealthy patron who, like his less well-to-do father, loved the signs of ambition and its success. Augustine's feelings toward Romanianus emerge in the address of a later book to his patron: "When I was but a poor boy setting out on my studies, you took me up, opening to me your house, your money, and, what is much more, your heart." Just what age Augustine was as this "poor boy" we cannot tell, but he acknowledges the importance of the interchanges when he was sixteen and his father died: "When I lost my father, you comforted me with your friendship, gave me life with your advice, and helped me from your resources."[13] The description of the vistas opened to him at Romanianus' home, if even half correct despite the usual hyperbolic praise of one's patron, shows what satisfactions to the earthly self this setting could provide:

> if your table were sumptuously laden for banquets every day; if any man might confidently ask of you and be assured of receiving whatever he needed or his fastidiousness desired, and if many

> benefits were lavished even upon such as did not ask for them; if your estate itself, carefully administered by your own people, were sufficiently large and organized to meet such great expenses; and if, meanwhile, you yourself were to pass your time in exquisite mansions, in splendid baths, occupying yourself with games of dice such as honour does not forbid, with hunting, and with feasting...would anyone, Romanianus, I ask you, would anyone dare to mention to you another happiness...?[14]

Romanianus' life matched that of many of the best swells of Italy and the Roman aristocracy itself.[15] His support enabled Augustine to study in Carthage until he was about twenty years old (IV.xvi.28).

In Carthage, at about age seventeen, Augustine, like many other young men of his era, formed a liaison with a young woman, most likely of lower social class, whose relatives could not hope to marry her legally to a man of prominence. The girl presumably was Catholic, and may well have remained so during Augustine's Manichaean years.[16] Augustine and she had a son not long after their relationship began. They named him Adeodatus, or "gift of God." Scholars assume that they began to practice contraception after the child's unplanned arrival.[17] He is the only child Augustine had. Adeodatus may have attended a grammarian's school, but his father took over his later education, as Augustine's books *The Happy Life* and *The Teacher* indicate.

At age eighteen, Augustine read Cicero's *Hortensius*, which entered into the curriculum as an example of fine rhetoric. But as Augustine said, "I did not turn my attention to the book to sharpen my tongue or my mode of expression, but because what it said convinced me" (III.iv.7).[18] He heard the call to philosophy, defined in the book by the Greek etymology, love of wisdom. Endeavoring to seek wisdom wherever he might find it, Augustine tried turning to the Bible:

> and only one thing restrained my blazing [for the *Hortensius*]— that the name of Christ was not there, since this name, by your mercy Lord, this name of my Savior, of your Son, my tender heart had hitherto piously drunk in with my mother's milk, and deeply retained it. Anything which was without this name, however literary or polished or truly spoken, could not seize me wholly. (III.iv.8)[19]

The Bible presented a different problem, though. It circulated in a Latin rustic at best, and Augustine's Greek was nowhere near good enough to appreciate it in that language even if he had had access to a copy. But unpolished Latin could not satisfy his intellectual longing (III.v.9).

The search proceeded through a nine-year sojourn, starting when Augustine was eighteen years old, in the religious world of the Manichees (III.iv.7; III.vi.10; and IV.i.1). How an amazingly intelligent man could have associated himself with a sect devoted to such fantastic teachings baffles many modern scholars.[20] He tells us little of the attraction of the Manichees for him. They did use the name of Jesus and regarded him as the Christ, although they did not really accept him as fully human and fully divine.[21] They also believed in the Holy Spirit with the Father and the Son (IV.vi.10).[22] Their explanation of evil spoke to Augustine's own discomfort with the topic. They believed in one force of good in the universe, the Christian God as reinterpreted by them, and one of evil, a force of darkness opposed to God's light.[23] This duality in the cosmos corresponded to a division in the soul, where each person was thought to have a good will and a bad will that would lead in different directions and account for human tendencies to act contrary to the good (VIII.x.23–24).[24]

The potential for assigning responsibility to something other than one's self and one's own, unitary will, which made Manichaeism attractive to Augustine, also enticed him to astrology. Astrology, too, assigned responsibility for action outside the person, although it did not need the theory of two wills at war within the person. Instead, it assured people that the planets and stars controlled behavior. Some years later while he lived in Milan much argument and disconfirming evidence led him to relinquish his fascination with astrology (IV.iii.4; VII.vi.8–10).[25]

Augustine mentions that he read Aristotle's *Ten Categories* without the help of a teacher when he was twenty years old. He matched the understanding of people who read the book in school under the direction of authorities on the subject:

> I had discussions with people who said they had understood the *Categories* only with much difficulty after the most erudite teachers had not only given oral explanations but had drawn numerous diagrams in the dust. They could tell me nothing they had learnt from these teachers which I did not already know from reading the book on my own... (IV.xvi.28)[26]

Evidently Augustine had begun to surpass his own teachers. The implication follows that by the time he was twenty, Augustine had exhausted the intellectual resources of one of the major centers of the empire. What was he to do? The answer was not simple. While such talent and accomplishment opened the possibility of higher attainments and, no doubt, maintained the interest of a man like Romanianus in him, it assured Augustine nothing, not even a clear road ahead in his career.

After several years' study of rhetoric at Carthage, Augustine returned to Tagaste (Brown says in 375),[27] apparently to open a grammar school at Romanianus' behest and with his support. Augustine's work there might almost have served as an informal, partial, but not monetary, repayment to Romanianus, because it would have elevated the status of their hometown. Augustine stayed with his mother again for part of the time he lived there, but at first she would not permit him to return to her house because she detested his affiliation with the Manichees. Yet she had a dream that she interpreted as God's word to her that Augustine would one day embrace

Catholicism and that she could in good conscience allow him to live with her (III.xi.19). While he lived again in Tagaste, an old friend died, and the mourning that beset Augustine led him back to Carthage (IV.vii.12). His ambition added to his interest in the move[28] but had proved an insufficient incentive until his friend's death augmented his desire to leave.

In Carthage Augustine taught rhetoric. He wrote a book *On the Beautiful and the Fitting* (*De pulchro et apto*, IV.xiv.23), when he was about twenty-six or twenty-seven years old (IV.xv.27). It did not bolster his reputation, as he tells us: "Although no one else admired the book, I thought very well of it myself" (IV.xiv.23).[29] In spite of the lack of praise from others for his argument, he maintained a position as a teacher of the highest-level students in the premier city of North Africa. His students would become government officials or lawyers, like Alypius (VI.ix.14, 16), who also became his friend. Their training in rhetoric opened the door for them to high office, prestige, and even wealth, for which Augustine himself still hoped in these years.

Augustine participated, apparently more than once, in verse competitions in Carthage (IV.i.1). He was not only a teacher, therefore, but also a performance artist. Just who were the greatest heroes of the public is hard to say—probably actors or charioteers—but short of those venues for notoriety, Augustine had achieved popular renown. He says that he won one of these competitions, although his scorecard for the rest of them has vanished completely. This victory allowed him to become a friend of the proconsul, Vindicianus. Proconsuls came to the city for a year at a time, according to Brown, and they seem to have circulated into other important cities and positions around the empire. Making friends with such a person brightened Augustine's social and economic prospects considerably.[30]

The routine life of a teacher could be much less glamorous, however. The students in Carthage caused much disturbance, both in and outside of the classroom. Augustine found their self-characterization as the "Wreckers" apt: "They would take out after the shyness of the unknown students, which they pursued so they could mock it for no good reason, and thereby feed their own malevolent exuberance" (III.iii.6).[31] Furthermore, some obnoxious behavior seems to have been open to any inconsiderate youngster: "At Carthage the licence of the students is foul and uncontrolled. They impudently break in and, with almost mad behavior, disrupt the order which each teacher has established for his pupils' benefit. They commit many acts of vandalism with an astonishing mindlessness, which would be punished under the law were it not that custom protects them."[32] They compromised teachers' control over the classroom and annoyed Augustine both as a student and as a teacher: "When I was a student, I refused to have anything to do with these customs; as a professor I was forced to tolerate them in outsiders who were not my own pupils" (V.viii.14).[33]

Augustine claims that this frustrating conduct by the students in Carthage led him to leave North Africa for Rome, where the reputation of better-behaved students appealed to him (V.viii.14). His departure in 383 at age twenty-eight led to the unforgettable scene of Monica's trailing him to the water's edge to plead with him not to go, his deception of her, and her praying at a local shrine while he went to the boat. He told her he would dissuade a friend from sailing at the wrong time, but in fact he left with his friends as Monica wept and begged God that he not go (V.viii.15).

Augustine fell deathly ill on his arrival in Rome (V.ix.16) but recovered and established himself as a teacher and more secretly as a Hearer in the Manichean community. Yet after a year he sought to leave Rome because the well-behaved students cheated their professors of the fees they owed. When the bill came due they simply never returned. Symmachus, a famous orator and patrician of an old Roman family, arranged for Augustine to audition for the position of teacher of rhetoric in Milan (V.xii.22—xiii.23). This was a public post that would take Augustine to the seat of the Western Empire at the time.[34] He would meet the powerful players in the imperial court and give speeches for at least two great figures—the emperor himself (VI.vi.9) and the proconsul.[35] Although they represented the heights of worldly power and kept his ambitions alive, the more formidable person to enter his life was Ambrose, bishop of Milan, an orator of some repute himself, a powerful actor in worldly affairs, and a deeply devout Christian. Augustine would never be the same after Ambrose's rhetoric revealed ideas that, like Cicero's, spoke to the heart when Augustine had intended that only his mind receive instruction.

As the years of adolescence ended, Augustine continued to struggle with the goal of wisdom, the lure of worldly success, and the echo of Christ's name, "drunk in with [his] mother's milk." With him in Milan were his brother, his friends Alypius and Nebridius, his concubine, his son, and, in fact, his mother. Monica had sailed to Italy, probably in the spring of 385,[36] and found Augustine in Milan. Cousins also arrived. In the face of major social upheaval, bound to affect the cultural direction of the empire, aware of the prospect of his own social advancement, in a shifting pool of familial contacts and friendly influences, Augustine entered the year 386.

Events of Augustine's Late Adolescence in Their Social Context

Augustine's remarkable abilities shone in the spotlight with greater glamour as he made his way from schoolboy to professor of rhetoric. Yet his own abilities would have remained undeveloped outside of social structures. Nor would they be intelligible to us without knowledge of the social context. We already make progress by knowing that his talents could begin to blossom because his father indulged more than ordinary ambition for him, and his mother supported his father's efforts in his behalf. Their social position would allow them to approach a wealthy man like Romanianus in their town in order to raise the funds for Augustine's advanced schooling. On the one hand, then, his family's social position supported his opportunities in ordinary ways within their social class. On the other hand, his parents' extra effort and ambition multiplied those opportunities and demonstrated for him the benefits of exerting oneself for a goal.

Brown and Kaster agree in their description of people trained in literature, grammarians as well as rhetors, as a class apart from the run-of-the-
mill people.[37] Augustine himself describes the pyramid of excellence: "We
see that very few attain consummate eloquence, though throughout the
whole world the schools of rhetoric thunder in the ears of crowds of young
men…Everyone wants to study Cicero's works because they are established
by the authority of our ancestors. The crowds of the unlearned endeavour
to learn what is prescribed for their learning by a few learned men. But
very few succeed."[38] Kaster confirms such a characterization in his more
extended study: "'Letters' or the like recurred as one of the three or four
most important marks of status—what Paulinus of Nola meant when he
referred to *honos, litterae, domus* [honor, letters, home] as the 'tokens of prestige in the world,' or what Jerome had in mind when he spoke of the 'noble
man, fluent of speech, wealthy,' a vivid figure flanked by an 'accompaniment of the powerful,' set off against the backdrop of the 'mob.'"[39] Markus
cites Marrou's characterization of "the ideal of the cultured man as a religious ideal…" Markus deems this evaluation a "ubiquitous tendency
among the literate classes of the late Empire…"[40] By helping him continue
his education, therefore, Romanianus funded half of Augustine's ticket to
social mobility. Augustine's success in his education completed the price
of admission to Romanianus' social setting, if not to his full wealth and
privilege.

Given these early backers—even stokers—of his ambitions, Augustine's
own desires to return to Carthage as a teacher of rhetoric from the grammar school at Tagaste, despite Romanianus' wishes to the contrary,[41] would
not be surprising. He had grown up with ambition, difficult choices made
by his parents, and their willingness to pour themselves into plans for his
worldly success. Tagaste for a young man with this family background
and education—and ample brain cells firing at the same time—would prove
too small.

The years in Carthage allowed a synergy of social and cultural influences on Augustine's thought and action to develop. The opportunities
available in Carthage shaped the guidance for life that Augustine found
there. He found guidance into competition, and thence access to further
secular achievement, through Vindicianus the proconsul and others whose
names are uncertain. He found guidance into spiritual fascination, both in
Manichaeism and astrology. He found intellectual sustenance. He had time
to read Aristotle and Cicero. Yet a twenty year old who could outthink his
teachers would have to move toward brighter intellectual lights. But years
passed before he exhausted his intellectual projects in North Africa and his
patience with his students.

Carthage was the primary city of the Roman empire in North Africa.
Its harbor welcomed boats from all around the Mediterranean, and sent
dietary staples, largely paid as taxes, across the sea to southern Europe and
Asia Minor. Some scholars call Carthage a university town, although the

university as we have known it only came into being in the Middle Ages. We have already seen, however, that Carthage was more full of lusts than of learning, as Augustine described it. It was also a home to theaters. It housed a circus, which we should picture as a Roman amphitheater, site of lascivious shows, the bloody chariot races, and gladiators' combats.

Augustine's relationship with his lover, whose name he never states, has given rise to much misinterpretation in our era, largely because we have no custom or institution like it in modern Europe or the U.S. The woman is usually called his concubine, less because the word accurately identifies their relationship for our common understanding, than because the term is cognate to the Latin and we have none that connotes the relationship more precisely.[42] Concubinage was a social institution in the sense defined in chapter 1—a pattern of human interaction of considerable duration and stability, for which the expected interactions are well established and reasonably well known to the people involved and to outsiders as well.[43] Concubinage, as Augustine practiced it, may best be understood for us today as a form of marriage.[44] Marriage would have to be conceived of as a two-tiered system at that time. The higher tier, marriage so called, was largely an economic arrangement between families to assure heirs of property and of the family's name, who would bear the responsibility for its continued honor.[45] It began with a ceremony of commitment, usually a dowry, and was sealed by a legal document and public recognition by both partners' families and the law. Concubinage did not require a ceremony for its initiation or legal action like divorce for its dissolution. It did not presuppose a transfer of wealth in the form of a dowry. It did not involve an explicit or public promise of fidelity or lifelong association, although we have already seen that such assumptions would have been misplaced in legal marriage with respect to the husband's side. Nonetheless, a concubine would be thought of as adulterous if she had sex with someone other than her partner.[46] Concubinage did, however, in Augustine's case result in a long-term, faithful, sexual relationship, and more than twelve years of shared responsibilities as parents. Laws of inheritance showed that a concubine's child could become the rightful heir to the father's property if no children by a formal, first-class marriage could claim it. The institution was expectable for young men, who were considered adolescent at least until their late twenties,[47] and who for many years could not establish themselves sufficiently socially or financially to be suitors acceptable to the prominent, affluent families of the girls they sought.[48]

Monica also played an important part in the years of social advancement for Augustine. She can be seen to have controlled the family money after Patricius' death (III.iv.7). She seems to have attained a status traditionally open to widows who had three children: she could exercise greater economic autonomy than most women under Roman law.[49] Yet clearly she had no desire for an existence separate from Augustine when she went to the port at Carthage to beg him to stay in North Africa or take her with him to Milan (V.viii.15).

While his departure without Monica conveys an attitude of haughty coldness to some readers, his social situation can make it more comprehensible, although nothing can recast it as more warm and considerate. First, we must take cognizance of the earlier claim that Augustine's future in Italy was uncertain when he departed (V.xii.22). On a strictly social level, he needed room to maneuver. Doing so would draw him into situations that his mother might well dislike. He would have to deal more directly with pagans, and he appears to have expected to depend on the Manichees in Rome (V.vii.14). If we remember that she would not let him live with her when he first returned as a Manichee from Carthage to Tagaste, we cannot reasonably assume that she would have welcomed the prospect of depending, with him, on the Manichees in Rome for her room and board.

Second, Monica was about fifty-one years old when Augustine sailed for Rome. Would uprooting her really present itself as a good thing to do? How would she fare on the voyage? Would she be happy in Italy? He mentions that she, like he, had a provincial accent.[50] He also had entree in Roman society that she would have lacked. How would an old woman with a funny accent manage in a new society, where, as we may recall, she would have been expected most often to stay home (in this case, with her son's concubine)? She would almost indubitably have set out to find the nearest church, and develop the relationship with her bishop there that she had had in North Africa. Yet this would raise again the conflict of religious commitments in the family, and might prove impracticable in a larger city where the bishop would have had the full range of prominent patrons and poverty-stricken parishioners to whom he would already be attending.[51] Arguably she continued to grow spiritually and intellectually to a surprising extent,[52] yet could Augustine reasonably be expected to have foreseen that development when he left Carthage? Finally, to the practical side of young Augustine, Monica's security in North Africa might have seemed sure. She had controlled at least some part of the inheritance left by Patricius and had enough money to take food to tombs for memorial feasts for the dead (III.iv.7; VI.ii.2). Had she found herself in need, Romanianus would not have let her starve.

These lines of reasoning, admittedly speculative, stand in contrast to the idea of filial piety. How the many men in government service who traveled on the empire's business honored that ideal is unclear. Despite the fact that Augustine does not advance the reasons above when he recounts his departure from his natal lands, such thoughts carry some weight. First, they negate nothing that he did say. Second, they open up for us some of the factors that he may have taken for granted, both as a young man and later as the author of the *Confessions*. Third, for those of us who do not share that social context, elucidation of social and cultural considerations can help refine our psychological inferences.

None of this argument should gainsay that taking leave of Monica etched itself vividly in Augustine's psyche. He may have been practical and even somewhat cold in his behavior, but not inert: "[my mother] wailed bitterly at my setting out and followed me to the edge of the sea. But I deceived her as she forcefully held on to me so that she could call me back or go with me" (V.viii.15).[53] This interaction would create quite a scene in the mind, as well as in society. Even if it happened that many other young men set sail for Rome and left weeping mothers on the shore to lament their sons' departures, such a scene would strike the senses. In fact Augustine seems to have intended it to do so as he recounted it in book 5 of the *Confessions*.

While Augustine says that he moved to Rome to find better-behaved students, and presumably a classroom atmosphere more conducive to the intellect, one can also believe that he hoped for the stimulation of the people he might meet and the sights he had never seen in that city of myth and empire. He does not claim to have wanted a simple life as a teacher. He did not know what Rome would bring. He seems to have wanted the chance to find a better life for himself, in whatever sense of "better" might arise. He admits as he tries to convey his reasons for going that "these considerations [of more money and higher status] had an influence on my mind" (V.viii.14).[54] In addition, his geographical change altered the context of predecessors and contemporaries who could push his intellect further. For instance, Ambrose's early life took place in a cultural depth and social breadth that Augustine's family could only desire, but not provide, for their son. Ambrose's training in grammar and rhetoric was supplemented by a family library, an educated brother and sister, travel around the north coast of the Mediterranean, and high government service.[55] The Romans and Milanese hovered near the pinnacle of the empire, perilous as those heights were. In Rome and Milan, a greater proportion of the men Augustine met would have been the people that the North Africans could only desire to be.

Guidance for Life in These Social Settings

Searching out the cultural influences on Augustine's thought and action during these years confronts us with some familiar problems. First, he simply alludes to much of his cultural heritage, and we, separated from it by a millennium and a half, must apply ourselves in order to understand his implicit references. Second, we have to unravel the references to his knowledge of culture contemporary with his writing and those contemporary with the time about which he wrote. Finally, we have to work with our own conceptions of culture, which, like those of society and the person, may require some refinement themselves. The refinement that I will suggest for our understanding of culture borrows from the notion of intertextuality. By this I mean, somewhat loosely, that great pieces of literature (and perhaps all texts) combine in themselves the patterns of presentation, the diction, the themes, and the images of other literary works. One way texts influence each other is by the earlier work's patterning of the later author's mind. An author may pore over a book so often or so carefully that its elements become part of that later author's thought, perception, and artistic judgment. This process adds to the ways we may think of culture making up psyche, and of authors' psyches helping to make up culture.

If we are to take the intertextual transmission of culture seriously as part of the study of Augustine's thought and life, we need to know still more about his education. The term "liberal studies" with which Augustine described his learning covered a much narrower range then than we might now expect. Peter Brown assesses it grimly: "It was frankly pagan... Vergil, Cicero, Sallust, and Terence were the only authors studied in detail. It was exclusively literary: philosophy, science, and history were, alike, ignored...It imposed a crushing load on the memory..."[56] He offers a partial explanation for the apparently unappealing way of teaching: "The content of this education was not as important as its aim. This aim had remained unchanged for some 800 years. It was still being vigorously pursued in the fourth century, in the crowded, noisy schoolrooms of the teachers of rhetoric, as far apart as Bordeaux and Antioch..." Brown concludes, "The ideal product of this education was the orator," whom he allows Augustine to describe: "a man that is, who could 'give pleasure throughout his argument, by his vivacity, by the feelings at his command, by the ease with which words came to him, perfectly adapted to dress his message in style.'"[57]

This training seems to have come to Augustine from manuals, including treatises like the *Hortensius* that he studied for other purposes.[58] Yet his culture should not fall victim to a reduction of its resources to these particular cultural artifacts. After all, North Africa had also been the home of Plotinus a century and a quarter before, even though he too had left for Italy, and Augustine would encounter his work only there. The southern rim of the Mediterranean also counted Tertullian and Cyprian among its offspring. In the second and third century they set the course of North African theology for the next several hundred years. Origen, whose readings of the scriptures heavily influenced Ambrose, had written from Alexandria, as did the church father Clement. Somewhere, as the anthropologist Obeyesekere has pointed out about culture more generally, lay images, ideas, stories that may have fallen out of popular use but could spur the minds and feelings of people who, seeking, might find them.[59] The failure of a whole culture did not propel Augustine from North Africa. Instead he seems to have encountered a paucity of immediately available resources or spastic communication of those that suited his particular needs and desires. These lacunae could have exacerbated the drawbacks of Carthage's distance from the centers of power and prompted his move across the Mediterranean.

This perspective should temper the psychological studies' claims that Augustine was fleeing Monica when he went to Rome.[60] In the discussion of culture and its effects on the psyche we should emphasize that August-ine may well have been consciously aware, when he sailed, of the similar-ity between his departure from his mother and Aeneas's desertion of Dido in the *Aeneid*. As Shweder and Much explain in their study of discourse in moral development, Hindus clarify their actions within their social system by reference to stories.[61] Other people may do likewise when they turn to literature, or theater, or religious rites for consolation, comprehension, and the marking of life transitions. In Augustine's literary world, the *Aeneid* spotlighted for people the heritage of the Roman empire and the image of the man of honor and success. Of course it would play into Augustine's construction of his life, both as he acted it and as he wrote it.[62] Aeneas's parting from Dido could serve as a blessing on the sacrifice of relation-ships by men on the move.

Another example of how Augustine's cultural heritage may have shaped his life while he lived it, as well as when he wrote it, comes from his comments on his friendship with the young man who died while Augustine taught grammar school in Tagaste. The language of the bishop looking back recalls quite directly the language of Cicero in his treatise on friendship, and both young men would have read this in school. Cicero himself reproduced and crystallized a discussion of friendship like that of Aristotle in the *Nicomachean Ethics*.[63] As the friendship continued its devel-opment after their schooling was over, one can imagine that Augustine and his friend recognized themselves as conforming to the Ciceronian model of friendship, or wished to be seen as such. Augustine as bishop revised that ancient model of friendship in writing this story, to a slightly different paradigm in which friends cling not only to the same ideal, but should love each other, consciously, with full awareness of that love, in God.[64] Yet the lines he wrote on the healing power of other friendships after the one friend's death make the classical image vivid through everyday instances and show a person understanding himself in his culture's terms:

> There were other things which occupied my mind in the company of my friends: to make conversation, to share a joke, to perform mutual acts of kindness, to read together well-written books, to share in trifling and in serious matters, to disagree though without animosity—just as a person debates with himself—and in the very rarity of disagreement to find the salt of normal harmony, to teach each other something or to learn from one another, to long with impatience for those absent, to welcome them with gladness on their arrival. These and other signs come from the heart of those who love and are loved and are expressed through the mouth, through the tongue, through the eyes, and a thousand gestures of delight, acting as fuel to set our minds on fire and out of many to forge unity. (IV.viii.13)[65]

Augustine tells us that these healing aspects of friendship eventually cleared his mind of the great grief that followed on his friend's death. These culturally transmitted themes, like those related to his move to Rome, will return in a depth psychological interpretation.

Self Psychological Reflections on Augustine's Later Adolescent Years

Augustine had learned enough of ancient Greek and Roman wisdom to have refined his desires somewhat according to high standards. Nonetheless, he still had his earlier longings. His famous prayer from his youth exemplifies his ambivalence: "Grant me chastity and continence, but not yet" (VIII.vii.17).[66] From a self psychological point of view, one would conclude that from the multitude of influences on him, the many urgings pushing him in many ways, he chose unknowingly the ones that spoke to his unconscious injured grandiosity. He included, but relegated to second place, those that spoke fairly loudly to his idealizing in its few but important distinctions from grandiosity. A careful look at Augustine's language and Kohut's theory suggests why Augustine's self, in the self psychological sense, was fragmenting in ways that could achieve representation in his language of the many and the One. In addition to problems with grandiosity and idealizing, concerns about alter ego selfobjects also came into view.

Before Milan and Ambrose, Augustine would seem to have maintained himself primarily from his grandiose side. He won the verse competitions. He heard the applause of the audience. Bright young pupils listened to him. He could carry on a double life, exercising his brain on rhetoric in public and on the Manichaean teachings in private. He could discuss the abstruse teachings of astrology with the proconsul. What could such a young man not do? A middle-class youth whose grandiosity had suffered injury in childhood could not hope for a better setup to return a full mirroring of his wonderfulness to him in adulthood. For a time, and to a certain extent, stoking his grandiosity worked to keep him in psychological balance.

Although his work and his social contacts could keep affirming his grandiosity, evidence for self-sustenance from sources other than his own grandiosity comes from Augustine's apparent idealizing of various men at this time in his life. We may infer that Augustine's relationships to the proconsul Vindicianus and his patron Romanianus included an element of idealizing, as Vindicianus' status and Augustine's later descriptions of Romanianus' wealth and munificence might suggest. Two other attachments of Augustine's to renowned men seem less easy to understand, however, strictly on the basis of their social relations with Augustine. In fact, most of the time he thought about them, neither of them had any social relations at all with him. One never did. That one was Hierius, an orator in Rome whose fame had reached Carthage. Augustine dedicated the book he wrote in his mid-twenties to Hierius, although they had never met. He contemplates his fascination with Hierius as he looks back while he writes the *Confessions*. What he loved in the man, he says, was the esteem with which other people spoke of him. He credits himself with having been able to sort out shining reputations to the extent that he would admire a man for eloquence but not for gladiatorial combat (IV.xiv.21–22). Nonetheless, he loved the marks of glory to which grandiosity could attach, without being able to discern anything about Hierius' heart. Speaking in the language of self psychology, one could say that despite the fact that Augustine had not the slightest experience of what Hierius was like, Augustine idealized him for his capacity to get affirmations of grandiosity.

Why would such an idealization develop for a man he had never met? It might come from a need to idealize very strongly. Kohut suggests that this need arises when early idealizations do not get a chance to moderate slowly but surely into realistic admiration.[67] If Patricius' ideals could not withstand the alternate ideals espoused by Monica, if Patricius behaved irrationally in his anger, if he died when his grandiose aspirations for Augustine still needed paternal backing, then Augustine would likely have suffered damage to his idealizing. His father's death when Augustine was about sixteen could have called the damaged idealizing back toward consciousness. Its approach to awareness could have been disguised by displacement onto these other men.

A similar line of thought suggests itself with regard to the Manichaean wise man Faustus. The absurdities of some of the Manichees' claims did not escape Augustine, but his inquiries about them drew one ultimate response, that he should wait till Faustus would come, that Faustus would be able to explain everything (V.vi.10). When he did arrive, he spoke pleasantly, but not with sufficient philosophical rigor to satisfy Augustine (V.vi.11–vii.12). This eventuality may be less surprising than the report that Augustine attributed to Faustus such a keen intellect that he would be able to unravel problems that Augustine himself could not solve. Augustine knew that he had understood Aristotle's *Categories* by himself. Why then should he expect to find a teacher for the Manichaean writings who had the intelligence to explain what Augustine himself could not understand? Perhaps because he had a need to idealize.

This line of self psychological interpretation is strengthened by Augustine's discussion of his interest in Ambrose and his preaching and thinking, and by his appreciation of Simplicianus and his ability to clarify the writings of the Neoplatonists.[68] But these experiences are part of the shift that came about in the self, as well as in his cultural resources and social situation, at the time leading up to his conversion. They will be taken up in the next chapter.

Augustine's feelings about the friend who died, and indeed about his other friends, have the ring of what Kohut calls an "alter ego transference." Originally this term referred to a stage in the development of grandiosity. It seemed to Kohut to develop after the child felt grandiose because she merged with the grandness of the parent. The parent's wonderfulness was not something external to be looked up to and drawn on as it would be in an idealizing transference. It simply *was* hers. Then would come the alter ego transference, when the other and the nascent self would seem to be somewhat separate, but essentially the same. Then, still very early in childhood, during the toddling years at the latest, would come the mirroring transference in which an adult would applaud what the little one thought of as wonderful in herself: "Oh, did you pick those dandelions all by yourself? Oh, what beautiful dandelions!" The foolishness of admiring the dandelions, otherwise weeds to be exterminated or greens to be eaten, highlights the point that the admiration is not for the value of the dandelions, but for the child and her initiative and achievement.[69]

Kohut later came to see the alter ego or "twinship" transference, as he then called it, as a distinct way that the self reconstitutes its wholeness. It would happen for some people, he thought, simply by sharing the presence of another being who would be like oneself in some way that seemed reliable. One example he gives is of a girl who felt calm and alive and comfortable when kneading dough next to her grandmother who was engaged in the same activity. The feeling tone of the memory did not include a strong element of her grandmother actively mirroring her, nor did she think that she and her grandmother were the same ball of power and might. No, they just worked together, and they felt contented in so doing. When this experience ended because the girl moved, she developed a fantasy of a genie who was just like her and lived in a bottle on her dresser and would listen to her thoughts and feelings and never cause a disagreement or distress. That fantasy seemed to help her respond to the loss that resulted from leaving her grandmother and to restore her self in a home with somewhat distant and cold parents.[70]

A friend could indeed fill for Augustine the role of what Kohut called an alter ego selfobject. The need for such an alter ego selfobject to sustain the unconscious self might be especially great in these tumultuous years when Augustine left home for the biggest city he had ever seen, when his father died, when he glimpsed an ideal but could not find a way to live by it, when he fell in with the heretical and proscribed Manichees. Augustine's friend also willingly joined the Manichees, so he and Augustine conformed to the classical ideal of friends sharing their vision of the good. They had grown up in the same town and played together as children and gone to school together—probably been beaten by the same schoolmaster—so they knew a great deal about one another and about one another's world. What a well-formed base for an alter ego relationship, a keel for an otherwise overstimulated and unrestrained self!

Kohut would say that everyone needs this sort of image of others like oneself to sustain the self, that we cannot carry on without continued sustenance for the self.[71] The pain Augustine mentions at his friend's death makes the case very well that his need for self-sustenance ran deep:

> I was in misery and had lost the source of my joy...I found myself heavily weighed down by a sense of being tired of living and scared of dying...I thought that since death had consumed him, it was suddenly going to engulf all humanity...I was surprised that any other mortals were alive, since he whom I had loved as if he would never die was dead. I was even more surprised that when he was dead I was still alive...(IV.v.10–IV.vi.11)[72]

Augustine in this passage appropriates the language of classical ideals of friendship, and in its disguise he expresses unconscious feeling.

This discourse on grief and friendship comes in the *Confessions* in a discussion of the years after Augustine's schooling had finished, and he had returned to Tagaste to live. Augustine's father had died a few years earlier, and Augustine describes his grief about his friend's death as a "torment" or even "punishment" in "his fatherland," and "his paternal home" as a "marvelous unhappiness" (IV.iv.9).[73] Several possibilities present themselves if we consider these allusions to a fatherland and his father's home psychologically. His father would have played a large role in his psychological makeup. That is, his father represented the cultural ideal of the grandiose man: Patricius admired, and may even have flaunted as best he could, the external flourishes that tip us off to archaic unconscious grandiosity. But when Patricius died, what would have happened to the idealized status of these flourishes? Death simply does not flatter a person. As these ideals glorified grandiosity, it would have dimmed too, at least temporarily when he died. Therefore, Patricius' death could have dealt a blow to Augustine's unconscious self both in its idealizing and in the display of grandiosity that it idealized.

With grandiosity and ideals clouding over at once, Augustine may have been especially susceptible to alternate modes of sustaining himself. He might have been more open to the power of friendship to heal one's heart and mind, and then all the more vulnerable when it disappeared with a friend's death. He also seems to have strengthened his feelings of admiration for Romanianus at this point. In fact, Romanianus seems by Augustine's later account to have shown empathy as Kohut would wish for it. That is, interactions with him seem to have demonstrated empathy to Augustine and to have helped the unconscious self remain stable. Finally, Augustine might have been more susceptible to the Manichees when he joined them a few years after his father's death, if he could comprehend his loss through their account of evils in this life. Their worldview could symbolically assuage the damage to grandiosity that could come from recognizing his and his father's powerlessness in the face of death.

All these changes in his personal relationships, in addition to the later upheaval of a move to a new country and disappointment in the realities of his new job, followed by a move to yet another city and another professional adjustment, make it easy for us to see how Augustine's grandiosity could have been nearly overwhelmed as the primary focus of his self's coherence. Once he got to Milan, an encounter with a strong mind focused on different ideals in a social and cultural world of much less stability even than Carthage could further the disruption of the cohesion he had formed for himself. He may first have undergone the disruption unconsciously, but soon it became apparent to his conscious awareness.

Augustine Recombining Symbols
in the Account of the "Confessions"

The comparison of Dido and Aeneas to Monica and Augustine can point us toward a more complete reading that lets us see how society, culture, and psyche combined to pattern Augustine's understanding of his life. The notion of intertextuality enters the interpretation here because a closer look at Augustine's presentation of the event, distinguished from the event itself, allows us to see how texts seem to have seeped deeply into his understanding of the world and himself, his harmonizing of them, his self-presentation, and his self-cohesion.

Aeneas pursues his fortunes by sailing from Carthage to Rome, much to Dido's dismay, and she, the queen of Carthage, commits suicide as her lover leaves. This story itself recalls numerous desertions of women by their lovers in ancient tales (for instance, in the *Odyssey*), as well as departures of many a son against his mother's wishes.[74] The hint that the love of mother and son might resemble that of the celebrated lovers has given rise to oedipal interpretations. Yet before exploring them, we might note the play of other texts in the same story.

Augustine seems to have the parable of the prodigal son in mind as he writes the *Confessions*, especially the narrative of his late adolescence.[75] The prodigal son's departure from his father's home may appear through the moment of Augustine's resettling in Carthage after his friend died in Tagaste,[76] or again through his voyage from Carthage to Rome. In this latter instance, we may note that he was taking his cultural inheritance and all that he had accumulated through boyhood, much as the prodigal collected the inheritance that his father had accumulated for him. In both cases, the young man finds himself worse off than before. The inheritance is not bad in either case, but it will not supply the young man's desires indefinitely. Becoming more absorbed in the allures of the wider world, each loses the certainty he had. Each finds himself entangled in a worldly situation he cannot sustain. Both return to their childhood home.

Differences between the story of Augustine's journey and that of the prodigal also prevent it from becoming an allegory, that is, a one-to-one match of a representation to what it signifies. The prodigal leaves his father as well as his father's house, whereas Augustine, going either to Carthage to teach or to Rome, took his leave several years after his father's death. The prodigal squanders a material inheritance, but Augustine does not. The prodigal enjoys promiscuous sex, but Augustine, although sexually active during these years, becomes faithful to one woman. Inasmuch as these aspects of the prodigal's story might represent Augustine's spiritual departure from God as his father, we could note that his journey away from his home in God had begun long before. The ocean voyage simply extends it, and, as Augustine seems to intend us to understand it, it actually helps to lead him back home. Instead of an allegory then, we find an extensive symbolic web, leading from one spiritual warning and reminder to another.

The motif of the journey ties the story of his departure not only to that of the prodigal and of Aeneas and Odysseus but also to the ideas of Plotinus, who uses the metaphor of a journey to discuss the soul's return to the One. If the soul falls away from the One, as the Neoplatonists would say, then it must journey back, as Plotinus said, not by feet or by boats, but by turning into itself and exploring itself.[77] There it might find the light of the One. Ambrose and other Christian Neoplatonists would identify this One with God. Augustine believed by the time he wrote the *Confessions* that all learning comes by the teaching of God from inside the soul (X.xl.65),[78] and so does knowledge of the way of return and its destination.

Yet clearly Augustine as a younger man did not turn inward for knowledge, but outward for a more exalted earthly life. The bishop shows through the story that the ancient Greek and Roman tales' ideals and modes of behavior contradicted the guidance for life available to people who set their hearts on God. He knows as he composes that his own arrival in Rome, where he fell terribly ill, did not match the glories of the achievements of Aeneas. Nor did his further route to Milan and return to his homeland.

Ricoeur emphasizes that symbols help bring thought to some concrete phenomenon.[79] This story of Augustine's journey does so too. A cultural symbol mixed with the others on the conscious level would appear to be the movement away from God, started by a precipitous fall, and the return trip, guided by the oft misperceived, but still powerful, hand of God. The fact that this story fit the social structure of power, wealth, and prestige in the late Roman Empire makes it all the more apt as a way of leading thought to concrete realities. While it allows the educated reader's mind to wander from text to text and take bearings from the various pointers in the literary tradition, it also deposits us boldly in a real world of sea coasts and hostels, nighttime sailings, tearful mothers, and illness as one adjusts to a foreign land.

None of these interpretations preclude the presence of unconscious material in disguised form in this story. As some scholars have held, Augustine may have wept when, as a boy, he read the story of Dido and Aeneas because he felt emotionally frustrated by a clinging mother. He may have expressed unawares his unconscious feelings about Monica by sailing away from her and by retelling the story later.[80] Nonetheless, these possibilities do not sustain a reductive reading of the story as primarily an oedipal struggle, nor do they tell us conclusively why Augustine did what he did or wrote what he wrote.[81]

Not only does the story itself not sustain such conclusions, but the evidence adduced to support the oedipal interpretation itself is weak. Two other vignettes that have turned up in oedipal readings should themselves be reconsidered. One is Monica's dream of the young man on the ruler and the other is the account of her many tears that led a bishop to predict Augustine's ultimate salvation.

First, we should note that in their cultural context both dreams and tears mark Monica as a pious woman guided by God.[82] Dreams and tears had greater currency in Augustine's and Monica's world than in Europe or America of the late twentieth century.[83] Later in the *Confessions* he tells us that he and Monica waited for her to have a dream to guide them in his course toward marriage (VI.xiii.23). He tells us that people cried in church, and their bishop, preaching, wept with them.[84] In their social context, these dreams and tears were not strictly idiosyncratic features of Monica's psyche.

The dream puts Monica in the category of those who have prophetic insight.[85] Worried constantly about Augustine's salvation, she dreamed one night that a radiant looking young man came to her standing on a wooden ruler. He assured her that where she was on the ruler, Augustine would also be. She interpreted the ruler as the rule of faith and the young man in the dream as a messenger from God. When she told Augustine of the dream, near the time it came to her, he challenged her interpretation with his own: that where he was as a Manichee, she would be. But she retorted that the young man did not say that, but the opposite. She caught the brilliant young rhetorician in a misapprehension of words. One might wonder how she could do this, but Augustine assures the reader that she did it by God's working in her awareness. The true teacher taught her the truth in this dream (III.xi.19–20).

Second, Augustine sees Monica's tears as a mode of correction by God. They are the "just whip of sorrows"[86] for her too earthly love of him. She still held too closely the ancient Roman values of family and earthly attachment to one's relatives, as Augustine saw her in retrospect. Just as he had to sail to Rome to suffer more from his own misapprehension of God, she had to weep until she came to the arrangement of her love that God would want, less bound, as Augustine puts it, by "the remnants of Eve, seeking with groans what she had brought forth with groans" (V.viii.15).[87] But the tears did what they should do according to Augustine's thoughts about God's correction of human beings: the chastisement led her to seek God.

Finally, interpretations of the dream as evidence of Monica's own sexual desire for Augustine should be toned down.[88] They tend not to follow the rules of interpretation, and they overlook alternate analyses. For instance, the first rule of dream interpretation is that the dream should be interpreted by free associations. Yet we have almost none of Monica's own thoughts about it. Those we do have, like the dream text itself, are recounted by her son some twenty years later. He assures us of the accuracy of his memory and we have no reason to think he lied, but we do have reason to think that memory could shift over time, and that distortion could creep in from his own unconscious into the creative process of writing his book. Second, in principle, the dream would be primarily about Monica's own oedipal conflicts. According to psychoanalytic theory, these could be expressed in disguised form in her relationship to Augustine and thence lead her to an overly strong attachment to him. But they could also have fostered a strong attachment to Patricius or to Navigius, Augustine's brother. Poor Navigius, he never seems to match his brother's brilliance (IX.xi.27). Could the shining, handsome young man on the ruler be a disguised image of Monica's desire for her other son to rub off his dullness and fulfill her fondest wishes for him? Might not her interpretation of the dream as a reference to Augustine provide just the cover needed for her unconscious desires for Navigius to reach conscious expression?

These proposals gently parody previous conclusions, yet without violating the text and the rules of dream interpretation set out by Freud. My more serious suggestion extends the thoughts already advanced, that Augustine may have had some unconscious oedipal desires that emerged in disguised form in his relationship to his mother and in his later writing about her. These may have lent conviction to certain thoughts or feelings and influenced his actions. But in the case of his departure for Rome, the social and cultural factors favoring his decision seem strong enough to let us see why he would have left as he did. He need not be seen primarily as fleeing Monica, not even if we take the unconscious into account. The self psychological factors also seem interesting and perhaps influential but not determinative. The expression of his own grandiosity would be likely in trying to make his fortune in the famed city from which the Empire extended and in behaving like the cultural hero Aeneas. The symbols of culture would allow his grandiosity to connect through a web of associations to oedipal feelings, literary images, and realistic if uncertain ambitions. So from reprehensible behavior by students, his own idealization of the outward appearances of grandiosity, his solid background in rhetoric, and his questioning disappointment in the Manichees, he "came to Milan," as he says, "to Ambrose, the bishop" (V.xiii.23).[89]

CHAPTER 6

Conversion at the Limits of the Self

At age thirty Augustine entered a time of confusion and upheaval. If he was ever a water buffalo listening to an orchestra, this was the time. He could not apprehend music in his life. His quest for wisdom never ceased, although it fell in second place behind his ambitions and sensual loves. His active pursuit of worldly security and success accelerated, while his search for a defensible system of thought to organize his view of the world took him into at least three intellectual arenas—skepticism, Neoplatonism, and Christianity. Any of these explorations would have kept a lesser mind busy. In the years between 384 and 386, a shift in geographical location, acceleration of his career, changes in his home life, and social unrest in the city added to Augustine's own tumult.

Neoplatonic denigration of attachment to the world and ambivalence about the body did not free Augustine from his desires for worldly success and sexual enjoyment.[1] Even after he committed himself to being a catechumen in the Catholic Church, he shifted toward now one delight, then another. His testimony to this variability punctuates the passages on these years: "These winds blew first one way, then the other, pushing my heart to and fro" (VI.xi.20);[2] "How fearful a fate for 'the rash soul' (Isa. 3:9) which nursed the hope that after it had departed from you, it would find something better! Turned this way and that, on its back, on its side, on its stomach, all positions are uncomfortable" (VI.xvi.26);[3] "My heart vehemently protested against all the physical images in my mind, and by this single blow I attempted to expel from my mind's eye the swarm of unpurified notions flying about there. Hardly had they been dispersed when in the flash of an eye (1 Cor. 15:52) they had regrouped and were back again..." (VII.i.1).[4]

These comments about intersecting waves of experience indicate that our gaze must scan the range of influences and events of these years and not stop to stare only at the conversion drama Augustine depicts in book 8 of the *Confessions*. Despite the fame of the scene, its fascination for readers of many centuries, and its effect on theories of conversion, his newfound willingness to make the full commitment of baptism is only one aspect of years of changes. Augustine returned to Africa some time in 389 or 390 as a baptized Catholic instead of a Manichee, but he grew into his explicitly Christian self for several years before and even more years after whatever experience he may have undergone in the garden at Milan in 386.

Augustine constructed the *Confessions*, including the scene of his conversion in the garden, as a theological statement, not simply as an account of events.[5] Yet the theological points it makes rely on the conviction that God works through particular people and events. Which people and which events matter. So if we are to hear and respect Augustine's authorial voice enough to try to follow his message, attention to the people and the events in their social and cultural contexts becomes crucial. Then we will have prepared our understanding to investigate the more personal dynamics in these years of his life and his story of them. This time encompasses a shift from idealizing the marks of fruitful grandiosity, to idealizing God the one good and muting grandiosity, although grandiosity reemerges in a counterpoint we call shame.

What Happened and How It Fit
Augustine's New Social and Cultural Settings

Arrival in Milan

A less precise statement of events than Augustine's little declarative sentence would be hard to achieve: "And so I came to Milan to Ambrose, the bishop..."[6] This claim captures the essence of the move to Milan as Augustine the author saw it theologically. Sentences following shortly confirm the role of hindsight in Augustine's emphasis on Ambrose in the *Confessions*: "Ambrose taught the sound doctrine of salvation. From sinners such as I was at that time, salvation is far distant. Nevertheless, gradually, *though I did not realize it,* I was drawing closer" (V.xiii.23).[7] But more simply stated, what Augustine the young teacher of rhetoric came to was Milan itself.

Milan comprised the imperial court, both Arian and Catholic Christians, the military, tradespeople and merchants, and a good job for Augustine himself and its concomitant demands. He had to meet the people who could advance his career and learn whom to avoid. He was establishing himself as worthy of the position he had attained, and preparing to advance to a yet higher position. Milan in the autumn of 384 burgeoned with people on the make. Their fates hung in one balance after another as conspiracies and invasions and emperors and their officers followed one on the other. Augustine sets out the situation vividly as he describes a friend of his friend Ponticianus:

He was amazed and set on fire, and during his reading began to think of...leaving his secular post in the civil service to be your [God's] servant...Angry with himself, he turned his eyes on his friend and said to him: "Tell me, I beg of you, what do we hope to achieve with all our labours? What is our aim in life? What is the motive of our service to the state? Can we hope for any higher office in the palace than to be Friends of the Emperor? And in that position what is not fragile and full of dangers? How many hazards must one risk to attain to a position of even greater danger? And when will we arrive there?" (VIII.vi.15)[8]

"Friends of the Emperor" were "honoured individuals in high office," according to Chadwick. In that era, they like "all high office holders were vulnerable to palace revolutions and conspiracies."[9]

At least in one sense Augustine did literally come "to Milan to Ambrose the bishop": he visited Ambrose early in his time in Milan. Courcelle describes their first meeting as "an exchange of official courtesies."[10] He infers that "the Catholic bishop of Milan, no matter how busy he might have been, would without doubt not have refused the official rhetor of his city several hours of confidential conversation..."[11] This first visit would have had less the character of intimacy, however, than of formal interchange. In the near future the aspirations of the young rhetorician could lead to an icy standoff if Augustine's verbal skills were called into service to support the young emperor Valentinian and his mother Justina.[12] Augustine himself may have realized that he entered a dicey situation, and his obligatory call on Ambrose may have seemed all the more reassuring when Ambrose welcomed him "like a father." One could even speculate that Augustine's further comment about his response to Ambrose alludes to the seriousness of the social setting of Milan in the mid 380s: "I began to like him, at first indeed not as a teacher of the truth, for I had absolutely no confidence in your Church, but as a human being who was kind to me" (V.xiii.23).[13] In a world of ambition and uncertainty, genuine kindness, even as befitted performance of an official social role, could relieve some pressure and allow momentary relaxation.

Relief and delight seem mixed in Augustine's description of his admiration of Ambrose's preaching:

I used enthusiastically to listen to him preaching to the people, not with the intention which I ought to have had, but as if testing out his oratorical skill to see whether it merited the reputation it enjoyed or whether his fluency was better or inferior than it was reported to be. I hung on his diction in rapt attention, but remained bored and contemptuous of the subject matter. My pleasure was in the charm of his language. (V.xiii.23)[14]

With this opening, Ambrose evidently succeeded in the classic aim of the rhetorician, to employ the delights of language to persuade people of one's point. Augustine, trained and able as he was, acknowledges Ambrose's victory: "Nevertheless together with the words which I was enjoying, the subject matter, in which I was unconcerned, came to make an entry into my mind. I could not separate them" (V.xiv.24).[15]

The interpretation of the stories of the Hebrew Bible primarily engaged Augustine's attention in his early attendance at Ambrose's sermons. The Manichees mocked these stories, and Augustine had ceded their point. Yet Ambrose operated according to a more sophisticated method of interpretation: "I heard first one, then another, then many difficult passages in the Old Testament scriptures figuratively interpreted, where I, by taking them literally, had found them to kill (2 Cor. 3:6)."[16] Hence from technique of expression, to content of the stories, to technique of interpretation, Augustine's mind kept moving under Ambrose's homiletic tutelage.

Augustine states carefully at the close of book 5 that he did not immediately accept the Catholic faith as expounded by Ambrose. He chose a cautious route. Intellectually, he adopted the position of the skeptics. The skeptics, as Augustine summarized their teachings, held

> that man could not have knowledge of the things which concerned philosophy…nevertheless, man could be wise and that the whole office of the wise man…was to seek for truth. It follows from this that the wise man will not assent to anything whatever. For if he assented to something uncertain, he must needs fall into error; and for the wise man this is a crime.[17]

Brown contends that Augustine's decision to adopt skepticism marks an important phase in his turning toward Catholicism: "This comparatively short period of uncertainty is one of the most crucial and little known turning points of his life. For it brought home to Augustine the ideal of 'Wisdom' as a prolonged quest. Cicero had never abandoned this ideal."[18]

Augustine chose a tentative course in his religious life also. He adopted a familiar position for a man with a desire for political advancement at that time: he aligned himself with the Catholic Church without committing himself to its full discipline.[19] Augustine enrolled as a catechumen in the Catholic Church during the approximately seven months between his arrival in Milan and his mother's joining him there in the late spring or early summer of 385 (V.xiv.25; VI.i.1).[20] Some time thereafter two important changes took place in Augustine's personal life. He became engaged to be married, and his concubine was sent away to facilitate the engagement. Yet his marriage had to be postponed two years until his fiancée had reached the age of twelve, the legal age of marriage. So Augustine found another woman for the interim. These two events cause much vexation in readers today. The social and cultural context, which can allay some distress about these behaviors, will be discussed in later sections. First, the historic sweep of the capital city will come into view.

Ambrose in Conflict with the Emperor and Empress

Milan underwent an upheaval during Augustine's few years of residence in the city. The teenaged emperor, Valentinian II, and probably his widowed mother, Justina the empress in the background, requested use of one of the Catholic basilicas for the Arians' worship. Ambrose's success in withholding it bolstered the strength of the church against the state for a long time to follow.

The exact timing of all the events is not clear; nor are all the motives.[21] An outline, however, can evoke the import of the events. A law favorable to the Arians dates from early 386.[22] Augustine says in the *Confessions* that before he was converted, while "we were still cold, untouched by the warmth of your Spirit," he was "excited by the tension and disturbed atmosphere in the city"(IX.vii.15).[23] Ambrose had been serving in an old basilica, while he oversaw the construction of a new one. Valentinian requested one of Ambrose's basilicas for use at Easter and backed up the request with military might. Soldiers were even sent to hang up the royal tapestries in one of the basilicas, an action that could signal the raising of a throne for the emperor in the church, or the seizure of property.[24] Ambrose bluntly refused the imperial request.[25]

The bishop judged that the confrontation risked bloodshed.[26] Soldiers had already arrived at one of the churches. This seemed like a threatening gesture, but Ambrose's letter to his sister about the events implies that the soldiers leaned toward deserting the emperor and supporting Ambrose.[27] When they heard that Ambrose had forbidden them to receive the eucharist, some of them did abandon the emperor's party and enter the church to ask "for prayers, presumably prayers of forgiveness."[28] The royal tapestries and hangings were removed, apparently on orders.[29]

Meanwhile, officials brought Ambrose word from the emperor: the emperor thought of Ambrose as a usurper.[30] While this may seem absurd, the emperor's point of view becomes clearer when one sees that he thought of Ambrose as impeding the exercise of imperial power by preventing him from appearing as he willed in public.[31] Ambrose pointed out that he lacked the usual weapons of a usurper, but then turned the word to his rhetorical advantage. He charged that the emperor could become a usurper of the powers granted by God to the clergy. Some soldiers still surrounded the basilica on the emperor's behalf, so Ambrose and his people stayed inside overnight.[32]

After the night of watch in the church and the next day's worship, the emperor ordered the soldiers to withdraw. Still, the emperor feared Ambrose. He said to some of the counts who urged him to give in to Ambrose: "If Ambrose ordered you, you will give me to him in chains."[33] Fortunately no greater upheaval ensued.

Augustine, summarizing the situation, signals a concern of his own: "The devout congregation kept continual guard in the Church, ready to die with their bishop, your servant. There my mother, your handmaid, was a leader in keeping anxious watch and lived in prayer" (IX.vii.15).[34]

Ambrose's letter suggests a complication that may have persuaded Augustine himself to stay outside the basilicas: "All the palace officials, the clerks, the agents of affairs, the attendants of various counts were ordered to avoid going out on the pretext that they were forbidden to take part in the rebellion. Men of high rank were threatened with many dire consequences unless they effected the surrender of the basilica."[35]

Within the next few months, bones were found that Ambrose believed to be the remains of the martyrs Protasius and Gervasius. Such relics could raise the prestige of a church and seemed a sign of God's favor toward the Catholics. The tomb Ambrose had prepared for himself in the new basilica would house the martyrs' bones instead.[36] While Augustine may overstate the closeness in time of the discovery of the relics to the conflict about the basilicas, he still makes a telling point when he says that the miracles attributed to the bones affected the persecutions. He blamed the oppressive measures in this passage on the Empress Justina, "The mind of that hostile woman, though not converted to sound faith, was nevertheless checked in its anger" (IX.vii.16).[37]

Changes in Augustine's Life

The guidance from Augustine's social milieu and the successful people in the world of the court and imperial politics no longer gave him hope of finding wisdom, or even peace with himself. So while he carried on as a teacher of rhetoric and public official, a man engaged to a girl whose family would help him make his way in government and politics, the lover of a less well-to-do woman, the friend of talented and busy men, the father of a precocious son, and the son of a devout and remarkable woman (VIII.vi.13), he also turned inward more fully. The story of his personal life diverges more sharply from his social setting than it has before, although the two never bifurcate completely. Cultural psychology, psychological anthropology, and systems theory would expect their interaction; yet the possibility of the various aspects of life, person, society, and culture becoming disjointed always remains.[38] At this time of Augustine's life the connections between these aspects seem to have loosened, and shifts got under way in his personal life, his part in social institutions, and the future of his culture.

In addition to the changes in Augustine's personal relations with other people and the social turmoil in his city, Neoplatonism posed a new set of challenges through Ambrose's Christian preaching. Augustine took the initiative not only to read the Neoplatonic works, but also to meditate on them and try to apply them to his own life. He recounts in book 7 of the *Confessions* a Neoplatonic ascent to a vision of the good, of God. He claims that this vision was of the true God, even though Augustine himself had not yet become a baptized Christian. Preaching and introspection and Neoplatonism could get him this far:

By the Platonic books I was admonished to return into myself...I entered and with my soul's eye, such as it was, saw above that same eye of my soul the immutable light higher than my mind— not the light of every day, obvious to anyone, nor a larger version of the same kind...It was not that light, but a different thing, utterly different from all our kinds of light...It was superior because it made me, and I was inferior because I was made by it. The person who knows the truth knows it, and he who knows it knows eternity. Love knows it. Eternal truth and true love and beloved eternity: you are my God...When I first came to know you, you raised me up to make me see that what I saw is Being, and that I who saw am not yet Being. (VII.x.16)[39]

Moreover, he glimpsed and retained an understanding of the relationship of good and evil. This vision and the teachings that informed his presentation of it allowed him to escape his old entanglement in the question, Whence comes evil? He began to believe that it issues from the wrongly oriented free will of human beings (VII.xxi.27).[40] But his own will seemed less than free.

Augustine describes the end of his vision as leaving him with assurance that he had not anticipated: "I was astonished to find that already I loved you, not a phantom surrogate for you." It did not leave him with the capacity to do what he wanted: "I was not stable in the enjoyment of my God. I was caught up to you by your beauty and quickly torn away from you by my weight. With a groan I crashed into inferior things. This weight was my fleshly habit. But with me there remained a memory of you. Nor was I doubting in any way that there was one to whom I was attached, but I was not yet myself who was attached" (VII.xvii.23).[41]

Some time in the following weeks or months, unable to get the attention he needed from Ambrose, Augustine turned to the bishop's "father" in the faith, Simplicianus. He was a learned man, well connected in the empire of the fourth century, and worthy of respect for his character. He enthusiastically received Augustine's mention of his readings of the Neoplatonists, and encouraged his participation in the church. This seemed a great problem to Augustine, so Simplicianus told him the story of Marius Victorinus, another famous rhetor who held office as a non-Christian, and eventually made a public profession of his faith. The promise of the interchange between Augustine and Simplicianus began to manifest itself immediately: "As soon as your servant Simplicianus told me this story about Victorinus, I was ardent to follow his example. He had indeed told it to me with this object in view" (VIII.v.10).[42]

Several other men and examples complemented Simplicianus' influence in the next weeks or months. Augustine continued the talks he had often had with his friends, especially Alypius and Nebridius. An acquaintance, Ponticianus, a court official who came to visit on business, told Augustine and Alypius the story of other government officials who became baptized Christians after they read the story of Saint Anthony. Anthony was a desert monk in the third century in Egypt, who had given up a prosperous life after the reading of the gospel in church that said to sell all one has, give to the poor, and follow Jesus (VIII.vi.15).[43]

Augustine depicts a great struggle battering him while Ponticianus spoke and after he left. Augustine says his mind reverted to the tension between his will toward sexual satisfaction and the desire of his now practiced philosophical intellect to move toward God. He turns over in his meditation the power of evil in himself, as in others, and the helplessness of knowledge in the face of a will bound by habit to do what the mind and heart hold as wrong. He recounts a sort of vision he had in the garden of his house after Ponticianus left, a reassurance about the possibility of continence even for simple people and the help they receive from God to maintain it. He mentions the verse of the Bible he read when he seized on the possibility that God might give to him what Anthony received, guidance from a particular verse of scripture, Romans 13:13–14: "Not in riots and drunken parties, not in eroticism and indecencies, not in strife and rivalry, but put on the Lord Jesus Christ and make no provision for the flesh in its lusts" (VIII.xii.29).[44] He reminds us of Alypius' faithful accompaniment through the struggle, his patient waiting as it unfolded, and his joining in the outcome by reading and accepting the next verse of scripture—"Receive the person who is weak in faith" (Rom. 14:1)[45]—for himself. Augustine crowns the event by the report of his mother's rejoicing, and even a purification of her own desires, now more delighted by his resolution to be baptized than by the earthly hope for grandchildren (VIII.xii.30).

Augustine does not report how he ended his engagement and his second love affair, but end them he apparently did. He and his friends Alypius, Nebridius, and Verecundus discussed their political and professional plans. They agreed that Augustine would resign his post in a few weeks, at the beginning of the vacation for the fall harvest. If he resigned sooner, he might become the focus of a fuss about such a public figure suddenly giving up a noteworthy career. If he did not resign, he would still be serving the lesser things that were keeping him from the One. Hence he would resign at the end of a term of classes. At that time, his action might even seem to result from his increasing difficulty in breathing and speaking, a physical ailment that plagued him from time to time over the course of his life (IX.ii.3–4).

The Social Context for Augustine's Personal Life

The social context of Augustine's private life greatly affected his story and his life as we know it. The two facts of his domestic life that are hardest to understand a millennium and a half later, many miles away, are his engagement to a ten year old and the sending away of his concubine. Both become more comprehensible, if not more palatable, when displayed in their social context.

Augustine wanted to find a wife from a family of means, who could help cover the expenses of higher civil office. If he were to rise in the Roman bureaucracy, he would assume more and more financial obligations of the kind that Romanianus had discharged toward Augustine himself. The court gorged itself on display. Its representatives in the "governorship of a minor province" (VI.xi.19),[46] the position to which Augustine aspired, bore responsibilities for entertainment. In families wealthy enough to advance Augustine's ambitions, the girls were married early.[47] In a world of high mortality rates where a family was not seen simply as a set of ties of affection or blood, but a lineage of accomplishment and honor, people preferred to bequeath their wealth through their daughters than to see it disappear.[48] The sooner they had children, the more likely an heir to the family's fortune would be assured.

Other influences also impinged on his decision. For instance, Monica, her social role as his mother, and her Christian views of marriage sustained another theme: "Her hope was that once married I would be washed in the saving water of baptism" (VI.xiii.23).[49] He could not receive that sacrament as long as he was allied with a concubine. Nor could he marry the concubine, as marriage across certain social classes ran afoul of the law.[50] To whatever extent Monica did long to see Augustine prepared for baptism, she would see herself as well placed to seek out a nice Christian bride, given her frequent attendance at the episcopal basilica in Milan.

Some scholars have seen Monica's efforts in finding a wife for her son as interference.[51] Yet the parents would have arranged a marriage in the upper classes,[52] and a woman in Monica's position could have been her own agent.[53] In other words, she would customarily take on the role of arranging for the marriage. The hint of her importance in the effort comes from the Latin: "and it was pursued diligently that I should take a wife" (VI.xiii.23).[54] By whom was it "pursued diligently"? By Monica, although the family with whom she was negotiating may have had their own interests in assuring that the city's rhetor would be their son-in-law.

Whether spiritual motives alone impelled Monica to seek a spouse for Augustine can never be known. Augustine implies that she wanted more grandchildren. While she could have had them through his concubine, she, as a Christian, would not approve of the parents' relationship. From his later Christian perspective, she did better by relinquishing the desire altogether (VIII.xii.30).

Who can imagine that romance propelled Augustine into this match with a ten year old at least twenty years his junior? In the *Soliloquies* he entertains the notion of a woman who could be a companion of the soul as well as of the body, but even once his fiancée became a marriageable twelve year old, she could not have fit the description until she grew up for several more years.[55] Yet he notes of her in the *Confessions*: "Since she was pleasing, it was awaited" (VI.xiii.23).[56] This sounds strange, but he uses the third person singular passive voice. The English translations that attribute to him a willingness to wait ring less true than the French, "As she was pleasing, one was waiting."[57] Perhaps, as O'Donnell suggests, the sense is that Augustine found his life beginning to pass out of his own control.[58]

Certainly Augustine himself was not waiting in all aspects of his life. He would not wait for sex, denied him now that his concubine had been sent away as "a hindrance to my marriage" (VI.xv.25).[59] So he took another concubine whom he intended to abandon with more forethought than he seems to have employed in rejecting the first.

Perhaps familiarity with society's support for divorce in most European and North American countries at the close of the twentieth century can help with comprehension of how Augustine could have allowed his first concubine to leave and then have expressed serious grief for her more than a decade later in the *Confessions*. His action rings heartless with regard to affection and unconscionable given the economic prospects for women in his society.[60] The example of attitudes toward divorce reminds us, however, that social arrangements support some, but not all, courses of action. The actions that receive social support may become the best decision an individual has the capacity to make in particular social circumstances. But the best choice in a situation cannot guarantee moral praiseworthiness or freedom from heartache. Many divorced people know this sorrow, whether they chose to leave a marriage or were themselves left behind.

I find myself here in the situation of Erik Erikson as he mulled over Gandhi's behavior in intimate relationships. Despite all the modes of understanding available to me, I still feel distress about both Augustine's parting from his first concubine and his taking of a second to whom he had no plans to be faithful. He seems to have utterly disregarded what would happen to the second young woman's social standing and reputation, not to mention her eligibility for baptism in the church toward which he himself was drawn. Erikson interrupted *Gandhi's Truth* to write the Mahatma a letter about the behavior that the psychoanalyst could not approve.[61] Similarly, I will take a step back from the material under consideration to highlight two points about the requirements of interpretation.

First, my search for understanding does not commit me to the idea that what is comprehensible is also morally justifiable. To the contrary, I hold that behavior and feelings that are comprehensible may at the same time be reprehensible. Therefore, I am not suggesting that we admire Augustine for his behavior toward his concubine, or even that we condone his actions. Instead, I am proposing that we come to a way of framing what he says about her and his behavior toward her so that we can imagine it might have been true, even if we think it was wrong.

This approach matches Augustine's own judgment in regard to his taking another woman after his concubine returned to Africa. He makes no concession to his feelings, strongly as he remembers them:

I, unhappy, not an imitator of the woman, impatient of delay—
because after two years I would get her for whom I was asking—
as I was not a lover of marriage but a slave of lust—I procured
another woman, not of course as a wife. By this liaison the disease
of my soul would be sustained and kept active, either in full vigour
or even increased, so that the habit would be guarded and fostered.
(VI.xv.25)[62]

The phrase "disease of my soul" speaks directly to his low opinion of his
character at the time. The word "unhappy" in this quotation carries both
an emotional and a moral tone that may escape the reader at the turn of the
twenty-first century. The emotional tone, more apparent to us, finds reinforcement in the descriptions of his feelings that precede it and that close
the passage: "My heart where she was clinging, was cut and wounded and
was trailing blood." He closes by recalling that even after he took another
woman to bed, "my wound, inflicted by the earlier parting, was not healed.
After the heat and very sharp pain, it was putrefying" (VI.xv.25).[63]

But the moral tone of "unhappy" also persists in the passage. Happiness in Augustine's era meant philosophically not simple contentment or
euphoria or enthusiasm, but something more akin to blessedness—a state
of moral probity that assured the ability to bear the trials and suffering that
may intrude in any life. Any man of the time would have assumed that his
moral capabilities surpassed those of a woman.[64] But Augustine had not
attained a moral rectitude that would allow him to endure the demands
and sacrifices of life while waiting for his marriage. He tells us that the first
concubine "had returned to Africa vowing that she would never go with
another man." But as for himself, he was "not an imitator of the woman…"
(VI.xv.25).[65] He portrays himself, in sum, as morally bankrupt in his behavior after his concubine's departure.

My second point about the requirements of interpretation is that the
understandings of social science do not require that cultural guidance and
social roles and institutions always meet the personal needs of individuals.
A number of scholars fault Talcott Parsons for relying too heavily on the
idea that person, society, and culture are congruent. Instead they argue
that social and cultural change spring from mismatches between these three
aspects of human existence.[66] So, some would add, does individual creativity, and, alas, mental illness.[67] This theoretical caution facilitates comprehension of Augustine's report of his past. We have reason in general to
think that society and culture could push someone in a direction to which
that person assents, only to find himself or herself later full of sorrow about
the implications of the decision as the action runs its course.[68] That Augustine should have escaped such consequences is not much more probable
than that we will ourselves.

Culture and Augustine's Intellectual
Conversion to Neoplatonism

We can appreciate Augustine's inner turmoil about the moral consequences of his relationships with his lovers if we realize how much the
philosophical ideas he sought out weighed against these relationships.
Moreover, the ideas of Neoplatonism, their inherent contradiction to much
of Manichaeism, their conviction compared with the Academics' skepticism, and their potential for fitting with Christian teachings, influenced his
conversion to Christianity quite strongly. Through Neoplatonic thought,
culture in the cumulative tradition worked with Augustine toward his
conversion, even though, as we have seen, culture as derived from the usual
social patterns exerted pressure on his secular career.

The problem of evil had so preoccupied Augustine that it not only made
the Manichees and their answer to it attractive to him, but reinforced his
attachment to them. Yet Plotinus' answer satisfied him more fully once he
found it. The notion that evil comes from the human soul's distraction from
the One by many sensual desires gave him a new vision of the world and
his place in it. It led to his mystical ascent to the One and also imbued him
with a new vision of human happiness.

Plotinus saw matter itself as a manifestation of evil, although not as
evil's source or full realization. His view contrasted with the Manichees'
dualistic understanding of both good and evil as implicated in physical
substances. He saw the real source of the universe as unitary, good, and
complete. Matter, by itself, he argued, lacks form. The form that matter
lacks must be some aspect of the good, because from the good comes everything that is. Any lack, any deficiency, must be a lack of good, thence at
least a taste of evil. The conclusion follows: "The nature of bodies, in so far
as it participates in matter, will be an evil, [although] not the primal evil."
Then Plotinus draws on the widely shared idea of ancient philosophy that
the soul is what gives a body life: "For bodies…are deprived of life [in and
of themselves], and in their disorderly motion they destroy each other…"
Orderly motion might benefit bodies, but disorderly motion wreaks havoc.
These ideas lead him to a point that we shall see Ambrose disseminating in
his treatises: "and they [bodies] hinder the soul in its proper activity…"[69]

Plotinus then raises a question, the answer to which would counter
Augustine's earlier Manichaean views: "Which, then, is the evil soul?" It is
not a separate soul, captive to a separate force of evil, as the Manichees
would say. It could not be, because good gives rise to everything that is.
Instead Plotinus argues for a soul that goes astray by one of its own forces:
"It is the irrational part of the soul which is receptive of evil, that is of
unmeasuredness and excess and defect, from which come unrestrained
wickedness and cowardice and all the rest of the soul's evil, involuntary
affections which produce false opinions, making it think that the things
which it shuns and seeks after are evil and good respectively."[70] But what

the irrational soul shuns is not necessarily evil, and what it seeks is not always good.

Plotinus believed that the distinctions of sense are not the relevant guides to understanding humanity and its place in the cosmos. Instead, what is important is understanding that souls must train themselves in virtue to rise above their entanglement with matter. Only then will they be able to see the good.

How then should the soul improve? Plotinus turns to interpreting Plato to discover an answer: "Not by movement in place, Plato says, but by winning virtue and separating oneself from the body: for in this way one separates oneself from matter as well, since the man who lives in close connection with the body is also closely connected with matter."[71]

A similar reference to escaping from the snares of the body and from the diversion into earthly things occurs in another *Ennead* that, like the one just quoted, Augustine would have read.[72] There Plotinus asks: "How shall we find the way? What method can we devise?…Let him who can, follow and come within, and leave outside the sight of his eyes and not turn back to the bodily splendours which he saw before." Then Plotinus' roots in Plato become obvious: "When he sees the beauty in bodies he must not run after them; we know that they are images, traces, shadows, and hurry away to that which they image." The words recall the idea of physical motion, but only as a metaphor, not as a concrete reality: "How shall we travel to it, where is our way of escape? We cannot get there on foot; for our feet only carry us everywhere in this world, from one country to another. You must not get ready a carriage, either, or a boat. Let all these things go, and do not look. Shut your eyes, and change and wake to another way of seeing, which everyone has but few use."[73]

Then Plotinus offers a route surmounting these obstacles blocking sight and leading to virtue: "And what does this inner sight see? When it is just awakened, it is not at all able to look at the brilliance before it. So that the soul must be trained, first of all to look at beautiful ways of life: then at beautiful works, not those which the arts produce, but the works of men who have a name for goodness: then look at the souls of the people who produce the beautiful works." This text exemplifies the famous Platonic ascent, the movement of thought from earthly experience to the abstract underpinnings of earthly experience to a vision of the truth behind the earthly appearances from which one started contemplation. Plotinus emphasizes the need to prepare the soul for the ascent and its goal:

> How then can you see the sort of beauty a good soul has? Go back
> into yourself and look; and if you do not yet see yourself beautiful,
> then, just as someone making a statue which has to be beautiful
> cuts away here and polishes there and makes one part smooth and
> clears another till he has given his statue a beautiful face, so you
> too must cut away excess and straighten the crooked and clear the

dark and make it bright, and never stop "working on your statue" till the divine glory of virtue shines out on you, till you see "self-mastery enthroned upon its holy seat."[74]

Perfected sight and self-mastery allow the person, understood as soul, hope for a great destiny: "You must first become all godlike and beautiful, if you intend to see God and beauty."[75] Such attainment permits arrival at the highest beauty.

This way of conceiving of good in the universe would separate Augustine still further from the Manichees. Good people would not be good because of their physical practices, like Manichaean ascetics eating to release particles of the good from matter. Instead, physical practices would help people attain the good, inasmuch as their physical restraint gave them freedom of the soul. That freedom, the soul's freedom to see correctly, would help them to return to the good. Evil, Augustine's old familiar bugbear, would now be comprehensible to him as a lack of the good, not its rival. Such thoughts would encourage Augustine to free himself from his many worldly distractions, his concerns about wealth and career, marriage and mistress.

Ambrose's preaching would only have reinforced Plotinus' point:[76]

And so the soul which desires to fly away is brought down by these allurements. But you must struggle like a good soldier of Jesus Christ; despise lesser things, forget the things of earth, strive for the celestial and eternal. Lift up your soul, so that the bait in the snares does not entice it. The pleasures of the world are a kind of bait—and what is worse—the bait of evils, the bait of temptations.

Ambrose then turns to topics encompassing Augustine's concerns, earthly pleasures, sex, wealth, although in more despicable forms than those into which Augustine fell: "While you seek pleasure, you are running into the snares. For 'the harlot's eye is the lover's snare...' The possession of what belongs to another, full of delight as it is, is a snare." He springs a trap for a young man like Augustine, who might try to exempt himself because he succumbed only to lesser evils: "Every path of life is filled with snares."[77]

Augustine said that no philosophy would have seemed true to him if the name of Christ were not there. It was not in Plotinus' writings, but it was in Ambrose's preaching. For instance, at the end of the sermons quoted above, known in published form as the treatise *Death as a Good*, Ambrose blends the theme of ascent with quotations from the Bible and invokes explicitly the name of Jesus: "We follow You, Lord Jesus, but summon us to follow, because without You no one may ascend. For You are 'the way, truth, life' [John 14:6], the power, faith, reward."[78] Ambrose embroiders this theme of going to God by ascent, and ends saying: "Let us therefore hasten to life...So let us seek Him there, where John sought and found

Him. He sought Him in the beginning and found Him living with the living, the Son with the Father."[79] The images of going somewhere to find the good flow together here from Plotinus and the Bible. Plotinus' One, and its emanation, the Intellect, resemble (although they do not perfectly match) Ambrose's understanding of the Father and the Son of the Christian Trinity.

Augustine describes himself as having needed words like these at this time, but as having assimilated at first only Plotinus' philosophical ideas. Augustine tried hard to turn himself toward the One, and in his mystical ascent succeeded more than most people. Still he lived at many months' remove from either a Neoplatonist or a Christian life ending his moral quandary about sex and its conflict with devotion to the ideals of philosophy.

All these passages bring out parts of a symbolic pattern that functioned as a symbol system in the hands of Ambrose, other Christian writers preceding him and contemporary to him, and later, Augustine himself. None of these writers intended the sort of systematic theology that would later focus the thought of a Thomas Aquinas. We see nonetheless a consistent series of overlapping significations. The body and sensory experience are thought of as lower. The soul and reason are thought of as higher, with a unitary source of all life and being as the highest point of thought. Moreover, the lower things are deemed deceptive and enticing, and the delights of beauty and the physical senses become a representation of everything that keeps the soul from recognizing and concentrating on the unitary source of life and being, which is also true beauty and the origin of all sensory beauty. Therefore, a person can be seen as trapped in many things, all of which are lower. The direction of escape is depicted as up. The image that follows is the flight of a bird. But people know they cannot fly like birds, so these prior significations set up a problem for the person who thinks with them. How can a person become airborne? In the set of symbols, asking about being airborne is asking how one can get free of the deceptions and enticements of the senses and approach the one source of all, the Good. The answer is in still more figures of speech—a mode of sight "which everyone has but few use."[80] To use this mode of sight one must turn inward. So "inside" or "internal" means of the mind or soul, and "outside" or "external" means of the physical world. Both form part of the network of images in the symbol system. A person must give up looking, figuratively speaking, "outside" to turn "inside" and go "up" toward the eternal, immutable, pure Good. Notice also that this good is one, be it the "One" for Plotinus and his pagan followers or "God" for Ambrose and Christian Neoplatonic thinkers. So the theme of the many and the One plays itself out both in pagan and Christian Neoplatonism in connection with ideas of deceptive senses, earthbound living, evil, lower experience, escape, flight to the good, virtue, sight, higher experience, truth, existence, and finally, happiness.

Plotinus' and Ambrose's discourses were vital to Augustine's conceptions of happiness. The topic can be seen as central in his thought,[81] as in that of all ancient philosophers, for happiness was considered to be the main aim of all human life. In two sermons, probably from the first half of 386, revised for publication as *Jacob and the Happy Life*,[82] Ambrose starts from classic philosophical notions and moves toward an explication of happiness in a Christian framework that preserves its connection with his philosophical forebears. We hear an echo of Plotinus on giving the mind to reason in order to achieve virtue and keep passions in check: "Necessary for the training of all men is good discourse, full of prudence, while the mind given to reason excels in virtue and restrains its passions, for virtue is teachable. Further, one seeks it by study and learning and loses it by neglect."[83] Ambrose proceeds through a number of familiar philosophical discussions, yet keeps in mind a Christian twist on the argument, that the help of God, as found in the Christian scriptures, would be necessary to achieve happiness.

For instance, Ambrose asks rhetorically, "For who is so great that he can rid himself of bodily passion?"[84] The philosophers might have pushed a person toward such an achievement, but Ambrose turns the reader, or originally hearer, of his words toward the scriptures for assistance in understanding human involvement in the passions. Ambrose will allow that passions need not flow into action: "The prudent mind can restrain and keep in check the assaults of the passions, even the severe passions, and cool all the heat of the most burning concupiscence, channel the emotions elsewhere, and by the use of right reason scorn the passions." He roots this philosophical stand in the idea of God's will in creating humanity: "For indeed, when God created man and implanted in him moral laws and feelings, at that time He established the royal rule of the mind over man's emotions, so that all his feelings and emotions would be governed by its strength and power."[85] He then advocates studying scripture to learn more about the virtues that come from reason in control of the passions,[86] but he does not give up on the philosophical line of thought.

This set of considerations lets fly another arrow to land in the heart of Manichaean teaching, although Ambrose appears not to address this heresy directly in this passage: "It is not that we can attribute our trouble to anything but our own will. No one is held to guilt unless he has gone astray by his own will. Actions which are imposed on those who resist contain no fault; the malevolence of sin follows only upon actions perpetrated voluntarily, and this fault we would divert to others."[87] But if we can divert it, he implies, it is ours at the outset.

Then Ambrose launches into interpretation of the human situation through biblical passages, especially difficult passages from the apostle Paul's letter to the Romans. In these discussions he recalls the prominence of the passions in human lives and the constant presence of sin. Yet he suggests, in a Christian turn on the Neoplatonist theme of escape from humanity's entrapment in the senses and the lower parts of life: "We are troubled by reason of frailty, but we escape by reason of Christ."[88] The crucifixion of Jesus and his sharing in human sufferings show, for Ambrose, the love of God for humanity. They also demonstrate the relative unimportance of earthly suffering compared to the great good of turning toward God. Having turned, one can live with the strength and equanimity that Christ exhibited and made possible for humanity through his crucifixion and resurrection. The good of union with God the Father that sustained Jesus would also sustain later Christians.

Ambrose closes in on identifying happiness with a life centered on God. He concludes: "Therefore, the motive for living well is not bodily pleasure, but the mind's sagacity."[89] The wise mind has tried to turn away from the many distractions of the body and its passions and learned that it needs God's help, found largely through study of the scriptures and meditation on the goodness of God that they reveal. He picks up Plotinian themes again, with a strong, immediate link to biblical language this time: "so the man who has been made perfect seeks nothing else but the only and admirable good. On this account the Scripture also says, 'One thing I have asked of the Lord, this will I seek after, that I may dwell in the house of the Lord all the days of my life and may see the delight of the Lord' [Psalm 27: 4]."[90]

The standard set for Augustine, as for Ambrose's other listeners, was overwhelmingly high. For instance, even the death of family members should not lessen happiness: "A man of such purpose is not diminished nor broken by adversities, nor restrained by barriers, nor made sorrowful by the loss of his dear ones." Ambrose does not deny that such sorrows exist, but he maintains philosophical consistency: "Now the man who is saddened by such misfortunes is not saddened in conformity with God's will, and what is not in conformity with God's will is filled with folly. Therefore, the sadness that is of this world and is not in conformity with God's will and every anxiety over distress of the body are not found in the man who has been perfected."[91]

Through such ideas from Plotinus and Ambrose, Augustine had acquired a systematic view in which to understand his own responsibility for action, his failures to meet his standards (standards he now believed he should have held from the outset), and the way his own behavior fit in the universe as a whole. He could let go of his desire for worldly success and especially of the notion that achievement might lead to happiness: "My secular activity I held in disgust, and now that I was not burning with my old ambitions in hope of honour and money it was burdensome to me to tolerate so heavy a servitude. By now those prizes gave me no pleasure in comparison with your gentleness and 'the beauty of your house which I loved' (Ps. 26:8)." His sexual involvement and pending marriage, however, overcame his capacity to dedicate himself to God. As he says in biblical language as he looks back on that time: "And now I had discovered the good pearl. To buy it I had to sell all that I had; and I hesitated (Matt. 13:46)" (VIII.i.2).[92]

Psychological Interpretation of the Years in Milan

Interpersonal and Cultural Psychological Dimensions of the Social and Cultural Milieu for Augustine

The more one reads the earlier books of the *Confessions*, the dialogues written at Cassiciacum, and the books Augustine wrote before he returned to North Africa, the less his acceptance of baptism in the Catholic Church looks like a single dramatic conversion experience. Instead it becomes an ongoing turmoil, a series of crosscurrents, an investigation that may not truly have ceased for the rest of his life.[93] Conscious elements of Augustine's thought are crucial to the meaning he found in his near-chaotic times. The most obvious psychological fact is that he changed his intentions. Perhaps the next most evident from his account is that various people profoundly influenced his altered perspective.

Augustine's shifts from Manichaeism to skepticism, from skepticism to Neoplatonism, and from Neoplatonism to Christianity centrally involved changes in his intentionality. They led him into what Shweder has called different "intentional worlds." Shweder identifies an intentional world most broadly with "a socio-cultural environment." He further specifies intentional worlds as "human artifactual worlds populated with products of our own design."[94] These products can be cognitive as well as physical, given that Shweder includes "traditional intellectual artifacts, representational schemes, and accumulated knowledge of some cultural or subcultural community."[95] While Augustine after age eighteen always pursued the goal of wisdom, he exchanged intellectual artifacts and representational schemes and added to his accumulated knowledge. The representational scheme of Manichaeism failed to account for the kinds of knowledge it claimed to include, such as astronomical science. When it ceased to coordinate Augustine's perceptions of the world, he had to find another route to the certain wisdom he desired. His shift to skepticism brought with it changes in ritual behaviors and social interactions. His adoption of Neoplatonic ideas posited an altogether different representational scheme of the universe and revised radically his notions of the good. Now he would seek the One from which everything derived, as Neoplatonism would have it, and he would learn the theme of the existence of evil only as a privation of good.

These changes of intention deserve note especially because Augustine prized them. Attention to them offers an opportunity to give Augustine credit for ideas about his own life and his own mind. Late antique culture greatly respected intention. That is why great philosophical minds applied themselves to the nature of happiness as the goal of life. In his early thirties, Augustine discovered a necessity of change in his intentionality precisely as he struggled with how to achieve the happiness he saw through Neoplatonism. He reflects on himself through his Neoplatonic vision of God: "Nor was I doubting in any way that there was one to whom I was attached, but I was not yet myself who was attached" (VII.xvii.23).[96] In other words, he wanted to approach a mode of being that was distinct from other goals he had held. It would lead him to further changes in himself, if he had a chance to reach it.

Augustine writes often in book 8, as he prepares the reader for the conversion story, of how he struggled and failed to do the good as he understood it. He says that he had known his own "iniquity...but deceived myself, refused to admit it, and pushed it out of my mind" (VIII.vii.16).[97] But he found himself unable to escape this knowledge during Ponticianus' story of the other government officials who had dedicated themselves to God. Still Augustine's intentions were divided. Those that drew him back into sexual pleasure were lust, formed, according to his famous metaphor, as a chain of habit (VIII.v.10). Those that kept him from asking for help were known in his later language as pride.

Augustine represents the overcoming of both the chain of sexual habit and pride as coming through an image of Continence, personified as a woman, accompanied by many other people. Whether this actually occurred to him in his inner struggle that day in the garden is uncertain. Perhaps he as an author creates in this scene for the first time an extended metaphor for his struggle. In any case, he seems to wish this vignette, like the rest of the conversion tale, to make vivid the truth of his psychological condition and his life in relation to God.

Continence confronts Augustine with the need to stop trying to achieve his contact with the good by himself. She proposes that he give up the effort and let God take away the bondage to sexual habit. The story suggests that if Augustine were to do this, he would certainly have given up a large amount of pride:

> Many boys and girls were there, there many youths and people of
> all ages, and serious widows and aged virgins, and in all these
> Continence in no way sterile, but the fruitful mother of children,
> of delights, from you her husband, Lord. And she was laughing at
> me with encouraging pleasantry, as if she was saying, "You can't
> do what these men and women can do? And truly, are they able to
> do it in themselves alone and not in their Lord God? The Lord,
> their God, gave me to them. Why do you stand in yourself and not
> stand? Throw yourself on him! Do not fear. He will not draw back
> so that you fall: be secure in throwing yourself! He will catch you
> and cleanse you."

But this hint of a change of intention—giving up on one's own accomplishment and allowing God to take over—was not its fruition. Augustine adds:

> And I was blushing greatly, because I was hearing the murmurings
> of those trifles even at this point, and I, delaying, was still hang-
> ing. And again she seemed to be saying, "Turn a deaf ear against

these members of yours on the earth, that they may be mortified. They are recounting delights to you, not just like the law of the Lord your God." That controversy in my heart was nothing if not from me against me myself. (VIII.xi.27)[98]

Augustine is leading up to the transformation that William James describes so adroitly as the shift in a person's "habitual centre of personal energy."[99] James's ideas point to a likely feature of intentional worlds: the intentional world constructed by a whole society will not all be present at once to an individual mind. As James describes the psychological process, some ideas, related to each other, move to the center of attention at one time, and to the periphery at another. When one set of related ideas moves to the periphery, another takes over the center.[100] Whether one would describe these ideas as related by association, as James does, or choose some other theoretical language, the point remains that the parts of a society's intentional world may shift in their predominance in a person's mind. In Augustine's world, the shifting happened as people who entered his life portrayed various ideas vividly enough to move them toward the center of his personal energy.

Drawing on Augustine's account, and others in the literature of personal conversion tales, James concludes that a person going through conversion will struggle toward a change and eventually give up.[101] Augustine depicts his own case as follows: "From a hidden depth a profound self-examination had dredged up a heap of all my misery and set it 'in the sight of my heart' (Ps. 18:15). That precipitated a vast storm bearing a massive downpour of tears. To pour it all out with the accompanying groans, I got up from beside Alypius...I threw myself down somehow under a certain figtree, and let my tears flow freely." Then Augustine shows himself giving up control to God. He no longer torments himself about what he will do, but draws on scripture to show what he had been feeling and thinking at the time: "Though not in these words, yet in this sense I repeatedly said to you: 'How long, O Lord? How long, Lord, will you be angry to the uttermost? Do not be mindful of our old iniquities' (Ps. 6:4). For I felt my past to have a grip on me. I uttered wretched cries: 'How long, how long is it to be?' 'Tomorrow, tomorrow.' 'Why not now? Why not an end to my impure life in this very hour?'" (VIII.xii.28).[102] Augustine pinpoints a realignment of ideas after he heard the sound of a child's voice saying, "Take, read, take, read." Although he debated what game might induce a child to say such a thing, he could not remember one and "interpreted it solely as a divine command to me to open the book and read the first chapter I might find." He says he read Romans 13:13–14: "'Not in riots and drunken parties, not in eroticism and indecencies, not in strife and rivalry, but put on the Lord Jesus Christ and make no provision for the flesh in its lusts'" (VIII.xii.28–29).[103] This passage set his heart at ease, according to the narrative, and helped him make the decision to change his way of life and receive baptism in the Catholic Church.

Here an interpersonal psychology helps us understand what Augustine is offering as a way of hearing harmony and order in the discord in our
world. Augustine becomes a somewhat different person by a shift in intentionality inspired by relationships and interchanges with other people. The
change is not exclusively intentional in a rational sense. It is not strictly
psychological in the sense of a mind operating only according to its own
principles. It is not strictly social, a way of going along with the crowd,
because he could have gone other ways with different crowds. But the
combination of people and ideas, social interaction, and guidance for life
in the traditions he encountered allowed him to alter his intentions and act
on them.

Preparation for Self Psychological Interpretation
of the Conversion Story

The previous discussion of Augustine's emotional responses to his conversion and decision to be baptized implies that self psychological interpretation has to account for a change in Augustine. His language about
this time, and from this time, so eschews joy in ambition, power, worldly
accomplishment, and money, that he does not appear any more to be someone whose unconscious self is sustained primarily by the marks of grandiosity. Instead, idealization seems to have taken over as the pole of the self
that allows him to find stability and continuity in his life. But the marks of
grandiosity do not disappear in his writings after this. Rather they resonate with shame, which is one of the indicators of wounded grandiosity
uncompensated by worldly success or personal power.

Augustine's changing balance of grandiosity and idealization bears a
striking resemblance to what Kohut calls the overcoming of a "vertical split"
in the personality. Substantiating this claim requires a somewhat technical
discussion that will enter piece by piece into the presentation of the changes
in Augustine's expressions of grandiosity and idealization.

Previous chapters have demonstrated how Augustine's grandiose self
and idealized parent imagoes could have suffered sufficient damage to lead
to a lack of coherence in his unconscious self. Yet Augustine's talents in his
social world and cultural milieu, as well as his parents' exertions in his
behalf, allowed him to succeed in the kinds of activities that might assuage
his injured grandiosity. His accomplishments put Augustine in a long line
of successful men, one of the most prominent being Cicero, his hero. Therefore, his accomplishments, while soothing his injured grandiose self, would
also conform to a cultural ideal. Augustine could readily idealize the marks
of affirmed grandiosity.

Nevertheless, the representations of affirmed grandiosity could not
prevent indications of a fragmented, incoherent self from slipping through
into his self-descriptions. He writes of himself even after his acceptance of
Neoplatonic ideas: "In my temporal life everything was in a state of

uncertainty, and my heart needed to be purified from the old leaven (1 Cor. 5:7f.). I was attracted to the way, the Saviour himself, but was still reluctant to go along its narrow paths" (VIII.i.1).[104]

These lines and the sentiments they express correspond to a disguised expression of Kohut's notion of a vertical split in the psyche. This "split," as he calls it, appears most distinctly in people who in one way or another lead a double life.[105] I would not contend that Augustine's inner division reached the same severity as Kohut's examples—people gripped by perversions—but the more clinically severe conditions provide a model for the dynamics of Augustine's life.[106]

The term "vertical split," like all the other theoretical language of self psychology, is a metaphorical way of speaking of expectable processes of the subjective life. First, Kohut means by it that division exists in the person. Second, he wants to contrast the division to a "horizontal split" in the psyche. The horizontal split refers to the barrier of repression that keeps painful memories from reaching consciousness in a clear form. The vertical split by contrast speaks of a division in the person's consciousness.[107] The word "split" in the psychoanalytic lexicon indicates a strong division, and one of which the person is usually unaware: "When this defense is in operation, the nonrecognized or unacknowledged aspects of mental activity do not lie behind a repression barrier; they are separated from the acknowledged parts of the self by a failure of synthesis or integration."[108] This founds the application of the notion of splitting to people caught up in perversions. People who engage in these behaviors are conscious, not unconscious, of what they are doing. But somehow they manage to see themselves as something other—really—than someone who practices perverse behavior. Their behavior is not integrated with their understanding of themselves at moments when they are not engaged in it.[109] In response to an accusation, they would mount a protest along the lines, "But that's not really me. That's just this thing that I sometimes feel I have to do. But it isn't me. Really, it isn't!"

Augustine, the author of the *Confessions*, looking back on those years, can see that it was really he who followed the outlawed Manichees and tried to advance a career in government, saw himself as a seeker of truth in an ascetic mode and as a lover and a social climber. But Augustine of his nineteenth to twenty-ninth year seemed to be unable to admit that these different sides of himself posed problems of irreconcilable dimensions.

The metaphor of a vertical split in the psyche applies to the interpretation of Augustine's life and writings because of the similarities between his situation and that of a patient of Kohut. The patient, Mr. X as Kohut called him, had a part of his personality that displayed "overt grandiosity," according to Kohut. On the other side of the vertical split, however, he was aware of being depressed, and his self, in Kohut's terms, felt "empty." He appeared as "isolated, lacking in initiative" [110] and therefore seemed in self psychological terms to live with "an unresponded-to grandioseexhibitionistic fragment…"[111] He also gave indications of an "incompletely organized nuclear self [that] seeks consolidation via idealization of [an] omnipotent selfobject (father as teacher and guide)."[112] Some of these particulars also fit Augustine, although we must acknowledge that he was not isolated and did not lack initiative for his worldly career, perhaps because he had found responses in his career to his grandiose self.

The overt grandiosity displayed by Mr. X appears in Augustine, or can be inferred from his self-descriptions: "My mind was intent on inquiry and restless for debate…" (VI.iii.3);[113] "I was panting after honours, money, marriage…How unhappy I was, therefore, and how you [God] acted to make me feel my misery, on that day when I was preparing to recite the praises of the emperor, in which I would lie about many things and for lying would gain the favor of people who knew the accolades were untrue…" Augustine will here tell the story of his encounter with a cheerfully drunk beggar and illustrate beautifully, although unawares, the idea of the vertical split. The grandiose side is implied in his comparison of their accomplishments: "Nor should I have put myself ahead of him because I was better educated, since I was not getting any pleasure out of my education; but I was seeking to please people, not so that I might teach them but just so that I could please them" (VI.vi.9).[114] He seems, as self psychologists might say, to have been seeking mirroring selfobjects for his grandiosity.

The other side of the split, depression for Mr. X, appears in Augustine's further comments about the drunkard: "And certainly he was having a good time, I was troubled; he was unworried, I was scared. And if anyone had asked me whether I would rather exult or fear, I would have responded, 'exult'; if anyone had questioned me further about whether I would rather be such as he or such as I was then, I would have chosen to be myself made up of worries and fears, but from perversity, surely not on account of the truth?" (VI.vi.9).[115] One might think that Augustine sounded so overwhelmed because he still had to deliver the panegyric. Isn't a person allowed to have jitters before a performance? But he closes this escape hatch with another reflection:

> And that beggar was going to have sobered up that same night, while I slept and got up, would be sleeping and getting up, with my inebriation with glory, see for how many days!…Certainly he was more happy, not so much because he was drenched in good humor, while I was eviscerated with cares, but even more because he had acquired wine by wishing people well, while I was seeking pride by lying. (VI.vi.10)[116]

One could also argue that for Augustine, as for Mr. X, an "incompletely organized nuclear self [sought] consolidation via idealization…" The importance of men whom Augustine could idealize was mentioned in the last chapter. These men seem to have been disguised representations in consciousness of the man Augustine wanted in Patricius. They were well known and successful and had many people's admiration. Yet they disappointed Augustine or remained out of reach. So he carried on with his life as though his own grandiosity, his ambitions, achievements, power, and other worldly assets, were the mainstay of his inner balance. Could Ambrose remedy the need for an idealized "omnipotent selfobject (father as teacher and guide)"? According to Kohut's ideas, yes, but only if the vertical split between overt grandiosity and more covert despondency could be overcome first.

Four different experiences can be seen as rattling the vertical divide in Augustine's conscious view of himself: encountering Ambrose, reuniting with Monica, sending away his lover of the last decade and more, and discovering the costs and benefits of success.

Ambrose Rattling the Vertical Divide

Ambrose could easily represent to Augustine the worldly success he wanted but would challenge that success explicitly and implicitly. Ambrose represented the possibility both of success in Augustine's chosen fields and of scorn for achievement as a measure of life's value. This revaluation of Augustine's values by someone who knew them well could damage the assumptions of Augustine's balance of grandiosity and secular idealizing. Moreover, Ambrose spoke of a philosophy and theology that would allow expression of Augustine's repressed and suppressed feelings, thus allowing them some access to consciousness. While they surfaced in disguised form, so did a different solution to inner division, one proposing unity in both the individual and the cosmos.

The marks of worldly success in Ambrose matched quite closely those Augustine cultivated for himself. Ambrose was eloquent, a rousing speaker, and thus succeeded in the kind of work that Augustine had chosen and largely perfected. Tremendous popularity for Ambrose among the people of Milan resulted from this eloquence. Popularity provides a grown-up kind of mirroring approval for the grandiose side of oneself, and that may have been a reason that Augustine cherished it for himself and admired it as it showered on Ambrose. In addition, Ambrose was smart, well-educated, undoubtedly more cultivated and better read than most of the clergy, and perhaps even the civic leaders and teachers, than Augustine would have met in North Africa (VI.xi.18). He came from a more prestigious and well-established family than Augustine did. Augustine would have known that Ambrose had served previously as the governor of the province of Aemilia-Liguria in which Milan lay.[117] His challenge to the imperial family's efforts to appropriate a basilica for Arian worship demonstrated Ambrose's political power and influence. In sum, Augustine says: "Ambrose himself I thought a happy man as the world judges things, for he was held in honour by the great and powerful. Only his celibacy seemed to me painful" (VI.iii.3).[118]

While Ambrose had achieved so much that Augustine and his parents had hoped he could accomplish, Ambrose represented something else even more strongly: Catholicism. He made plain the possibility of combining a different set of ideals with the worldly strengths Augustine had so idealized. Ambrose was a living combination of attainments for which Augustine longed and the wisdom that he sought. Ambrose's life would challenge Augustine's particular conflation of the ideal with the marks of grandiosity. Ambrose's mode of being would suggest that Augustine did not need to separate so much his abilities and accomplishments from his less worldly ideal, the search for wisdom. Implicitly, Ambrose's life would persistently raise for Augustine the question, "Why not go on with my own philosophical ideals?"

In addition, Ambrose's language and the expression of the philosophical and theological ideas he preached would have challenged Augustine's idealizations. In a self psychological framework this challenge appears as intellectual and emotional, and both conscious and unconscious. Battering at desires for goods in a worldly sense, Ambrose's preaching would tell Augustine on the unconscious level that his self would not cohere. This is big news in anybody's life, no matter how it is delivered. But hearing it from a man so easily idealized would probably increase its force and shake the vertical division in Augustine's psyche.

The language Ambrose used to make these points could allow the expression of Augustine's unconscious desires. For instance, when Ambrose preached the following themes, he would have introduced the ideas of fragmentation of the self, and of a grandiosity that would not survive life's buffeting: "And so the needs of the body beget many concerns and introduce pursuits that impede the strength of the soul and hinder its concentration...life itself is in the slime. There is no stability of thought, no constancy."[119] These metaphors from Ambrose, "stability,""constancy," overlap with Kohut's. Augustine, hearing these words as conscious evocations of the problems of the many and the need for the One, could also have had unconscious currents, of the kind described by Kohut, attach to them. Feelings of shame might find a safe escape from explicit memories by shifting their associations and attaching themselves to a phrase like "life itself is in the slime." The experience of feeling torn apart and powerless by being embarrassed in front of other people could detach itself somewhat from its roots in childhood and find expression in the phrases, "There is no stability of thought, no constancy."

Yet symbolic language and symbolic images, according to psychoanalytic schools of thought, not only present the problem, but also propose solutions. Augustine's childhood anguish might not have gotten free of repression so it could be expressed in Ambrose's words if he had not also spoken in ways that could have expressed the desired outcome. But he did, for example, when he said in his Christian Neoplatonic train of thought:

"The soul that cleaves to the invisible God, good and immortal, flees from the things of this body, abandons earthly and mortal concerns, and becomes like to the object of its desire, in which it lives and has its sustenance."[120] According to self psychological interpretation, these words could convey that the upset feeling can be left behind. One can instead become like the idealized parent imago—"becomes like the object of its desire"— and the self can survive and be nurtured. What more could one ask? How provocative of, yet soothing to, unconscious distress.

This set of ideas came not only through a person, but also through society and cultural artifacts. Augustine, intrigued by Ambrose's preaching, also met people, a small group but an important one in the crosscurrents of Milanese society, who had given themselves over to reading Plotinus.[121] In the *Enneads* he would have found these ideas without the Christian elements. He would have been able to absorb them at leisure as he read. He would have seen them in the texts without the Christian ideas and symbols that he still eschewed, but in the language of the pagans, who formed an important part of his past. Yet the language was new enough to him that it could make the ideal borrowed from Cicero, to seek after wisdom wherever he might find it, alive again and full of its earlier luster. As he wrote later to Romanianus: "For since as yet we were untouched by that great fire which was to consume us, we thought that the slow fire with which we burned was the greatest. But lo! when certain books full to the brim…had let a very few drops of most precious unguent fall upon that meagre flame, they stirred up an incredible conflagration, incredible, Romanianus, incredible…"[122]

Ambrose promised something more that could have spoken to Augustine's unconscious longings. Ambrose preached assurance of help from an idealized source: "We are troubled by reason of frailty, but we escape by reason of Christ."[123] How much this contrasts to the childhood blows to Augustine's grandiosity and idealizing! When Augustine was beaten at school, he suffered because of frailty, but he was not given an escape, even by the parents he idealized at home. Yet through Ambrose's words, culture provided a mode of expression and resolution of psychological distress: we may suffer but we will be helped by the ideal being.

The same sort of ideas could excite repressed recollections of a different aspect of Augustine's life, the loss of his father's assistance when his father died. Romanianus filled the gap somewhat, but Ambrose promises more: "Are you afraid of the uncertain twists of life and the plots of the adversary? You have the help of God, you have His great liberality…" The safety of merger with an ideal for which Augustine may well have longed since childhood finds consummate expression in Ambrose's assurance about God's generosity expressed in terms of the closeness of a father and a son: "The Son could not feel death's bitterness, because He was in the Father; for Himself He gave up nothing, on your behalf He offered everything. In the fullness of His divinity He lost nothing, while He redeemed you."[124]

The ideal is secure, it loses nothing, and it extends itself to the uncertain or captive one who needs it. If this were the case, and Augustine came to treasure it because of its unconscious, as well as conscious, appeal, then why would he need a vertical split in the psyche to keep his grandiosity in balance between its noisy and depressed manifestations? Why not let the longing to idealize emerge in disguise from the unconscious and shift the balance from worldly success to idealization? The conscious psyche could afford to begin to merge and integrate because assurance in the person of Ambrose would soften the blow, as would the words he preached and the words of Plotinus, especially as they were accepted by other influential men in Milan. They would allow change to eventuate, not in destruction but in fruition of other parts of himself with which Augustine had been struggling for so long and that would no longer be kept at bay by a vertical divide.

Monica Rattling the Vertical Divide

Augustine most likely listened to Ambrose preach for about half a year before the time when Monica arrived in Milan. The effect of Ambrose's preaching and person on Augustine overlapped with the effect of Monica's reappearance on the scene of Augustine's life and perhaps with her own style of preaching. Her arrival coincided with a time of psychological upheaval, not just in the ways apparent from the evidence left us by Augustine, but also in ways we would expect from Kohut's description of the psyche. Kohut points out that the self can find its cohesion and continuity challenged throughout life, at times when circumstances require adjustments, such as "moves…from the small town to the big city."[125] When Augustine went to Carthage he became a Manichee, and when he went to Milan, just a year after leaving his homeland for Italy, he became a Christian catechumen and a Neoplatonic thinker. Shortly after this change in his life, when Kohut would expect the self to be unstable and likely to regress to an older form of cohesion, Monica came to his side. Closeness to the mother is usually the oldest form of self-cohesion from the self psychological point of view, and it seems again to have become available to Augustine just as reassurance for his self would probably have been necessary. Longings for, and difficulties of, closeness with her could well have become unconsciously active at that time. The unconscious remains of memories of early childhood would presumably make her ways and her ideals more attractive.

On the other hand, Monica may have rekindled some difficulties for Augustine. As far as we can tell, she was not enthralled with his worldly success. Nor did she respond joyfully to what he offered to her as spiritual progress. He seems to recall his disappointment in her reaction: "When I informed her that I was not now a Manichee, though neither was I a Catholic Christian, she did not leap for joy as if she had heard some unexpected news." Far from exulting in his new position in the public eye, she concentrated on a more religious concern: "In her mind she was offering me before you on a bier, so that you could say, as you said to the widow's son 'Young man, I say to you, arise' (Luke 7:12)…" She may have told him this later, but even if she did wait to disclose this point of view, she probably did not exude a mirroring pleasure in Augustine's spiritual steps: "Very calmly and with her heart full of confidence she replied to me that she had faith in Christ that before she departed this life, she would see me a baptized Catholic believer" (VI.i.1).[126] Well intentioned as she may have been about this, she could have administered another blow to Augustine's grandiosity if it was beginning to switch from pleasure in worldly success to pleasure in the progress of his soul.

A narcissistic injury to Augustine as a man about town may have come from Monica's relationship to Ambrose. Augustine mentions in both the *Confessions* (VI.iii.3–4) and in the *Soliloquies*[127] that he did not have the opportunities he wanted to speak to Ambrose. Yet he reports that his mother caught Ambrose's attention: "When he saw me, he often broke out in praise of her, congratulating me on having such a mother…" (VI.ii.2).[128] Augustine does not comment directly on his response to Ambrose's laudatory remarks about Monica, but we can note that she seemed to have been the beneficiary of more of Ambrose's concern than her son was, despite the fact that she had achieved so much less social status and education than Augustine. If his self was still trying to cohere through grandiosity and delight in his own wonderfulness, these interchanges could not have supported that effort.

Finally, Monica's energies for Augustine's salvation extended to his marital status, "because the saving water of baptism would wash me, once married" (VI.xiii.23).[129] Again, she exhibited an attitude that would not rest content with what Augustine had achieved and with the goodness he offered as he was. He may have agreed with her at the time, and certainly did so later, but the repetition of at least small psychological blows to his grandiose self would have continued.

These blows to his grandiosity would tend to undermine a strong vertical split in his personality. The prominent grandiose part of himself would have trouble maintaining itself while Monica always wanted something better for him or of him. The success in schooling she had wanted in his childhood no longer satisfied her. Perhaps she herself had changed. A careful reading of the *Confessions* shows that Augustine depicts her as growing in her faith (II.iii.8; IX.xi.28). Maybe Christian ideals were more important to her now.[130] Or maybe his delays in living up to them caused her greater anxiety as they both aged. In any case, she could easily have hindered his maintenance of his previous inner balance and its vertical split in the psyche.

Lovers Rattling the Vertical Divide

A self psychological look at Augustine's separation from his concubine shifts the understanding of it, and leads me finally to speculate that

Augustine was what we today would call "in love" with his concubine,[131] but that his culture would not readily have supported such an understanding.

The reflection that Augustine did not act as if he felt wounded by his concubine's departure can be understood through self psychology. If he was still operating with a vertical split in the psyche and with grandiosity as the noisiest side of it, then his self, unconscious as well as conscious, might have rallied to the idea that his marriage and advancement in his career would keep him coherent and energetic and responsive to life's unfolding. This outcome could have been especially important to him, because the other side of the vertical split seems to have been active when Monica joined him in Milan, when, he says, he "despaired of the discovery of the truth" (VI.i.1).[132] Maybe a marriage and the opportunities it would bring could help him. If so, the concubine could not.

In any case, the language he uses to describe his feelings expresses exquisitely in conscious terms the feelings of a fragmented and incoherent unconscious self: "Torn from my side as an impediment to my marriage was she with whom I was accustomed to sleeping; my heart, where she was clinging, was cut and wounded and was trailing blood…After the heat and very sharp pain, it was putrefying, and it was hurting, as it were, more frigidly but more desperately" (VI.xv.25).[133] Kohut often mentions injured grandiosity as giving off an air of coldness. Partings tend to hurt the unconscious self, to reopen its old wounds, even if the reasons for separation are unassailable, sometimes chosen by the person who later suffers.[134] Of course Augustine would not have been aware of the words as revealing an unconscious self, but they could allow old divisions to make their way into consciousness with just enough disguise to escape repression.

The apparent lack of caring in Augustine's initiation of sexual relations with another woman looks like more than callousness from a self psychological point of view. It suggests an effort to heal an injured self. Kohut suggests that intense physical activity, especially related to sex, can lend a sense of coherence to the self.[135] Yet after that, Augustine could not claim to have much control over his sexual appetite, strongly enjoined as that was by Plotinus, Ambrose, and the Stoics. How would his overt grandiosity stand up to the witness of such feelings?

If on the silent side of the vertical split lay empty depression, perhaps it intensified through Augustine's experience of being in love without a socially acceptable expression for the value of the love relationship. The awareness that the relationship would have to end may have been undermining it for both partners and creating a sense of foreboding.

Augustine's text and the law and mores of the time might make my analysis seem anachronistic. Yet his phrase about her being "torn from my side…" takes up the imagery Genesis 2:21–24, in which God takes a rib from Adam's side in order to make him a helpmate. Augustine, in writing this way, alludes to his first concubine as his married partner.[136] Instead of having a wife and helpmate, after she left he had only a bleeding side. In addition, he points out that sexual relations with another woman did not heal the wound, and that the pain lasted a long time in different forms. In later works when he talks about what marriage should be he condemns concubinage but leaves a small opening for a woman to have been a concubine without being unpardonable. The conduct that would mitigate his judgment of her resembles the behavior of his first long-term lover.[137] More than one academic has gently noted that tenderness from his own experience seems to survive in this judgment.[138] Might that experience have been romantic love, unnamed and unbeknownst to him?

This argument underscores a theoretical point in the larger attempt in which we are here engaged, to understand how life might be perceived as a symphony rather than a cacophony: an individual's pain and sorrow can issue in a creative new representation of an aspect of human life. Augustine's language in this passage is arresting, gripping if one dwells on it. How did he write so of someone his culture said he should regard as beneath him, unworthy of his rank and of being his spouse? Why use language reminiscent of the creation of woman in Genesis? Why would he grieve so when his culture and social circle would have said he had done right to send her away? Perhaps the answer is that the psychological life is not fully determined by society and culture: shaped, yes; determined, no. This event, which fit rather nicely in Augustine's culture, has bequeathed to the culture that we inherit a passage both amazing and annoying; genuinely touching language pairs with truly unflattering action for our further rumination as we guide our own lives on waters that may, alas, become similarly rocky at some time.

Success Rattling the Vertical Divide

The costs and benefits of success seemed to shift for Augustine as he got closer to the center of power. We have already seen the passages in which young men in the civil service decided that the glory for which they hoped would cost too much in anxiety and perhaps in physical well-being to be worth the price. Others of Augustine's thoughts on the matter have also been cited. One further comment comes from his reflections after encountering the drunk who seemed happier than he:

> I often observed their [my friends'] condition to be much the same as mine, and my state I found to be bad; this caused me further suffering and a redoubling of my sense of futility. If success ever smiled on me, I would feel that it was not worth the effort to take the opportunity, since, almost before I had grasped it, the chance flew away.

> The group of us who lived together as friends used to deplore these things. (VI.vi.10—vii.11)[139]

Clearly, if the joys of ambition and success were to support his grandiose side, they had failed, and Augustine needed something else.

As the vertical split slowly disintegrated, Augustine had to confront two parts of himself that had remained in the shadows while his grandiose self had predominated. One was his idealizing. The other was his desire to be close to a woman physically and emotionally. The former had many culturally approved outlets. The latter was not so likely to be satisfied in normal social channels and could not be incorporated in a life adhering to his highest philosophical ideals. Having to reorient these aspects of his life now that overt grandiosity failed to maintain his stability would be a psychologically painful and difficult process. More shifts would have to occur to allow Augustine some psychological relief and to release his talents into a direction that promised some greater peace of mind.

Grandiosity Escaping the Repression Barrier

The marks of grandiosity no longer sustained Augustine, but the signs of grandiosity continue to appear as a theme of his writing. These signs take the forms of injured grandiosity: they manifest themselves as shame and rage. The language about shame prevalent in book 1 of the *Confessions*, when Augustine recounts for the reader the sorrows of schooling, tends to disappear in his descriptions of his feelings in the following years of his life. It reappears in his discussion of the months in Milan and thereafter.

An important distinction must be kept in mind here. The language of shame in describing his feelings of the interim years becomes minor, while language of shame permeates the author's voice throughout the whole of the *Confessions*. When Augustine recalls how listening to Ambrose's preaching began to change his mind about the truths and falsehoods of the Catholic faith, he ends without suggesting that he felt ashamed at the time:

> Even so I did not think I ought to hold to the Catholic way. Granted it could have educated people who asserted its claims and refuted objections with abundant argument and without absurdity. But that was not sufficient ground to condemn what I was holding. There could be an equally valid defence for both. So to me the Catholic faith seemed not to have been defeated but also did not yet appear as the conqueror.

> I then energetically applied my critical faculty to see if there were decisive arguments by which I could somehow prove the Manichees wrong…Accordingly, after the manner of the Academics, as popularly understood, I doubted everything, and fluctuating among all things, I decided the Manichees must be left…

The only hint he gives of the sense of unworthiness or inadequacy that characterizes shame appears in the lines, "But to these philosophers, who were without Christ's saving name, I altogether refused to entrust the

healing of my soul's sickness" (V.xiv.24–25).[140] Yet his words do not clearly
indicate the label "sickness" as applying to his evaluation at the time of his
indecision. He portrays himself much more as having felt rational and calm,
even proud and self-confident, in his way of approaching the challenge
presented by Ambrose's preaching.

By the next book's recital of further developments, words evocative of
shame begin to enter the descriptions of his feelings at the time. He proceeded bit by bit toward a change of the manifestations of what we can see
self psychologically as grandiosity. For instance, he says that even in the
time after his mother's arrival in Milan, "I had not yet come to groan in
prayer that you might come to my aid. My mind was intent on inquiry and
restless for debate" (VI.iii.3).[141] He seems to have remained in the grandiose mode of proving himself to achieve status and bolster his sense of himself. Yet as he continued to hear Ambrose's preaching, his feelings, as well
as his mind, changed: "Every Lord's day I heard him 'rightly preaching
the word of truth' (2 Tim. 2:15) among the people...I was glad, if also
ashamed, to discover that I had been barking for years, not against the
Catholic faith but against mental figments of physical images"(VI.iii.4). [142]
The same kind of language appears twice more in the next chapter:

> My concern to discover what I could hold for certain gnawed at
> my vitals the more painfully as I felt shame to have been suffering
> so long from illusion. Deceived with promises of certainty, with
> childish error and rashness I had mindlessly repeated many un-
> certain things as if they were certain...Even if it was not yet evi-
> dent that the Church taught the truth, yet she did not teach the
> things of which I harshly accused her. So I was confused with
> shame. I was being turned around. (VI.iv.5)[143]

As the overt expressions of grandiosity failed, the old pains of shame
seem to have arisen. Augustine's own attribution of these pains to his embarrassment about misunderstanding the teachings of the church makes
sense. But the intensity of his distress suggests that they received fuel from
another fire. Shame about childhood mistakes and the reactions to them
could quite easily express itself through these intellectual struggles and
the emotional responses they drew forth.

Augustine's depiction of his conversion in the garden also supports
the view of shame as arising both from the present and from the past. We
have already seen the language he used to display his feelings to Alypius
after Ponticianus came and told them stories of other people who had
adopted ascetic Christian ways of life: "Uneducated people are rising up
and capturing heaven (Matt. 11:12), and we with our high culture without
any heart, see where we roll in the mud of flesh and blood..." (VIII.viii.19).[144]
Education and failure are again mixed in this passage, not exactly in the
way they were in childhood, but in a way that allows both shame and fear
of failure regarding education to come to expression without his having to
revisit childhood embarrassments explicitly.

Idealizing Escaping the Repression Barrier

Language of shame in another vignette from the conversion permits us to see how idealizing could shift to prominence and act as a solace. As Augustine describes his anguish continuing after Ponticianus left, he admits that sexual desires tormented him. They had less force than previously, but they pulled him away from his urge to give up his old ways and turn to a Christian life. He presents them as plural, like the many delights of the senses that Plotinus and Ambrose said would lead a person away from the One. They refer to the lower aspects of life as these two teachers and most ancient authorities saw it. They are "the mud of flesh and blood" of the previously cited passage.

The words related to shame intensify as Augustine inscribes the vision, what the psychoanalytically inclined would see as an extended fantasy, of continence appearing to him personified as a lovely woman. As noted above, this vignette speaks on the conscious level of giving up pride and a sense of being able to do everything for oneself by oneself. The possibility that the fantasy might reveal Augustine's own childhood pains seems supported by the idea that Continence speaks to him as if he were a child.[145] Augustine calls the people he pictures accompanying her "children...from you, her husband, Lord." Then she, as he imagines her, suggests that he respond like a child learning to stand up and walk: "Why do you stand in yourself and not stand? Throw yourself on him! Do not fear. He will not draw back so that you fall: be secure in throwing yourself! He will catch you..." Augustine confirms the suspicion of shame: "And I was blushing greatly..." (VIII.xi.27).[146] Shame appears to be a large part of this representation of the moments of his conversion, but idealizing has also appeared in the descriptions of God and womanly Continence.

As Augustine moved more deeply into Christianity, he had readily available to him the ideal of the mother church and the father God. These two supported each other as idealizable figures, instead of undermining each other as Monica and Patricius did. Moreover, other figures from Augustine's life and culture could attach themselves to the meanings of the mother church and father God.[147] These can be reinterpreted self psychologically as offering Augustine's unconscious self the coherence it needed to sustain a conscious change in his way of life.

First, the mother church has a correlate in the figure of Continence in the conversion vignette. The naming of God as the husband of Continence makes her God's wife, just as the New Testament calls the church the bride of Christ. The image painted by Augustine says that Continence approaching him has "pious hands full with flocks of good examples" and the people of the church then as now often were referred to as "flocks." The possibility that she might represent to Augustine an idealized figure of his mother gains plausibility when we see that he pictures Continence "extending to me, who was to be upheld and embraced, pious hands..." Such might be a memory of some time in childhood, and a remembered longing from any childhood, a desire "to be upheld and embraced." The psychological promise of the idealized parent imago resounds in the statement of her purpose: "so that I might come and not doubt..." (VIII.xi.27).[148]

The mother's upholding of the father, instead of diminishing his values, appears clearly in the words, "Throw yourself on him! Do not fear. He will not draw back so that you fall: Be secure in throwing yourself! He will catch you and cleanse you." Years before Monica had implied that Patricius would lead adolescent Augustine astray, but this new image of the father grows more admirable with the mother figure's praise. Hence the example shows fully the theoretical base of the interpretation: a psychological symbol emerges out of the material of culture, disappointment or injury in one's feelings, and an imagined resolution of the sorrow.

One might notice similar features in the image of God presented here. This is not a God who has fits of temper and becomes unreasonable, nor a God who laughs at a child's discomforts. It is not a God who is unfaithful, nor one who denigrates the child's mother. A harmony between God, this father, and Continence, the mother, can unroll smoothly. This, too, would create a symbolic solution to Augustine's childhood disappointments in parents who could not always contribute to each other's idealizations and sometimes lived, without admitting it, at odds with each other. Certainly Augustine claims that his father admired his mother greatly, and that his mother always spoke calmly after the storm subsided when Patricius' hot-headedness had gotten the better of him (IX.ix.19). Nonetheless, parental disagreements communicate themselves to children, even if parents handle them peacefully. We see the child's awareness in Augustine's case because he knew that Patricius committed adultery and that Monica exercised self-control to deal with her husband's anger.

The vignette sketches a solution on the cosmic level to Augustine's problems of idealizing his parents. It also shows a father image that could collect around it various images of men who influenced him strongly. As Augustine has Continence describe her husband God, the divine appears as the kind of idealizable male Augustine had looked for in Faustus and Hierius and Ambrose. In fact, what he says he longed for from Ambrose is promised in God. He described his desire vehemently: "My hot passions required a considerable period when he could be free for me to pour out my story to him, and that was never found" (VI.iii.4).[149] But God, as presented by Continence, would not fail to catch him. If Augustine would jump, precipitously cast himself on God, God would readily save him, rather than being preoccupied with books or a congregation.

After Augustine met Ambrose, at least two other symbolic male figures came into his life. One was Simplicianus. He helped Augustine understand better the connections between Neoplatonism and Christianity, and he introduced him to the story of Marius Victorinus. Simplicianus and Marius Victorinus, like the government officials Ponticianus mentioned and the desert monk Anthony whose story he told, could suggest to Augustine in both his conscious and unconscious thoughts that a person could relinquish worldly accomplishments and the recognition that comes with them. One could rely instead on God for personal stability, confidence, and inspiration. For the self psychologists these same words would imply that idealizing can take over from grandiosity the function of assuring adequate coherence and continuity of the self.

The language of the many and the One suits this shifting terrain of Augustine's psychological and spiritual life. Each of these examples called Augustine back from the belief that success as a government official would give him what he wanted. They also represented the possibility that giving up the many commitments and rewards of his career would gain for him the wisdom for which the *Hortensius* had set him on fire. Rather than being lost by giving up the many delights of a life of glory and wealth, he would discover a unity within himself as he focused on the One through whom everything exists.

The call of Plotinus to turn inward toward oneself and to seek there for access to the One might well have played an important role in the change in Augustine's life. It would have done so in that it encouraged him to turn away from the many, but it also could have affected him by giving him time for himself. Major changes in a person's direction in life generally require considerable time and energy. This demand is reflected in the amount of time invested in psychoanalysis or the length of time in recovery from physical addictions before the former addict can have some confidence about not succumbing again to the lure of the substance. When Augustine takes time for the changes happening in himself, goes to hear Ambrose preach, seeks out Simplicianus, reads Plotinus and the letters of Paul, he opens the opportunity for the events he recounts from his meeting with Ponticianus to happen. He is ready so that something might occur that he would later characterize in these memorable words:

> But while he was speaking, Lord, you turned my attention back to myself. You took me up from behind my own back where I had placed myself because I did not wish to observe myself (Ps. 19:13), and you set me before my face (Ps. 50:21) so that I should see how vile I was, how twisted and filthy, covered in sores and ulcers. And I looked and was appalled, but there was no way of escaping from myself. If I tried to avert my gaze from myself, his story continued relentlessly, and you once again placed me in front of myself; you thrust me before my own eyes so that I should discover my iniquity and hate it. I had known it, but deceived myself, refused to admit it, and pushed it out of my mind.

> But at that moment the more ardent my affection for those young men of whom I was hearing, who for the soul's health had given themselves wholly to you for healing, the more was the detestation and hatred I felt for myself in comparison with them. (VIII.vii.16–17)[150]

Even as the language of shame crescendos in this passage, Augustine recounts the discovery of an ideal that might be in his reach, might be near enough to be incorporated into himself, might allow him to become stable, both from his point of view and from that of a self psychologically oriented interpreter. But the process as a whole would take time, including that spent at Cassiciacum.

CHAPTER 7

Christian Life up to 397 C.E.

Many years would pass, nearly as many as this book will cover, before Augustine's life would settle down. Even then, it would include trips, visitors, ecclesiastical conflicts, and political strife. The years immediately after his conversion were filled with a remarkable number of personal upheavals. He traveled with friends and family back to North Africa, suffered the death of his mother, son, and at least two friends, entered the priesthood, and soon became bishop.

The language of the Bible and the church would come to predominate in the music of Augustine's life. It would guide him as an individual, as a pastor of his diocese, and as a leader in the region. It would also permit expression of a pattern of unconsciously held thoughts and feelings. In the terms of self psychology, these patterns derived on the one hand from shame, which seems to have followed on injured grandiosity, and on the other from merger with an ideal that could compensate for that injury. So often, consciously and in Christian terms, he laments his own weaknesses and his inability to apply his talents and skills rightly. Many of these plaints, if not all, introduce praise in the language of the Bible and of Christian Neoplatonism for God's ability to make good Augustine's defects and for God's power to bring about a harmony of motives and actions in the larger social arena. If this would not happen in the present life, and he became increasingly convinced that it would not, then God would assure it in the future.

An unusual opportunity presents itself in Augustine's works from these years to see culture and psyche making each other up. As the many, identified by his cultural sources with sensual distractions, are reined in to approach the One, they seem from our point of view constantly threatened with repression and continually ready to reassert themselves in disguised forms. His responses to his own psychological dynamics were reinforced by the theories of the psyche prevalent in his culture and elucidated for

137

him by his philosophical readings and Ambrose's preaching. Their views of the psyche focused him on the happiness that would come from adherence to the One. Love, Augustine believed, like the movement of the Platonic *eros* toward beauty, would draw us toward the One. It becomes a major theme in Augustine's writings for others' edification. But believing that Plotinus had overestimated the human capacity to raise the soul toward God, and agreeing instead with Ambrose that we humans need God's help, Augustine constantly enjoins turning to God for assistance. So the One seems ever greater, and we could allow that this sense accurately reflects the universe. But Augustine's self will not become dependably smaller. Its idealizing would spill from longing for parents' reassurance into praise for God, and its grandiosity would find disguised expression in the symbols and practices of Augustine's Christian life.

Changes in Augustine's Social Environment

Augustine underwent important changes in his social circumstances between 386 and 395. When he and Alypius decided to make a full commitment to the church, Nebridius and Verecundus were not yet ready to be baptized, but their friendship with Augustine and the others endured. Verecundus offered his villa at Cassiciacum, outside Milan, to Augustine, his pupils, friends, cousins, and mother (IX.iii.5–6). There in the fall of 386 and the winter of 387 they studied and discussed philosophy. A guide for this way of life came from the well-to-do people who retreated from their busy public lives to their country estates to study the Bible and the writings,[1] usually commentaries and letters, of famous bishops and clergy. This pattern of Christian contemplation and study could help Augustine and his friends form a community reminiscent of philosophical leisure but dedicated more directly to God.

Augustine turned several of their conversations into books in dialogue form. We see in these books discussions of the questions about which Ambrose preached in Milan and that Plotinus addressed in the *Enneads*. Relatively few references to the Bible appear, and virtually none to the writers of the early church or to theologians of the fourth century. These sorts of cultural transmissions were still largely unfamiliar to Augustine. Indeed, he had lived in Milan over a year and a half before he learned from Ponticianus that Ambrose had formed a monastic community outside the walls of Milan. How much more he had to learn!

Surprisingly, the writings from Cassiciacum show no incontrovertible evidence of Augustine's having recently had the struggle and experienced the relief of the episode in the garden at Milan as depicted in the *Confessions*. The dialogues are often called strictly philosophical by scholars; they even gave rise to a lengthy debate about whether he had converted to Christianity at all in 386 or whether he had simply become thoroughly Neoplatonist.[2] Yet their Christian tone appears in references to Jesus Christ as the main authority for Augustine's thought[3] and to Ambrose's preaching.[4]

But later works contrast with them by the abundant biblical citations and allusions that mark his indisputably Christian compositions.

By the beginning of Lent in March 387 Augustine and his family and friends returned from Cassiciacum to Milan so that Augustine, his son Adeodatus, and Alypius could attend the instruction for catechumens soon to be baptized by Ambrose (IX.vi.14).[5] After the baptism, they started a journey back to North Africa, where they hoped to live a quiet life of leisure and service to God. As they waited in Ostia to sail, Monica and Augustine shared a religious experience that Augustine describes clearly as a Christian Neoplatonic ascent (IX.x.24–25). Yet even this consolidation of his Christian and philosophical apprehensions does not complete his development in Christianity.

His mother died shortly after the vision she shared with him at Ostia. Family and friends gathered to bury Monica and help with the rituals, the grieving, and the household routine. Presumably assistance came from the church in Ostia, for Augustine and his companions would not have been in the city for a long time and would not have had the full circle of acquaintances that they had had in Milan or Tagaste. Other people were there to check Adeodatus' weeping, to give Augustine an opportunity to alleviate his grief by speaking on "subjects fitting for the occasion" (IX.xii.31),[6] and to prepare Monica's body for burial.

Augustine and his family and friends left Ostia and went to Rome for approximately another year. He makes no mention of these dates in the *Confessions.* In Rome in 388 he wrote two substantial works against the Manichees: *On the Morals of the Catholic Church* (*De moribus ecclesiae catholicae*) and *On the Morals of the Manichees* (*De moribus manichaeorum*). He began to compose several other books also. As he returned from Italy to North Africa,[7] the Manichees were never far from his mind nor removed from allusions in his treatises.

The leisured pursuit of wisdom and study of philosophy in which Augustine could indulge with his friends at Cassiciacum remained their way of life as much as possible during their travels and after their arrival in Tagaste. Although Augustine and his friends formed a wider web of relationship than the "one soul in two bodies" of classic models of friendship, the close sharing of so many of the important aspects of their lives could follow that pattern. Their bonds were close enough that Alypius and Evodius moved with Augustine to Hippo after he was pressed into service as a priest and set up a monastery at the church there.[8] The community at Tagaste was not yet a genuine monastery, however.[9]

Augustine's letters show that he corresponded with Nebridius during these years, but the death of Nebridius came before Augustine's ordination to the priesthood in 391. Adeodatus' death also intervened in the early years back in North Africa, but not before Augustine had an opportunity to discuss learning with him and recount their conversation in the philosophical dialogue *The Teacher* (*De magistro*).

Not long after Adeodatus' death, Augustine went to Hippo Regius, a major seaport about fifty miles northwest of Tagaste,[10] one hundred fifty miles west of Carthage.[11] By his own account he wanted to investigate establishing a monastery there[12] and, according to his biographer Possidius, he was responding to a cry for spiritual help from a government official.[13] These goals led him into a risky situation, one in which some people believe he veritably courted being snatched by the people of the town and led to the bishop for ordination as a priest.[14] Whatever his intentions, such was the outcome. Bizarre as the procedure may seem to us, it happened to other men as well.[15] Some of the recruits demonstrated remarkable unwillingness, as, for instance, had Ambrose when the people of Milan called for him, not even baptized at the time, to assume the vacant episcopal chair in their city.[16] Rarely did their responses deter the people, however, as the subsequent career of Ambrose attests.

Augustine, the well-known orator, was destined by his bishop, Valerius, for higher duties than the priesthood. Valerius was an older man of Greek background who spoke Latin with an accent that sometimes confused his people. Their own accent would have come from the Punic language of the region. Very few orators could match Augustine in any case. So Valerius asked Augustine to preach, although the right to speak to the people in the cathedral normally pertained only to the bishop.[17]

Augustine protested insufficient knowledge of the scriptures and petitioned Valerius for time to study them before he undertook the role of preacher. Valerius gave in.[18] By the time Augustine began to preach he had already worked on commentaries on Genesis and the Psalms. Starting not long thereafter and finishing before 400 C.E. he began writing interpretations of Galatians, Romans, and the Sermon on the Mount. He encountered both of the major Christian controversies of his early priesthood during those years: the continued debates with the Manichees and the opposition of the Donatist sect. He began to preach not only to the locals, but also to the assembled bishops of North Africa, many of whom had served as clergy for a much longer time than he had.[19]

When Valerius had Augustine made coadjutor bishop in 395, some North African Christians were disturbed because they believed that he had not followed the canons of the Council of Nicaea.[20] This irregularity touched a sore spot, because the church in North Africa had lived for eighty years and more with the Donatist schism, occasioned by contradictory claims about the grounds for validity of bishops' consecrations. Yet Valerius and Aurelius, the important bishop of Carthage, supported Augustine for the post, and he moved without any disruption in his service to the bishop's chair when Valerius died in 396.

These changes encouraged a new familiarity with cultural resources. At the beginning of his priesthood, Augustine spent extended time in biblical study. As he entered into the Donatist controversy he read the earlier North African clerical leaders, like Cyprian, the revered bishop of Carthage of the mid-third century, and the Donatist layman and biblical scholar Tyconius. He exercised his knowledge of these sources in sermons, letters and treatises, and public debates.

The bishopric added duties to Augustine's already busy life. He would continue preaching, now following custom, as the bishop of the town. He would also adjudicate many matters that would fall under civil law and revert to government magistrates today. He represented Hippo at the church councils called regularly by Aurelius and usually held in Carthage. Moreover, his correspondence with his friends, and increasingly with strangers, mounted as people sought his opinions on matters of scriptural interpretation, doctrine, and conduct of personal and ecclesiastical matters.[21] Augustine finally aged and died in this role, often examining and changing his thought in response to the conflicts it put in his way.

Augustine's Thought, Shaping and Being Shaped by Culture

Philosophy and Christianity at Cassiciacum

Augustine allowed the Christian and Neoplatonist bases of his thought to consolidate, then to expand in the years after his baptism. At the same time, he tried to win to Christianity the many friends he had encouraged to become Manichees. In the years of Augustine's entry into ecclesiastical circles his thought clearly continued to respond to the challenges posed by the Manichees, but also began to engage issues of the nature of the church, prompted by his encounters with the Donatists. Throughout he displayed an urgency of feeling about the need for the many to return to the One and, what he later pictured as his own experience in the garden in Milan, the need for the One to help the person mired in the many.

The titles of the works written in the fall of 386 at Cassiciacum give away much of Augustine's line of thought at the time. The works themselves show the influence of Christian culture as Christian themes entered into Augustine's philosophical understanding. [22] *Against the Academics (Contra academicos)* claims to be a philosophical treatise against a specific school of philosophy, the skeptics who had recently claimed Augustine's allegiance. His refutations of their opinions led him to the affirmation that the truth found in reasoning will match both the teachings of Christianity and the philosophy of the Neoplatonists.[23] *The Happy Life (De beata vita)* discusses classic philosophical positions on happiness. Yet Augustine's concern with Christianity enters clearly as the discussion turns, with his approval, toward how happiness depends on having God, whether, because of God's omnipresence, it is possible not to have God, in what ways one might have God (propitious toward one or not), and so on. Christian conviction is underscored by Monica's interjection into the dialogue of many of the most important points, wisdom that Augustine claims she could only have attained as a result of her life of faith.[24] *On Order* (or *Divine Providence and the Problem of Evil; De ordine*) also reviews standard philosophical arguments on how one can believe that order reigns in a universe so dominated by evil and suffering. Augustine proceeds directly from sounding altogether Neoplatonic in explaining the source of everything that is and its relationship to Intellect and its manifestation in being, to identifying these terms with the Christian Trinity.[25]

A striking assimilation of Augustine's new philosophical ideas and intentions appears in the *Soliloquies* (*Soliloquia*). The philosophical nature of the text manifests itself in many ways. These soliloquies take the form of an internal dialogue in which his interlocutor is Reason. Augustine's goal is to know God and the soul.[26] While these may seem like distinctly Christian terms to some people, they were not necessarily so in Augustine's culture. As he pursues the goal, he begins to speak of desiring wisdom above all else: "Wisdom alone I love for her own sake."[27] Certainly the Christian tradition had long identified wisdom with God, but Augustine does not here make that identification explicit.[28] Moreover, as O'Connell has shown, his other language in this passage matches fairly closely Plotinus' discourse on the approach to the beautiful, the good, and the true in *Ennead* 6.5.10.[29] The metaphors of sight, the need to purify the eyes to see the good,[30] the inevitability of turning away from the world and looking into the soul if one wants to reach truth[31] soon appear in the *Soliloquies*, as in the *Enneads*.

The clearly Christian elements of the assimilation that appear in the *Soliloquies* are many fewer, and often follow closely on the Neoplatonic images. The prayer that opens the *Soliloquies* displays these convergences. For instance, Augustine addresses God as "Father of Truth, of Wisdom, of the True and Perfect Life, of Beatitude, of the Good and the Beautiful, of the Intelligible Light…" Calling the ultimate a Father is common to both Christianity and Neoplatonism. Yet these last references to the Good and the Beautiful and the Intelligible Light sound more Plotinian than biblical. Neoplatonic themes continue as Augustine rings the changes on evocations of God's identity: "from whom to be turned is to fall; to whom to be turned is to rise…" Soon after, this allusion to the Neoplatonic ascent notwithstanding, Augustine adds a variation on a biblical verse: "God, to whom faith calls us, hope lifts us, and charity unites us…"[32] The Neoplatonic teachings about the distractions found in earthly delights move to another Neoplatonic concern, that the better part of a person not be subject to the inferior part. Yet again a Christian tone creeps in as Augustine indicates that God frees the better part of the person from subjection to the inferior part, and draws in the biblical phrase "death is swallowed up in victory."[33]

A conjunction of images from Augustine's writings at Cassiciacum and the *Confessions* speaks of the turning of a person to God. O'Connell has identified this as an implicit unity that he calls the *fovere* complex. In Latin *fovere* means "to care." It is the word for a mother bird taking care of her young. By extension it comes to mean "to cherish," "to caress," "to foster." One of the images of the fovere complex O'Connell calls Eros, the drawing power or pull of desire. His examples are not of the Cupid-like figure of erotic enticement, however, but of wisdom and philosophy, each pictured as an alluring woman. Another image of the *fovere* complex is the head that has to turn to see wisdom and beauty. The third is God's hand that may pull a person's hair in order to turn the head or, more gently, stroke the head to relax the person beset by anxiety, or soothe the eyes that still cannot see once the head is turned. Each of these symbols evokes for the reader a part of God's ability to care.[34]

Augustine's search for wisdom at Cassiciacum leads him to images of philosophy similar to the widespread personification in his culture of a virtue as a woman. In *Against the Academics*, philosophy is sometimes a mother and sometimes a lover. As Augustine speaks of his own turning for wisdom to philosophy, she appears maternal. He says that he found "refuge in the lap of philosophy. She now nourishes and cherishes me… she teaches, and teaches truly, that nothing whatever that is discerned by mortal eyes, or is the object of any perception, should be worshipped, but that everything such should be contemned…I speak of philosophy from whose breasts no age can complain that it is excluded."[35] Here she is the nurturing mother, teaching that the many should not preoccupy people. But later Augustine refers to philosophy as an alluring lover who could attract even an enemy: "to her beauty a flattering and holy lover, marveling, panting and burning, he would fly."[36]

In the *Soliloquies* Augustine discusses philosophy in female metaphors with Reason as his interlocutor. Reason encourages him to describe the goal of his search. He claims that it is to know God and the soul.[37] Augustine equates God with wisdom as the passage continues, and a very feminine wisdom allures him:

> [Reason:] But now what kind of man are you to be Wisdom's lover, desirous of seeing and embracing her, as it were, without any covering garment but yet most chastely? That privilege she allows only to a very few chosen lovers. If you burned with love for some beautiful woman, she would not rightly give herself to you if she found you loved anything else besides. So that most chaste beauty, Wisdom, will not show herself to you unless you burn for her alone.

In this speech Augustine as the author of the text implies again that a person must give up the many to attain to the One. He responds as a character in the dialogue:

> A[ugustine]: …What bounds can be set to love of so great a beauty, in which not only do I not envy others but also wish to have as many as possible along with me seeking her, panting after her, holding and enjoying her, in the belief that they will be my friends all the more because love for her is shared by us in common?

> R[eason]—Such should the lovers of Wisdom be. Such she seeks, with whom intercourse is truly chaste and without defilement.[38]

In this passage, the sensuality that has been such a snare in the flesh is pictured as transcended and transformed so that it draws Augustine's attention to the One, identified with wisdom. Clearly this beautiful Wisdom has the drawing power that O'Connell calls Eros.[39] Her image as a personification of a desirable quality allows Augustine also to maintain the classic ideal of friendship in which friends are "friends all the more," or true friends at all, as they pursue the same good. The *Soliloquies* then continue with Reason's discourse on how the eye must be trained to see properly. The explanation echoes Plotinus and recapitulates a Platonic ascent.[40] At the end it turns, as do Ambrose's discourses, toward the need for God's help to accomplish what Neoplatonic philosophy recommends. It shows the confluence of cultural sources available to Augustine, for despite the feminine personification of wisdom, by the end of the passages male pronouns refer to God, in distinctly Christian tones with Ambrose's statement of the theme not far removed.[41]

At the beginning of *Against the Academics* common ancient personifications of a quality or force as a woman shift to a reference to God as male. One personification is virtue, a second, fortune. Augustine signals that virtue is protective, yet she seems in part a forcible recruiter, who would "take away...the man suited to her purpose." The hand image of the fovere complex enters, not to nourish and cherish but to snatch: "She would already have put her hands on you..." Who is she who would put her hands on people, instead of having them long to fly to her? She is in some way an owner, a possessor, in a sense of Roman law, more nearly a father or *pater familias* with rights to physical control over his children and responsibility to provide for their needs: "She would have proclaimed you her own by right; and leading you into possession of the most secure goods, would not have permitted you to serve chance even if it were favorable to you."[42] She is both mother and father, perhaps. In either case she has to allow control to remain with fortune until the person reaches wisdom: "The port of wisdom never receives the divine spirit inhering in mortal bodies, where no wind of fortune, either favoring or opposing it, can move it, unless fortune herself, either favoring it or seemingly opposed to it, conduct it there." The care exercised by virtue changes into a more powerful fruition in God, as Augustine goes on: "Nothing remains to us in your behalf other than prayers, by which, from that God to whom these things are concerns, we might (if we are able) win his returning of you to yourself; for so, readily, he will also return you to us, and that he might permit that mind of yours, which has already long been in labor to catch its breath, to emerge at length into the air of true liberty."[43]

Interestingly, while this passage makes no mention of the head part of the fovere complex, it brings up several of the ideas that O'Connell noticed in the image's source in Plotinus and its functions in Augustine's other writings. Plotinus introduces an image of one head with many faces to describe the person distracted by externals:

So therefore, when we look outside that on which we depend we do not know that we are one, like faces which are many on the outside but have one head on the inside. But if someone is able to turn around, either by himself or by having the good luck to have his hair pulled by Athene herself, he will see God and himself and the All; at first he will not see as the All but then...he will stop marking himself off from all being and will come to the All without going anywhere, but remaining there where the All is set firm...[44]

The question of individual effort or luck effecting the movement toward wisdom foreshadows the reference to virtue and fortune in Augustine's words. The possibility of turning around to see God and oneself and the All has the same sense as Augustine's interest in bringing his reader (Romanianus in the first instance as his addressee) to his true self and to his friends. Yet here the intertwining of Neoplatonism and Christianity in Augustine's thought was still only beginning.

A Moment of Experience

Augustine continued his spiritual and Christian development while he stayed at Ostia several months after leaving Cassiciacum. He waited there with his mother, son, and compatriots to sail back to North Africa. During their sojourn, Monica and he had an afternoon's conversation that he describes as turning into an ascent to God, often understood in later centuries as a joint mystical ascent. Augustine's language describing it in the *Confessions* clearly draws on the Neoplatonism he had found in Milanese intellectual culture:

And when the conversation had come to the conclusion that whatever delight of the bodily senses, in whatever physical light, was not worthy even of comparison or mention, given the rejoicing of that life, raising ourselves by more ardent affection to the Selfsame, we were walking step by step through all created things and that sky where the sun and moon and stars shed light over the earth. And then we were ascending more internally by thinking and speaking and admiring your works. And we came into our minds and we went beyond them, so that we touched lightly the region of unfailing richness, where you feed Israel eternally with truth for nourishment, and there life is wisdom, through which all things are made...and while we spoke and panted after it, we touched it lightly with a whole beat of the heart. And we sighed and left behind, tied there, the first fruits of the spirit and we came back to the sound of our mouths...(IX.x.24)[45]

Biblical allusions, such as the reference to God's feeding of Israel, as well as the quotation from Romans 8:23 ("the first fruits of the spirit"), show that Augustine wants the experience to be understood as Christian, despite the Neoplatonic form of the ascent.[46]

Many Cultural Weapons, All against the Manichees

Writings that Augustine completed in Rome attest to the major themes of his use of, and contribution to, his cultural resources. In *On the Morals of the Catholic Church* he consolidates some of his Christian and philosophical resources. The concept of love expands in these texts beyond the sense of erotic drawing power. It begins to extend to a concern for, and good action toward, other human beings. In each instance Augustine wants to convince his audience that true happiness issues from adherence to the One, God, rather than the many distractions of earthly life.[47]

On The Morals of the Catholic Church begins with Augustine's concern to teach the Manichees, especially in regard to the validity of the Hebrew scriptures adopted by the Catholic Church, or in his words, Testamentum Vetum, the Old Testament. He is no doubt trying to draw the Manichees away from their dualities toward the One. He holds that he can establish the Catholic view of morals by using texts from the New Testament, which the Manichees will accept. He can match those passages with others from the Old Testament in order to demonstrate that his opponents cannot fairly reject its books if they accept those of the New Testament. Then, believing that he can launch his argument from the use of reason, he adopts standard arguments from his philosophical culture for happiness as the criterion of a good life. If happiness comes from possession of something, then that thing must be something that one can love and cannot lose. This guarantor of happiness, he thinks, is God: "If we follow [God] we live well, and if we reach [God] we live not only well, but even happily."[48] Following God would school the soul in virtue so that it in turn could regulate the body well.

But he talks about reason using all of its capacity and failing to maintain the sight of God: "It turns away: it cannot gaze; it throbs; it boils up; it gapes with love; it is beaten back from the light of truth, and to the familiarity of its own shadows, not by choice but by exhaustion, it is turned back."[49] The problem is that the eyes that would see God to gain in virtue must already be purified, as Plotinus had it, to see the light clearly. Into this predicament comes authority, which Augustine describes as a "shade,"[50] something to cool down the glare of the sun until the eye can look at it in small glimpses in order to gain the capacity to take it in at large. Authority comes from the scriptures, clearly a Christian, not a Neoplatonic, agency. Then he sketches a brief, Christianized Neoplatonic ascent to God: "we shall never be able to perceive, unless, beginning with things human and at hand, and holding by the faith and the precepts of true religion, we continue without turning from it in the way which God has secured for us…"[51] As promised, Augustine quotes passages which in the New Testament bring their authority to bear on the primacy of love of God: the first of the love commandments ("Thou shalt love the Lord thy God with all thy heart, and soul, and mind") and the assurance of the apostle Paul that "all things issue in good to them that love God."[52] He points out that the first of these is itself a quotation of the Old Testament. Layering quotations on each other, he tries to show the Manichees that they are caught in the interconnection of the Old Testament with the New if they intended to accept the New at all, as they did.[53]

After challenging the Manichees further regarding their specific beliefs, Augustine returns to his main theme: "Following after God is the desire of happiness; to reach God is happiness itself." Still jabbing at the Manichees' doctrines about materiality, he adds, "We follow after God by loving Him; we reach Him, not by becoming entirely what He is, but in nearness to Him, and in wonderful and *immaterial* contact with Him, and in being inwardly illuminated and occupied by His truth and holiness. He is light itself; we get enlightenment from Him."[54] These phrases echo parts of *The Happy Life*, written a little over a year earlier, about God's being the greatest good, the One who would make people happy, and about people's being separated from and needing to proceed toward God.[55] The language of *On the Morals*, however, develops these ideas with more references to Christian scriptures than did *The Happy Life*. Specifically, Augustine begins to support his claim that the two great commandments recognized by Jesus in Matthew 22:37–39 are the foundation for all Christian morals: "The greatest commandment, therefore, which leads to happy life, and the first, is this: 'Thou shalt love the Lord thy God with all thy heart, and soul, and mind.'" This quotation will lead him to the answer of the ancient philosophical question of what is the chief good: "Our chief good, which we must hasten to arrive at in preference to all other things, is nothing else than God…"[56]

Augustine argues that we cannot lose this good, God, against our wills. Love keeps the mind focused on God, "love…the only security for our not turning away from God, and for our being conformed to Him rather than to this world…"[57] Love for God is, in fact, a gift of God, as Augustine proves by quoting Paul: "the love of God is shed abroad in our hearts by the Holy Spirit, which is given unto us."[58] This assertion implies what Augustine will later state in the *Confessions*, that although the philosophy his culture offered him through Plotinus helped him see where he should direct his life, it could not assist him in getting there (VII.xxi.27). He needed the help of God to discover how to turn his attention from worldly things, like sexual desire, toward God, much as Ambrose's preaching had proclaimed all people would need such assistance.

Augustine has not forgotten the second great commandment: "Thou shalt love thy neighbor as thyself."[59] In his explication of it he assumes the classical view of friends seeking the same good and the Neoplatonic ideas of the many and the ascent to the One: "What, then, you do with yourself is to be done with your neighbor; that is, let him delight in God with a perfect love. For you do not love him as yourself if you do not make an effort to lead to that good which you yourself are striving to reach." This One can unite the many: "For this is one good which does not become constricted when all are striving for it with you." It not only unites individual people, but also expands to link and order human obligations: "From this precept the duties of human society are born…"[60] Although Augustine alludes little to the scripture in the *Soliloquies* when he pictures himself and the many approaching wisdom,[61] he proceeds, in *On the Morals,* with further scriptural resources. Love of neighbor may itself be obscure, but Augustine finds Paul elucidating it: "Hear also what Paul says: 'The love of our neighbor,' he says, 'worketh no ill.'" He expands on this briefly and ends by turning to another passage, "'We know that all things issue in good to them that love God.'"[62]

Augustine elaborates on how the many different people and ways of life can flow into God if they follow the commandments and seek to love God with all their heart, soul, and mind, and their neighbors as themselves. He draws on examples of Christians who have dedicated their lives to God and contrasts them with the Manichees. Scripture supports the ways of life of other Christians living alone or in community, he says.

Augustine writes of the life in community of the monks about whom Ponticianus told him. Here we see a pattern of social relations providing culture's guidance for life to Augustine, who appears to have investigated further and discovered the existence of other such communities.[63] This guidance combines with the Bible as a cultural resource and allows him to explain that the many practices can be evaluated under one law: "They [the monks] bear in mind how strongly Scripture enjoins charity on all; they bear in mind, 'To the pure all things are pure…' Accordingly, all their endeavors are concerned not about the rejection of kinds of food as polluted, but about the subjugation of inordinate desire and the maintenance of brotherly love."[64] This whole way of life of Christian community, which contrasts with Manichees' dietary restrictions, he sums up under the principle of charity, *caritas*, Christian love: "Charity is principally taken care of. Their diet is fitted to charity, their speech to charity, their dress to charity, their countenance to charity; they meet in and agree on one charity. To injure it is taken to be as criminal as injuring God."[65] Later, as his years of service as a priest and a bishop progressed, he became unavoidably aware of the weaknesses of the clergy and monks. Yet even their sins he attributed to a lack of the charity[66] that he here apostrophizes as "principally taken care of" in the lives of the exemplars on whom he reflects.

Augustine began *On Free Will* (*De libero arbitrio*), another effort to counter Manichaean teachings, at Rome and finished it after his ordination to the priesthood.[67] Augustine does not address this work to the Manichees, but he takes up the question, proposed in dialogue form by Evodius, of whether God is the author of evil. Not far behind it lies the question of why we do evil. Augustine mentions that this question had bothered him immensely when he was younger and had led him to his former allegiance to the Manichees. He affirms that he wishes to spare Evodius the same trouble.[68] They discuss how evil might come from a person's free will. This argument implicitly undermines both the need for a second power in the universe, an evil force of darkness opposing God's good force of light, and the notion that human beings are bound by such an evil force and bear no responsibility for their wrongdoing.

The form of *On Free Will* resembles more the dialogues at Cassiciacum than *On the Morals of the Catholic Church*. Not only does it match the genre of philosophical dialogue, but it depends much more heavily on arguments well known in his philosophical culture than does *On the Morals*.[69] The book does not make the transition, so pronounced in *On the Morals of the Catholic Church*, from what can be learned by reason to what requires the assistance of the friendly authority of the scriptures. Its references to the Bible are sparse.

More important to understanding the persistent intermingling of Christian and philosophical cultural influences in Augustine's continuing conversion to Christianity is the recognition that he finished books 2 and 3 of *On Free Will* after his ordination to the priesthood.[70] They, especially book 2, continue similarly to the dialogues composed at Cassiciacum. Although he often abandoned writing projects, notably his commentaries on Genesis, he continued *On Free Will* in much the same vein as he started it. Strongly Neoplatonic themes return, including the difficulty of discovering a unity in the multiplicity of sense perceptions unless reason uncovers it for the mind,[71] the drawing power of the truth,[72] the possibility of ascending in the mind from sense perceptions to the truth to which they bear witness,[73] and the snares for the eye that fall out of practice in seeing the truth.[74]

Despite Augustine's intervening study of the Bible, such strongly philosophical elements of the treatise should not surprise us. He depicts both Evodius and himself in *On Free Will* as trying to exercise understanding of what they already believe, in the hope that the Septuagint's rendering of Isaiah 7:9, "Unless ye believe ye shall not understand," might come to fruition for them in both believing and understanding. Philosophy qualified as the arbiter of understanding, although the truth rested in God.[75] Therefore, Augustine would want to demonstrate understanding in good philosophical form. In addition, the cultural influence of his training in rhetoric impressed on him the importance of persuading his reader by using the tools that would reach the audience.[76]

The Usefulness of Belief (*De utilitate credendi*), written in about 392, is a long letter to a friend from his youth, Honoratus, whom he led during their school days in Carthage into Manichaeism. The awareness of his friend's learning seems to influence Augustine to launch sophisticated comments about scriptural interpretation, beyond what he uses in *On the Morals of the Catholic Church*, to persuade Honoratus to change course as Augustine himself had. He sets out the idea of a fourfold interpretation of the scriptures, which he seems to assume his friend will understand, but not already have at his command. Augustine wants Honoratus to see how an allegorical interpretation will allow a spiritual reading based on figurative understanding of biblical texts. It will circumvent the problems of relying alone on the other three: the "historical," what we might call "literal"; the aetiological, what we might call "causal," to indicate that it shows why something was said or done in the Bible; and the "analogical," what we might call prophetic, to indicate how the Old Testament might foretell the events recounted in the New Testament.[77]

Augustine also aligns other forms of knowledge with the argument against Manichaean doctrine. He talks about kinds of error possible in any reading, even of secular materials. He mentions the necessity of sympathetic readings of texts in order to avoid distortion of their meaning. He affirms that a teacher also sympathetic to the text may be required in order for someone to understand it.[78] He appeals to experience, his own, that which they have in common and that of other people.[79] In short, he tries all forms of argument that he thinks might convince Honoratus. By bringing all these cultural resources to Honoratus' attention, he also incorporates them more fully into the strains of his own thought.

The cultural influence of rhetorical technique on Augustine's thought appears more clearly yet in the comparison of *The Usefulness of Belief* to a document recording a different rhetorical demand: his debate with Fortunatus the Manichee. The debate took place in 392 in Hippo at the baths when Augustine was a priest. In it both Augustine and Fortunatus quoted the letters ascribed to the apostle Paul. They and their audience shared this cultural ground. If Augustine had turned more to Plotinus and the ancient philosophers in this debate he would have lost his audience and failed to make the most telling points against his opponents: to wit, that Fortunatus' arguments failed on the basis of texts to which Fortunatus himself subscribed.

The question that Augustine presses until Fortunatus gives way essentially duplicates one Evodius raised and Augustine debated with him and recorded in *On Free Will*. As noted in *Acts or Disputation Against Fortunatus the Manichaean*, Augustine takes up the Manichees' question, "Why did God, omnipotent, inviolable, immutable, whom nothing could injure, send hither the soul, to miseries, to error, to those things that we suffer?"[80] The question implies that God is the author of the evil humans suffer, because God did not have to "send hither the soul" to its sufferings. From Augustine's point of view the reasonable answer is that God did not send the soul hither to its sufferings, but that the soul, by turning from God, brought these sufferings as punishments on itself.[81]

Augustine drew on his knowledge of the symbol system and teachings of the Manichees to debate Fortunatus. The extent to which Fortunatus invokes scripture and the name of Christ confirms that Augustine as a young man seeking wisdom may well have expected to find it along with the name of Christ, which he "had drunk in with [his] mother's milk" (III.iv.8), in the company of the Manichees.[82] Yet Augustine ascribes now to a more humble view of humanity, a view of human frailty and sin:

God is one thing, the soul another. That God is inviolable, incorruptible, and impenetrable, and incontaminable, who also could be corrupted in no part and to whom no injury can be done in any part. But we see also that the soul is sinful, and is twisted about in hardship, and seeks truth, and is in need of a liberator. This changing condition of the soul shows me that the soul is not God.[83]

On the second day of the disputation he describes how this could be the human condition. Free will was most available to Adam, he argues, "But after he voluntarily sinned, we who have descended from his stock were plunged into necessity." Nonetheless, some inkling of free will remains to those who contemplate that they have choice about specific actions, at least until they allow a bad habit to form: "Today in our actions, before we are implicated by any habit, we have free choice of doing anything or not doing it. But when, by that liberty, we have done something and the pernicious sweetness and pleasure of that deed has taken hold upon the mind, by its own habit the mind is so implicated that afterwards it cannot conquer what, by sinning, it has fashioned for itself." Augustine adduces the example of the difficulty in leaving off swearing once one is accustomed to do so,[84] and his analysis of the mechanism of habit will serve as well for the difficulty of letting go of sexual activity when the issue returns in book 8 of the *Confessions*.

The answer to the problem of overcoming habit also corresponds to that in the *Confessions*, although it is less developed. Augustine uses citations from the apostle Paul's letters to point out the need for God's help, or grace, to counteract the force of habit: "When the grace of God has breathed the divine love into us and has made us subject to His will, to us it is said: 'Ye are called for freedom,' and 'The grace of God has made me free from the law of sin and of death.'"[85] Again, he turns to the theme of God's help for the person who is trying to shake off the many sensual influences and form a close attachment to the One who is God.

Two years later, Augustine produced two short commentaries on Paul's Epistle to the Romans: *Propositions from the Epistle to the Romans* (*Expositio quarundam propositionum ex epistola ad romanos*) and *Unfinished Commentary on the Epistle to the Romans* (*Epistolae ad romanos inchoata expositio*). The former is an edited record of a discussion with other clerics.[86] The latter starts as a commentary but ends abruptly after examining Paul's greeting to the Romans and discussing the sin against the Holy Spirit. In both works Augustine stays close to the text of Romans, and when he wanders, his path almost always leads to other scriptural texts.[87] He concentrates so fully on interpreting scriptures that an otherwise expectable cultural influence, a quotation from Vergil's *Ecologues*, comes as a surprise,[88] despite our awareness of the great Latin poet's prominence in Augustine's culture and educational regime. These are the last scriptural interpretations Augustine wrote before his further study of Romans led to a major change in his thought.

The new interpretation of Romans would support the whole pattern of return to God displayed in the *Confessions*.

Paul's words require Augustine's attention to symbol systems of the Hebrew as well as Greek background of the New Testament. In the *Propositions* Augustine draws attention to Romans' theme of "the works of the Law and of grace."[89] This leads him to pressing issues, such as the justice of God's punishing human beings, a question posed also by Evodius in *On Free Will*. Augustine identifies the predicament: "Such statements must be read with great care, so that the Apostle seems neither to condemn the Law nor to take away man's free will."[90] He introduces an interpretive schema to support this effort to preserve a reasonable view as well as the apostle's teaching: "Therefore, let us distinguish these four stages of man: prior to the Law; under the Law; under grace; and in peace. Prior to the Law, we pursue fleshly concupiscence; under the Law, we are pulled by it; under grace, we neither pursue nor are pulled by it; in peace, there is no concupiscence of the flesh."[91]

This proves to be a formative and versatile interpretation of the next chapters of Romans, both in this work and in others that follow. It allows him to return to ideas about habit, like those he mentioned in the *Acts or Disputation Against Fortunatus*. He explains the time "prior to the Law" as a time dominated by desires born of the mortality of the flesh. These desires receive satisfaction and build habits based on repeatedly seeking the pleasure of satisfaction, much as Aristotle describes it.[92] Although Augustine knew these ideas from their currency in his culture and not from Aristotle's text, he agrees with Aristotle that the person gets stuck in the habit of doing the things that brought satisfaction and cannot give them up without external intervention. According to Augustine, even people who acknowledge the rectitude of God's law are still "pulled by" fleshly concupiscence, that is, by desire reinforced by habit. Augustine recommends a way for this person to move from this second stage to the third:

> Let the man lying low, when he realizes that he cannot rise by himself, implore the aid of the Liberator. For then comes grace, which pardons earlier sins and aids the struggling one, adds charity to justice, and takes away fear. When this happens, even though certain fleshly desires fight against our spirit while we are in this life, to lead us into sin, nonetheless our spirit resists them because it is fixed in the grace and love of God, and ceases to sin. For we sin not by having this perverse desire but by consenting to it.[93]

The fourth stage, perfect peace, he believes to be possible only after the resurrection, when earthly desires will cease.[94]

Expansion of this four-stage schema allows Augustine to account for many of the most perplexing sayings of Paul in Romans. But still the question of why some people ask for the help of the Liberator and some do not confronts him, because the kinds of questions Evodius asked appear also in Romans itself. The apostle Paul wrote:

As it is written: "Jacob I have loved, but Esau I have hated." What shall we say then? Is there injustice with God? God forbid. For he saith to Moses: "I will have mercy on whom I will have mercy; and I will shew mercy to whom I will shew mercy." So then it is not of him that willeth nor of him that runneth, but of God that sheweth mercy. For the scripture saith to Pharao: "To this purpose have I raised thee, that I may shew my power in thee, and that my name may be declared throughout all the earth." Therefore he hath mercy on whom he will and whom he will, he hardeneth.[95]

Does God impede some people from asking, as some Old Testament stories imply? If so, how can God punish such people justly? Augustine answers that Esau lacked faith and that Pharaoh had not responded to God prior to God's hardening of Pharaoh's heart. Therefore, both of them merited the damning outcome.[96] During the writing of the *Propositions from the Epistle to the Romans* Augustine holds that people can obey the Law, that is, do the good works enjoined in both Testaments, only by God's grace. But they can believe in God by their own effort:

For unless each one believes in [God] and perseveres in willing-ness to receive, that one does not receive the gift of God, that is, the Holy Spirit, whose pouring forth of love enables him to do good. Therefore God did not elect anyone's works (which God Himself will grant) by foreknowledge, but rather by foreknowledge He chose faith, so that He chooses precisely him whom He foreknew would believe in Him; and to him He gives the Holy Spirit, so that by doing good works he will as well attain eternal life...Belief is our work, but good deeds are His who gives the Holy Spirit to believers.[97]

This position would soon change, as we will see in the next chapter.

The *Unfinished Commentary on the Epistle to the Romans* shows how Augustine received the cultural legacy of the Bible and harmonized it with more common practice of the guidance for life in his own secular experience. Some themes similar to those in the *Propositions* appear, such as the need for God's help to avoid sin.[98] But other topics enter. For instance, Augustine spends more time on the hope for some peace in this life and not only after the resurrection: "Grace then is from God the Father and the Lord Jesus Christ, by which our sins, which had turned us from God, are remitted; and from them also is this peace, whereby we are reconciled to God. Since through grace, once sins are remitted, hostilities dissolve, we now in peace may cling to him from whom our sins alone had torn us."[99] Here the theme of help from God is again emphasized. In addition, the unifying power of the return to God, its ability to free people from many sins and hostilities to adhere to the One, echoes again.

But grace and peace do not come easily. Two indications of this bear special notice. First, Augustine enters on several pages of defense of God's punishment of human beings. Augustine, holding that God is just, assumes that human beings merit the penalties they receive. In studying the Bible he finds backing for this point of view:

> so steadfast is divine justice that even though the spiritual and eternal penalty will be relaxed for the man who repents, nevertheless, the bodily afflictions and torments, which we know troubled even the martyrs, and finally death itself, which our nature has merited by sinning, are relaxed for no one. For since even just and pious men pay these penalties, one must believe that they stem from the just judgments of God. This, which not even one of the just may avoid, the sacred scriptures call discipline. Indeed Paul exempted no one when he said, "He whom God loves, he corrects, and he whips every son whom he receives" (Heb. 12:6).[100]

This idea receives scriptural backing from the Gospel of John: "For even when the Lord promised his peace, he said, 'I have said these things so that you might have peace in me, but affliction in the world' (Jn 16:33)."[101] Augustine does not give up on the idea that God's correction is in fact tied up inextricably with God's gifts to humanity: "these trials and tribulations purge them [good and just people] completely of every stain. For the perfect peace of the body will be confirmed in due time, if now our spirit holds unshakeably and unchangingly to the peace which the Lord has deigned to give us through faith."[102] Many trials may plague even the person desiring a return to the One.

The second indication of the difficulty with which grace and peace come to human beings during their life on earth appears through Augustine's references to his relatively new engagement with the Donatists. These were the schismatics who held that the sin of handing over the scriptures to the persecutors back at the beginning of the fourth century had invalidated the ordination of the clergy who gave in to the coercion and that all ordinations and consecrations that could be traced back to those fallen clergy were invalid. The Donatists' separation from the Catholic Church occasioned much unrest in their geographical base, North Africa, and some scholars see "peace" as the key word in Augustine's desire for reunion with the schismatics.[103] Hence the idea that forgiveness allows peace with God suggests that Augustine might have the Donatists in the back of his mind as he wrote. Grace, not works like holding out against persecutors, would lead to forgiveness. Forgiveness and the remission of sins would dissolve hostilities. Peace might follow in both the spiritual sense of life with God and the more earthly sense of good relations between neighbors. These two senses would be related, of course, in Augustine's thought: we have seen him saying that love of neighbor is the surest step toward love of God.

Later in the *Unfinished Commentary*, Augustine refers to the church's teaching authority, to repentance, and the sinner's acceptance by the Church and God: "That great authority of the Catholic Church, the mother of all the saints by that same gift of the Holy Spirit, spread with such fecundity throughout the whole world—to what heretic or schismatic has she ever cut off the hope of salvation, if he correct himself?" Then he uses images that appeared in a popular song he wrote to encourage the Catholics in Hippo in their resistance to Donatism: "Does she not with tears call back to her breast all who in proud haughtiness have left her?"[104] A little later in the text he again makes his reference to the Donatists clear: "Others blow away the Spirit's sacraments and do not hesitate to baptize again those already baptized in the name of the Father and of the Son and of the Holy Spirit."[105] Augustine here interprets Romans, like other scriptures, not just for his own life, or the life of his congregation or even for his fellow clergymen, but for the church in its wider conflicts. The difficulties of life in the church in its struggles in North Africa coincide with an end of an era of Augustine's thought wherein peace and unity in spite of diversity could seem a possibility on earth, albeit only through the aid of the One God, who created all and would bring all Christians back to God's self.[106]

Psychological Dynamics of Augustine's Early Christian Years

Augustine's writings from 386 through 395 give evidence for further self psychological interpretation of his life and work. The manifestations of psychological dynamics occur in the context of his social relations and his cultural influences and contributions and appear to interact with them. Through Ambrose's preaching and Augustine's own reading of the Neoplatonists and through the representatives of the way of life Ambrose proposed, idealizing seems to have come to the fore in establishing Augustine's self. His grandiosity shows up in more muted tones than it did before his conversion. Sometimes grandiosity seems to appear as an expression of shame from some injury to his narcissism, to his sense of wholeness and continuity over time. Sometimes it appears as rage, the other common expression of injury to grandiosity. Sometimes grandiosity seems to find mirroring in the responses of his audiences when he speaks. The deaths of his friends and relatives, the change in his social status, and the pressures of ecclesiastical life all seem to have affected his psychological life.

Dynamics of the Self and Personal Relations at Cassiciacum

The three dialogues from Cassiciacum, *Against the Academics*, *The Happy Life*, and *On Order*, show how deeply Augustine allowed the ideas on which he ruminated to permeate his own feelings. The influence of other people on Augustine's being, conscious and unconscious, is unmistakable. The interaction of culture and psyche also stands out clearly, as both emotions and ideas express themselves in culturally prescribed patterns.

An example comes from the dedication of *The Happy Life*. Augustine gives us a hint that his personal stability is undergoing stress—"What firmness do I possess?"—he asks his addressee, Theodore. The problem is not simply the upheaval in his career and his religious commitments. It is also his intellectual response to his cultural resources: "For, up to now, in my mind even the question of the soul is uncertain and changeable." But he does not expect to resolve this problem strictly intellectually. Instead he will also invoke friendship, goodness, and fellow feeling: "Hence, I beg of you by your virtue, by your kindness, by the ties and the familiarity that bind our souls to each other, to give me your helping right hand..." Nor is Augustine's request needy and self-absorbed, because his rhetorical flourishes imply mutuality: "for this means that you love me and believe also that you are in turn loved and cherished by me..." Then Augustine turns to that great pained query that resonates in his works: How may one soul be truly open to another? He seems to feel bereft of some closeness, perhaps, as Kohut would name it, of closeness to unconscious alter ego selfobjects:

> That you may know what I do and how I gather my friends at the port [of philosophy], and that you may more clearly understand my soul—since I cannot find any other signs through which to reveal myself to you—I have thought it well to address to you one of my disputations that seems to me to have become rather of a more religious sort and more worthy of your standing, and indeed to dedicate it to your name.[107]

Culture pervades these passages as Augustine turns to philosophy, disputation, the dialogue form of intellectual prose, and the literary device of a dedication to reach out to Theodore, who may serve, in self psychological terms, as a selfobject.

Augustine reshapes his culture's standards as he seeks more intellectual "firmness," and later he shows a similar warmth and concern for the people whom he would help:

> On the Ides of November fell my birthday...I asked all those of us who, not only that day but every day, were living together to have a congenial session in the bathing quarters[108]... Assembled there— for without hesitation I present them to your kindness, though only by name—were first, our mother, to whose merit, in my opinion, I owe everything that I live; my brother Navigius; Trygetius and Licentius, fellow citizens and my pupils; Lastidianus and Rusticus, relatives of mine, whom I did not wish to be absent, though they are not trained even in grammar, since I believed their common sense was needed for the difficult matter I was undertaking. Also my son, Adeodatus, the youngest of all, was with us, who promises great success, unless my love deceives me.[109]

Neither his mother, a woman, nor his cousins, all untrained in grammar, should have attended a philosophical disputation if the group followed cultural models, but he draws them in by keenly perceiving their virtues—his mother's "merit" and his relatives' common sense. Thereby he remolds slightly the borders of culture.[110]

At the end of the discussions a few days later, Trygetius exclaims: "How deeply I wish you would feed us every day with the same measure.'" Augustine's somewhat elliptical response shows, despite its obscurity, his emotional engagement with his friends and family: "'This measure,' I answered, 'is to be observed everywhere and everywhere to be loved, if our return to God is in your heart.'"[111] Here Augustine portrays the life of friendship across gender and educational boundaries as they pursue the good together, holding each other's good in their hearts. Here also, Augustine is shaping culture, for the Neoplatonic idea of a return to the One clearly takes on a social dimension as people cherish another person's approach to the divine.

Yet not every emotion in the period of assimilation of Neoplatonism and Christianity partook of the warmth and pleasure of the interchanges from *The Happy Life*. Augustine writes in the dialogues of lying awake thinking at night and trying to understand his new life.[112] And in the *Confessions* he describes how emotions roiled as he read Psalm 4:

> My God, how I cried to you when I read the Psalms of David, songs of faith, utterances of devotion which allow no pride of spirit to enter in!…how they kindled my love for you! I was fired by an enthusiasm to recite them, were it possible, to the entire world in protest against the pride of the human race…What vehement and bitter anger I felt against the Manichees! But, then, my pity for them returned, because they were ignorant of your remedies, the sacraments. They were madly hostile to the antidote which could have cured them. As I read the fourth psalm during that period of contemplation, I would have liked them to be somewhere nearby without me knowing they were there, watching my face and hearing my cries, to see what that Psalm had done to me…
>
> I trembled with fear and at the same time burned with hope and exultation at your mercy, Father (Ps. 30:7–8). All these emotions exuded from my eyes and my voice when "your good Spirit" (Ps. 143:10) turned towards us to say: "Sons of men, how long will you be dull at heart? And why do you love vanity and seek after a lie?" (Ps. 4:2). (IX.iv.8–9)[113]

Sometimes the more distressing emotions spill over into his interchanges with other people. In one segment of the discussion recorded in *On Order*, his pupils Trygetius and Licentius begin to try to trump one another. Augustine's response is not only intellectual and pedagogical but also emotional and personal: "Then I said to both of them: 'Is this the way you act?…Oh, that you could see, even with as bleary eyes as mine, in what dangers we lie, and what heedlessness of ills this laughing indicates! Oh, if you were to see, then how quickly, how instantly, and how much more persistently you would change it into weeping!...'" He carries on about his sorrow in response to the boys' behavior and the concern they owe him based on his love for them.[114] He stops only when "tears imposed moderation on [him]" and he could not say more.[115] Yet he has not quite yet finished with them, for he adds shortly thereafter: "Both of you... are nevertheless trying to introduce and to implant the pest of enfeebling jealousy and empty boasting—the lowliest of the pests, to be sure, but even more pernicious than all the others—into that philosophy which I rejoice to have made my own." [116] The intersection of intellect and emotion appears in this statement as his philosophy yields rejoicing for him, and interference with his philosophy upsets him. Is Augustine also displaying, unbeknownst to himself, some narcissistic rage in this interchange? Some grandiosity may be in disguise sneaking into his joy in having made philosophy his own. The boys' bickering would challenge this grandiosity. And, as the notion of overdetermination might suggest about symbolic statements, perhaps his sorrow also reflects a damaged ideal in those early idealizing moments with his mother and father. Did his father's jealousy and boasting tarnish the loveliness of the attractive female figure from his early childhood, his mother? Is he then more susceptible later to dismay about tarnishing of the culturally idealized female personification of philosophy?

Ostia Vision and Cultural and Psychological Understanding

The themes from Augustine's childhood can still be discerned in his adult language; but the Ostia vision recounted in book 9 of the *Confessions* suggests that his conversion and its continuation through the following months and years did not result in regression from adulthood, as some psychological interpreters would have it.[117] Instead, the childhood experiences leave only small traces in the account of the experience, an experience that may have happened in cultural terms.[118] Augustine also reshaped culture through the narrative of the experience.

The psychodynamic terms analyzing Augustine's unconscious childhood recollections as transformed into adult symbols can elucidate the accounts of the Ostia vision. Augustine writes of ascending with Monica to "the region of unfailing richness where you [God] feed Israel eternally..."[119] The infantile sense of the idealized parent appears in this phrase, all the more so as the Latin for "region of unfailing richness" is *"regionem ubertatis indeficientis,"* the region of inexhaustible fertility, or, at its root, of the inexhaustible breast. The child's approach to the idealized parent may also appear disguised in the embedded explanation: "raising ourselves by more ardent affection to the Selfsame..." (IX.x.24).[120] The longing of a very young child for merger with the idealized parent appears again: The created things of the world left behind, a person would find that God "alone would speak, not through them but through himself, so that we would hear his word, not through the tongue of the flesh, nor through the voice of an angel, nor through the sound of thunder, nor through the obscurity of a symbolic utterance, but him whom in these things we love, himself without them, we would hear" (IX.x.25).[121] The person "without them" hears God as in a parent's enveloping embrace; nothing impedes contact.

Yet Augustine also famously transforms culture through these passages. First, he renders the Neoplatonic ascent in memorably Christian terms. The ascent in book 7, Augustine's turning to Neoplatonism and rising to a vision of God, is stated in less overtly Christian terms than are the accounts in book 9.[122] Secondly, book 9 includes Monica, so that it expands the Neoplatonic view of the potential for a person to rise to the One. A person need not qualify as a learned philosopher to participate in the Neoplatonic ascent.[123] Moreover, Plotinus thought of the ascent as the "flight of the alone to the Alone,"[124] but drawing on his use of Monica as a representation of the church, Augustine suggests through his ascent with her the unity of the church approaching God. Humanity rises together, not alone, to touch the eternal.[125] Yet the scene also brings the many experiences of Augustine's earlier life, a paradigm for other lives, into connection with what he believed to be "touched" in the figurative language of the passage (the One). As a vision of the mystical truth, it may have given him a kind of knowledge of potential union of the many with the One. In all events, it is the brilliant distillation of the beautiful sounds that he continued to hear in the great orchestration of life.

Much as the model of interpretation I am using holds that culture and psyche make each other up, we may also explore the thought that the relationship of mystical experience and the psyche may be seen as a two-way street. The psyche may influence mystical experience and mystical experience the psyche. For, if we are to believe Augustine's main point in the narration, something more than the running of grist through the cultural and psychological mills happened at Ostia. He claims that he and Monica "extended [their] reach and in a flash of mental energy attained the eternal wisdom which abides beyond all things" (IX.x.25).[126] For the self psychological interpreter, this phrase sounds like an evocation of what Kohut called "cosmic narcissism." "Cosmic narcissism" on the conscious level manifests itself as an acceptance of life's transience and of one's own death.[127] Kohut describes it on the unconscious level as "the achievement…of a shift of the narcissistic cathexes from the self to a concept of participation in a supraindividual and timeless existence…" Kohut also attributes such a capacity to an identity with the mother in early infancy.[128] An experience of a joint mystical ascent with one's mother can be seen as reinstating such an identity and hence facilitating the development of cosmic narcissism.

The achievement of cosmic narcissism in Augustine remains an open question, however. One might argue that Augustine never fully achieved such a shift of cathexes: on his deathbed in 430, he absorbed himself in penitential psalms that he had asked to have copied out and hung on the walls of his bedchamber. He secluded himself from his congregation and his clergy. Perhaps at that time he was regrouping narcissistic energies to face the prospect of his own death.[129] Certainly the intervening years had rained many blows to the self on his grandiosity and idealizing. We have already seen some of them in the controversial setting of the disputation with Fortunatus. We will see others outlined in the discussion of the Donatist controversy in chapter 9. Perhaps under the duress of the conflicts from 400 to 430 his narcissism never fully reached a transformation to Kohut's image of "cosmic narcissism." Alternately, informed as he was by the tradition of the desert monks, he may have participated in a different form of spiritual change over the years and spiritual expansion in the days before his death.[130] He surmises in *On the Morals of the Catholic Church* that the anchorites live without seeing other human beings by contemplating "something transcending human things..."[131]

Whatever the evaluations of the end of his life, the description of the experience at Ostia and several other passages of the *Confessions* disclose "a concept of participation in a supraindividual and timeless existence..." In addition, Augustine also senses exquisitely the pathos of living in relation to that existence: "If only it could last, and other visions of a vastly inferior kind could be withdrawn!" (IX.x.25).[132] The tension between the present life in the morass of the senses and the future life in the enjoyment of God permeates his works. Its presence in the later books of the *Confessions* will become clear in the next chapter.

For now, I will add one thought to the psychological study of mysticism. A person who has had a mystical experience, whatever one may believe about the divinity or humanity of its source, would come away from the experience with a very strong magnet for idealizing. If a person had a strong desire for an ideal and then sensed herself encountering it, she would have a knowledge, beyond everyday cognition, of what the self strove for. And if the self were seeking coherence through an emphasis on idealizing, its impetus would increase. Augustine's experience with Monica at Ostia can thus be seen to have reinforced the shift in his self from reliance on grandiosity to reliance on the idealizing pole of the unconscious core of his being. This interpretation in no way precludes the possibility that they did touch in a moment of total absorption "eternal wisdom which abides beyond all things." The mystics' claims that such experience strengthens the psyche could be understood in part through the psychological concept of idealizing.

If that moment at Ostia capped unconscious wishes related to infancy and childhood, a great idealized being who feeds people "eternally," if it includes mention of the delight of the senses which is so evident in children, if it recollected being brought up to the level of a much stronger power, and if it adds the possibility of complete merger with that person, it does not simply amount to these things, or even the sum of them. It becomes something more, not only mystically but even psychologically and culturally. It allows mother and son to share an experience no longer cast in terms of their genetic and social relationship and allows Augustine to recall it a decade and more after her death. It brings archaic feelings into the languages of Neoplatonism and Christianity. It makes available to Augustine's readers the union of what Ricoeur calls the archaic and the sublime, the childhood and the knowing creativity of the person, in poetic language that may capture the phenomenon better than any technical exposition of it.[133]

The Death of Monica

Augustine emphasized in the story of Monica's death, as throughout the *Confessions*, his theological points about the work of God in other people's lives and in his own. Many of the details seem accurate, perhaps because at the culmination of her life Monica would have focused more and more on her relationship with God and the promises of her faith.[134] For instance, Augustine says that not long before she died she gave up her desire to be buried in the tomb she had constructed for Patricius and herself (IX.xi.28). He thus can use her death as a testimony to God's ability to separate people from the many sensual reassurances of earthly life so that they may more wholly devote themselves to the One God.

Augustine's portrayal of Monica's death has prompted comments that he appears cold on the occasion.[135] Yet we can also note that the emotional responses Augustine describes at his mother's death shift complexly. Few psychologically attuned readers could be surprised by turbulence following the loss of a selfobject as formative as a mother. Interpreted self psychologically, the fluctuating emotions would seem to indicate a need for even greater idealization of his mother and for greater idealization in general in order to respond to the challenges posed to his self by her death.

The comments on Augustine's coldness have a basis in the text of the *Confessions*:

> On the ninth day of her illness, when she was aged 56, and I was 33, this religious and devout soul was released from the body…

> When the news of what had happened got about, many brothers and religious women gathered…I myself went apart to a place where I could go without discourtesy, and with those who thought I ought not to be left alone, I discussed subjects fitting for the occasion. I was using truth as a fomentation to alleviate the pain of which you were aware, but they were not. They listened to me intently and supposed me to have no feeling of grief. (IX.xi.28 and XI.xii.31)[136]

Augustine continues to protest that his feelings threatened to overwhelm him, but he sounds even more solipsistic because of some of his reactions to his feelings: "Because it caused me such sharp displeasure to see how much power these human frailties had over me, though they are a necessary part of the order we have to endure and are the lot of the human condition, there was another pain to put on top of my grief, and I was tortured by a twofold sadness" (IX.xii.31).[137]

Here again "culture and psyche make each other up." Awareness of the cultural ideal of the Stoics and the Neoplatonists, that a fully developed philosophical spirit should not be moved by the attachments of ordinary life,[138] allows us to see Augustine depicting his deeply internalized cultural standards. His expression of feeling meets instantly with his conceptions, absorbed from culture, of the proper way to express oneself. In addition, cultural understandings lay down a second sorrow on top of the first, the sorrow of recognizing that a certain human limitation overtook him.

We also see in this scene an instance of the communication to the next generation of the culture's constructions of emotion. Adeodatus sees his grandmother die: "Then when she breathed her last, the boy Adeodatus cried out in sorrow and was pressed by all of us to be silent. In this way too something boylike in me, which had slipped toward weeping, was pressed by the youthful voice of my heart and became silent." We cannot tell how much of an explanation Adeodatus received along with the admonition to be quiet. Augustine says immediately:

> We did not think it right to celebrate the funeral with tearful dirges and lamentations, since in most cases it is customary to use such mourning to imply sorrow for the miserable state of those who die, or even their complete extinction. But my mother's dying meant neither that her state was miserable nor that she was suffering extinction. We were confident of this because of her virtuous life, her 'faith unfeigned' (1 Tim. 1:15), and reasons of which we felt certain (IX.xii.29)[139]

Did they say all this to Adeodatus as they hushed him? Or did this reasoning reveal itself later as the burial was prepared? Or is Augustine introducing for the first time this summary of tacit understandings? Perhaps at the time they went on quickly: "After the boy's tears had been checked, Evodius took up the psalter and began to chant a psalm. The entire household responded to him: 'I will sing of your mercy and judgement, Lord' (Ps. 101:1)" (IX.xii.31).[140]

Opportunities for culture to allow personal expression ensued as the people at Monica's deathbed began to sing Psalm 101. It would easily foster the expression of some grief for Monica, as it evoked recollections of the Christian household she managed. For instance, verse 2 says: "I walked in the innocence of my heart, in the midst of my house." Would it bring to mind her Christian faithfulness during Patricius' infidelity and the slander of the slave girls who had badmouthed her to her mother-in-law early in her marriage (IX.ix.20)? The catalogue of the faithful person's conduct proceeds: "I did not set before my eyes any unjust thing: I hated the workers of iniquities. The perverse heart did not cleave to me: and the malignant, that turned aside from me, I would not know."[141] Augustine's own comments about Monica refusing to have him in the house when he was a Manichee could echo here and in verse 7: "He that worketh pride shall not dwell in the midst of my house: he that speaketh unjust things did not prosper before my eyes." Just how these verses sounded in the ears of the people assembled at Monica's deathbed we cannot know, but surely the psalm could have offered an opportunity for both feeling and expressing their sense of loss.

The claim of the interpretive approach I am using is that culture does more than shape the outward expression of feeling and perhaps even create or add to feelings that well up spontaneously: it also leads to repression of some feelings, which then survive unconsciously and recombine with each other to form compromise expressions of both an unsatisfied desire and a longed-for result. Donald Capps has examined the implications of repression for shame in Adeodatus, hushed as he began to cry at his grandmother's death. Capps suggests that Augustine's own responses to Adeodatus must have been shaped by a similar shame.[142] The possibility of ongoing shaming, long past childhood, crops up in Augustine's comments about critics who might accuse him of not responding rightly to his mother's death:

> If he finds fault that I wept for my mother for a fraction of an hour, the mother who had died before my eyes[,] who had wept for me many years that I might live before your eyes, let him not mock me but rather, if a person of much charity, let him weep himself before you for my sins; for you are the Father of all the brothers of your Christ.

> My heart is now healed of that wound in which I could have been guilty of carnal affection…(IX.xii.33—xiii.34)[143]

Indeed we have already seen that Ambrose had reproached people for giving in to grief about the death of loved ones.[144]

The fact that Augustine had these tears to worry him attests to his active emotions after his mother's death. After her burial he went to the baths and hoped that their warmth would relieve him of his grief. But it did not. He slept and awoke feeling better. Then he remembered a hymn by Ambrose that sings of the healing powers of sleep. It seems to have reminded him again of sorrow; its lines include the thought that rest "lightens weary minds and releases the anxious from their grief" (IX.xii.32).[145] No doubt it recalled Monica and her reliance on Ambrose her bishop, as well as her faith in God. Augustine confesses:

> From then on, little by little, I was brought back to my old feelings about your handmaid, recalling her devout attitude to you and her holy gentle and considerate treatment of us, of which I had suddenly been deprived. I was glad to weep before you about her

and for her, about myself and for myself. Now I let flow the tears which I had held back, so that they ran as freely as they wished. My heart rested upon them, and it reclined upon them because it was your ears that were there, not those of some human critic who would put a proud interpretation on my weeping. (IX.xii.33)[146]

Here Augustine seems to evoke a child's comfort in crying on his mother's shoulder, cradled near her breast where as a baby he had nursed. Psychoanalytic thought expects grief to lead to regression, if not in behavior, then in the stirring of thoughts and feelings repressed during childhood. After gentle physical care of the body in the warm water of the bath, after sleep (a phenomenon to which Freud drew our attention as a weakening of the repression barrier), Augustine begins to recall his mother's "holy gentle and considerate treatment of us..." He seems to feel its loss like a child whose mother has gone away when he describes himself as having "suddenly been deprived." Then his tears flow, like a little one's. His heart, like a baby's head, rested and reclined, because God, in Augustine's characterization, would listen and show compassion. After Monica's death, and more likely when he wrote about it a decade later, he seems to have experienced a compromise formation, in which the possibility of being laughed at for human weakness, like Monica and Patricius laughed at his sorrows about beatings at school, and the ensuing injury to his grandiosity could express themselves, but now receive an empathic and soothing response.

No self psychological interpreter would expect the unconscious stirrings of injury to subside simply. The evidence for applying this bit of theory to Augustine's experience comes in compressed reminiscence, which must derive its fuller meaning from its relationship to the repeated theme of friendship. Augustine asks himself why he felt such painful sorrow. He conjectures about the answer with little hesitation:

It must have been the fresh wound caused by the break in the habit formed by our living together, a very sweet and precious bond suddenly torn apart. I was glad indeed to have her testimony when in that last sickness she lovingly responded to my attentions by calling me a devoted son. With much feeling in her love, she recalled that she had never heard me speak a harsh or bitter word to her...Now that I had lost the immense support she gave, my soul was wounded, and my life...[was] torn to pieces, since my life and hers had become a single thing. (IX.xii.30)[147]

The words echoing friendship occur in the first and last sentences of the quotation, hinted at by the phrase "the habit formed by our living together," and affirmed in its sequel, "a very affectionate and precious bond..." The phrase "my life and hers had become a single thing" confirms Augustine's reference to his culture's ideal of friendship.

These turns of speech recall Augustine's comments about his friend-ship in his early twenties in Tagaste with the young man who died. In that passage he adopted the classical expression that he and his friend had shared one soul in two bodies (IV.vi.11).[148] Although he does not say in so many words that his life was "as it were torn to pieces" in book 4, he describes his life compellingly as though that were true. He speaks of his hometown as an "immense torture" (IV.iv.9).[149] He recalls a fear that "since death had consumed him [the friend], it was suddenly going to engulf all humanity." His own life seemed unreal: "I was even more surprised that when he was dead I was still alive, for he was my 'other self'" (IV.vi.11).[150] While the language of book 9 recounting his inner life in response to Monica's death is less bitter and less hopeless than the words of book 4, it evokes a similar sort of rending of the soul in response to the loved one's death.

The key to the diminished bitterness and despair in book 9 may well be the Ostia vision and Augustine's portrayal of it. For the ancient view of friendship required friends to be pursuing the same good. In book 4, as Augustine recalls the friend of his youth in Tagaste, he laments that they had not sought God, the true good, together, but had fixed their search for the good on the Manichees' teachings:

> As a boy he had grown up with me, and we had gone to school together and played with one another. He was then not yet my friend, and when he did become so, it was less than a true friend-ship which is not possible unless you bond together those who cleave to one another by the love which "is poured into our hearts by the Holy Spirit who is given to us" (Rom. 5:5). Nevertheless, it was a very sweet experience, welded by the fervour of our identi-cal interests. (IV.iv.7)[151]

The sweetness that Augustine attributes to this experience is the same as that he ascribes to his habit of living together with his mother (*"dulcis"*[152] and *"dulcissima"* [IX.xii.30][153]). But the adjective for life with his mother is in the superlative while the description of life with his friend is not. The lack of "the love which 'is poured into our hearts by the Holy Spirit who is given to us' (Rom. 5:5)," which he laments in his relationship to his friend, had been supplied in his relationship with Monica and made itself plain through the Ostia vision: "We touched it lightly with a whole beat of the heart" (IX.x.24).[154] Again, "at that moment we extended our reach and in a flash of mental energy attained the eternal wisdom which abides beyond all things" (IX.x.25).[155] In speaking of this profound experience as ascent to God, Augustine assures us that he and his mother had not only sought the same good together, but in a moment found it.[156]

The experience at Ostia signals the reader that a fundamental change has come to Augustine's human relationships. He now has had an experi-ence that showed him that people can be joined fully because of their relationship to God. After such a moment of intense communion with God, the possibility of hope in spite of the end of earthly life may have become a reality for him.[157] If so, it would attest to the noetic quality of the mystical experience beyond what the social-scientific, hermeneutic approach can unravel from the expression in language of the experience itself. Grief comes over him, but the listless wandering about town and looking for someone who fails to return is not prominent (IV.iv.9). The prayers to God for the person's soul and the thanks to God for the person's life begin.

One more layer of meaning in this depiction requires notice from the self psychological point of view. Augustine's comments about his soul being "wounded, and my life, as it were, torn to pieces" recall also his separation from his concubine.[158] He uses different Latin words for "wound" in the two passages, but in both cases indicates a perilous rupture. The fleshly metaphor is stronger in the passage about the departure of his concubine, for he says that she was torn "from his side" and that his "heart" was wounded. To speak of Monica's death he uses the word for "soul."[159] Yet the similarity deserves comment for another reason. In both cases he notes a "habit" of being connected to the woman. He says he "was accustomed to sleep" with the concubine, and refers to the desire for sex with a woman as a "habit" (VI.xv.25).[160] His mother and he were in the "habit" of living with one another (IX.xii.30).[161]

A comparison of his concubine and his mother in this way of course begs for an oedipal interpretation, but first we should reflect on the possibility that Augustine's concubine was to some extent an alter ego selfobject for him. O'Donnell mentions that the language about Augustine's concubine's departure bears similarities to his choice of words in book 4 about his friend's death,[162] and certainly the way he writes of the loss of his friend allows him to be seen as an alter ego selfobject. The further similarity of language about the loss of his friend, his concubine, and his mother implies some similarity in his feelings about them.[163] Why would they not have been alter ego selfobjects for him at the same time that they filled other roles in his life? All three of these people provided constancy in his life. This is what Kohut seems to refer to when he describes the woman who had worked in childhood quietly with her grandmother and later imagined a genie in a bottle on her dresser to whom she could talk with confidence and an imagined full understanding. Somehow this woman felt more whole and consistent either remembering her grandmother or talking to her "genie." Augustine's friend, concubine, and mother all seem to have sustained his sense of wholeness and continuity as well. Their effect is most noticeable in his description of their separation from him. This fits the working of any good selfobject—when it sustains us it is nearly unnoticeable.

Monica as an alter ego selfobject would not have to eradicate Monica as a mirroring selfobject for Augustine's grandiosity or as an idealized parent imago. Despite her flaws in both aspects of her relationship to him, she probably remained a bit of each as long as she lived. Arguably, she became more an idealized selfobject in his psyche after her death. Her double role in the *Confessions* as his mother and as a figure of the church certainly idealizes her.

The association of Monica with the church in the *Confessions* allows one to suspect that Augustine's feelings about her may have appeared in earlier characterizations of the church in his writings. Not long after she died, he wrote *On the Morals of the Catholic Church*. In it, the role of the mother church in bringing the "many," the still ignorant people, back to the One, to God, through obedience to God's laws receives beautiful rhetorical treatment. A bit of praise of Monica, some idealizing of her unconsciously through the conscious depiction of the power of the church, seems easy to discern in this passage:

> Rightly...Catholic Church, most true mother of Christians, you not only proclaim that God alone, the attainment of whom is the most happy life, is to be worshipped most purely and chastely,...but you also embrace love and charity for the neighbor...

> You teach boys through childlike means, youths forcefully, old people peaceably, according not only to the age of the body but also the age of the soul...You carefully teach to whom honor is owed, to whom liking, to whom reverence, to whom fear, to whom consolation, to whom admonition, to whom encouragement, to whom discipline, to whom rebuke, to whom punishment... [164]

The laudatory words allow Monica to participate in a perfection of the maternal role that she foreshadowed in Augustine's life but never fully achieved. The injury to his idealizing could be overcome in this passage. For instance, Monica may well have succeeded in teaching him intellectually that "God alone, the attainment of whom is the most happy life, is to be worshipped most purely and chastely" and she would seem, as Augustine portrays her, to have achieved the capacity to "embrace love and charity for the neighbor..." Moreover, she probably contributed clearly and sensibly to teaching him "to whom honor is owed, to whom liking, to whom reverence," and so on. But she seems to have been less skilled as an empathic instructor when she laughed at the beatings he received at school, and when she warned him in his teens, more solemnly than he could accept, not to commit adultery. Augustine's unconscious resolution for her incapacity and wish for an upbringing more finely tuned to his development may appear in the phrases, "You teach boys through childlike means, youths forcefully, old people peaceably, according not only to the age of the body, but also the age of the soul..." If so, this passage becomes symbolic in the sense proposed by Ricoeur. It puts guidance for life into a form to which people can turn again and again. At the same time it represents a wish and a desired fulfillment sufficiently disguised to escape unconscious repression.

These many descriptions of Monica and of a mother could certainly allow expression of sexually charged feelings that would be amenable to an oedipal interpretation. As I suggested in chapter 4, the social situation seems to have included enough elements of the classic oedipal triangle for sexual desire for the mother to have developed and later been repressed. Once repressed, those feelings could come out in disguise. The praise for the church, identified with Monica, may well include unconscious feelings of sexualized love for Monica. The passage will not sustain an oedipal explanation, however. That is to say, its true cause is not oedipal. Its true cause is unknowable. Or, if Augustine were writing this, he might say, "Unknowable." Whether one attributes it to God, or strictly to earthly sources, the passage appears to have allowed Augustine to express various aspects of his experience simultaneously. Such a concatenation of memory and direction for the future would help bind these images and ideas together in the intellectual and emotional resources through which he understood his life.

The Deaths of Nebridius and Adeodatus

The deaths of Nebridius and Adeodatus remind us of the shrinking circle of loved ones during Augustine's early years as a Christian. Exactly what either death meant to him remains a mystery. Yet who can doubt that the loss of their interactions with him created a loss of sustenance for his self?

Peter Brown's reference to "the lost future" captures the significance of this near surd in Augustine's life.[165] The self of Augustine in his social role of teacher, friend, philosopher, and father lost a future with each death. Not only had he separated from his career and the grandiosity implicated in it, but when he left Milan he left friends, among them Verecundus, who had allowed him the use of the estate at Cassiciacum. Augustine tells us that Verecundus died not long afterward. One tie to his recent past broke. Nebridius separated from the group of Augustine and his friends when they returned to North Africa but corresponded with him regularly. Then Nebridius died. Another tie to the past loosened. Another person who may have served as an alter ego selfobject was missing.

Then followed the death of Adeodatus. The end of his life draws no specific lament from Augustine in the *Confessions*. Yet he implies there and in the dialogue *The Teacher* that they felt very close to one another. In discussing his baptism and that of Alypius, Augustine notes, "We associated him [Adeodatus] with us, so as to be of the same age as ourselves in your grace." Augustine seems quite comfortable with this association, perhaps finding in his son yet another partial alter ego figure. Certainly if the father is to be believed, Adeodatus matched his keenness of mind. Augustine extols his son's intelligence, saying that when Adeodatus was fifteen "his intelligence surpassed that of many serious and well-educated men...His intelligence left me awestruck" (IX.vi.14).[166]

They seem to have shared admiration for each other. A student of self psychology would have to note that Kohut implies that a father's pride in his son is an expectable expression of grandiosity.[167] If Patricius demonstrated such pride in Augustine, Augustine's own pride in Adeodatus would have received social reinforcement from behavior and feelings learned long before. *The Teacher* shows Augustine and Adeodatus complimenting each other from time to time. "Most acutely stated,"[168] Augustine responds to Adeodatus' exposition of how we could demonstrate the reality to which verbs refer. "You have been most attentive."[169] "I see you are well armed against that adversary."[170] Adeodatus says to his father, "Go on as you have begun, for I shall never think unworthy of attention anything you may think it necessary to say or to do."[171] This quotation offers an interesting example of how the idealizing of the younger generation, which helps them maintain their own unconscious wholeness, can support the grandiosity of the older generation and their unconscious wholeness.[172]

A similar instance shows in addition that when Augustine must disagree with Adeodatus, he praises first, then corrects: "An acute observation. But you are wrong." This blunt rejoinder precedes an empathic recognition of the difficulty of the subject they engage: "To correct your error, listen attentively to what I say, if I can manage to express myself as I wish." The father acknowledges that he too faces pitfalls on the way to articulating abstractions: "To use words to treat of words is as complicated as to rub fingers together and expect someone else to distinguish which fingers tingle with warmth and which help others to tingle." Then Adeodatus can reflect Augustine's skill back to him: "I give you all my attention, for your similitude has aroused my interest."[173]

Augustine confirms at the end of the dialogue his contention that God assures us of every truth we come to know. Adeodatus' last response must raise the question of how much of this dialogue is to be believed: "I am specially grateful that latterly you have spoken without the interruption of questions and answers, because you have taken up and resolved all the difficulties I was prepared to urge against you. You omitted nothing at all that caused me to doubt; and in every case the Secret Oracle [God] of which you have spoken has answered me exactly according to your words."[174] Certainly scholars have contended that Augustine tended to lose control of the dialogue form[175] and one cannot deny that the last pages of *The Teacher* lose the voice of Adeodatus entirely until the final paragraph. Augustine may well have written his son's grateful coda to create a graceful exit from an argument clumsily tacked onto its original genre. Nor must we believe that the compliments cited above record exactly the words used by father and son. Nonetheless, even if Augustine is trying to portray Adeodatus as respectful and admiring, the portrayal suggests that Augustine found him admirable, and as someone deserving to be remembered as meeting the cultural standards for a boy in relationship to his father.

But Augustine does not turn his son into a sycophant. He allows us, in addition, a glimpse of Adeodatus as spunky, nearly impertinent. In one instance Adeodatus answers a challenge from Augustine: "I am surprised that you do not know, or rather that you pretend not to know, that what you ask cannot be done in conversation, where we cannot answer questions except by means of words. You ask for things which, whatever they may be, are certainly not words, and yet you too use words in asking me. First put your questions without using words, and I shall reply on the same terms."[176] Augustine concedes: "I admit your challenge is just. But..." and he elaborates the point differently. The sharp reply from Adeodatus is not peculiar to him, except perhaps in its cleverness. In the dialogues written at Cassiciacum and in *On Free Will* the students disagree openly with Augustine. Well they might, for he shows himself sometimes posing questions in order to provoke contradictory answers.[177] He allows a little sparring in the literary presentation of these exchanges and suggests that such sparring could have been part of the discourse as it occurred.

From the self psychological point of view one might say that Augustine is constructing a mirroring selfobject in *The Teacher*. To make this interpretation, one would remember that representations affected by the unconscious are always thought to represent a lack and the fulfillment of the wish for the aspect now missing from life. This would not mean, however, that the main unconscious influence on the dialogue would be Augustine's lack of and wish for a respectful, admiring son. The interpretation would have to focus in a different direction, because another tenet of a depth psychological interpretation is that the longed-for outcome derives fundamentally from childhood. The main representation in the dialogue would be Augustine's relationship to his own father, Patricius. This construal offers several advantages. It suggests that Adeodatus' more laudatory comments may not betray a stilted relationship between himself and Augustine, a quality of relationship that would contrast sharply with the *Confessions'* intimations about their life together. Instead, the words would let us know something about the desire that Augustine may have had to idealize Patricius, and to satisfy with an intellectual discussion Patricius' needs for mirroring—perhaps a hopeless task. Augustine may also unconsciously be representing the kind of teacher he wished he had had, one who would have admired and confirmed his abilities and been able to correct him gently. His schoolteachers could not, and he suggests in the *Confessions* that his father neglected correcting him at all in his adolescence (II.ii.4, II.iii.6). But in this dialogue he can show the world, as well as himself, a father who can remain close to his son, share his son's best gifts of intellect, and teach his son gently and strongly.

Moreover, the depiction of the relationships in *The Teacher* leads at the end to acclamation of God as the one true teacher. It allows Augustine to portray the relationships of father and son returning to God, much as the

Ostia vision creates a sense of the relationship of mother and son returning to God. The idealization of both mother and father also fits the conjunction of culturally female and male images of Virtue and Wisdom at Cassiciacum: comforting, erotically alluring, forceful, providing, directing. Augustine sets out the notion of God as teacher fairly simply: "When the teachers have expounded by means of words all the disciplines which they profess to teach, the disciplines also of virtue and wisdom, then their pupils take thought within themselves whether what they have been told is true, looking to the inward truth, that is to say, as far as they are able. In this way they learn." Here we may have more evidence that he did not think of his students, or his son, as sycophants. He goes on to complete the argument:

> At another time, if God permit, we shall inquire into the whole problem of the usefulness of words...we must not attribute to them a greater importance than they ought to have, so that now we should not only believe, but also begin to understand, how truly it is written by divine authority that we are to call no one on earth our teacher, for One is our teacher who is in heaven (cf. Matt. 23:10). What is meant by "in heaven" he will teach us, by whom we are admonished by human agency and by external signs to be inwardly converted to him and so to be instructed. To know and to love him is the blessed life, which all proclaim that they are seeking but few have the joy of really finding. But I should like you to tell me what you think of my whole discourse.[178]

Augustine's and Adeodatus' discussion thus returns to the idea of God as the One. That One exceeds both teachers and fathers, who are surpassed by the inner God who can instruct everyone who turns inward.

In small hints in this passage both the Neoplatonic and the biblical background of Augustine's thought crop up. They allow him to represent a brief sketch of a perfect idealizing of the perfect teacher, who also is called father elsewhere in the tradition. If the self psychological interpretation advanced above is correct and a more idealized Patricius is unconsciously represented in this dialogue, then all three, Patricius, Augustine, and Adeodatus can be seen as unconsciously drawn into the idealizing that in turn allows Augustine a measure of continuity and wholeness of his self.

Injuries to Grandiosity as an Impetus to Idealizing

As we have seen, Augustine had given up many of the social supports for grandiosity when he resigned from his teaching post. To some extent he could also rely on alter ego selfobjects, but we have seen how the people who could have been such selfobjects were lost to him. Moreover, elevation to bishop would be likely to leave him with fewer companions who spent time with him regularly and personally as a person who functions as an alter ego selfobject would probably do.

We have already seen some passages that highlight idealizing in *On the Morals of the Catholic Church*. They emphasize God as the One toward whom many human characteristics and modes of life can hope to flow. All the virtues tend toward God. The prayers of the desert monks direct themselves always to love for God. The way of life of monks in community focuses on love for neighbor and love for God. Love for neighbor will direct any Christian heart to God. And all hearts, strengthened in virtue to see God, cling by love to God if they are truly happy. The depiction of God and love for God cannot exalt God much more than does *On the Morals of the Catholic Church*.

Language that could represent injured grandiosity appears in *On the Morals*. Augustine uses the same notions he will later use in the *Confessions* (VII.xvii.23) to speak of his own feebleness in trying to hold to the truth he found in the Neoplatonic vision. Reason cannot maintain its accomplishments: "It cannot gaze;...to the familiarity of its own shadows, not by choice but by exhaustion, it is turned back."[179] It needs the aid of authority, according to Augustine. This language can serve as an excellent disguise for the childhood experience of needing the strength and knowledge of adults to help. His laments about the lack of able authority to guide him in his youth suggest experiences of insufficient adult guidance that can reach symbolic expression in these quotations.

Moreover, rather than elevating the human condition by glorifying its importance, Augustine later in the work also considers the second great commandment, to love one's neighbor as oneself, as hierarchically lower than the command to love God. Why love one's neighbor as oneself? Because such love is the surest "step towards the love of God...".[180] Hence, even though love for one's neighbor is the second great commandment, nothing human equals the love for God. Symbolically, this idea can represent the limitations of grandiosity: a human being, like Augustine, is a step on the way of another person to God. This secondary condition finds a solace in the gifts of God, such as the scripture, that can lead the less-than-ideal self back to the One, to the divine ideal, to God.

Each of the other anti-Manichaean writings discussed above also shows the high idealization of God and the relegation to a much lesser value of the things related to human beings. In *The Usefulness of Belief* Augustine locates the Manichees' repudiation of Old Testament stories not in the fantastic tales, but in the Manichees' inability to interpret the scripture. In *Acts or Disputations against Fortunatus* Augustine holds that no problem of God's sending people to suffer in their human bodies exists, but that the human soul has merited its sufferings. In the commentaries on Romans he argues that God has not been unfair in judging against Pharaoh or Esau but has foreknown their lack of faith and has justly responded to their unwillingess to call for help. In all these arguments Augustine bends his efforts to show how, despite all human questioning, God is just and good. He paints a picture of people as having jettisoned any well-merited claim to affirmation of their grandiosity. Yet he allows the possibility of help from, and a return to, an all-good and all-powerful God.

The scheme of four stages of humanity drawn from Romans forms an important background to Augustine's theology and self-portrait in the *Confessions*,[181] so their potential for expressing and resolving injured grandiosity through the idealizing of God can serve as an instructive example. Augustine says of the first stage: "Prior to the Law, we pursue fleshly concupiscence…" Within his cultural terms, even the non-Christian ones of Plotinus or other ancient philosophies, this phrase announces a blow to human grandiosity. He says in effect that we pursue that which is subject to corruption and weakness, that which makes us a slave to our bodies and desires for physical satisfaction. Even in our own day, those who indulge their lusts rarely think of their behavior as slavery and would not feel proud to do so.

Unfortunately for grandiosity, progress in knowledge leads to a worse situation and a greater blow, according to Augustine: "Under the Law we are pulled by it," that is, by fleshly concupiscence or lusts of various sorts. We have formed the habits that we find excruciating to break or embarrassing to rectify. Struggling against the restraints created by our own efforts to enjoy reality leaves us clumsily exposed to disappointment in both our original efforts for happiness and our endeavors to overcome the resulting imprisonment.

Augustine talks about overcoming the problem of human habits of slavery to lust by using language that again can represent a baby responding to discomfort: "Let the man lying low, when he realizes that he cannot rise by himself, implore the aid of the Liberator." The Liberator as an idealized figure certainly recalls the parent or caring adult helping a child: "For then comes grace, which pardons earlier sins and aids the struggling one, adds charity to justice, and takes away fear." "Grace," Latin "*gratia*," meant for Augustine primarily "help." God's grace is God's assistance to humanity. The sense of grace as "gratis," that is, "free of charge," is important to Augustine. It facilitates the representation of a parent's help, for this parental intervention comes without a requirement for payment. Moreover, grace "adds charity to justice, and takes away fear." Charity here should be construed as Christian love. The gracious, loving God is seen as helping the person without making the assistance depend on the person's fault in "lying low." So too would an idealized parent help the fallen child first and allow care to balance any criticism about the possibility of the child's action having caused the fall.

The fourth stage of perfect peace allows a continued representation of struggle in this life and a heightening of the idealization of God and God's working, for perfect peace will come only after this life, when God, the idealized figure, will have raised both the soul and the body prostrated by death.

This sequence of a person lying low and being helped to rise can serve Augustine well in his narration of his own life. It could certainly represent his own feelings about being beaten in school and the response he would have desired from the parents and other adults he did idealize. It might speak also to childhood fears in response to Patricius' hot temper, and the reassurance of a return of his goodhearted demeanor. It can make sense to many people as an explanation of frustrations of our efforts to live well. It can express at the same time the hope for an idealized parental figure salving the injuries to grandiosity that could have occurred in childhood. It expresses the smarting of many small defeats and disappointments and the hope for their happier resolution. By expressing such different aspects of human life, including unpleasant unconscious feelings escaping repression, it can orchestrate a range of human thoughts and feelings and speak to and for both conscious concerns and unconscious desires.

Residual Grandiosity and the Cultivation of Alter Ego Selfobjects

Idealizing may have served as Augustine's primary route to unconscious psychological wholeness, but it was not the only strategy that self psychology would make apparent to a psychological observer. While injury to grandiosity often seems to be represented in Augustine's writings by a downplaying of human capacities and an emphasis on human weakness, it also can appear to emerge in what Kohut calls "narcissistic rage." This, like other manifestations of unconscious desires, does not announce itself straightforwardly, but in disguise. It can be seen in Augustine's interaction with Fortunatus the Manichaean. Similarly, the third form of selfobject interaction proposed by Kohut, the alter ego selfobject, seems to have remained important to Augustine. He may have unconsciously sought through his writings to replenish the circle of alter ego selfobjects.

Narcissistic rage seems to manifest itself as Augustine hounds Fortunatus in their disputation. He returns relentlessly to the question of why God sent human beings into the body. The answer, of course, supports the image of the perfect God, but the constant pursuit of the point suggests that he finds, unconsciously, a psychological threat to himself in Fortunatus' position. His unconscious might be right about this danger. Fortunatus speaks for a position that Augustine once held, but which he has come to regard as foolish. This personal history could embarrass him. He later believed that his Manichaean views had left him more in error than a poorly educated woman like his mother. For him, what a blow to his remembrances of what we consider grandiosity! Having come to look down on his past beliefs, he would still suffer an injury to his grandiosity because of them, an injury that Fortunatus would call to mind in public, where the very publicness of the occasion could increase Augustine's shame. On such occasions, Kohut warns us, overt rage, or its more subtle manifestations such as sarcasm,[182] can recreate a sense of wholeness and continuity for the unconscious self. Augustine's tendency to go on the attack against his adversaries is quite open to this self psychological interpretation at the same time that his conduct fit in his social milieu and his cultural framework.

Finally, *The Usefulness of Belief* can be seen as an attempt to win back a friend, not just from religious error but also for an alter ego selfobject. The very effort involved in trying to persuade someone to see one's own point of view can also create a sense of likeness that reassures us unconsciously about the value of our self.[183] Kohut emphasizes that selfobject interactions keep everyone alive psychologically throughout the life span. When Augustine wants to draw Honoratus back into friendship that pursues the same ideal, he also can attempt to gain a friend who restores the unconscious self. Manichaeism itself can then be seen as a threat to his unconscious self, because it stands between him and the selfobject relationship he might want unconsciously to reestablish with his old friend.

None of these considerations disappear from the writing of the *Confessions*. A look at *To Simplicianus* (*Ad Simplicianum*) will help us understand the development of Augustine's ideas about God's grace and how these might have added to his unconscious idealizations of God and expressions of shame about humanity that so permeate the *Confessions*.

CHAPTER 8

Augustine and *Confessions,* Books 10–13

The many and the One is a theme that draws together both Augustine's conscious intentions for the *Confessions* and what appear to have been the unconscious strains of his life. Comprehensive as this claim is, it does not mean that the *Confessions* can or should be read only in this way. It is not a claim that this is the only valid culturally informed psychological reading of the *Confessions.* It is instead a hermeneutic effort to lead minds at the turn of the twenty-first century to an educated comprehension of the *Confessions* that addresses psychological hypotheses of our time.

This reading requires not only the support of the last seven chapters, but some attention to the *Confessions* and claims about the work in psychobiographical essays and historical, theological, and literary studies. Several points deserve notice immediately. First, Augustine had incorporated many of the intellectual resources from his culture—for example, Neoplatonic philosophy, biblical interpretation, and Roman literature— in his patterns of thought and self-expression before he ever initiated the project of writing the *Confessions.* Second, the *Confessions* does not conform to the generalization that it is primarily a personal piece of writing. Its concern with persuading an audience of a theological worldview is much too great for such a characterization to hold true.[1] Third, books 10 through 13 of the *Confessions,* which follow the overtly autobiographical books, remain autobiographical although less obviously so than the first nine. Bearing these considerations in mind, we can interpret the last four books of the *Confessions,* those that pertain most to the time of its writing, by relying on the tools of analysis that have proven their hermeneutic value thus far.

Social Circumstances of the Writing of the *Confessions*

Augustine had succeeded Valerius to the episcopacy in Hippo before he began the *Confessions*. His former life, his participation in the councils of the North African church, his letters, his conflicts with the Manichees and the Donatists had augmented his fame as a Christian leader. He recognized that his letters would be circulated.[2] He might at any time have reached a larger public than he knew he addressed while he was writing.

Evidence of his standing in the Christian world comes from the request from Simplicianus that Augustine explicate some passages from Romans for him. Simplicianus had counseled Augustine in the mid-380s. Augustine addresses him in *To Simplicianus* as "Father Simplicianus" and thereby acknowledges his role as more advanced in the Christian life.[3] Despite this salute to Simplicianus, we can tell that the man who first offered answers, not only to Augustine but previously to Ambrose, now sought instruction from his former student.

Augustine wrote the *Confessions* themselves in answer to a request of Paulinus of Nola, which Paulinus had originally made of Alypius.[4] In the *Confessions*, as we saw in chapter 1 above, Augustine struggles with the question of how to open his heart to someone else as he fills Paulinus' request. Brown suggests that Augustine decided to "select as important incidents and problems that immediately betray the new bishop of Hippo. He had come to believe that the understanding and exposition of the scriptures was the heart of a bishop's life."[5] As he does this in his interpretation of Genesis in *Confessions'* books 11 through 13, he differentiates his position from that of the Neoplatonists about the way the universe came into being. Similarly his ongoing debates with the Manichees (book 12) about the interpretation of scripture reveal the life he led as a bishop. These two concerns, interpretation of scripture and debate with opponents, motivate many of his literary accomplishments during the rest of his episcopacy. In the last books of the *Confessions*, then, Augustine does not so much describe himself at work as allow us to see him living out his role.[6]

Cultural Considerations in the *Confessions*

Cultural considerations in reading the *Confessions* outlast the resources available to enumerate them. Fortunately, they encompass thoughts already advanced in this book, which now may recombine in somewhat shorter form. They also include a reinterpretation of Romans that must enter the picture, for the answers about Romans that Augustine wrote in *To Simplicianus* form the theological skeleton of the *Confessions*.[7] Before the understanding of Romans and its relationship to the *Confessions* will make sense, the form of the book itself requires discussion.

The form of the *Confessions* has raised many questions in modern scholarship. The relationship of narrative to theology and philosophy, or the relationship of story to digression as sometimes seems to be the case, often provokes confusion. The lack of comment on many aspects of Augustine's life perplexes people. The relationship of books 10 through 13 to the previous nine books mystifies many readers. As Robert McMahon says of scholarly opinion: "All Augustine scholars, it would seem, can agree on this one thing, at least: if there is a latent design to the *Confessions*, it is very latent indeed." He adds comfortingly, "We are not obtuse readers."[8] When we begin to suspect that he may have overestimated our competence, we can reassure ourselves with the thought that eminent scholars have placed blame for confusion about the form of the *Confessions* squarely on Augustine.[9] Yet insight into its structure can help orient the reader to the whole of the book and the cultural influences on it.

First, several understandings widely held in late antiquity can be seen as illuminating structure in the book. Introspection, derived from Neoplatonism and Stoicism, as well as Christian practices of confession,[10] shapes much of the rhetoric of the *Confessions*. The Neoplatonic sources of Augustine's thought also imply that the memories of Augustine's youthful experiences are not of themselves revelatory, but have to be referred through his introspection to larger truths. Neoplatonic ascent only begins with attention to what people experience in the world; it does not end there. It becomes an ascent precisely because it moves beyond the earthly experience toward an intellectual and spiritual realm. Augustine's apparent digressions, then, correspond to the reflection on experience that leads the soul to a realm of higher truth. They, therefore, serve to keep the book from becoming primarily personal. Instead he expects that they will lead away from his personal experience to the kind of truth that any mind trained to the ascent can understand.

Several scholars have commented that the movement from Augustine's experiences to an ascent corresponds to an *exercitatio animi*, that is, an "exercise of the soul." The exercise conforms to the Neoplatonic idea, reflective of much ancient philosophical thought, that the mind must be trained to see the truth. Not only does Plotinus enjoin such training, but Augustine himself can be seen to refer to it in his dialogues. For instance, in *The Teacher* he apologizes to Adeodatus for taking him through seemingly pointless mental games because of the exercise they need for future work: "You will pardon me, therefore, if I play with you to begin with, not for the sake of playing, but in order to exercise and sharpen our mental powers so that we may be able not merely to endure the heat and light of the region where lies the blessed life, but also to love them."[11] O'Connell favors regarding the whole of the *Confessions* as one great *exercitatio animi*,[12] but Weintraub sees each episode as the start of such an exercise. One by one, he notes, they help the reader to exercise the mind on particular concepts, such as the nature of words, the interpretation of God's word, and the recognition of God's Word.[13] From either point of view, the lack of comment by Augustine on certain major topics becomes comprehensible as part of his effort to choose incidents to discuss so that he can make particular intellectual and spiritual points. He wants to use them to guide the reader and to strengthen the reader's soul by exploring the experience and its implications. He surely could have accomplished the same task with other incidents, but, just as surely, he would not need to achieve the results for the soul by recounting all the facts in which we today, or the curious reader in his own day, might be interested.

The idea of the *exercitatio animi* also helps illuminate the relationship of books 10 through 13 to books 1 through 9. In books 10 through 13 Augustine continues the exercises of the soul. The books focus, however, on the present of his life. Book 10 does this most obviously, as Augustine reflects on the inquiries he wants to put to God, the distractions that lead him back to the world of the senses and away from God, and the gifts of God that give him hope for and a taste of a happy life. Book 11 asks about the nature of time and eternity, and thus about the nature of the soul, which appears, as Augustine says, "distended" in time and yearning for eternity (XI.xxix.39).[14] Such an abstract reflection would not speak to the untrained reader. A reader who had traversed the first ten books of the *Confessions*, however, might begin to follow the general point of book 11, even if its more complex philosophical turns would still confound a philosophical neophyte. Book 12 discusses the origin of the whole of creation in time, what God's creating it means, what sort of being it has, how it stands in relation to heaven, and so on. Again, this is a much more abstract reflection than those in the earlier books. Augustine has already prepared the reader, however, for the idea of the spiritual interpretation of the scriptures. He helps the reader see in this book how such an interpretation might work, the pitfalls it encounters, and how Augustine can hope to answer the problems that arise. Book 13 then moves the reader through further interpretation of creation into a biblical understanding of society, the role of Christians and the church in it, and how Christians can progress toward the happy life of living rightly with God and other human beings. It suggests an allegorical reading of the Bible that sketches a general scheme of human life in society that mirrors aspects of Augustine's own individual life. For instance, it talks about the importance of examples of Christian lives and the need for people authoritative in the spiritual life to guide people less mature in it so that they can grow into wisdom. The biblical allegory thereby echoes the influence of people like Ambrose and Simplicianus and Monica on Augustine. But his personal experience has been raised again to a more universal and intellectual level.[15]

Yet another important aspect of the relationship of books 10 through 13 to books 1 through 9 is the development of an approach to Augustine's effort to understand God and himself and the inversion of that approach. In books 1 through 9, and somewhat in book 10, Augustine searches through his own experience to find God. In books 11 through 13 especially, he seeks to understand the things that he believes God has taught humanity through creation and the scriptures' story of it. By doing so he can understand himself. In the earlier books he writes from himself toward God and in the later books from a perspective of revelation by God, as he sees it, toward himself.[16]

This pattern that Augustine suggests in his own reflection extends to other people as well. Augustine is proposing that his own life exhibits the pattern of all people's lives.[17] Broadly speaking, it is a Neoplatonic fall of the soul away from the goodness of life with the One, whom Augustine saw as the Christian God, into a life of distraction and dispersal among the many diversions suggested by sense perception. In its Christianized form, it is the life of humanity after Adam, with the hope of God's calling the person to return to God and attain the blessedness imagined in eternity and pictured with the help of the Bible. Other lives Augustine portrays in the *Confessions* also exhibit this pattern. Monica's life story demonstrates it (IX.viii.17—xi.28), as, arguably, does Alypius' (VI.vii.11—x.17; VIII.viii.19; VIII.xii.30), and even that of Augustine's unnamed friend who becomes a Manichee by the urging of Augustine and returns on his deathbed to God by God's ineffable action in baptism (IV.iv.7–8).[18]

Augustine weaves other motifs into the overall pattern of fall and return. Any one scene can recall several of them. For instance, the conversion scene in the garden in Milan brings up literary parallel after literary parallel: the calling of Nathaniel by Jesus,[19] the garden of Eden,[20] the apostle Paul on the road to Damascus,[21] and, by Augustine's frank admission, the story of Anthony. The whole of the *Confessions* recalls the wanderings of Odysseus and Aeneas, the Israelites in the desert, and many other stories of travels toward home. It is an image for the Christian life that Augustine could borrow from Plotinus and Ambrose and that he used frequently both at the time when he wrote the *Confessions* and later.

These parallels return us to the issue of intertextuality. The interpretive framework for this book does allow some thought about intertextuality, or the play of one text in another and the meaning that arises by the interchange, juxtapositions, and contrasts of ideas, allusions, and images between the texts in question. Books, texts of all kinds, compose part of the material of culture, the substance in which guidance for life perdures. The content of books thus becomes available from one author to another, one generation to another, one society to another. The stories, terms, themes, images, and literary structures of one person or group of people pass to another. Often they move from person to person by means of a system of formal education. Such a social institution occupied much of Augustine's time for about twenty-five years. His grasp of literary motifs and models can hardly surprise us. As a great rhetorician, Augustine loved the interplay of words, quotations, and ideas. He paid attention to genre as he wrote. He considered his audience and adapted his address to their interests and capacities. He transformed the genre of the life story by writing his *Confessions*.[22] He understood that he might be in error (XII.xxxi.42—xxxii.43), that truth might appear differently in different times and places, and even that specific moral truths appropriate to one generation might not fit another.[23]

Yet these literary interests, which in our day intrigue people who explore intertextuality, formed part of a network of concepts for Augustine that differ sharply from those of students of literature at the turn of the twenty-first century. Augustine had taken seriously Cicero's recommendation that a person seek the truth in whatever philosophical school might hold it (III.iv.8). In the long run he concluded that such a truth exists, and counseled the readers of *On Christian Doctrine* that "every good and true Christian should understand that wherever he may find truth, it is his Lord's."[24] This statement contradicts crucial considerations implied in today's term "intertextuality."

Therefore, the concept of intertextuality can help uncover intelligent, illuminating, and satisfying interpretations of the *Confessions*. It can also help us think about how Augustine's mind worked in writing the *Confessions*. But it cannot exhaust the interest of Augustine's *Confessions*. Such issues will become clearer as we reflect on the change of Augustine's thought represented by *To Simplicianus*. The study of Romans advanced his thinking and helped him describe a pattern that lies behind every book of the *Confessions*. It is more than a literary pattern, however. It is an interpretation of and a recommendation for life, as well as an orchestration of conscious and unconscious thought and feeling.

To Simplicianus: Augustine's Struggle with the Cultural Legacy of Two Biblical Texts

The passages from Romans that Simplicianus asked Augustine to explicate can be seen as part of the guidance for life that I call culture. Simplicianus' request led Augustine to a reappropriation of the cultural source on which he had so recently commented in *Propositions from the Epistle to the Romans* and *Unfinished Commentary on the Epistle to the Romans*. His next treatment of these passages recapitulated in more detail some of his previous conclusions, but certain crucial ideas seemed to tighten like a vise and hold his thought to new determinations: first, God chooses who will have faith and who will not have it, and second, good works follow from faith and allow a person to attain the reward of eternal life. That is to say, he no longer proposes God as the foreknowing deity who chooses people, like Moses and Jacob, because God knows they will have faith while other people will not. Rather, they receive faith because God chooses them.

In *To Simplicianus* Augustine is trying to explain passages from Romans 7, including the following: "'For sin,' he says, 'finding occasion through the commandment deceived me and thereby slew me…We know that the law is spiritual but I am carnal…Not what I would, that do I practise [*sic*], but what I hate that I do.'"[25] To explain these quotations, he points out that human desire prompts people to act in the hope of attaining some sweet-ness or pleasure.[26] Repeating these actions solidifies them into habits. The habit may even appear to be good because of the sweetness that follows on the action. Augustine speaks of a "constant attendance on pleasure," which Burleigh aptly translates "addiction to pleasure." To Augustine's way of thinking, this is a penalty for "repeated sinning."[27] Moreover, much like the boys stealing the pears whom he describes in *Confessions* book 2, the sinners enjoy doing the wrong all the more when they know that the law forbids it. But these people enjoy doing what is forbidden only for a while. The thought of bitterness appears in his language, just as it does in his denigration of the pleasures of sex to the level of slavery in *Confessions* book 8. In *To Simplicianus* he says in general terms: "The price of deadly pleasure includes the sweetness which deceives, and gives delight in do-ing contrary to the law, which is all the more pleasant the less it is lawful. No one can enjoy that sweetness as the price of his condition without be-ing compelled to serve lust as a chattel slave. He who knows that an act is prohibited and rightly prohibited, and yet does it, knows that he is the slave of an overmastering desire."[28] He interprets the biblical writings of the apostle Paul through the classical philosophical notion of the body en-slaving the soul, of physical desires and delights becoming slave drivers of the unwise.

The Law assists a person in gaining awareness of slavery to desire and sin, according to Augustine's interpretation of Romans 7:16: "'If what I would not, that I do, I consent unto the Law that it [the Law] is good.'" Augustine explains the reason the person still does wrong: "He is over-come because he is not yet free by grace, but he already knows through the Law that he is doing wrong, and he does not really want to do that."[29] Paul casts the predicament as an inner war: "I delight in the law of God after the inward man…But I see another law in my members warring against the law of my mind, and bringing me into captivity under the law of sin which is in my members." Augustine gravitates to calling the Law in the mem-bers a burden on the soul. He notes: "So it often happens that what is not right gives pleasure and cannot be resisted."[30] Paul's famous plaint, "Who shall deliver me from the body of this death?" leads to the phrase that Augustine sees as the indication of God as the giver of grace, of help, to overcome the compulsion of the body of death: "The grace of God, by Jesus Christ our Lord." [31] Augustine summarizes these thoughts simply: "Those who have received the Law break it, unless through grace they obtain power to do what it commands. So it is that the Law does not exercise dominion over those who are under grace, and fulfil it by love, though they were condemned when they were under the fear of the Law."[32]

The whole struggle of Augustine with sexual desire, the chain or bond of lust, which he describes in *Confessions* book 8, works out to an application of this theory of human sin and salvation. What a striking depiction he offers of himself living as if saying, "Wretched man that I am, who will deliver me from the body of this death?" The grace of God as the helper comes in that scene as the image of Continence and all her children given her by God, as the voice of the child saying, "Take, read, take, read," and as the passage of scripture he finds in Romans 13. But the theory of why he could not submit to God's will simply by his own decision receives its own discussion as Augustine answers Simplicianus' second question.

Simplicianus' second question regards Romans 9:10–29, where Paul reinterprets the stories of Jacob and Esau and of Moses and Pharaoh. Augustine opens the commentary on this portion of scripture much as he did his remarks on Romans 7. He does not deviate far, at first, from his earlier writings. He starts in respectable hermeneutic form:

> First, I shall try to grasp the apostle's purpose which runs through the whole epistle, and I shall seek guidance from it. It is that no man should glory in meritorious works, in which the Israelites dared to glory…The Jews did not understand that evangelical grace, just because of its very nature, is not given as a due reward for good works. Otherwise grace is not grace…No man is to think that he has received grace because he has done good works. Rather he could not have done good works unless he had received grace through faith.

Augustine then hints at a mechanism that might incite a person to faith: "A man begins to receive grace from the moment when he begins to believe in God, being moved to faith by some internal or external admonition."[33] Such admonitions recur continually throughout the *Confessions* as Augustine recounts his past to make his theological points. When he discusses Patricius' response to Augustine's sexuality at the baths, he presents Monica's voice as speaking to him about the importance of not committing adultery, God as speaking through her, and himself as scorning God's admonition when he rejects Monica's advice. He portrays the friend who died as delivering a message forbidding Augustine to mock the efficacy of baptism. He concedes that the dismissed concubine set him an example of chastity that he would not follow. Of course the more obvious admonitions come from Ambrose in his preaching, Simplicianus in his encouragement about what philosophers to read and the course a famous rhetorician might follow in becoming a Christian, and Ponticianus in his stories of Anthony and the government officials who decided for baptism and chastity. Then finally the scene in the garden depicts internal and external admonitions to call Augustine effectively to faith.

But Augustine confronts the question in *To Simplicianus* of why not everyone responds to such calls. His exegesis of Romans 9 forces this question because Paul quotes both Genesis 25:23, "The elder [Esau] shall serve the younger [Jacob]," and Malachi 1:2, "Jacob have I loved, but Esau have I hated."[34] Augustine follows Paul in noting that the former quotation is attributed to God from before the birth of the twin brothers. They could not have shown faith or works before birth, nor accrued different merit because of anything Esau would have done before the birth of Jacob. Paul turns to a passage, then, in which the inscrutability of God's will stands out in bold relief: "For he saith to Moses: 'I will have mercy on whom I will have mercy; and I will shew mercy to whom I will shew mercy.'"[35] Augustine raises the question: "Who would dare to affirm that the Omnipotent lacked a method of persuading even Esau to believe?"[36] He then quotes Romans 9:17, "The apostle himself goes on. 'The Scripture saith unto Pharaoh, For this very purpose did I raise thee up, that I might show in thee my power, and that my name might be published abroad in all the earth.' The apostle adds this as an example to prove what he had said above, that 'it is not of him that willeth, nor of him that runneth, but of God that hath mercy.'"[37] Augustine knows that this scripture will make God seem unjust, so he exhorts Christians, "Let us believe that this belongs to a certain hidden equity that cannot be searched out by any human standard of measurement…"[38]

Recognizing that the question of God's justice still remains after this explanation, Augustine offers a line of Christianized Neoplatonic reasoning. God as the creator made everything good and loves the goodness in it, but humanity sinned in a way Neoplatonism would understand: "Sin in man is perversity and lack of order, that is, a turning away from the Creator who is more excellent, and a turning to the creatures which are inferior to him." That is to say, humans turn from the One to the many. The completion of this line of argument returns step by step to God's inscrutability:

> But God loved in him [Jacob], not the sin which he had blotted out, but the grace which he had freely given him. Christ died for the ungodly, not that they should remain ungodly, but that they should be justified and converted from their impiety, believing in him who justifies the ungodly. For God hates impiety. In some he punishes it with damnation, in others he removes it by justification, doing what he judges right in his inscrutable judgments.[39]

Toward the very end of the discussion of Romans 9, Augustine confesses why his own standard for how God should judge would fail in God's sight. He links the thought indirectly to another Pauline passage: "But if I set up this standard of judgment, he will deride me who has chosen the weak things of the world to confound the strong, and the foolish things of the world to confound the wise. Looking to him I should be ashamed; and being corrected, I, in turn, would mock at many who are pure by comparison with some sinners, and many who are cultivated orators by comparison with certain fishermen."[40] These words seem almost intended to set up the story he will recount in the *Confessions*, that the standards he learned in his worldly training did not help him reach God, that he suffered shame and still could be motivated by it, that purity does not necessarily rest where one would expect it, and that cultivated orators cannot hold a candle to fishermen who follow the Christ.

Thoughts on Culture and Mysticism

William James listed the "noetic quality" of mystical experience as one of its distinguishing features, in addition to its "ineffability," "transiency," and "passivity."[41] The noetic quality is the mystical experience's apparent imparting of knowledge. The mystic knows something after the mystical experience that had escaped her awareness before it. The play of texts from Augustine's culture will make sense of much of the *Confessions*, but if one is to learn from James, one should ask as well if the mystical experiences mentioned by Augustine are not also at work in the text of the *Confessions*.[42] We cannot verify Augustine's accounts of his mystical experience, even less the experiences themselves, but we can grant credence that they might have happened. We can take them, as James does, as data of human experience, whatever that experience might be. Certainly we cannot falsify them.

But how should a person put a mystical insight into words? This is a great and unsolvable problem of mystical experience. One might use the words at hand already in cultural works, which might themselves have been shaped by some such experience. And one might also find that the experience floats as another text, a wordless text, perhaps even an imageless text, shaping the flow of the other words, and reinforcing the conviction with which they are offered to their public.

Augustine's wrestling with the book of Romans seems quite likely to have been in large part intellectual, rational, painstaking, like all thorough wrestling with a difficult text. In this case we know the passages evaded the intellect of a man as wise and well-schooled as Simplicianus. Yet in reading the struggle with Romans in *To Simplicianus*, and rediscovering it in the *Confessions*, one can still hold that it takes some of its power in Augustine's thought from its resonance with his mystical experience and with the challenges of bringing it into his thought about his more mundane experience. How can he tell of his life with God without it? How can he tell of his life with God with it? And why, given all he knows of himself, did he receive divine assistance, God's grace? For all the play of texts, we have reason to believe that a major interchange in Augustine's writing takes place between words and experience. One lives a life of feeling, touching, tasting, hearing, seeing, smelling, as he says in book 10. One may also live a life with God and less oriented to matter and the senses. But this second aspect of life is, according to Augustine, itself a matter of introspection and dedication, and of the grace of God.

Cultural Themes in Confessions Book 10

At the beginning of this book, we saw that Augustine starts book 10 of the *Confessions* by evoking the presence of the church as his audience. The

Christian themes of the opening fade, although they do not disappear, as Augustine continues the book with a search of his memory. He will wend his way back to concentration on the explicitly Christian themes by the end of book 10.

Augustine's discussion of memory is influenced by Platonic schools of thought, and he ponders their notions with many examples from his own reflections. His engagement in a step-by-step ascent to God (X.viii.12) proceeds through this exploration of memory. Clearly he is moving through the many toward the One. As he says in a momentary summation of his project: "Great is the power of memory. I don't know what kind of wonder it might be, my God, a profound and unending multiplicity. And this is mind, and this is I myself. What, then, am I, my God? What is my nature? It is diverse, a life of many forms, powerfully immeasurable."[43] But he realizes that animals also have memory, albeit of limited power, and he does not want to arrive only at the level of beasts: "So I will also go beyond memory to touch him who 'set me apart from quadrupeds and made me wiser than the birds of heaven' (Job 35:11). I will also go beyond memory, so that I may find you where?—true good and sure sweetness—so that I may find you where?" (X.xvii.26).[44]

Augustine exercises the mind to review its own path and invokes the theme of the many without mentioning it explicitly:

> You conferred this honour on my memory that you should dwell in it. But the question I have to consider is, In what part of it do you dwell? In recalling you I rose above those parts of the memory which animals also share, because I did not find you among the images of physical objects. I came to the parts of my memory where I stored the emotions of my mind, and I did not find you there. I entered into the very seat of my mind, which is located in my memory, since the mind also remembers itself. But you were not there because, just as you are not a bodily image nor the emotional feeling of a living person such as we experience when we are glad or sad, or when we desire, fear, remember, forget, and anything of that kind, so also you are not the mind itself. For you are the Lord God of the mind. All these things are liable to change. But you remain immutable above all things, and yet have deigned to dwell in my memory since the time I learnt about you. (X.xxv.36)[45]

After all these memories, then, Augustine returns us to the One. In fact he seems almost to chide himself for his previous question: "There is no place, whether we go backwards or forwards; there can be no question of place. O truth, everywhere you preside over all who ask counsel of you. You respond at one and the same time to all, even though they are consulting you on different subjects" (X.xxvi.37).[46] The omnipresence of God and God's eternity would make multiplicity the human lot and Oneness the constant feature of God, no matter how widely human interactions with the divine might vary.

But like Augustine's taste of the One in the previous ascents in book 7 and with Monica in book 9, this hint of the One does not persist as a pure experience. Rather, Augustine begins to recall the distractions of the senses that led to the fall of the soul away from the One. The pull of the eternal and the contrary draw of the temporal, the appreciation of what is, eternally, and the recognition of excellence in the timebound lead into an exquisite passage: "Late have I loved you, beauty so old and so new: late have I loved you. And see, you were within and I was in the external world and sought you there, and in my unlovely state I plunged into those lovely created things which you made. You were with me and I was not with you. The lovely things kept me far from you, though if they did not have their existence in you, they had no existence at all." The theme and variations of human separateness from God and God's seeking the soul to return it home resound in Augustine's language transfiguring the dangers of the senses and God's overpowering of them: "You called and cried out loud and shattered my deafness. You were radiant and resplendent, you put to flight my blindness. You were fragrant, and I drew in my breath and now pant after you. I tasted you, and I feel but hunger and thirst for you. You touched me, and I am set on fire to attain the peace which is yours" (X.xxvii.38).[47]

Acknowledging that he remains internally divided, Augustine reviews the sensual pleasures that still tempt him. Painstakingly, sense by sense, he considers how these manifestations of the many distract him from the One. In almost torturous detail he catalogues his shortcomings derived from these distractions. Yet before he starts he already gives the reader the clue to the solution as well as the problem: "By continence we are collected together and brought to the unity from which we disintegrated into multiplicity." The force of this idea in his life is captured by Miles: "Continence was, on the one hand, a literal practice, a positive commitment to abstaining from sexual activity. As a practice it was, for Augustine, I emphasize, not an inactivity, a *not* doing. It was…simultaneously a gathering and centering of the self and an energetic resistance. But…[i]t was also symbolic of a unified and unifying affection and attention…"[48] God, the source of continence, can provide the love by which Augustine will rise, like the heat from fire:[49] "O love, you ever burn and are never extinguished. O charity, my God, set me on fire. You command continence; grant what you command, and command what you will" (X.xxix.40).[50]

Augustine returns at the end of book 10, after the rehearsal of his sensual temptations and failings, to the theme of God's gifts that make his approach to God possible. Continence is no longer the name given to what human beings need, although the idea is not lost. Rather, in response to a grouping of his failings under three forms of lust—of the flesh (sensual desires), of the eyes (curiosity), of ambition (pride; X.xxx.41, X.xli.66)[51]—he seeks someone to mediate a reunion with God (X.xlii.67). That someone he identifies in clearly Christian language, using the cultural resource of the Bible, as Jesus Christ. As in the gift of continence, God gives in Christ what

God requires: "For us before you he is priest and sacrifice..." (X.xliii.69).[52] Knowledge and return to God come as one: "Your only Son 'in whom are hid all treasures of wisdom and knowledge' (Col. 2:3) had 'redeemed me by his blood' (Rev. 5:9)." As he moves on to his contemplation of God's nature and work in the cosmos, he sets his tone for the investigation: "'And they shall praise the Lord who seek him' (Ps. 22:27)" (X.xliii.70).[53]

Cultural Themes in Book 11

In book 11, Augustine seems to move further from his work as autobiographer and into more philosophical abstractions about the nature of time. Yet his use of the cultural model of a long direct address to God[54] at the beginning of the book should be taken seriously as a mode of expressing his personal intellectual and devotional involvement in the understanding of time, which was implicated in his interpretation of the opening of Genesis. At the end of book 11 he revisits how his own life can be comprehended in these terms.

The first paragraph of book 11 demonstrates Augustine's continual turning over of the scriptures. He rolls them about on his tongue and in his mind so that they weave through his thoughts apparently constantly. He either quotes or refers to them moment to moment:

> I am stirring up love for you in myself and in those who read this, so that we may all say "Great is the Lord and highly worthy to be praised" (Ps. 48:1)...We pray, and yet the truth says "Your Father knows what you need before you ask him" (Matt. 6:8). Therefore we lay bare our feelings towards you, by confessing to you our miseries and your mercies to us (Ps. 33:22)...For you have called us to be "poor in spirit," meek, mournful, hungering and thirsting for righteousness, merciful, pure in heart, and peacemakers (Matt. 5:3–9). (XI.i.1)[55]

The cultural resource of philosophy also enters the discussion early. For example, Platonic notions of the imperfection of the changeable enter into Augustine's search for the creator: "See, heaven and earth exist, they cry aloud that they are made, for they suffer change and variation" (XI.iv.6).[56] From the ancient Greeks onward, philosophers thought that if something were changeable it was imperfect, because either it had lacked something before the change and was imperfect for that reason or it lacked something after the change and became imperfect then.[57]

The counterpoint of biblical and philosophical cultures continues throughout the book. As Augustine seeks the Bible's creator God he returns, unsurprisingly, to scripture, for example, to this idea from the Psalms: "Therefore you spoke and they were made, and by your word you made them (Ps. 33:6,9)" (XI.v.7).[58] But a philosophical turn follows immediately, as Augustine asks, "But how did you speak?" As he moves toward a philosophical contemplation of the understanding of Genesis 1 he shifts without warning to a quotation from the New Testament: "Surely not in the way a voice came out of the cloud saying, 'This is my beloved Son' (Matt. 17:5)." He is not offering a proof text, however, for he goes on in a fairly straight-forward, reasoned example, a philosophical argument based on the widely shared experience of hearing: "That voice is past and done with; it began and is ended. The syllables sounded and have passed away, the second after the first, the third after the second, and so on in order until, after all the others, the last one came, and after the last silence followed" (XI.vi.8).[59] This direction of thought can lead him back to the question of the words of creation to which Psalm 33 attests, to wonder how God's word might have made heaven and earth. His considerations allow rich interplay with the first chapter of the Gospel of John, where Jesus Christ is identified with the Word or Logos of God, which "was in the beginning with God" and "was God" (XI.vii.9).[60] The gospel then returns the reader to the creation story: "All things were made by him: and without him was made nothing that was made."[61]

Not long after these first references to John, Augustine alludes to his earlier narrative life story by saying, "Even when we are instructed through some mutable creature"—like Monica, Ambrose, or Simplicianus—"we are led to reliable truth when we are learning truly by standing still and listen-ing to him. We then 'rejoice with joy because of the voice of the bride-groom' (Jn. 3:29), and give ourselves to the source whence we have our being." This conclusion of Christ as the true teacher appears in his dia-logue with his son in *The Teacher* and often earlier in the *Confessions*. The allusions to his earlier life and to notions of the true teacher interior to the soul do not preempt his other themes, however. For instance, Christ weaves into the pattern of platonic ascent and philosophical notions of the immu-table God: "And in this way he is the Beginning because, unless he re-mained when we were wandering, there would be no place to which we would return. But when we return from error, we return by knowing. But in order that we may know, he teaches us, for he is the Beginning and he speaks to us" (XI.viii.10).[62]

Augustine has not forgotten his own difficulties in learning, however. The challenges of trying to get his opponents to comprehend his Christian understanding of creation brings him to laments that resound with the words he has used to describe his own earlier confusion: "They attempt to taste eternity when their heart is still flitting about in the realm where things change and have a past and future; it is still 'vain' (Ps. 5:10). Who can lay hold on the heart and give it fixity, so that for some little moment it may be stable, and for a fraction of time may grasp the splendour of a constant eternity?" (XI.xi.13).[63] That this also infects his present life Augustine at-tests at the end of book 11: "I am scattered in times whose order I do not understand. The storms of incoherent events tear to pieces my thoughts, the inmost entrails of my soul, until that day when, purified and molten by the fire of your love, I flow together to merge into you. Then shall I find stability and solidity in you, in your truth which imparts form to me" (XI.xxix.39—xxx.40).[64] Here we see evidence for Peter Brown's claim that Augustine as autobiographer did not present himself as a wholly changed human being, but writes so that the reader "senses the tension between the 'then' of the young man and the 'now' of the bishop. The past can come very close… "[65]

Cultural Themes in Book 12

Augustine returns to the words of Genesis 1 as he begins book 12 of the *Confessions*, but he also tries as an interpreter of the Bible to coordinate them with other biblical passages. For instance, he notes that Psalm 115:16 speaks of "The heaven of heaven [which] belongs to the Lord…"[66] This raises a question for him: if God created heaven and earth, then "where is the 'heaven of heaven,' Lord, of which we have heard in the words of the psalm…?" (XII.ii.2).[67] Later he links this to the idea of a "'wisdom [that] was "created before everything' (Eccl. 1:4)" (XII.xv.20).[68] But his notions of God's eternity and perfection will not allow him to see this wisdom, "created before everything," as God's own wisdom: "Your wisdom is manifestly coeternal and equal with you…" God's own wisdom is, in sum, Christ. Augustine concludes: "Evidently 'wisdom' in this text [Eccl. 1:4] is that which is created, an intellectual nature which is light from contemplation of the light."[69] He elaborates using other texts, this time from the New Testament, and returns to the passage from Psalm 115:16:

> So there was a wisdom created before all things which is a created thing, the rational and intellectual mind of your pure city, our "mother which is above and is free" (Gal. 4:[26]) and is "eternal in the heavens" (2 Cor. 5:1). In this text "heavens" can only be "the heavens of heavens" which praise you (Ps. 148:4); this is also the Lord's "heaven of heaven" (Ps. 113:16). (XII.xv.20)[70]

The reader familiar with cultural influences not only from the Bible but from philosophy can hear Neoplatonic notions still in these passages. The idea of a created, rational wisdom, which gains light by gazing on the light, recalls Plotinus' idea of Nous, or Mind or Intellect, which derives from the One and maintains its being by its relationship to the One.[71] Moreover, the whole of book 12's concentration on the heaven of heavens and the heaven and earth created by God moves the reader closer to the goal of the Neoplatonic ascent. In fact, McMahon points out that it can be seen as part of a longer ascent in the literary structure of the *Confessions*:

> Kenneth Burke has argued that books 10–12 trace "the kind of dialectical progression that is traditionally, in Neo-Platonist thought, called the Upward Way."[72] Book 10 largely concerns the principle of Memory; book 11 inquires into the nature of time; and book 12 dwells on God's sempiternal "heaven of heaven." Here, clearly, is a progression upward on a "return to origins." Time is a principle

anterior to memory, just as God's sempiternal heaven proves anterior to time.[73]

That ascent in the *Confessions* culminates in book 13.

Cultural Themes in Book 13

Book 13 of the *Confessions* continues the interpretation of Genesis through a seemingly bizarrely overdrawn allegorical reading of the creation story. Yet the allegorical passages make their own kind of sense, and the themes from philosophy still show in them, as does Augustine's own life story. Moreover, Augustine can use these verses of Genesis to move from familiar themes of the *Confessions* to contemplation of the nature of the church, of social life in the larger world, and of the relationship of Christians and the church to the rest of human society. Ultimately, Augustine draws the story of the creation of the many back to the evocation of their final resting place in the One. The symphonic themes of culture—and psyche, as we shall see later—nowhere sound stronger than in this book.

As in previous books, the opening chapter displays these themes. Augustine starts by recapitulating his autobiography, including its opening in confession—the confession of praise of God's goodness and of Augustine's own sin. Unsurprisingly, he finds a grounding in scripture for such thoughts: "I call upon you, my God, my mercy (Ps. 59:17). You made me and, when I forgot you, you did not forget me. I call you into my soul which you are preparing to receive you through the longing which you have inspired in it." Here we see Augustine alluding to the "many" of creation used by God to call Augustine back. But the references to scripture go on without quotation, as the reader aware of Augustine's exegesis of Romans 7 and 9 in *To Simplicianus* can realize. Augustine revisits here God's ability to call the person, which goes beyond using creation and includes the power to initiate the person's change of heart:

> Before I called to you, you were there before me. With mounting frequency by voices of many kinds you put pressure on me, so that from far off I heard and was converted and called upon you as you were calling to me. Moreover, Lord, you wiped out all the evils which merited punishment, so as not to bring the due reward upon my hands (Ps. 17:20), by which I fell away from you. In any good actions of mine you were there before me; in my merits you were rewarding "the work of your own hands by which you made me" (Ps. 119:73).

As he continues, the view in Genesis of the Creator God and of the goodness of creation sounds strongly, as does the perfection of God and God's aseity, God's being by God's self and without assistance from any external support, as required by Augustine's culture's philosophical tradition:

Before I existed you were, and I had no being to which you could grant existence. Nevertheless here I am as a result of your goodness, which goes before all that you made me to be and all out of which you made me. You had no need of me. I do not possess such goodness as to give you help, my Lord and my God. It is not as if I could so serve you as to prevent you becoming weary in your work, or that your power is diminished if it lacks my homage. (XIII.i.1)[74]

As Augustine continues his meditation on Genesis 1 he arrives at the assertion that the Spirit of God was "borne above the waters" (Gen. 1:2). Augustine himself recapitulates his exegesis and explanation thus far:

We have said a lot about "the heaven of heaven" (Ps. 113:[16]), about "the earth invisible and unorganized," and about the "dark abyss"...And now where the name of God occurs, I have come to see the Father who made these things; where the "Beginning" is mentioned, I see the Son by whom he made these things. Believing that my God is Trinity, in accordance with my belief I searched in God's holy oracles and found your Spirit to be borne above the waters. There is the Trinity, my God—Father and Son and Holy Spirit, Creator of the entire creation. (XIII.v.6)[75]

Mixed in this heavily trinitarian language is also a reference to the Neoplatonic notion of the lesser good of formlessness, which Augustine recalls as he talks about the "dark abyss."

On this notion of a trinitarian God discerned in the opening lines of Genesis depends a famous metaphor that displays central points of Augustine's theology. Augustine asserts: "My weight is my love. By it I am carried wherever I am carried. By your gift we are set on fire and carried upwards; we grow red hot and we go" (XIII.ix.10).[76] For this remark to make sense, one must recall the Neoplatonic ascent toward the One. We have seen that this ascent can occur through meditation on the earthly aspects of life, the evidence of the senses, and the reason that lies behind them. Yet daily life and the senses and reason were not enough, Augustine tells us, to draw him back to God. God's own action was needed. In this passage he signals symbolically God's help through the Holy Spirit. He can refer through the creation story to God's greatness as height. He can call on the idea of God as a helper, extending the divine Oneness to humanity through the biblical idea found in Acts 2:38 that the Spirit is God's gift. Then if the Spirit is helper and the Spirit is borne above the waters, the person borne by the Spirit can also hope to ascend to the One. Immediately after the reference from Acts to the Spirit as gift, Augustine claims: "In your gift we rest. There we enjoy you. Our rest is our place." The Spirit's activity in this attainment is clear in the next lines, as is the ongoing Neoplatonic theme: "Love lifts us there, and 'your good Spirit' (Ps. 143:10) exalts 'our humble estate from the gates of death' (Ps. 9:13)" (XIII.ix.10).[77]

Everyday examples from another aspect of culture—late antiquity's physics—help Augustine elaborate his symbols. He explains in passing the metaphor of weight, which has a different referent than it would today: "A body by its weight tends to move towards its proper place. The weight's movement is not necessarily downwards, but to its appropriate position: fire tends to move upwards, a stone downwards" (XIII.ix.10).[78] A human's weight is not a function of mass, as Augustine develops the metaphor. People's weight, their movement toward their appropriate place, depends on their love, says Augustine. And if people are to return to the One with whom they were made to be, they do so by the fire of God's love. Fire was seen as the lightest of the elements,[79] the one that rises as smoke up a chimney. Yet this fiery love comes not from the human being's own heart, but by the gift of God. Augustine reasserts this in the same passage and brings the metaphor together with the idea of the heaven of heavens as a heavenly Jerusalem: "Lit by *your* fire, your good fire, we grow red-hot and we go, as we go upwards 'to the peace of Jerusalem' (Ps. 122:6)" (XIII.ix.10).[80]

McMahon describes Augustine as creating himself as a speaker distinct from himself as author in the *Confessions*[81] and as having that speaker in book 13 take on the voice of conviction that comes from the mystical experience of meditating on the Trinity. The meditation appears for the reader in chapters xii–xvi,[82] although when it happened in Augustine's life is not clear, except that it occurred before the final revision of these chapters. Granting McMahon's point, we still find that Augustine's language in these passages admits of a cultural and social interpretation. The mystical experience, voiced in these passages, opens up understanding of the earthly influences on Augustine's self-expression.

For instance, as Augustine interprets the light created by God, according to Genesis 1:14, he brings together his own interpretation of the two great commandments and the platonic ascent. He has just finished mentioning "loving our neighbour in the relief of physical necessities..." He alludes to the second great commandment, loving one's neighbor as oneself, as he explains: "Aware of our own infirmity we are moved to compassion to help the indigent, assisting them in the same way as we would wish to be helped if we were in the same distress" (XIII.xvii.21).[83] He lines these ideas up with the image of light from Genesis and more closely with the ascent from Neoplatonism in the next chapter: "Let our light which lasts but a short time 'break forth.' Passing from the lower good works of the active life to the delights of contemplation, may we 'hold the word of life' which is above and 'appear as lights in the world' (Phil. 2:15) by adhering to the solid firmament of your scripture." God then appears as a philosophical teacher: "For there you hold conversation with us to teach us to distinguish between intelligible and sensible things as between day and night, or between souls dedicated to the intelligible realm and souls dedicated to the material world of the senses." Moreover, God succeeds admirably as a teacher, bringing pupils to God's own wisdom: "Then it is not only you in the secret place of your judgment who divides between light and darkness as you did before the making of the firmament; it is also your spiritual people established in the same solid firmament and distinguished by your grace manifested throughout the world. May they 'give light over the earth and divide day and night and be signs of the times' (Gen. 1:14)" (XIII.xviii.22).[84]

Augustine reminds the reader of why people taught by God are necessary. His analysis shows that he believes his view of the truth of Genesis' account of the creation can clarify the situation of the human race: "May your ministers now do their work…May they be an example to the faithful by the life they live before them and by arousing them to imitation (1 Thess. 1:7). Thereby hearing them is no mere hearing but leads to doing" (XIII.xxi.30).[85] These words can recall for the reader the people in Augustine's own life who helped lead him back to God. Although Augustine never heard Marius Victorinus, he heard of Victorinus' doing, which inspired him to imitation. Monica's words often fell on deaf ears, but the example of her piety reached her son, as it had her husband. The preeminent example behind these words of Augustine may well be Ambrose, whom Augustine heard, but also saw in action in his humble dress and his daily habits and in his defense of the Catholic church. Moreover, from Ambrose's preaching Augustine learned the figurative interpretation of the scripture and in the present he does the same kind of work that Ambrose did in interpretation.

Augustine goes on in this passage in biblical phrases that almost amount to an injunction not to fall into the errors in which he had lived so long. He takes up Neoplatonic notions of the value of the mind over the senses, biblical recommendations, cautions about undue trust in philosophy and dubious religious teachings, and, finally, their connection to the animals mentioned in the creation story:

> "Seek God and your soul shall live" (Ps. 69:32), so that the earth may "produce a living soul." "Be not conformed to this world" (Rom. 12:2). Restrain yourselves from it. By avoiding this world the soul lives; by seeking it the soul dies. Restrain yourselves from the savage cruelty of arrogance, from the indolent pleasure of self-indulgence, and from "knowledge falsely so called" (I Tim. 6:20). Then the wild animals are quiet and the beasts are tamed and the serpents are rendered harmless: in allegory they signify the affections of the soul. (XIII.xxi.30)[86]

Augustine allows that a soul may ascend very far with God's help, to perception of the Trinity. He builds on the apostle Paul's words, "Be renewed in the newness of your mind to prove what is God's will,"[87] as he suggests that individuals may surpass imitation of other good people and attain their own awareness of God: "Because such a person now has the capacity, you teach him to see the Trinity of the Unity and the Unity of the Trinity" (XIII.xxii.32).[88]

But even these people are limited in their judgments, and Augustine believes that God restrains them to exercising these judgments in the social setting of the church. He points out that God in Genesis gave human beings dominion over earthly things, but not things in the firmament above. Therefore, people, even spiritually wise ones, cannot judge things seen only from God's perspective, such as the interior of someone's heart or the future of someone's salvation. But some judgments appear to be possible even for the laity, because they too can see external works, although their conclusions may not have the force of the clergy's, given that the priests are charged with the power of correction:[89]

> The spiritual person also judges by approving what is right and disapproving what he finds wrong in the works and behavior of the faithful in their charitable giving—like the fruitful earth. He judges the "living soul" in its affections made gentle by chastity, by fasting, by devout reflection on things perceived by the bodily senses. And lastly he is said to exercise judgement on questions where he possesses a power of correction. (XIII.xxiii.34)[90]

In the last chapters of the *Confessions*, the phrase "morning and evening" recurs, keeping the reader in the language and cadence of Genesis 1 while Augustine evokes other biblical images. He draws us to the idea of rest at the end of time, as at the end of his book, a rest very much like the fruit of a Neoplatonic ascent:[91]

> For our sins were over us, and we had abandoned you to sink into a dark depth. Your good Spirit was "borne over" it to help us "in due season" (Ps. 142:10). You justified the ungodly (Rom. 4:5), you separated them from the wicked, and you established the authority of your book between those in higher authority who were submissive to you and those below who were subject to it. You gathered a society of unbelievers to share a single common aspiration, so that the zeal of the faithful should "appear" and so bring forth for you works of mercy, distributing to the poor their earthly possessions so as to acquire celestial reward.

That celestial reward is peace which is the gift of God:

> All these things we see, and they are very good, because you see them in us, having given us the Spirit by which we see them and love you in them.

> "Lord God, grant us peace; for you have given us all things" (Isa. 26:12), the peace of quietness, the peace of the sabbath, a peace with no evening (2 Thess. 3:16). (XIII.xxxiv.49—xxxv.50)[92]

Yet a brief reprise of his life, which he would also see as a reprise of every Christian's life, enters into the final repetitions of the themes of Christianity and Neoplatonism: "At one time we were moved to do what is good, after our heart conceived through your Spirit. But at an earlier time we were moved to do wrong and to forsake you. But you God, one and good, have never ceased to do good. Of your gift we have some good works, though not everlasting. After them we hope to rest in your great sanctification." Still, at the close, after the last confession of sin in the book, Augustine offers the confession of praise and of God's goodness: "What man can enable the human mind to understand this? Which angel can interpret it to an angel? What angel can help a human being to grasp it? Only you can be asked, only you can be begged, only on your door can we knock (Matt. 7:7–8). Yes, indeed, that is how it is received, how it is found, how the door is opened" (XIII.xxxviii.53).[93]

These beautiful words have made such a symphony of Augustine's conscious thought that the play of the personal unconscious life in them may seem irrelevant. But to understand how the different strands of our lives accomplish their deeper work we can still look for the traces of the activity of the unconscious. Here in conscious poetry and intellectual skill the effects of unconscious processes might be most powerful: where it is most veiled the unconscious can move most boldly. As the personal elements of Augustine's confessions and the reminiscences of his life story have been reiterated thus far in this chapter, the remainder will be devoted to the signs of the unconscious in the material he drew from culture and his social experience and formed into his theology.

Self Psychological Interpretation of Augustine as He Wrote the *Confessions*

The self psychological themes in Augustine's writings should be clear by now, but clarification and reinforcement of their appearance in *To Simplicianus* and the *Confessions* will emphasize how they shifted and persisted up through his early middle age. If the early wholeness of his self seems to have been built on grandiosity and ideals that supported it, his life from his early thirties onward seems to have derived its unconscious cohesion from his idealizing, in terms of which his grandiosity could achieve some expression. The emphasis on God's action in his life and in the universe allows a heightening of idealizing. His corresponding understanding of the human condition and his own experience could not support grandiosity openly. But in accord with the psychoanalytically grounded insight that painful experiences undergo repression and come to expression in distorted forms later, we can infer that Augustine's injuries to grandiosity did emerge in his work, as did the continuing injuries to it that he would have administered by viewing his own faults in such a harsh light. However, idealizing would not have had to sustain the self alone, for Augustine could also seek out alter ego selfobjects through his invocations of the church.

The Conscious Shift and Unconscious Intensification in To Simplicianus

Augustine made his small but drastic shift in his view of human nature in *To Simplicianus*, written in 396. He gave up the notion that human beings chose to respond to God's calling or not to answer it and conceded that the power to initiate faith comes from God alone. The obvious outcome of this position is that human beings have even less on which to congratulate themselves. This view would unconsciously deliver a blow to grandiosity. Given so little reinforcement for their own worth, people would have much to gain from idealization of someone else. In Augustine's case, this someone else was God.

The last chapter has already pointed out that Augustine's view of people as needing help from God to get free of their bondage to sin almost necessarily represents a blow to grandiosity. In *To Simplicianus* he does not relinquish this analysis. He only intensifies the view of human helplessness. God chooses who will receive the grace necessary to attain the freedom from the chains of sin and the capacity to do the good.

The response to objections that God does not seem to act fairly in these decisions resonates with the voice of an authoritarian human being: "Through all this you can hear as an undertone, 'Who art thou that repliest against God?' That must be understood as a recurring refrain—if God, willing to show his wrath, endured vessels of wrath, who art thou that repliest against God?"[94] People are ready to credit Augustine with this voice, and rightly so, but he did not take it up because it seemed the best thing to do in a world of infinite options. One would conclude much more reasonably that such authoritarian tones had rung in his ears at least since he went to school. The lament of unfairness still sounds in Augustine's plaint in the *Confessions*: "The schoolmaster who caned me was behaving no better than I when, after being refuted by a fellow-teacher in some pedantic question, he was more tormented by jealousy and envy than I when my opponent overcame me in a ballgame" (I.ix.15).[95] Teachers and pupils seem to have undergone their respective injuries to grandiosity, and in the *Confessions*, as in *To Simplicianus*, Augustine appeals from the sense of unfairness to the grandeur of God. So it would seem that the review of Romans, like the review of his school days, allows him to express injury to grandiosity and to assuage it by taking comfort in idealizing the God to whom he now clings.

Admittedly, a little bit of childhood grandiosity seems to come out as Augustine recognizes his failure to understand God's judgment: "Looking to him I should be ashamed; and being corrected I in turn would mock at many who are pure by comparison with some sinners…"[96] He seems still to have some of the arrogance noted by Kohut in those who have suffered blows to grandiosity. Yet the main theme of the passage is an exaltation of God. Augustine quotes Paul and later paraphrases the same text: "Inscrutable are his judgments, and his ways past finding out."[97] This verse starts with the famous line, "O the depth of the riches of the wisdom and of the knowledge of God!" (Douay). Seen sometimes as a cheat of the real difficulties of justifying God's ways to humanity,[98] it fits in the depth psychological context as a way of supporting idealizing that can then allow coherence to the self, even the self that has been wounded by authoritarianism and labors under the unconscious as well as conscious burdens of awareness of failure.

The Confessions

These themes of the low value of the self and the great worth of God run throughout the *Confessions*, as does the dependence of the self on God in order to reach salvation. The self without God is scattered and strewn about the world. Throughout the story Augustine testifies to God's calling him back to cling to God's oneness and to have some of his own oneness restored by so doing. The last four books of the *Confessions*, permitting a glimpse of the time when he was actually writing the work, continue these themes. The ideas of injury to grandiosity and the need for idealization appear quite strongly in them. Earlier they appeared in the voice of Augustine as author, but they did not seem to dominate Augustine at the time about which he was writing. In the later part, the two voices become much closer, even if, following McMahon, we do not believe that they completely coincide. So the end of the *Confessions* shows, as does the beginning, that Augustine in his later years depended heavily on his idealization of God for the sustenance of his unconscious self, as well as for the direction of his conscious meditation and writing.

The apparent intent to provide the reader with *exercitationes animi* demonstrates the overall theme. Something is wrong with the reader, as with all human beings, as we grow up. We are not born perfect, according to Augustine's argument in book 1. Nor will we begin to achieve perfection unless the soul works for it, although Augustine believes this work will lead to recognition of God's having made the first efforts in the person's behalf. Therefore, the goodness of the soul on its own is limited. Recognition of this idea, borrowed from parts of Augustine's culture, could induce a blow to grandiosity, just as the language about human imperfection could express such a blow. But exercise aims to take the soul closer to the one God, and it holds out hope of approaching an ideal. That is to say, the diminution of grandiosity is matched immediately by an offer of idealizing and hope for the well-being of the person through the strengthening of the ideal as it becomes clear within the person.

In book 10, for instance, we see that Augustine asserts something wonderful about memory: "Great is the power of memory—I don't know what kind of wonder it might be—my God, a profound and unending multiplicity." These words might well carry some hidden grandiosity, as the next phrase implies: "And this is mind, and this is I myself." But the threat of unconscious inner division can also be seen as coming to expression, perhaps because the marvelous qualities of memory assuage the pain of division sufficiently for the unconscious injuries to reach consciousness in somewhat altered form. Augustine mentions not just once as above, but again in the same paragraph, the idea of himself as scattered and divided:

"What then am I, my God? What is my nature? It is diverse, a life of many forms, powerfully immeasurable."[99] This need not necessarily be a drawback, as Augustine believed that God made creation good, as well as various (VII.xii.18–xiii.19). Yet as we recall the dangers he saw in his own scattered life and his desire to return to God, we cannot see such a reference as simply positive. Moreover, the rest of the passage shows that however great memory is, and whatever it might offer his unconscious grandiosity, Augustine wants to move on toward the ideal, toward God: "I will also go beyond memory, so that I may find you where?—true good and sure sweetness—so that I may find you where?" (X.xvii.26).[100]

Augustine believes that the great ideal God can be found within the human being, and this sets up another way that injured grandiosity might be assuaged. What a claim a person, consciously aware of limitation and unconsciously carrying many blows to grandiosity, makes in saying to God, "You conferred this honour on my memory that you should dwell in it..."! But Augustine maintains the tension between God within and God outside himself: "But you remain immutable above all things, and yet have deigned to dwell in my memory..." (X.xxv.36).[101]

The theme of internal division among the many replays itself through the rest of the chapter. Nothing that Augustine senses is good in and of itself. Everything depends on God. Even the continence that would reunite the person must be sought from God. The human's strength is not enough to achieve it. This, as we have already seen, constituted an aspect of life in which Augustine found himself incapable. He felt very ashamed of his own inability. As the book ends, God's extension of the divine self to humanity through Jesus gives Augustine the hope of being able to return and find his unity in reunion with God.

The idealization of God, seen as an outpouring of the unconscious self and the lament for blows to grandiosity, may seem by now to be almost surface content in book 11. That is, issues of idealizing and grandiosity may seem evident in what Augustine had consciously in mind as he wrote. Of course, they are not. Unconscious grandiosity and idealizing were not his terms, nor was the repressed unconscious his concept. But the language of his opening of book 11 is heavily layered with symbols as multiple meanings abound, and some of them are about a relatively small self and a rather great ideal to which to attach oneself. The language that could carry idealizing starts with the opening words: "Lord, eternity is yours..." The cultural material of the Bible makes more phrases available to him: "'Great is the Lord and highly worthy to be praised' (Ps. 48:1)" (XI.i.1).[102]

But of course the discussion of time highlights these ideas most brightly. The whole notion that time is a distention of the soul allows the expression of an unconscious self threatened with fragmentation. The claim that God is the eternity to which all time returns allows an immutable ideal of perfection, to which Augustine hopes consciously to return. It could also unconsciously function as an idealizable selfobject, God as the unchangeable one who will sustain the soul "when purified and molten by the fire of your love, I flow together to merge into you." Until that unification with God, the self might find greater coherence, if not perfect wholeness, in gravitating toward that ideal.

The language of book 12 would allow the same sort of unconscious currents to find expression. A vivid image for the ideal comes in the long exploration of the idea of the "heaven of heavens." Again and again Augustine tries to clarify what sort of goodness and perfection such a creation might have. He heaps the values he deems excellent on it: a "rational and intellectual mind," status as God's "pure city," freedom, and eternity. Moreover, its goodness is confirmed by its praise of God and its possession by God ("this is also the Lord's 'heaven of heaven' [Ps. 115:16]") (XII.xv.20).[103]

The allusion to the heaven of heavens as "our 'mother which is above and free'" especially encourages psychological interpretation. The explication should attend to the cultural context of the phrasing: Augustine is quoting the Bible, Galatians 4:26. The apostle Paul has designated Sarah, the wife of the patriarch Abraham, as the exalted mother in that text. He has used her as a literary type, or representation, of the Christian church saved by God. She contrasts with her maid, Hagar, the type of the people still slaves to sin. Therefore, Augustine cannot be deemed the inventor of this image of the exalted mother "above and free." It does not correspond simply to the unconscious workings of his mind. Yet it does make available an image by which his unconscious desires to idealize Monica might find expression. The heaven of heavens is secondary to God, as Augustine presented Monica taking a role subordinate to her husband. Augustine can say regarding it, in contrast to the attributes of God, "in principle mutability is inherent in it." But it escapes that imperfection by devotion to God like the faithfulness that Augustine so prized in Monica's bearing toward Patricius: "It would grow dark and cold if it were not lit and warmed by you as by a perpetual noonday sun (Isa. 58:10) because it cleaves to you with a great love" (XII.xv.21).[104]

If the heavenly city, heaven of heavens, carries this sense of an idealized image of Monica, it might also carry some hidden meaning of oedipal attachments, as Augustine goes on to picture the heaven of heavens and its relationship to God: "O House full of light and beauty! 'I have loved your beauty and the place of the habitation of the glory of my Lord' (Ps. 26:8–9), who built you and owns you. During my wandering may my longing be for you!" The relationships of Augustine to this "home," a nice recollection of an image of a mother, and to its superior have their mention also: "I ask him who made you that he will also make me his property in you, since he also made me" (XII.xv.21).[105]

But those who would see an oedipal triangle in such a passage should read through the next few chapters and consider its fuller representation:

"Jerusalem my fatherland, Jerusalem my mother (Gal. 4:26), and above it yourself, ruler, illuminator, father, tutor, husband, pure and strong delights and solid joy and all unutterable good things, all at the same time, since you are the one greatest and true good" (XII.xvi.23).[106] If the oedipal triangle makes a disguised appearance in this passage, it does so with the father and husband in control of the situation and the son clearly in a subordinate position. Perhaps, as psychoanalytic theory would have it, this is the resolution of the oedipal conflict that Augustine wanted and did not get. His dissatisfaction would make the resolution of the oedipal conflict a candidate for this kind of disguised representation. Let us assume it was so. We still may have an Augustine who did not "win" the oedipal conflict so much as find in it a variation on the more usual resolution: losing out to the father, but without quite the satisfaction and security that Augustine wanted in identification with Patricius. This interpretation would account for the disagreements he seems to have sensed between his parents and the difficulties in the household that might have followed from them.[107]

But this oedipal interpretation need not replace the self psychological understanding of these same sentences. Clearly they could add the idealization of Patricius to the idealization of Monica. Not only does he state the association of God with father, but he also allows an association between the heaven of heavens and the father, because he calls it the *patria*. This can be translated the "homeland," but more explicitly it evokes the idea of "fatherland." Evidently that heavenly home is androgynous. In addition to the paternal element in the heaven of heavens, the father God is represented in a way that could also speak of restoring the self: "You gather all that I am from my dispersed and distorted state to reshape and strengthen me forever, 'my God my mercy' (Ps. 59:17)" (XII.xvi.23).[108]

Nor is the mother image left out of this part of the sentence, for Augustine has already proclaimed, "I shall not turn away until in that peace of this dearest mother, where are the firstfruits of my spirit (Rom. 8:23) and the source of my certainties, you gather all that I am..." (XII.xvi.23).[109] Mother as the source of certainties: what better expression of the self psychological notion of the function of parents as ideals? For the small child they reassure the endangered self. And the damage to the self can also find expression here, in the phrase, "from my dispersed and distorted shape." A self psychologist could hope to find only rarely such a literary recapitulation of the symbols of the damaged self relying on parental selfobjects for restoration to wholeness.

Augustine calls on God at the opening of book 13, as at the beginning of books 10 through 12. His longing for God and confession of his own humbleness in relationship to God again resound with the tones of injured grandiosity: "You had no need of me. I do not possess such goodness as to give you help, my Lord and my God" (XIII.i.1).[110] Yet the book repeats image after image of ways God brings the unworthy to communion with God. The gift of the Holy Spirit can bear people up above the earth, bringing them close to God. They can approach the ideal by moving from ordinary good works to contemplation. Not only could they—and Augustine—thereby find unconscious cohesion in God as an idealizable selfobject, but they are promised that their own goodness could be increased, and that hope could have an unconscious effect of soothing injured grandiosity: "may we...'appear as lights in the world' (Phil. 2:15) by adhering to the solid firmament of your scripture. For there you hold conversation with us..." (XIII.xviii.22).[111]

But Augustine's ideas also speak of relationships to other people, similar to himself. These allow the inference that people of the church represent alter ego selfobjects to him. As he evokes the examples that spiritual people can offer and the behaviors in which they engage and the judgments they can render, he conjures up images of people like himself. Even the people who have not attained standing as spiritual can be seen as representations of what Augustine himself once was, and so serve as distorted images of earlier alter ego selfobjects: "They pursue the same end of temporal and earthly felicity. This purpose dominates everything they do, even though the innumerable variety of their anxieties makes them fluctuate from one thing to another" (XIII.xvii.20).[112] What description could more closely resemble Augustine in his earlier years?

Yet, as one would expect in a psychoanalytically interpreted symbol, the statement of the problem appears with the sketch of the solution. Augustine can imagine other people like himself and calm his unconscious concerns about the instability of his deepest unconscious coherence. As he moves himself and his readers on the conscious level closer and closer to the final images of rest in the One, he also reviews the problem: "For our sins were over us, and we had abandoned you to sink into a dark depth" (XIII.xxxiv.49).[113] These words could easily cloak an expression of failed idealizing. And the inability to do good, which would speak of injured grandiosity, reappears near the very end of the book—and includes unsuccessful idealizing at the same time: "At one time we were moved to do what is good, after our heart conceived through your Spirit. But at an earlier time we were moved to do wrong and to forsake you...Of your gift we have some good works, though not everlasting." So the words could communicate some healing to grandiosity—"we have some good works"—but they move quickly to further idealizing. No human agency, no angelic power, can help people to understand this. Only God can do so: "Only you can be asked, only you can be begged, only on your door can we knock (Matt. 7:7–8)" (XIII.xxxviii.53).[114] In depicting God as the only help for the human race, Augustine can also arrive at a disguised representation of the help for his unconscious self, sometimes teetering on the brink of fragmentation.

While Augustine would produce many more representations in which we could perceive his unconscious, threatened self over the course of his life, he allows us to see here how the ills of the human race, understood in conscious, culturally available, and not unreasonable terms, could also represent his own inner turmoil. They seem to give him enough unconscious cohesion, as well as conscious intellectual satisfaction, to carry on his work of writing, preaching, and helping to lead the church in times of threat and division. They allow him to make a certain peace with his own discomfort and to accept a level of distress that many a psychologist today would see as illness. They render a powerful symphony in the *Confessions*, not without discord, but also not without glorious force and remarkable passages of resolution.

CHAPTER 9

Reflections on Hearing
Music in Life

We have studied how the psychological themes of the many and the One could have been established in Augustine's early childhood, then shifted and rearranged themselves throughout his early adulthood. Would these insights apply to other aspects of our knowledge of Augustine, such as his later texts or early texts not addressed in this book? Surely the analysis just completed finds limits to its validity in the strengths and weaknesses of the application of its conclusions to the rest of Augustine's life. As Margaret Miles suggests in her own musical metaphor for the interpretation of the *Confessions*, "Necessarily discussed seriatim, text, context, and subtext must subsequently be mixed, as the separate instruments on different soundtracks are mixed, if the music of the text is to be heard in its full strength and beauty."[1] How much more this observation fits the study of a life, and how much more difficult it becomes.

Summarizing the understandings developed thus far and testing them against a few of Augustine's other writings is possible, but checking all of them at once is not. So let us look at a brief set of examples, then see if the insights from analysis of Augustine's writings will generalize further. This would be a step toward the appropriation that Ricoeur says will bring the interpretive process to a close, if only for the moment.[2] Can we discover something to appropriate for our own lives? What can this study imply for those of us who would rather not spend our whole lives as water buffalo listening to an orchestra?

Regarding Augustine

Briefly reviewed, what we have seen is that "the many and the One" was a theme that became available to Augustine through Neoplatonic philosophy when he was about thirty years old. It fit with Ambrose's preaching of the gospel, which made more sense than any biblical exposition he had heard before. It allowed the expression and resolution in symbolic words and ideas of certain unconscious distresses that appear to have persisted since his childhood. Before he had these words available, he had a hint of them in the idea of philosophy or wisdom as a beauty drawing him to itself. But most often in his late adolescence, his life seems to have been absorbed by the many aspects of culture, society, and himself. These, according to his own account, kept him preoccupied, but not happy. He was ambitious and successful and seems to have maintained his energy and creativity by means of what Kohut and self psychology have taught us to call grandiosity. His ideals themselves promoted his grandiose aspirations. Yet, under pressure from the many demands of his successful life and the representation to him of a Christian life by people he loved and admired, especially Monica and Ambrose, and with the intellectual assistance of Christian Neoplatonism, he substituted new ideals for his old ones. These new ideals allowed grandiosity to assume a secondary position in his psyche as they took over the guidance of his ambitions and projects. Yet the analysis of the last books of his *Confessions*, written when he was in his mid-forties, suggests that the unconscious distresses persisted and expressed themselves in disguised form. Although his adherence to Christianity and his devotion to the Christian God maintained the balance of idealizing over grandiosity and helped channel his energies in service to the church, its people, and its God, Christianity did not allow him to escape the unconscious distresses of his past.

The debt to interpretive theory in this psychological interpretation of Augustine's life and work deserves recollection. I acknowledged at the outset that Paul Ricoeur's view of symbols in *Freud and Philosophy* influenced my treatment of symbols. The key point in Ricoeur's work for the study of Augustine is the idea that symbols express in a single, transmittable structure both unconscious meanings and conscious guidance for human life. This understanding has an affinity to views that conceive of culture as a system of symbols, but I have held out for a conception of culture as more than that also. The naming of culture as "guidance for life" comes from Ricoeur, but I have expanded and specified his conceptualization by drawing on other understandings. Similarly, his acceptance of Freud's techniques for interpreting the unconscious influences in symbols has become my own, except that I add to it other potential meanings than the sexual ones on which Freud concentrated.

This approach to symbols has several important implications for a psychological study of historical figures. It suggests the importance of looking at symbols in the products that people of the past have bequeathed to us, for example in Augustine's texts. It endorses trying to understand the surface content of these products, that is, what the person meant them to communicate and accomplish, their intersections with other aspects of culture, and their role in the social world. It also implies that a person's legacy may encompass much more than a straightforward account of an activity or a moment. Hence, autobiographical writings, like the *Confessions*, ought not to be thought of primarily as historical records. Instead they come to our awareness as personal reconstitutions of cultural materials that already exist, as social and political tools and compromises, as statements of value in the material and moral aspects of our lives. Given Ricoeur's understanding, they also contain disguised expressions of unconscious distresses and intimations of the solution desired for that distress. Similar considerations would apply to other contributions by the person being studied to the cultural storehouse, contributions like treatises, sermons, letters.

European and American schools of psychology lose track too easily of this dynamic interchange between individuals and their milieu. To understand Augustine psychologically requires tracing not only the unconscious influences in his life, but also the ideals that the ancient world had held up to its schoolchildren for generations, the patterns of self-expression encouraged for learned people, the possibilities that Neoplatonism offered his thinking, and the openings for it to intersect with Christianity. One must also develop at least an awareness of the social pressures, the genuine possibilities for exercise of abilities, the unavoidable restrictions fashioned by the predecessors of the society in which Augustine lived and by the society in his own time. We sharpen our accounts of him by taking seriously the facts that he encountered Neoplatonism at a time when he had developed his own intellectual skills by training in rhetoric, that a bishop showed him a way of life and thought that he could not previously conceive coherently, that government service did not offer him a more rich and thoughtful occupation, that marriage was not an institution focused on personal satisfaction, that women were not likely to meet him as intellectual equals and soul mates, and that advancement in a career in either church or state meant relinquishing his relationship with his concubine. We see him less as an individual, thinking about love relationships and choices of careers in the ways we might think. We realize that in response to his society and culture, he was not a child in a candy store who sampled treats, kept some, and threw others, wrapper and all, on the floor. He was a young man of desires of many kinds in a world that presented him a range, but not an infinity, of satisfactions and disappointments. Sometimes the variety of satisfactions obscured the ones that would fulfill his own emotional and intellectual longings. Sometimes the plethora of options still remained devoid of a way for his thoughts and feelings to come to full expression and resolve themselves peacefully.

The theoretical base of my interpretation points us to the idea that cultural and social possibilities and limitations could actually have shaped Augustine's unconscious. The directions and forms of grandiosity and idealizing depended on the openings in society and cultural forms of thought and expression. Where options were closed, then repression would occur and supply both the material and energy for an altered, even distorted, expression of certain urges. Might he not have turned out to be a different person if his family, like Ambrose's, had been rich enough to support his attainment of a provincial governorship without marriage into a wealthier family? Then he would have been able to advance in that career track without courting so many people in high places. Perhaps some of his distress would have eased without the radical change of sending away his concubine, as his engagement presupposed. After all, some other well-known public figures lived for years with concubines; they did not, however, seek to marry into a wealthy family. What if Augustine's philosophical yearnings had met with satisfaction by a system of thought developed by someone other than Plotinus? How different his thoughts might have been if the ideas of Plotinus about the body had been a little less disparaging than the words he offered to one of his followers in response to a request for a painting or sculpture of him: "Why really, is it not enough to have to carry the image in which nature has encased us, without your requesting me to agree to leave behind me a longer lasting image of the image...?"[3]

But, in fact, to aspire in his career meant for Augustine an effort to court powerful and well-to-do friends and a bride and her family. To aspire in philosophy meant to learn from philosophers and theologians who could be read as denigrating the body. In such a world, only some expressions of grandiosity and idealizing would have been open to him, and so his unconscious distresses and desires would have to take routes to conscious expression different from those that, based on our social and cultural backgrounds, we might believe to have been more worthy.

One of the most challenging questions about Augustine, given my interpretation of his life and thought, asks whether he remained bound by his childhood experiences and his infantile unconscious dynamics, or whether he moved on to a mature adult redirection of them, perhaps even a transcendence of them.[4] The answer, I believe, is that the dichotomy is overdrawn. It derives from an old debate in psychological circles about whether Freud's view of the person and other psychoanalytic offshoots of his understanding leave an image of a person bound by unrealistic childhood desires and disappointments. Freud's own view of sublimation has been adduced to suggest that people can actually escape their repressed childhood conflicts through creative or scientific endeavors. Yet the concept of sublimation is itself vexed, and the relationship of repressed infantile conflicts to their supposed sublimation is not always clear in Freud's own writings. I conclude that Augustine still was moved, unknowingly, by his repressed childhood desires and disappointments, even as he became able to draw love of God and love of neighbor into one relatively healing pattern of life and thought.

The alignment of childhood injuries and disappointments as energies flowing into usually mature, sometimes exquisite, forms of adult expression remains very important in this formulation. As Don Browning has pointed out, the terms of psychoanalytic thought, or psychological thought more generally, can never furnish completely the standards to which they allude. What counts as "healthy" or "mature" or "neurotic" depends on judgments that stem from conceptions of the person heavily influenced by philosophy, theology, and other forms of moral and religious thought.[5] Whether Augustine was neurotic, whether he attained to health, what level of maturity he seems to have achieved, all can be answered competently only in terms of more complex systems of thought about persons, society, normalcy, the worth of what passes for normal, standards of the good life, and so on. For Augustine, the changed alignment of childhood injuries and disappointments as they emerged in his adult expression helped him to answer challenges to his ideals and thereby to shape much of the rest of Christian thought. Childhood injuries and disappointments seem to have come to his consciousness, sometimes through veiled apprehensions, in images of longing and visions of what people have longed for—the heaven of heavens, the ascent, the journey back to God—that have moved readers for a millennium and a half.[6]

But complete freedom from residues of childhood experience does not seem to have come to Augustine any more than it does to the rest of us. Why would any of us want it? While these experiences and their unconscious remainders may preserve some of our sorrows and anger and disappointment, they also hold some of the sweetest fantasies of satisfaction, old inarticulate memories of tenderness that never found full conscious expression and understanding, affection still offered if not accepted, and imagination that breathes with hope even if not with realism.

Possibilities for these Thoughts' Illumination of Augustine's Other Writings

Augustine's enduring distresses may seem minor or trivial in the context of the beautiful pattern of expression of the *Confessions*, especially as it has been discussed thus far. Yet other works by Augustine contrast with the *Confessions* in their much less pleasing tone. We have already seen in chapter 7 some evidence of these stresses in Augustine's debate with Fortunatus, the Manichee. An urge to assert himself by hounding Fortunatus suggests to the self psychological observer that he sought unconsciously to redress injured grandiosity. Not all of the injured feelings would have to have arisen from the immediate situation; some could have been called up again from the depths of the unconscious.

Similarly, Augustine goes on the offensive against the Donatists, as for example in the "Psalmus Contra Partem Donati," a song he composed for popular consumption. He accuses the Donatists of trading their souls to Satan and blaming others for their own wrongs.[7] As they emphasized the purity of the church and their uprightness in guarding the church's tradition, they could not help but have felt Augustine's charges as insults. The voice in the *Confessions* beseeching the people of the church who love him to hear him does not resound in his addresses to the Donatists. Pugnacity emerges as he defends his own viewpoint and stands up for what he holds dear. Some of this reaction may well have been a reasonable response to the strife caused by the Donatist controversy, but part of it at least may be the disguised voice of a young child saying, "You're no better than I am," perhaps saying that even to the schoolmasters who beat him for trivial mistakes when they committed greater spiritual wrongs. His wounded and repressed grandiosity may have spoken of its injuries as it displaced its responses onto other people.

In a book written against the Donatist position, *Against the Letters of Petilian, Donatist Bishop of Cirta*, Augustine lets the insults fly. He composed this book after the *Confessions*, so one cannot advance the interpretation that he had not yet developed the beauty of expression or spirit exhibited in the *Confessions*. One should admit, however, that his adversary, Petilian, provokes him. By the same token one must concede that Augustine does not succeed in rising much above Petilian's insulting level. In one passage, Petilian has called the Catholics snakes, because they had cooperated with an imperial campaign, eventually backed by arms, against the schismatic Donatists: "They have truly become vipers, who by their bites have vomited forth death against the innocent people." Augustine's answer sounds here, as in the "Psalmus," as though it carries the tone of a schoolyard taunt: "Pronounce the same judgment against yourselves as coming from us to you." Our inarticulate but expressive childhood phrase, "Same on you," comes to mind. But Augustine the rhetorician and preacher develops the point so far that we cannot really think of his retaliation as just a moment's slip: "For be well assured that this very fact marks in you the nature of vipers, that you have not in your mouth the foundation of truth, but the poison of slanderous abuse, as it is written 'The poison of asps is under their lips.'"[8] Might all the energy in these responses reflect not only his adult annoyance with his long-winded and obstreperous adversaries, but also his own unconscious injured grandiosity? In fact Augustine's language does sometimes sound like it might reflect the schoolmasters' touchy debates that he mentioned in the *Confessions*. For instance, he answers Petilian not just on the facts of the dispute or the grounds for it, but also in regard to his style: "But let us look at how garrulously he has set these things out, as though he will very easily uproot and overthrow our points."[9] If his schoolmasters argued about such things, then we could see here a cultural pattern that, beyond its general application, allows the individual expression of an offended sense of his own goodness, that is to say, a representation of injured grandiosity.[10]

Yet some of the beauty in the rhetoric of the *Confessions* does occur in other works. *On Christian Doctrine*, written during the same years as the *Confessions*, includes themes drawn from Augustine's cultural resources that show up also in his theological autobiography. For instance, in explaining his famous distinction between use and enjoyment (*uti* and *frui*),

Augustine develops a simple definition through an accessible and lovely metaphor. He notes: "To enjoy something is to cling to it with love for its own sake. To use something, however, is to employ it in obtaining that which you love, provided that it [what you are trying to obtain] is worthy of love." A more intuitive elaboration builds on these ideas:

> Suppose we were wanderers who could not live in blessedness except at home, miserable in our wandering and desiring to end it and return to our native country. We would need vehicles for land and sea which could be used to help us reach our homeland, which is to be enjoyed. But if the amenities of the journey and the motion of the vehicles itself delighted us, and we were led to enjoy those things which we should use, we should not wish to end our journey quickly, and, entangled in a perverse sweetness, we should be alienated from our home country, whose sweetness would make us blessed.

In this passage, Augustine is talking about human error as much as he is in his debate with Petilian. But here he implicitly includes himself gently in the people in error by using the first person plural. He lets the reader see why erring would appeal to "us," instead of treating it as an abhorrent aberration: it is filled with delights, although his point is clear that they constitute "a perverse sweetness." In addition, he has reminded his readers of their putative desire for their "home country," of its "sweetness [that] would make us blessed." The chiding tone and combative attitude shown toward Petilian have no place in this passage as Augustine returns the reader to a way of avoiding this predicament: "Thus in this mortal life, wandering from God, if we wish to return to our native country where we can be blessed we should use this world and not enjoy it, so that the 'invisible things' of God 'being understood by the things that are made' may be seen, that is, so that by means of corporal and temporal things we may comprehend the spiritual and eternal."[11] He returns here to the scripture, as he does in his response to Petilian, but only to draw the reader into the ascent toward God that he saw also in Neoplatonism. In fact, he uses cultural resources we have already seen: Plotinus' metaphor of life as a journey back to God and the story of the prodigal son.

If both restorative and distressful images and ideas appear in Augustine's writings, why can we discern different balances of them in these various works? The reason that might be advanced by a reading of surface content alone also offers a key to the self psychological interpretation: Augustine replies in *Against the Letters of Petilian* to an attack on his thoughts and reasoning. While he also replies to critics in the *Confessions* and *On Christian Doctrine*, his main focus lies elsewhere, on confession of sin, praise, and God's goodness, or on instructing people about how to read the Bible. These latter goals engage his strengths for the ends that he would like to pursue. They invite him to use his treasured capacities for meditation and introspection, for study of the scripture and its exposition. They bring to mind the value of an appeal to other people's love. All of these activities could also facilitate moments of unconscious narcissistic wholeness. Concentrating on one's gifts and skills can reverberate with unconscious grandiosity. Grandiosity, as Kohut explains it, gives people a sense of their own goodness, but does not need to imply a sick preoccupation with oneself. Drawing up his strengths in these writing projects could afford him an unconscious as well as conscious self-satisfaction that would manifest itself in the development of verbal symbols of restoration and wholeness. By the same token, Petilian's insulting approach to Augustine could threaten his internal sense of well-being, at the same time that it consciously provoked him. The unconscious recollections of injured grandiosity then would express themselves easily in disguise through the sarcasm, anger, and attack seen in *Against the Letters of Petilian*.

Social as well as personal dimensions of these works also bear reflection as we try to understand how they might manifest different tones and different implications of the work of the unconscious in Augustine's writings. Augustine wrote the *Confessions* with a Christian and generally charitable audience in mind, although he notes that some unfriendly readers may peruse his book. He composed *On Christian Doctrine* for young people learning to be preachers or teachers of Christianity. The audiences for both of these works, then, could serve as alter ego selfobjects or mirroring selfobjects.[12] Augustine could imagine people as he wrote who either bore an essential likeness to him in their Christianity and their efforts to live a life pleasing to God, or who would reflect back to him the value of the ideals he espoused in his books.

Petilian and the Donatists would have represented an opposite kind of person. They reflected an essential unlikeness in their insistence on maintaining a separate communion from the Catholic Church. They also opposed the value of the church that Augustine saw in its inclusion of humanity tainted by a history of sin. Petilian, moreover, later attacked Augustine's personal history.[13] The Donatists of the early 390s may have stirred up even more unconscious feeling for Augustine by evoking the image of church as mother,[14] an image we have seen replayed in the *Confessions* and Augustine's aligning of Monica with the church. Therefore, when they condemned the Catholic Church, they also struck unwittingly at Augustine's unconscious association of Monica with the church and his idealization of her, which would have helped him compensate for the diminution of her idealized status resulting from her lower social standing. The self, Kohut would lead us to believe, often will not submit to such threats. Instead the person consciously, without knowing all the unconscious sources of his or her demeanor, retaliates in coldness, arrogance, or aggression. Accounting for Augustine's tone in these works can encompass these considerations of potentials for blows to his unconscious self.

Appropriations

Peter Brown has called the *Confessions* the "self-portrait of a convalescent,"[15] of Augustine trying to heal himself of all the stresses and sorrows of his earlier life. Brown by no means reduces the book to this feature only, but highlights it as a particular function of the work for Augustine. Brown's comment has made sense to many scholars, especially to those psychoanalytically inclined, as he encourages us to think about the readjustment of life at a time near its halfway point.[16] But to Augustine healing meant the collection of the soul by continence, as that was given lovingly by God, and as it facilitated the soul's loving return to God. Only by loving rightly, using what should be used and enjoying what should be enjoyed, being "an unprejudiced assessor of the intrinsic value of things," as one who "neither loves what should not be loved nor fails to love what should be loved,"[17] could a person ascend back toward God. And only by God's loving gift of the Holy Spirit and the continence it bestowed (X.iiix.40) could one love rightly. In this love one would love one's neighbor, caring, as book 13 says, for the neighbor's bodily needs and for justice. Such love would serve as a step toward loving God, the only true source of satisfaction for all our human desires, the only object of love we could have without danger of its loss. As he says in *On Christian Doctrine*: "Thus, loving his neighbor as himself, he refers the love of both to that love of God which suffers no stream to be led away from it by which it might be diminished."[18] Hence the many delights that might draw people away, or the duties that they might allow to distract them from God, should all be funneled back toward God by being joined and ordered under the direction of love for God helped by God's grace.

I would urge, therefore, that we learn from the study of Augustine something about human life more generally. A descriptive study like the present one can show us that the meaning in Augustine's life appears to resonate with injuries to grandiosity and disappointed idealizing that can persist into middle age. We also see that such injuries and disappointments need not detract from meaning, but can give a passion to expression of thoughts and desires that appeals to later readers. The unconscious materials may also highlight possibilities and directions in conscious adult thought that otherwise would have escaped attention. Once brought to notice, even in disguise, they can be available for added development. They enter, as Ricoeur argues, into creative activities that shape culture by leading to new direction and guidance for human life.

So how could we finish our lives without resembling water buffalo listening to an orchestra? The events of our lives may still outstrip our ability to comprehend them, but we retain also the capacity to hear simpler or more complex discords and harmonies and perceive them, or maybe just experience them, in a symphonic whole. The essential contributors to our doing so seem to be terms and images that help to give a conscious perspective on the larger issues of life and to encompass its smaller occurrences in so doing. These terms and images, however, are most likely to attain to harmonic fullness when they can absorb, transform, and redefine our unconscious injuries and disappointments and help us to carry on our lives with other people. As our unconscious injuries and disappointments lead us to refine consciously the terms and images we discover in our culture, our contributions to culture can carry more experience and wisdom to our human kindred who encounter the expressions and ways of life we have shaped.

Many of our relationships with other people, even our simple interchanges, could become more instructive to us and lead us to greater empathy and wisdom if we applied more widely this model developed to understand Augustine. Empathy and wisdom, Kohut suggested, come from transformed narcissism. Narcissism for each of us could undergo transformation as we work with this model. For instance, it suggests that someone with whom we disagree may draw on very different cultural resources from our own. Although that person's disagreement might feel like a blow to our grandiosity or ideals, we can assimilate the hurt more easily if we realize that the opposing viewpoint expresses less a desire to upset us than a piece of a complex and interrelated view of the world and a manifestation of disguised aspects of the person's own past. Similarly, alas, with our triumphs. The urge to see ourselves, obnoxiously at times, as the best and most important person on the block, most worthy of admiration and most privy to the truth, can subside to manageable proportions—without having to be clubbed into submission—if we recognize again that other people's laudatory responses to us and our accomplishments derive from their own history of desire, disappointment, and wishes for fulfillment, as well as from a social and cultural background.[19] Persuasion and conflict might both have a better chance of delicacy and successful outcomes if a wider vision of the factors leading to people's present perspectives could be taken into account.

Yet despite the lovely words and the hope they mean to convey, our symphonies are fragile compositions at best. Whether they can withstand the Vandal invasion of Hippo, or cataclysms nearer our own day, like the Holocaust, genocide, or totalitarianism, can never be known in advance. Perhaps they should not be asked to do so. They are dependent creations, as we are, drawing on knowledge, imagination, cultural resources, social interchange, and patterns of human interaction. Destruction of cultural patterns and social life, or even simple but intense discouragement, can endanger these sources of meaning. Sometimes damage from the larger social and cultural environment can impinge so deeply on the psyche as to disrupt the human capacity to use the sources that remain and to develop new ones.

Nonetheless, Augustine's life and thought and this study of it unite with other human expressions to suggest that our fragile compositions of meaning in life can speak to those we love or could want to love. Here I propose that we learn something from Augustine's own view of healing. Recombination and elaboration of meaning can be nurtured by our lives with each other. The results can be passed from land to land and from generation to generation. Institutions today, like the church in his era, have important roles as preparers of people to discover and then to make this meaning. Institutions can guard the meaning already made. They can, although they often do not, preserve and nurture the people who preserve and nurture other people as they shape meaning. Cultural products, even if ignored for decades or misunderstood for centuries, lie waiting in cultural storehouses to help someone expand a theme of hardship or joy into a harmony of life. Perhaps we can love, in the sense of doing the good with respect to each other, by promoting justice in and through our institutions and preserving and nourishing the opportunities for cultural resources to incorporate discords and use them as leading tones resolving into new harmonies.

If I had a water buffalo that seemed to like the symphony—or jazz or rock and roll, for that matter—I would turn on a stereo in its vicinity with its favorite music. Having been taught by Augustine, we could do a great deal more for each other than we would for our animal kindred. We could act on love for our neighbors, offer care for their bodies and instruction for their minds, and discover joy in their apprehension of music in their lives. We could apply our conscious efforts to hearing the music of our own lives, even if we never perceive its unconscious sources. We might even discover in these efforts an approach to God in the company and service of our neighbors—human, animal, inanimate, and those already hallowed beyond this earthly life.

Bibliography

Primary Sources

Ambrose. *Death as a Good.* Translated by Michael P. McHugh. *Fathers of the Church,* vol. 65. 69–113. Washington, D.C.: Catholic University of America Press, 1972. *De bono mortis (On the Good of Death).* Edited by Jacques Paul Migne. *Patrologiae Cursus Completus, Series Latina,* vol. 14. 539–568. Paris, 1845.

————. *Jacob and the Happy Life.* Translated by Michael P. McHugh. *Fathers of the Church,* vol. 65. 117–184. Washington, D.C.: Catholic University of America Press, 1972. *De Jacob et vita beata.* Edited by Jacques Paul Migne. *Patrologiae Cursus Completus, Series Latina,* vol. 14. 597–640. Paris, 1845.

————. *Letters.* Translated by Mary Melchior Beyenka. *Fathers of the Church,* vol. 26. New York: Fathers of the Church, 1954. *Epistolae.* Edited by Jacques Paul Migne. *Patrologiae Cursus Completus, Series Latina,* vol. 16. Paris, 1845.

Aristotle. *Nicomachean Ethics.* Translated with an Introduction and notes by Terence Irwin. Indianapolis, Ind.: Hackett Publishing, 1985.

Augustine. *Acts or Disputation Against Fortunatus the Manichaean.* Translated by Albert H. Newman. Edited by Philip Schaff. *Nicene and Post-Nicene Fathers of the Christian Church,* vol. 4. 113–124. Grand Rapids, Mich.: William B. Eerdmans Publishing Co., 1887 (1979). *Acta seu Disputatio Contra Fortunatum Manichaeum.* Edited by Jacques Paul Migne. *Patrologiae Cursus Completus, Series Latina,* vol. 42. 111–130. Paris, 1841 (392).

————. *Against the Academics.* Translated and annotated by John J. O'Meara. *Ancient Christian Writers,* no. 12. New York and Ramsey, N.J.: The Newman Press, 1951. *Contra academicos.* Edited by Jacques Paul Migne. *Patrologiae Cursus Completus, Series Latina,* vol. 32. 905–958. Paris, 1841.

————. *Answer to the Letters of Petilian, Donatist Bishop of Cirta.* Translated by J. R. King. Edited by Philip Schaff. *Nicene and Post-Nicene Fathers of the Christian Church,* vol. 4. 519–628. Grand Rapids Mich.: William B. Eerdmans Publishing Co., 1887 (1979). *Contra litteras petiliani donatistae Cirtensis episcopi.* Edited by Jacques Paul Migne. *Patrologiae Cursus Completus, Series Latina,* vol. 43. 245–388. Paris, 1846.

————. *City of God.* Translated by Marcus Dodds. Introduction by Thomas Merton. New York: The Modern Library, 1950. *De civitate dei, Libri XXII.* Edited by Jacques Paul Migne. *Patrologiae Cursus Completus, Series Latina,* vol. 41. Paris, 1845.

————. *Confessions.* Edited with an Introduction by James J. O'Donnell. Vol. 1, *Introduction and Text.* New York: Oxford University Press, Clarendon Press, 1992.

————. *Confessions.* Translated with an Introduction and Notes by Maria Boulding. Edited by John E. Rotelle. *The Works of Saint Augustine: A Translation for the 21st Century* vol. 1. Hyde Park, N.Y.: New City Press, 1997.

————. ————. Translated with an Introduction and notes by Henry Chadwick. Oxford and New York: Oxford University Press, 1991; World's Classics, 1992.

————. ————. Translated with an introduction by R. S. Pine-Coffin. New York: Dorset Press, 1961.

————. ————. Texte de l'édition de M. Skutella. Introduction et notes par A. Solignac. Traduction de E. Tréhorel et G. Bouissou. *Bibliothèque*

Augustinienne, Oeuvres de saint Augustin. 13–14. Paris: Desclée de Brouwer, 1962.

_____. _____. Translated by Rex Warner. Introduction by Vernon J. Bourke. New York: The New American Library, Mentor Books, 1963.

_____. _____. Translated by William Watts. The Loeb Classical Library, vols. 26 and 27. Cambridge: Harvard University Press and London: William Heinemann Ltd., 1989 (1631).

_____. *Divine Providence and the Problem of Evil.* Translated by Robert P. Russell. *Fathers of the Church,* vol. 5. 239–332. New York: Cima Publishing Co., 1948. *De ordine (On Order).* Edited by Jacques Paul Migne. *Patrologiae Cursus Completus, Series Latina,* vol. 32. 977–1020. Paris, 1841.

_____. *Faith and the Creed.* In *Augustine: Earlier Writings.* Translated and edited with Introductions by John H. S. Burleigh. Library of Christian Classics. 349–369. Philadelphia: Westminster Press, Ichthus Edition, 1953. *De fide et symbolo.* Edited by Jacques Paul Migne. *Patrologiae Cursus Completus, Series Latina,* vol. 40. 181–196. Paris, 1845.

_____. *The Good of Marriage.* Translated by Charles T. Wilcox. In *Treatises on Marriage and Other Subjects,* Roy J. Deferrari. *Fathers of the Church,* vol. 27. 9–51. Washington, D.C.: Catholic University of America Press, 1969 (1955). *De bono conjugali.* Edited by Jacques Paul Migne. *Patrologiae Cursus Completus, Series Latina,* vol. 40. 373–396. Paris, 1845.

_____. *The Happy Life.* Translated by Ludwig Schopp. *Fathers of the Church,* vol. 5. 43–84. New York: Cima Publishing Company, 1948. *De beata vita.* Edited by Jacques Paul Migne. *Patrologiae Cursus Completus, Series Latina,* vol. 32. 959–976. Paris, 1841.

_____. *Letters.* Translated by Sister Wilfred Parsons. In *Saint Augustine: Letters,* volume 1 (1–82). *Fathers of the Church,* vol. 12. New York: Fathers of the Church, 1951. *Epistolae.* Edited by Jacques Paul Migne. *Patrologiae Cursus Completus, Series Latina,* vol. 33. Paris, 1845.

_____. *On Baptism, Against the Donatists.* Translated by J. R. King. Edited by Philip Schaff. *Nicene and Post-Nicene Fathers,* vol. 4. 411–514. Grand Rapids, Mich.: William B. Eerdmans Publishing Co., 1887 (1979). Edited by Jacques Paul Migne. *Patrologiae Cursus Completus, Series Latina,* vol. 43. Paris, 1841.

_____. *On Christian Doctrine.* Translated by D. W. Robertson, The Library of Liberal Arts. Indianapolis: Bobbs-Merrill Educational Publishing, 1958. Edited by Jacques Paul Migne. *Patrologiae Cursus Completus, Series Latina,* vol. 34. 15–122. Paris, 1845.

_____. *On Free Will.* In *Augustine: Earlier Writings.* Translated and edited with Introductions by John H.S. Burleigh. The Library of Christian Classics. 102–217. Philadelphia: Westminster Press, Ichthus Edition, 1953. *De Libero Arbitrio.* Edited by Jacques Paul Migne. *Patrologiae Cursus Completus, Series Latina,* vol. 32. 1121–1310. Paris, 1841.

_____. *On the Morals of the Catholic Church.* Translated by Richard Stothert. Edited by Philip Schaff. *Nicene and Post-Nicene Fathers,* vol. 4. 41–63. Grand Rapids, Mich.: William B. Eerdmans Publishing Co., 1887 (1979). *De moribus ecclesiae catholicae.* Edited by Jacques Paul Migne. *Patrologiae Cursus Completus, Series Latina,* vol. 32. 1309–1378. Paris, 1841.

_____. *(On the Psalms). St. Augustine on the Psalms.* Translated and annotated by Scholastica Hebgin & Felicitas Corrigan. *Ancient Christian Writers,* nos. 29 and 30. New York and Ramsey, N.J.: Newman Press, 1960. *Ennarationes in Psalmos.* Edited by Jacques Paul Migne. *Patrologiae Cursus Completus, Series Latina,* vol. 37. Paris, 1845.

_____. *Propositions from the Epistle to the Romans (Expositio quarundam propositionum ex Epistola ad Romanos).* In *Augustine on Romans: Propositions from the Epistle to the Romans; Unfinished Commentary on the Epistle to the Romans.* Translated and edited by Paula Fredriksen Landes. Society of Biblical Literature, Texts and Translations, no. 23. Early Christian Literature Series, no. 6. 2–49. Chico, Calif.: Scholars Press, 1982.

_____. ("Psalm Against the Party of Donatus.") "Psalmus contra Partem Donati." Edited by Jacques Paul Migne. *Patrologiae Cursus Completus, Series Latina,* vol. 43. Paris, 1841.

_____. *Retractations.* Translated by Mary Inez Bogan. *Fathers of the Church,* vol. 60. Washington, D.C.: The Catholic University of America Press, 1968. *Retractationes.* Edited by Jacques Paul Migne. *Patrologiae Cursus Completus, Series Latina,* vol. 32. 583–656. Paris, 1841.

_____. *Sermons I (1–19) on the Old Testament.* Introduction by Michele Pellegrino. Translated with notes by Edmund Hill. Edited by John E. Rotelle. *The Works of Saint Augustine: A Translation for the 21st Century.* Brooklyn, N.Y.: New City Press, 1990. *Sermons II (20–50) on the Old Testament.* Translated with notes by Edmund Hill. Edited by John E. Rotelle. *The Works of Saint Augustine: A Translation for the 21st Century.* Brooklyn, N.Y.: New City Press, 1990. *Sermones.* Edited by Jacques Paul Migne. *Patrologiae Cursus Completus, Series Latina,* vol. 38. Paris, 1841.

_____. *Soliloquies.* In *Augustine: Earlier Writings.* Translated and edited with Introductions by John H. S. Burleigh. Library of Christian Classics. 23–63. Philadelphia: Westminster Press, Ichthus Edition, 1953. *Soliloquiorum, libri II.* Edited by Jacques Paul Migne. *Patrologiae Cursus Completus, Series Latina,* vol. 32. 869–904. Paris, 1841.

_____. *The Teacher.* In *Augustine: Later Works.* Translated with Introductions by John Burnaby. Library of Christian Classics. 69–101. Philadelphia: Westminister Press, Ichthus Edition, 1955. *De Magistro.* Edited by Jacques Paul Migne. *Patrologiae Cursus Completus, Series Latina,* vol. 32. 1193–1220. Paris, 1841.

_____. *Ten Homilies on the First Epistle General of St. John.* In *Augustine: Later Works.* Translated with Introductions by John Burnaby. Library of Christian Classics. 259–348. Philadelphia: Westminister Press, Ichthus Edition, 1955. *In Epistolam Joannis ad Parthos Tractatus X.* Edited by Jacques Paul Migne. *Patrologiae Cursus Completus, Series Latina,* vol. 35. 1977–2062. Paris, 1845.

_____. *To Simplician—on Various Questions.* Book I. In *Augustine: Earlier Writings.* Translated and edited with Introductions by John H. S. Burleigh. Library of Christian Classics. 376–406. Philadelphia: Westminster Press, Ichthus Edition, 1953. *De Diversis Quaestionibus ad Simplicianum.* Edited by Jacques Paul Migne. *Patrologiae Cursus Completus, Series Latina,* vol. 40. 101–148. Paris, 1841.

_____. *Unfinished Commentary on the Epistle to the Romans (Epistolae ad Romanos Inchoata Expositio).* In *Augustine on Romans: Propositions from the Epistle to the Romans; Unfinished Commentary on the Epistle to the Romans.* Translated and edited by Paula Fredriksen Landes. Society of Biblical Literature, Texts and Translations, no. 23. Early Christian Literature Series, no. 6. 52–89. Chico, Calif.: Scholars Press, 1982.

_____. *The Usefulness of Belief.* In *Augustine: Earlier Writings.* Translated and edited with Introductions by John H. S. Burleigh. Library of Christian Classics. 284–323. Philadelphia: Westminster Press, Ichthus Edition, 1953. *De Utilitate Credendi.* Edited by Jacques Paul Migne. *Patrologiae Cursus Completus, Series Latina,* vol. 42. 65–92. Paris, 1841.

Ausonius. *Ausonius: Volume II*. Translated by Hugh G. Evelyn White. Loeb Classical Library, 115. Cambridge: Harvard University Press, and London: William Heinemann Ltd., 1967 (1921).

Cicero. *Laelius sive De amicitia dialogus*. Edited with an Introduction by H. E. Gould and J. L. Whiteley. London: Macmillan and New York: St. Martin's Press, 1968.

Codex Theodosianus. In *Corpus iuris Romani anteiustiniani*, vol. 2. Preface by Eduard Böcking. Darmstadt: Scientia Verlag Aalen, 1987.

Gregory of Nyssa. *Life of Macrina*. In *St. Gregory of Nyssa: Ascetical Works*. Translated by Virginia Woods Callahan. *FOC*, 58. 163–191. Washington, D.C.: Catholic University of America Press, 1967.

Paulinus of Milan. *Vita Ambrosii*. In *Paulin de Milan et la "Vita Ambrosii": Aspects de la religion sous le Bas-Empire*. Translated and edited by Émilien Lamirande. Paris: Desclée, and Montréal: Bellarmin, 1983.

Plotinus. *Enneads*, I.1–9. In *Plotinus. I: Porphyry on the Life of Plotinus and the Order of His Books, Enneads I.1–9*. Translated by A.H. Armstrong. Loeb Classical Library, vol. 440. 89–325. Cambridge: Harvard University Press, 1989. *Enneads*, V. In *Plotinus. V: Enneads V.1–9*. Loeb Classical Library, vol. 444. Cambridge: Harvard University Press, and London: William Heinemann, 1984. *Enneads*, VI. In *Plotinus. VI: Enneads VI.1–5*. Loeb Classical Library, vol. 445. Cambridge: Harvard University Press, and London: William Heinemann, 1988.

Porphyry. *On the Life of Plotinus*. In *Plotinus. I. Porphyry on the Life of Plotinus and the Order of His Books, Enneads I.1–9*. Translated and edited by A. H. Armstrong. Loeb Classical Library. 89–325. Cambridge: Harvard University Press, 1989.

Possidius. *Sancti Augustini Vita Scripta a Possidio Episcopo*. Edited with revised text, Introduction, notes, and an English version by Herbert T. Weiskotten. Princeton: Princeton University Press, 1919.

Schaff, Philip, Ed. *A Select Library of the Nicene and Post-Nicene Fathers of the Christian Church. Vol. IV: St. Augustine: The Writings against the Manichaeans and against the Donatists*. Grand Rapids, Mich.: Wm. B. Eerdmans Publishing Company, 1979 (1887).

Teresa of Avila. *The Life of Teresa of Jesus: The Autobiography of St. Teresa of Avila*. Translated and edited with an Introduction by E. Allison Peers. Garden City, N.Y.: Doubleday, Image Books, 1960.

Secondary Sources

Archambault, Paul J. "Augustine's *Confessiones*: On the Uses and the Limits of Psychobiography." In *Collectanea Augustiniana: Augustine: "Second Founder of the Faith."* Edited by Joseph C. Schnaubelt and Frederick Van Fleteren. 83–99. New York: Peter Lang, 1990.

Asmussen, Jes P., editor and translator. *Manichaean Literature: Representative Texts, Chiefly from Middle Persian and Parthian Writings*. Persian Heritage Series, no. 22. Ehsan Yar-Shater, General Editor. Delmar, N.Y.: Scholars' Facsimiles & Reprints, 1975.

Babcock, William S. "Patterns of Roman Selfhood: Marcus Aurelius and Augustine of Hippo." *Perkins Journal* 29 (Winter 1976):1–19.

Bakan, David. "Some Thoughts on Reading Augustine's *Confessions.*" *Journal for the Scientific Study of Religion* 5 (October 1965): 149–152.

Barbour, John. *Versions of Deconversion: Autobiography and the Loss of Faith.* Charlottesville and London: University Press of Virginia, 1994.

Bauman, Zygmunt. "Class, Social." In *The Social Science Encyclopedia*, 2nd ed. Edited by Adam Kuper and Jessica Kuper. London: Routledge & Kegan Paul, 1996.

Bennett, Camille. "The Conversion of Vergil: The *Aeneid* in Augustine's *Confessions.*" *Revue des Études Augustiniennes* 34 (1988):47–69.

Berger, Peter L., and Luckmann, Thomas. *The Social Construction of Reality: A Treatise in the Sociology of Knowledge.* Garden City, N.Y.: Doubleday & Company, Anchor Books, 1967 (1966).

Binns, J. W., Ed. *Latin Literature of the Fourth Century.* Greek and Latin Studies: Classical Literature and its Influence. Edited by C. D. N. Costa and J. W. Binns. London and Boston: Routledge and Kegan Paul, 1974.

Bonner, Gerald. *St Augustine of Hippo: Life and Controversies.* The Library of History and Doctrine. Philadelphia: Westminster Press, 1963.

Brett, Michael, and Elizabeth Fentress. *The Berbers.* Oxford: Blackwell, 1996.

Brittan, Arthur. "Society." In *The Social Science Encyclopedia.* Edited by Adam Kuper and Jessica Kuper. 794–795. London: Routledge & Kegan Paul, 1985.

Brown, Peter. *Augustine of Hippo: A Biography.* Berkeley and Los Angeles: University of California Press, 1967.

————. *The Body and Society: Men, Women, and Sexual Renunciation in Early Christianity.* Lectures on the History of Religions, N.S. 13. New York: Columbia University Press, 1988.

————. "Religious Coercion in the Later Roman Empire: The Case of North Africa." *History* 48 (October 1963): 283–305.

————. *The World of Late Antiquity: From Marcus Aurelius to Muhammad.* London: Thames and Hudson, 1971.

Browning, Don S. "The Psychoanalytic Interpretation of St. Augustine's *Confessions*: An Assessment and New Probe." In *Psychiatry and the Humanities*, vol. 2, *Psychoanalysis and Religion.* Edited by Joseph H. Smith, associate editor Susan A. Handelman. 136–159. Baltimore and London: The Johns Hopkins University Press, 1990.

————. *Religious Thought and the Modern Psychologies: A Critical Conversation in the Theology of Culture.* Philadelphia: Fortress Press, 1987.

Burnaby, John. *"Amor Dei": A Study of the Religion of St. Augustine.* London: Hodder & Stoughton, 1938.

Burns, J. Patout. *The Development of Augustine's Doctrine of Operative Grace.* Paris: Études Augustiniennes, 1980.

Burrell, David. "Reading *The Confessions* of Augustine: An Exercise in Theological Understanding." *The Journal of Religion* 50 (October 1970): 327–351.

Capps, Donald. "Augustine as Narcissist: Some Comments on Paul Rigby's 'Paul Ricoeur, Freudianism and Augustine's *Confessions.*'" *Journal of the American Academy of Religion* 53 (Spring 1985): 115–127.

————. "Augustine's *Confessions*: The Scourge of Shame and the Silencing of Adeodatus." In *Hunger of the Heart.* Edited by Donald Capps and James E. Dittes. 69–92.

_____. "Parabolic Events in Augustine's Autobiography." *Theology Today* 40 (October 1983): 260–272.

_____. "Symposium on Augustine's *Confessions*." *Journal for the Scientific Study of Religion* 25 (March 1986): 56–115.

_____ and James E. Dittes, editors. *The Hunger of the Heart: Reflections on the "Confessions" of Augustine*. Society for the Scientific Study of Religion Monograph Series, no. 8. West Lafayette, Ind.: Society for the Scientific Study of Religion, 1990.

Chadwick, Henry. "History and Symbolism in the Garden at Milan." In *From Augustine to Eriugena: Essays on Neoplatonism and Christianity in Honor of John O'Meara*. Edited by F. X. Martin and J. A. Richmond. Washington, D.C.: Catholic University of America Press, 1991.

_____. "On Re-reading the *Confessions*." In *Saint Augustine the Bishop*. Edited by Fannie LeMoine and Christopher Kleinhenz. 139–160. New York and London: Garland Publishing, 1994.

Clark, Elizabeth A. "Friendship Between the Sexes: Classical Theory and Christian Practice." In *Jerome, Chrysostom and Friends*. 35–106.

_____. "Introduction to 'The Life of Olympias' and 'Sergia's *Narration Concerning St. Olympias*.'" In *Jerome, Chrysostom and Friends*. 107–126.

_____. "Holy Women, Holy Words: Early Christian Women, Social History, and the 'Linguistic Turn.'" *Journal of Early Christian Studies* 6 (1998): 413–430.

_____. *Jerome, Chrysostom and Friends: Essays and Translations*. Studies in Women and Religion, vol. 2. New York and Toronto: Edwin Mellen Press, 1979.

_____. "Theory and Practice in Late Ancient Asceticism: Jerome, Chrysostom, and Augustine." *Journal of Feminist Studies in Religion* 5 (Fall 1989): 25–46.

Cochrane, Charles N. *Christianity and Classical Culture: A Study of Thought and Action from Augustus to Augustine*. London: Oxford University Press, 1940 (paperback 1957).

Courcelle, Pierre. *Recherches sur les Confessions de saint Augustin*. Paris: Éditions de Boccard, 1950.

_____. "Source chrétienne et allusions païennes de l'épisode du 'Tolle, Lege' (Saint Augustin, *Confessions*, VIII, 12, 29)." *Revue d'Histoire et de Philosophie Religieuses* 32 (1952): 171–200.

Cranz, F. Edward. "The Development of Augustine's Ideas on Society before the Donatist Controversy." In *Augustine: A Collection of Critical Essays*. Edited by R. A. Markus. 336–403. Garden City, N.Y.: Doubleday & Company, Anchor Books, 1972.

Crespin, Rémi. *Ministère et sainteté: Pastorale du clergé et solution de la crise donatiste dans la vie et la doctrine de saint Augustin*. Paris: Études Augustiniennes, 1965.

Daly, Lawrence J. "Psychohistory and St. Augustine's Conversion Process: An Historiographical Critique." *Augustinian Studies* (1978): 233–254.

_____. "St. Augustine's *Confessions* and Erik Erikson's *Young Man Luther*: Conversion as 'Identity Crisis.'" *Augustiniana* 31 (1981): 183–196.

Decret, François. *Essais sur l'Église manichéenne en Afrique du Nord et à Rome au temps de saint Augustin: Recueil d'études*. Rome: Institutum Patristicum Augustinianum, 1995 (1989).

_____. "L'utilisation des Épîtres de Paul chez les Manichéens d'Afrique." In *Essais sur l'Église manichéenne en Afrique du Nord et à Rome au temps de saint Augustin: Recueil d'études*. 55–106.

Dittes, James E. "Augustine's Search for a Fail-Safe God to Trust," *Journal for the Scientific Study of Religion* 25 (March 1986): 57–63.

_____. "Continuities Between the Life and Thought of Augustine." *Journal for the Scientific Study of Religion* 5 (October 1965): 130–140.

Dixon, Sandra Lee. "Faith Receiving Understanding: On the Proposition that Augustine's Mother Learned Something." Paper presented to the Rocky Mountain-Great Plains Regional Meeting of the American Academy of Religion and Society of Biblical Literature. Denver, Colo. April 27, 1996.

_____. "The Many Layers of Meaning in Moral Arguments: A Self Psychological Case Study of Augustine's Arguments for Coercion." Ph.D. diss., University of Chicago, 1993.

_____. "Monica and the Psychological Interpretation of Augustine's *Confessions*." 1996.

Dixon, Suzanne. "Infirmitas Sexus: Womanly Weakness in Roman Law." *Tijdschrift Voor Rectsgescheidenis* 52 (1984): 343–371.

Dodds, E.R. "Augustine's Confessions: A Study of Spiritual Maladjustment." *The Hibbert Journal* 26 (1927–1928): 459–473.

Douël, Martial. *L'Algérie romaine: Forums et basiliques*. Paris: Société d'Éditions Géographiques, Maritimes et Coloniales, 1930.

Dudden, F. Homes. *The Life and Times of Saint Ambrose*. 2 Vols. Oxford: Clarendon Press, 1935.

Duval, Noël. "'L'Inhumation privilégiée' en Tunisie et en Tripolitaine." In *L'Inhumation privilégiée du IVe au VIIIe siècle en Occident*. edited by Y. Duval and J.-Ch. Picard, 25–42. Paris: De Boccard, 1986.

Duval, Yvette. "L'Inhumation privilégiée, pour quoi?" In *L'Inhumation privilégiée du IVe au VIIIe Siècle en Occident*. 251–254. Edited by Y. Duval and J.-Ch. Picard Paris: De Boccard, 1986.

Elledge, Paul W. "Embracing Augustine: Reach, Restraint, and Romantic Resolution in the *Confessions*." *Journal for the Scientific Study of Religion* 27 (March 1988): 72–89.

Elson, Miriam, Ed. *The Kohut Seminars on Self Psychology and Psychotherapy with Adolescents and Young Adults*. New York and London: W. W. Norton & Company, 1987.

Erikson, Erik H. *Childhood and Society*. 2nd ed. New York and London: W. W. Norton & Company, 1963.

_____. *Gandhi's Truth: On the Origins of Militant Nonviolence*. New York and London: W. W. Norton & Company, 1969.

_____. *Insight and Responsibility: Lectures on the Ethical Implications of Psychoanalytic Insight*. New York and London: W. W. Norton & Company, 1964.

_____. *Young Man Luther: A Study in Psychoanalysis and History*. New York: W. W. Norton & Company, The Norton Library, 1962.

Fenn, Richard. "Magic in Language and Ritual: Notes on Augustine's *Confessions*." *Journal for the Scientific Study of Religion* 25 (March 1986): 77–91.

Ferrari , Leo C. "The Boyhood Beatings of Augustine," in *Hunger of the Heart*. Edited by Capps and Dittes. 56–67.

Février, Paul-Albert. "Tombes privilégiées en Maurétanie et Numidie," In *L'Ihumation privilégiée du IVe au VIIIe Siècle en Occident*. 13–23. Edited by Y. Duval and J.-Ch. Picard. Paris: De Boccard, 1986.

Finaert, G. "La législation impériale sur le Donatisme jusqu'en 400." In *Traités anti-Donatistes*, vol. 1, *Bibliothèque Augustienne, Oeuvres de saint Augustin*, 28. Paris: Desclée de Brouwer, 1963.

Fredriksen, Paula. "Augustine and his Analysts: The Possibility of a Psychohistory." *Soundings* 61 (Summer 1978): 206–227.

_____. "Beyond the Body-Soul Dichotomy: Augustine on Paul against the Manichees and the Pelagians." *Recherches Augustiniennes* 22 (1988): 87–114.

_____. "Paul and Augustine: Conversion Narratives, Orthodox Traditions, and the Retrospective Self." *Journal of Theological Studies* 37 (April 1986): 3–34.

Freeman, Mark. "History, Narrative, and Life Span Developmental Knowledge." *Human Development* 27 (1984): 1–19.

Frend, W. H. C. *Donatist Church: A Movement of Protest in Roman North Africa*. Oxford: Oxford University Press, 1952.

_____. *The Rise of Christianity*. Philadelphia: Fortress Press, 1984.

Freud, Sigmund. *Civilization and its Discontents*. Translated and edited by James Strachey. New York: W. W. Norton and Company, 1961 (1930).

_____. *Dora: An Analysis of a Case of Hysteria*. Edited with an Introduction by Philip Rieff. New York: Macmillan Publishing Company, Collier Books, 1963 (1905).

_____. *The Ego and the Id*. Translated by Joan Riviere. Revised and edited by James Strachey. New York and London: W. W. Norton and Company, 1960 (1923).

_____. *The Interpretation of Dreams*. Translated and edited by James Strachey. New York: Avon, Discus Books, 1965 (1900).

_____. *The Standard Edition of the Complete Psychological Works of Sigmund Freud*. Translated and edited by James Strachey. Vol. 11, *Leonardo da Vinci and a Memory of his Childhood*. 59–137. London: The Hogarth Press and the Institute of Psychoanalysis, 1957 (1910).

_____. *The Standard Edition of the Complete Psychological Works of Sigmund Freud*. Translated and edited by James Strachey. Vol. 14, *On Narcissism: An Introduction*. 69–102. London: The Hogarth Press and the Institute of Psychoanalysis, 1957 (1914).

_____. *The Origin and Development of Psychoanalysis*. Introduction by Eliseo Vivas. Washington, D.C.: Regnery Gateway, 1965 (1910).

_____. *On Dreams*. Translated by James Strachey. New York: W. W. Norton and Company, 1952 (1901).

_____. *The Standard Edition of the Complete Psychological Works of Sigmund Freud*. Translated and edited by James Strachey. Vol. 14, *The Unconscious*. 161–215. London: The Hogarth Press and the Institute of Psycho-analysis, 1957 (1915).

_____. *Totem and Taboo: Some Points of Agreement between the Mental Lives of Savages and Neurotics*. Translated by James Strachey. New York: W. W. Norton & Company, 1950 (1913).

Gay, Peter. *Freud for Historians*. New York and Oxford: Oxford University Press, 1985.

Gay, Volney. "Augustine: The Reader as Selfobject." *Journal for the Scientific Study of Religion* 25 (March 1986): 64–76.

Gedo, John E., and Arnold Goldberg. *Models of the Mind: A Psychoanalytic Theory.* Chicago and London: University of Chicago Press, 1973.

Geertz, Clifford. *The Interpretation of Cultures.* New York: Basic Books, 1973.

_____. *Islam Observed: Religious Development in Morocco and Indonesia.* Chicago and London: University of Chicago Press, 1968.

_____. "Religion as a Cultural System." In *The Interpretation of Cultures.* 87–125.

_____. "Thick Description: Toward an Interpretive Theory of Culture." In *The Interpretation of Cultures.* 3–30.

Geertz, Hildred. "The Vocabulary of Emotion: A Study of Javanese Socialization Processes." In *Culture and Personality: Contemporary Readings.* Edited by Robert A. Levine. 249–264. Chicago: Aldine Publishing Company, 1974.

Gergen, Kenneth. "Social Understanding and the Inscription of Self." In *Cultural Psychology: Essays on Comparative Human Development.* Edited by James W. Stigler, Richard A. Shweder, and Gilbert Herdt. 569–606. New York: Cambridge University Press, 1990.

Gilson, Étienne. *The Christian Philosophy of Saint Augustine.* Translated by L. E. M. Lynch. New York: Random House, 1960.

Hamman, A.-G. *La vie quotidienne en Afrique du Nord au temps de saint Augustin.* Nouvelle édition. Paris: Hachette, 1979. (Préface 1985.)

Havens, Joseph. "Notes on Augustine's *Confessions.*" *Journal for the Scientific Study of Religion* 5 (October 1965): 141.

Henry, Paul. *The Path to Transcendence: From Philosophy to Mysticism in St. Augustine.* Translated with an Introduction by Francis F. Burch. The Pittsburgh Theological Monograph Series, no. 37. Pittsburgh, Pa.: The Pickwick Press, 1981.

Hopkins, M. K. "Social Mobility in the Later Roman Empire: The Evidence of Ausonious." *Classical Quarterly* 11 (1961): 239–249.

James, William. *The Varieties of Religious Experience: A Study in Human Nature.* Introduction by Reinhold Niebuhr. New York: Macmillan, Collier Books, and London: Collier Macmillan Publishers, 1961 (1902).

Jonte-Pace, Diane. "Augustine on the Couch: Psychohistorical (Mis)readings of the *Confessions.*" *Religion* 23 (1993): 71–83.

Kakar, Sudhir. *The Inner World: A Psycho-Analytic Study of Childhood and Society in India.* 2nd ed. Delhi: Oxford University Press, 1981.

Kaster, Robert A. *Guardians of Language: The Grammarian and Society in Late Antiquity.* Berkeley: University of California Press, 1988.

Kliever, Lonnie D. "Confessions of Unbelief: In Quest of the Vital Lie." *Journal for the Scientific Study of Religion* 25 (March 1986): 102–115.

Kligerman, Charles. "A Psychoanalytic Study of the Confessions of St. Augustine." *Journal of the American Psychoanalytic Association* 5 (1957): 469–484.

Kohut, Heinz. *The Analysis of the Self: A Systematic Approach to the Psychoanalytic Treatment of Narcissistic Personality Disorders.* The Psychoanalytic Study of the Child, Monograph no. 4. New York: International Universities Press, 1971.

_____. "Forms and Transformations of Narcissism. In *The Search for the Self,* vol. 1. Edited with an Introduction by Paul Ornstein. 427–460.

_____. *How Does Analysis Cure?* Edited by Arnold Goldberg with the collaboration of Paul Stepansky. Chicago and London: University of Chicago Press, 1984.

_____. "Introspection, Empathy and the Semi-Circle of Mental Health." *International Journal of Psycho-analysis* 63 (1982): 395–406.

_____. "A Note on Female Sexuality." In *The Search for the Self*, vol. 2. Edited with an Introduction by Paul Ornstein. 783–792.

_____. "'On the Adolescent Process as a Transformation of the Self' by Ernest S. Wolf, John E. Gedo, and David M. Terman: Discussion." In *The Search for the Self*, vol. 2. Edited with an Introduction by Paul Ornstein. 659–662.

_____. "The Psychoanalytic Treatment of Narcissistic Personality Disorders: Outline of a Systematic Approach." In *The Search for the Self*, vol. 1. Edited with an Introduction by Paul Ornstein. 477–509.

_____. "Remarks about the Formation of the Self—Letter to a Student Regarding Some Principles of Psychoanalytic Research." In *The Search for the Self*, vol. 2. Edited with an Introduction by Paul Ornstein. 737–770.

_____. *The Restoration of the Self.* New York: International Universities Press, 1977.

_____. *The Search for the Self: Selected Writings of Heinz Kohut: 1950–1978*, vols. 1 and 2. Edited with an Introduction by Paul Ornstein. New York: International Universities Press, 1978.

_____. *Self Psychology and the Humanities: Reflections on a New Psychoanalytic Approach.* Edited with an Introduction by Charles B. Strozier. New York and London: W. W. Norton & Company, 1985.

_____. "Thoughts on Narcissism and Narcissistic Rage." In *The Search for the Self: Selected Writings of Heinz Kohut: 1950–1978, vol. 2*. Edited with an Introduction by Paul Ornstein. 615–658.

_____. "The Two Analyses of Mr. Z." *International Journal of Psycho-analysis* 60 (1979): 3–27.

_____ and Ernest S. Wolf. "The Disorders of the Self and their Treatment: An Outline." In *Essential Papers on Narcissism*. Edited by Andrew P. Morrison. New York and London: New York University Press, 1986 (1978).

Lamarre, Jean-Marc. "Les Confessions divisées. Discourse du Maître et discours de l'Hystérique dans les *Confessions* de Saint Augustin." In *Saint Augustin*. Edited by Patric Ranson. 337–347. *Les Dossiers H.* Edited by Jacqueline de Roux, Jean-Marie Benoist, and François Denoël. L'Age d'Homme, 1988.

Landes, Paula Fredriksen, Ed. "Introduction." In *Augustine on Romans: Propositions from the Epistle to the Romans; Unfinished Commentary on the Epistle to the Romans.* Society of Biblical Literature, Texts and Translations, no. 23. Early Christian Literature Series, no. 6. ix.–xvi. Chico, Calif.: Scholars Press, 1982.

Legewie, Bernhard. *Augustinus: Eine Psychographie.* Bonn: A. Marcus & E. Webers Verlag, 1925.

_____. "Die körperliche Konstitution und die Krankheiten Augustins." *Miscellanea Agostiniana.* vol. 2 Edited by A. Cassamassa. 5–21. Rome: Tipografia Poliglotta Vaticana, 1931.

MacCormack, Sabine G. *Art and Ceremony in Late Antiquity.* Berkeley: University of California Press, 1981.

_____. *The Shadows of Poetry: Vergil in the Mind of Augustine.* Berkeley: University of California Press, 1998.

MacMullen, Ramsay. *Christianity and Paganism in the Fourth to Eighth Centuries.* New Haven and London: Yale University Press, 1997.

McGinn, Bernard. *The Presence of God: A History of Western Mysticism.* Vol. 1, *The Foundations of Mysticism.* New York: Crossroad, 1992.

McGuire, Brian Patrick. *Friendship and Community: The Monastic Experience 350-1250.* Cistercian Studies Series no. 95. Kalamazoo, Mich.: Cistercian Publications, 1988.

McHugh, Michael P. Introduction. *Jacob and the Happy Life.* In *Saint Ambrose: Seven Exegetical Works. Fathers of the Church* vol. 65. Washington, D.C.: 1972.

MacKendrick, Paul. *The North African Stones Speak.* Chapel Hill, N.C.: University of North Carolina Press, 1980.

McLynn, Neil B. *Ambrose of Milan: Church and Court in a Christian Capital.* Berkeley: University of California Press, 1994.

McMahon, Robert. *Augustine's Prayerful Ascent: An Essay on the Literary Form of the "Confessions."* Athens, Ga., and London: University of Georgia Press, 1989.

McNamara, Marie Aquinas. *Friendship in Saint Augustine.* Studia Friburgensia, edited by H. O. Luthi. n.s. 20. Fribourg, Switzerland: The University Press, 1958.

Madec, Goulven. "Le neveu d'Augustin." *Revue des Études Augustiniennes* 39 (1993): 149–153.

Mahler, Margaret S., Fred Pine, and Anni Bergman. *The Psychological Birth of the Human Infant: Symbiosis and Individuation.* New York: Basic Books, 1975.

Markus, Robert A. "Augustine. Biographical Introduction: Christianity and Philosophy." In *Cambridge History of Later Greek and Early Medieval Philosophy.* Edited by A. H. Armstrong. 341–353. Cambridge: Cambridge University Press, 1967.

_____. "Paganism, Christianity, and the Latin Classics in the Fourth Century." In *Latin Literature of the Fourth Century.* Edited by J. W. Binns. 1–21.

_____. *Saeculum: History and Society in the Theology of St. Augustine.* Cambridge: Cambridge University Press, 1970.

Marrou, Henri-Irénée. *Saint Augustin et la fin de la culture antique.* Paris: Éditions de Boccard, 1938.

_____. *Saint Augustin et la fin de la culture antique* with "Retractatio." Paris: Éditions de Boccard, 1949.

Mayer, Cornelius Petrus. "Confessio—Der Weg des Christen aus der Verflochtenheit von Schuld und Schuldgefühlen bei Augustinus." In *Cassiciacum* vol. 46. *Traditio Augustiniana: Studien über Augustinus und seine Rezeption.* Edited by Adolar Zumkeller and Achim Krümmel. 3–17. Würzburg: Augustinus-Verlag, 1994.

Mead, George Herbert. *On Social Psychology: Selected Papers.* Edited with an Introduction by Anselm Strauss. Chicago and London: University of Chicago Press, 1977.

Melman, Charles. "Saint Augustin antipsychanalyste." In *Saint Augustin.* Edited by Patric Ranson. 332–336. *Les Dossiers H.* Edited by Jacqueline de Roux, Jean-Marie Benoist, and François Denoël. L'Age d'Homme, 1988.

Miles, Margaret R. *Augustine on the Body.* American Academy of Religion Dissertation Series, 31. Series edited by H. Ganse Little, Jr. Missoula, Mont.: Scholars Press, 1979.

_____. *Desire and Delight: A New Reading of Augustine's Confessions.* New York: Crossroad, 1992.

_____. "Infancy, Parenting, and Nourishment in Augustine's *Confessions.*" *Journal of the American Academy of Religion* 50 (September 1982): 349–364.

Monceaux, Paul. *Histoire littéraire de l'Afrique chrétienne depuis les origines jusqu'à l'invasion arabe.* Vol. 4, *Le Donatisme.* Brussells: Culture et Civilisation, 1966; Paris: 1912.

_____. *Histoire littéraire de l'Afrique chrétienne depuis les origines jusqu'à l'invasion arabe.* Vol. 7, *Saint Augustin et le donatisme.* Paris: Éditions Ernest Leroux, 1923.

Nauroy, Gérard. "Le fouet et le miel: Le combat d'Ambroise en 386 contre l'arianisme milanais." *Recherches Augustiniennes* 23 (1988):3–86.

Niño, Andrés G. "Restoration of the Self: A Therapeutic Paradigm from Augustine's *Confessions.*" *Psychotherapy* 27 (Spring 1990): 8–18.

Obeyesekere, Gananath. *Medusa's Hair: An Essay on Personal Symbols and Religious Experience.* Chicago and London: University of Chicago Press, 1981.

_____. *The Work of Culture: Symbolic Transformation in Psychoanalysis and Anthropology.* Chicago and London: University of Chicago Press, 1990.

O'Connell, Robert J. *Art and the Christian Intelligence in St. Augustine.* Cambridge: Harvard University Press, 1978.

_____. *St. Augustine's Confessions: The Odyssey of Soul.* Cambridge: Harvard University Press, Belknap Press, 1969.

_____. *St. Augustine's Early Theory of Man, A.D. 386–391.* Cambridge: Harvard University Press, Belknap Press, 1968.

_____. "The Visage of Philosophy at Cassiciacum." *Augustinian Studies* 25 (1994):65–76.

O'Donnell, James. J. *Augustine: Confessions II: Commentary on Books 1–7. Confessions III: Commentary on Books 8–13.* New York: Oxford University Press, Clarendon Press, 1992.

O'Donovan, Oliver. *The Problem of Self-Love in St.Augustine.* New Haven and London: Yale University Press, 1980.

O'Ferrall, Margaret More. "Monica, the Mother of Augustine: A Reconsideration." *Recherches Augustiniennes* 10 (1975): 23–43.

O'Meara, John J. "The Historicity of the Early Dialogues of Saint Augustine." *Vigiliae Christianae* 5 (July 1951): 150–178.

Outler, Albert C. Introduction. In *Augustine: Confessions and Enchiridion.* Translated and edited by Albert C. Outler. Library of Christian Classics vol. 8. Philadelphia: Westminster Press, 1955.

Parsons, Anne. "Is the Oedipus Complex Universal?" In *Belief, Magic, and Anomie.* 3–63. New York: Free Press, 1969.

Parsons, Talcott. "Psychoanalysis and the Social Structure." In *Essays in Sociological Theory.* 2nd ed. 336–347. Glencoe, Ill.: Free Press, 1954.

Parsons, William B. "St. Augustine: 'Common Man' or 'Intuitive Psychologist'?" *Journal of Psychohistory* 18 (Fall 1990): 155–179.

Poland, Lynn M. "Augustine, Allegory, and Conversion." *Literature and Theology* 2 (February 1988): 37–48.

Power, Kim. *Veiled Desire: Augustine on Women.* New York: Continuum, 1996.

Pruyser, Paul. "Psychological Examination: Augustine." *Journal for the Scientific Study of Religion* 5 (Spring 1966): 284–289.

_____, ed. "St. Augustine's Confessions: Perspectives and Inquiries." *Journal for the Scientific Study of Religion* 5 (October 1965 and Spring 1966): 130–152, 273–289.

Rambo, Lewis R. *Understanding Religious Conversion*. New Haven and London: Yale University Press, 1993.

Ricoeur, Paul. *Freud and Philosophy: An Essay on Interpretation*. Translated by Denis Savage. New Haven and London: Yale University Press, 1970.

_____. "The Model of the Text: Meaningful Action Considered as a Text." In *Interpretive Social Science: A Reader*. Edited by Paul Rabinow and William M. Sullivan. 73–101. Berkeley: University of California Press, 1979.

_____. *Time and Narrative*, vol. 1. Translated by Kathleen McLaughlin and David Pellauer. Chicago and London: The University of Chicago Press, 1984.

Rigby, Paul. "Paul Ricoeur, Freudianism, and Augustine's *Confessions*." *Journal of the American Academy of Religion* 53 (Spring 1985): 93–114.

Rizzuto, Ana-Maria. *The Birth of the Living God: A Psychoanalytic Study*. Chicago: The University of Chicago Press, Phoenix Books, 1979.

Rosaldo, Michelle Z. "Toward an Anthropology of Self and Feeling." In *Culture Theory: Essays on Mind, Self, and Emotion*. Edited by Richard A. Shweder and Robert A. LeVine, 137–157. Cambridge: Cambridge University Press, 1984.

Rouselle, Arline. *Porneia: On Desire and the Body in Antiquity*. Translated by Felicia Pheasant. Oxford: Basil Blackwell, 1988 (1983).

Saller, Richard. "Corporal Punishment, Authority, and Obedience in the Roman Household." In *Marriage, Divorce, and Children in Ancient Rome*. Edited by Beryl Rawson. 144–165. Oxford: Oxford University Press, 1991.

Shanzer, Danuta. "Pears before Swine: Augustine, *Confessions* 2.4.9." *Revue des Études Augustiniennes* 42 (1996): 45–55.

Shaw, Brent D. "The Family in Late Antiquity: The Experience of Augustine." *Past and Present* 115 (May 1987): 3–51.

_____. "The Age of Roman Girls at Marriage: Some Reconsiderations." *Journal of Roman Studies* 77 (1987): 30–52.

Shweder, Richard A. "Cultural Psychology—What Is It?" In *Cultural Psychology: Essays on Comparative Human Development*. Edited by James W. Stigler, Richard A. Shweder, and Gilbert Herdt. 1–43. New York: Cambridge University Press, 1990.

_____, Manamohan Mahapatra, and Joan G. Miller. "Culture and Moral Development." In *The Emergence of Morality in Young Children*. Edited by Jerome Kagan and Sharon Lamb. Chicago: University of Chicago Press, 1987.

_____ and Nancy C. Much. "Determinations of Meaning: Discourse and Moral Socialization." In *Moral Development Through Social Interaction*. Edited by William Kurtines and Jacob Gewirtz. 197–244. New York: Wiley & Sons, 1987.

Solignac, Aimé. "Augustin et la mère d'Adéodat." In *Confessions. Bibliothèque Augustinienne, Oeuvres de saint Augustin* vol. 13. 677–679, n. 22. Paris: Desclée de Brouwer, 1962.

_____. "Doxographies et manuels dans la formation philosophique de saint Augustin." *Recherches Augustiniennes* 1 (1958): 113–148.

_____. "L'Éducation à l'époque d'Augustin." *Bibliothèque Augustinienne, Oeuvres de saint Augustin* vol. 13. 659–661, n. 5. Paris: Desclée de Brouwer, 1962.

_____. "Introduction aux *Confessions*." *Bibliothèque Augustinienne, Oeuvres de saint Augustin* vol. 13. 9–268. Paris: Desclée de Brouwer, 1962.

_____. "Primitiae spiritus." *Bibliothèque Augustinienne, Oeuvres de saint Augustin* vol. 14. 552-555, n. 11. Paris: Desclée de Brouwer, 1962.

Suchocki, Marjorie. "The Symbolic Structure of Augustine's *Confessions*." *Journal of the American Academy of Religion* 50 (September 1982): 365–378.

Sundén, Hjalmar. "Augustine at Cassiciacum: Hearing the Words of Another." *Hunger of the Heart*. Edited by Capps and Dittes. 289–301.

Taylor, Charles. "Interpretation and the Sciences of Man." In *Interpretive Social Science: A Reader*. Edited by Paul Rabinow and William M. Sullivan. 25–71. Berkeley: University of California Press, 1979.

TeSelle, Eugene. "Augustine as Client and Theorist." *Journal for the Scientific Study of Religion* 25 (March 1986): 92–101.

Van der Meer, Frederic. *Augustine the Bishop: The Life and Work of a Father of the Church*. 2nd ed. Translated by Brian Battershaw and G. R. Lamb. London: Sheed and Ward, 1978.

Weintraub, Karl Joachim. "St. Augustine's *Confessions*: The Search for a Christian Self." In *Hunger of the Heart*. Edited by Capps and Dittes. 5–30.

_____. *The Value of the Individual: Self and Circumstance in Autobiography*. Chicago and London: University of Chicago Press, 1978.

Wetzel, James. *Augustine and the Limits of Virtue*. Cambridge: Cambridge University Press, 1992.

Williams, Daniel H. *Ambrose of Milan and the End of the Nicean-Arian Conflicts*. Oxford: Clarendon Press, 1995.

Willis, Geoffrey Grimshaw. *Saint Augustine and the Donatist Controversy*. London: S. P. C. K., 1950.

Winnicott, D. W. *Playing and Reality*. Harmondsworth, Middlesex, U.K.: Penguin Books Ltd., 1980 (1971).

Woollcott, Phillip, Jr. "Some Considerations of Creativity and Religious Experience in St. Augustine of Hippo." *Journal for the Scientific Study of Religion* 5 (Spring 1966): 273–283.

Yarbrough, Anne. "Christianization in the Fourth Century: The Example of Roman Women." In *Studies in Early Christianity*. Edited by Everett Ferguson. Vol. 14, *Women in Early Christianity*. Edited with an Introduction by David M. Scholer. 319–335. New York and London: Garland Publishing, 1993.

Ziolkowski, Eric J. "St. Augustine: Aeneas' Antitype, Monica's Boy." *Literature and Theology* 9 (March 1995): 1–23.

Zumkeller, Adolar. "Die geplante Eheschliessung Augustins und die Entlassung seiner Konkubine: Kulturgeschichtlicher und rechtlicher Hintergrund von conf. 6, 23 und 25." In *Signum Pietatis: Festgabe für Cornelius Petrus Mayer*. Edited by Adolar Zumkeller. 21–35. Würzburg: Augustinus-Verlag, 1989.

Notes

Chapter 1: Augustine for His Time and Ours

[1]*Islam Observed: Religious Development in Morocco and Indonesia* (Chicago and London: University of Chicago Press, 1968), p. 101.

[2]"Religion as a Cultural System," in *The Interpretation of Cultures* (New York: Basic Books, 1973), pp. 119–123.

[3]*Islam Observed*, pp. 111–113.

[4]Capps and Dittes also use music as a metaphor for the *Confessions*, but their preference is jazz, specifically contrasted to symphonic music. Introduction in *The Hunger of the Heart: Reflections on the "Confessions" of Augustine*, ed. Donald Capps and James E. Dittes, Society for the Scientific Study of Religion Monograph Series, no. 8 (West Layfayette, Ind.: Society for the Scientific Study of Religion, 1990), p. xiv.

[5]*Sol.*, I.ii.7.

[6]*The Varieties of Religious Experience: A Study in Human Nature*, with an Introduction by Reinhold Niebuhr (New York: Macmillan, Collier Books, and London: Collier Macmillan Publishers, 1961 [1902]), pp. 147–148.

[7]*Young Man Luther: A Study in Psychoanalysis and History* (New York: W. W. Norton & Company, The Norton Library, 1962), p. 43.

[8]E.g., *The Life of Teresa of Jesus: The Autobiography of St. Teresa of Avila*, trans. and ed. with an Introduction by E. Allison Peers (Garden City, N.Y.: Doubleday, Image Books, 1960), chap.9, pp. 117–118. See the place given to Augustine's conversion—and deconversion—in John Barbour's *Versions of Deconversion: Autobiography and the Loss of Faith* (Charlottesville and London: University Press of Virginia, 1994), pp. 1, 10, 15–16, 140–141.

[9]Karl Joachim Weintraub, *The Value of the Individual: Self and Circumstance in Autobiography* (Chicago and London: University of Chicago Press, 1978), p. 1.

[10]Citations to the *Confessions* will be given in parentheses in the text. Specific information about translations used and the Latin text of quotations will appear in the endnotes.

[11]A useful collection of articles taking these different approaches, as well as an excellent annotated bibliography, is found in Capps and Dittes, eds., *The Hunger of the Heart*.

[12]Paul Henry, *The Path to Transcendence: From Philosophy to Mysticism in St. Augustine*, trans. with an Introduction by Francis F. Burch, Pittsburgh Theological Monograph Series, no. 37 (Pittsburgh, Pa.: Pickwick Press, 1981), pp. 11, 90, 93–94, 100; see also McMahon, who builds his analysis of the *Confessions* on book 13. Robert McMahon, *Augustine's Prayerful Ascent: An Essay on the Literary Form of the "Confessions"* (Athens, Ga., and London: University of Georgia Press, 1989).

[13]Bernhard Legewie, *Augustinus: Eine Psychographie* (Bonn: A. Marcus and E. Webers Verlag, 1925), pp. V, 1–3, and 119–131, esp. n. 9, p. 127, and n. 13, p. 128; see Capps and Dittes, eds., *Hunger of the Heart*, pp. 345–346. A slightly later article by Legewie ("Die körperliche Konstitution und die Krankheiten Augustins," *Miscellanea Agostiniana*, ed. A. Cassamassa (Rome: Tipografia Poliglotta Vaticana, 1931), 2:5–21), is cited by Gerald Bonner, *St. Augustine of Hippo: Life and Controversies*, Library of History and Doctrine (Philadelphia: Westminster Press, 1963), p. 56, n. 1.

[14]E. R. Dodds, "Augustine's Confessions: A Study of Spiritual Maladjustment," *Hibbert Journal* 26 (1927–1928): 466.

[15]Charles Kligerman, "A Psychoanalytic Study of the Confessions of St. Augustine," *Journal of the American Psychoanalytic Association* 5 (1957): 470–471, 475, 480–484.

[16]Ibid., pp. 470–472.

[17]Paul Pruyser, ed., *JSSR* 5 (October 1965):130–152; *JSSR* 5 (Spring 1966): 273–289.

[18]*JSSR* 5 (Spring 1966): 284, 285, 287.

[19]*JSSR* 5 (October 1965): 151.

[20]Ibid., p. 150.

[21]Ibid.

[22]A source available on this point at the time Bakan wrote is Frederic Van der Meer, *Augustine the Bishop: The Life and Work of a Father of the Church*, 2nd ed., trans. Brian Battershaw and G. R. Lamb (London: Sheed and Ward, 1978), pp. 200, 206–208, 571.

[23]*JSSR* 5 (Spring 1966): 283.

[24]Ibid., p. 273.

[25]Ibid., p. 283.

[26]Ibid., p. 276.

[27]Sigmund Freud, *Civilization and its Discontents*, trans. and ed. James Strachey (New York: W. W. Norton and Company, 1961/1930), pp. 70–80; *The Ego and the Id*, trans. Joan Riviere, rev. and ed. James Strachey (New York and London: W.W. Norton and Company, 1960[1923]), pp. 24–25.

[28]"Psychological Examination," pp. 285–287.

[29]Ibid., p. 288.

[30]*JSSR* 5 (October 1965): 138–140, p. 135.

[31]Ibid., p. 137.

[32]Ibid.

[33]"Some Considerations," p. 276.

[34]Ibid., p. 283.

[35]"Continuities," p. 138.

[36]*St. Augustine's Early Theory of Man, A.D. 386-391* (Cambridge: Harvard University Press, Belknap Press, 1968), pp. 68–69, 71–73, 77–79, 82–84.

[37]"Some Thoughts," p. 150.

[38]*JSSR* 5 (October 1965): 143.

[39]"Reading *The Confessions* of Augustine: An Exercise in Theological Understanding," *Journal of Religion* 50 (October 1970): 327–351.

[40]Ibid., pp. 328–329.

[41]Ibid., pp. 336–340.

[42]Ibid., pp. 329–330, 339–340.

[43]"Augustine and his Analysts: The Possibility of a Psychohistory," *Soundings* 61 (Summer 1978): 206–214.

[44]Ibid., pp. 219–223.

[45]"Psychohistory and St. Augustine's Conversion Process: An Historiographical Critique," *Augustinian Studies* (1978): 234–240.

[46]"St. Augustine's *Confessions* and Erik Erikson's *Young Man Luther*: Conversion as 'Identity Crisis,'" *Augustiniana* 31 (1981): 188–196.

[47]Margaret R. Miles, *Augustine on the Body*, American Academy of Religion Dissertation Series, no. 31, series ed. H. Ganse Little, Jr. (Missoula, Mont.: Scholars Press, 1979), e.g., pp. 1, 6, 8, 39, 41, 128.

[48]Margaret R. Miles, "Infancy, Parenting, and Nourishment in Augustine's *Confessions*," *Journal of the American Academy of Religion* 50 (September 1982): 349–351, 360–362. Miles also poses a question much like my own as the setting for her study: "How does a person organize experience so that life does not appear to be a series of unrelated emotion-generating incidents?" (p. 350).

[49]"Parabolic Events in Augustine's Autobiography," *Theology Today* 40 (October 1983): 260–272. Capps cites Fredriksen's "Augustine and his Analysts."

[50]"Paul Ricoeur, Freudianism, and Augustine's *Confessions*," *Journal of the American Academy of Religion* 53 (Spring 1985): 93.

[51]Ibid., p. 94.

[52]Ibid., pp. 99, n. 3, 106, 111.

[53]In addition to the analysis below, see Don S. Browning, "The Psychoanalytic Interpretation of St. Augustine's *Confessions*: An Assessment and New Probe," in *Psychiatry and the Humanities*, vol. 2, *Psychoanalysis and Religion*, ed. Joseph H. Smith, associate editor Susan A. Handelman (Baltimore and London: The Johns Hopkins University Press, 1990), pp. 136–159.

[54]Donald Capps, ed. "Symposium on Augustine's *Confessions*," *JSSR* 25 (March 1986): 56.

[55]"Augustine as Client and Theorist," *JSSR* 25 (March 1986): 92–101.

[56]"Confessions of Unbelief: In Quest of the Vital Lie," *JSSR* 25 (March 1986): 102–115.

[57]"Magic in Language and Ritual: Notes on Augustine's *Confessions*," *JSSR* 25 (March 1986): 77–91.

[58]James E. Dittes, "Augustine's Search for a Fail-Safe God to Trust," *JSSR* 25 (March 1986): 57–63.

[59]"Augustine: The Reader as Selfobject," *JSSR* 25 (March 1986): 64–76.

[60]Lynn M. Poland, "Augustine, Allegory, and Conversion," *Literature and Theology* 2 (February 1988): 37–48.

[61]Paul W. Elledge, "Embracing Augustine: Reach, Restraint, and Romantic Resolution in the *Confessions*," *JSSR* 27 (March 1988): 73.

[62]Ibid., e.g., pp. 75 and 77 for earlier Freudian studies, pp. 77 ("play out her [Monica's] script"), and 83 ("the primacy of authentic feeling") for language reflecting twentieth-century assumptions.

[63]Charles Melman, "Saint Augustin antipsychanalyste," in *Saint Augustin*, ed. Patric Ranson, *Les Dossiers H*, ed. Jacqueline de Roux, Jean-Marie Benoist, et François Denoël (L'Age d'Homme, 1988), pp. 332–336; and Jean-Marc Lamarre, "Les Confessions divisées. Discours du Maître et discours de l'Hystérique dans les *Confessions* de Saint Augustin," in *Saint Augustin*, ed. Patric Ranson, pp. 337–347.

[64]"Augustine's *Confessiones*: On the Uses and the Limits of Psychobiography," in *Collectanea Augustiniana: Augustine: "Second Founder of the Faith*," ed. Joseph C. Schnaubelt and Frederick Van Fleteren (New York: Peter Lang, 1990), pp. 84–90.

[65]Ibid., pp. 91–95.

[66]"St. Augustine: 'Common Man' or 'Intuitive Psychologist'?" *Journal of Psychohistory* 18 (Fall 1990): 170–177.

[67]Ibid., pp. 166–168.

[68]"Restoration of the Self: A Therapeutic Paradigm from Augustine's *Confessions*," *Psychotherapy* 27 (Spring 1990): 8–18.

[69]"The Psychoanalytic Interpretation of St. Augustine's *Confessions*: An Assessment and New Probe," in *Psychiatry and the Humanities*, vol. 2, *Psychoanalysis and Religion*, ed. Joseph H. Smith, associate editor Susan A. Handelman (Baltimore and London: Johns Hopkins University Press, 1990), pp. 156–157.

[70]Ibid., pp. 145–154.

[71]See note 4 above. See the editors' interesting comments on the origins of the psychological study of Augustine in a seminar conducted by Dittes and attended by Capps (p. ix).

[72]"St. Augustine's *Confessions*: The Search for a Christian Self," in *Hunger*, pp. 5–30; originally published in Weintraub's *The Value of the Individual*, pp. 18–48.

[73]In *Hunger*, pp. 86–87.

[74]"Augustine on the Couch: Psychohistorical (Mis)readings of the Confessions," *Religion* 23 (1993): 72.

[75]*Hunger*, p. viii.

[76]For some of the problems, see, for instance, Paul Ricoeur, "The Model of the Text: Meaningful Action Considered as a Text," in *Interpretive Social Science: A Reader*, ed. Paul Rabinow and William M. Sullivan (Berkeley: University of California Press, 1979), pp. 78–80, 91, 97–101; Charles Taylor, "Interpretation and the Sciences of Man," in *Interpretive Social Science*, ed. Rabinow and Sullivan, pp. 31–39; and by extension from the field of the original argument, Clifford Geertz, "Thick Description: Toward an Interpretive Theory of Culture," in *The Interpretation of Cultures* (New York: Basic Books, 1973), pp. 9–10, 28–30.

[77]The additional, very serious issue of whether one ought to expect any unity of the person, as implied by the question "Who is Augustine?" will be taken up in the next chapter.

[78]Capps and Dittes also use a musical metaphor to capture some of the complexity of Augustine's thought; they apply it to his composition of the *Confessions* (*Hunger*, p. xiv).

[79]Paul Ricoeur, *Freud and Philosophy: An Essay on Interpretation*, trans. Denis Savage (New Haven and London: Yale University Press, 1970), pp. 514–524; see also Gananath Obeyesekere, *Medusa's Hair: An Essay on Personal Symbols and Religious Experience* (Chicago and London: University of Chicago Press, 1981), pp. 33–37, 115, 120; and idem, *The Work of Culture: Symbolic Transformation in Psychoanalysis and Anthropology* (Chicago and London: University of Chicago Press, 1990), pp. xviii, 15–17, 22–23.

[80]This understanding is fairly close to Parsons' definition of "social structure." See "Psychoanalysis and the Social Structure," in *Essays in Sociological Theory*, 2nd ed. (Glencoe, Ill: Free Press, 1954), 337. See also Arthur Brittan, "Society," in *The Social Science Encyclopedia*, ed. Adam Kuper and Jessica Kuper (London: Routledge & Kegan Paul, 1985), 794–795.

[81]Parsons, "Psychoanalysis and the Social Structure," p. 337.

[82]Peter L. Berger and Thomas Luckmann, *The Social Construction of Reality: A Treatise in the Sociology of Knowledge* (Garden City, N.Y.: Doubleday & Company, Anchor Books, 1967 [1966]), pp. 72–73.

[83]Parsons, "Psychoanalysis and the Social Structure," pp. 337–338; Berger and Luckmann, *Social Construction*, pp. 54–55.

[84]Saint Augustine, *Confessions*, trans. with an Introduction and notes by Henry Chadwick, World's Classics (Oxford and New York: Oxford University Press, World's Classics, 1992 [1991]), p. 181. "sed quis adhuc ego sim, ecce in ipso tempore confessionum mearum, et multi hoc nosse cupiunt qui me noverunt et non me noverunt, qui ex me vel de me aliquid audierunt…" Augustine, *Confessions*, vol. 1, *Introduction and Text*, 3 vols., ed. James J. O'Donnell (New York: Oxford University Press, Clarendon Press, 1992), p. 120. Chadwick's translation and O'Donnell's Latin editions will be the texts of the *Confessions* most often quoted. Chadwick's is the most readily available of the more recent English translations and O'Donnell's text is the most recent and certainly one of the most authoritative editions of the Latin.

[85]See Ricoeur, *Freud and Philosophy*, pp. 509–510, 521–524.

[86]Obeyesekere, *Medusa's Hair*, pp. 33, 36–37, 169–182.

[87]Chadwick, p. 181. "indicabo me talibus…amet in me fraternus animus quod amandum doces, et doleat in me quod dolendum doces. animus ille hoc faciat fraternus, non extraneus, non filiorum alienorum quorum os locutum est vanitatem et dextera eorum dextera iniquitatis, sed fraternus ille, qui cum approbat me, gaudet de me, cum autem improbat me, contristatur pro me…" (O'Donnell, I:120).

[88]Sigmund Freud, *The Interpretation of Dreams*, trans. and ed. James Strachey (New York: Avon, Discus Books, 1965/1900), pp. 313, 318, 328, 355–356, 364–365, 634–635.

[89]Ibid., pp. 340–343.

[90]Ibid., pp. 584–588.

[91]Sigmund Freud, *The Origin and Development of Psychoanalysis*, with an Introduction by Eliseo Vivas (Washington, D.C.: Regnery Gateway, 1965/1910), pp. 46–59; among others, see also *Dora: An Analysis of a Case of Hysteria*, ed. with an Introduction by Philip Rieff (New York: Macmillan Co., Collier Books, 1963/1905), pp. 22, 39; and *Interpretation of Dreams*, pp. 360–361, 382; but see disclaimers on pp. 194–195, and p. 194, n. 1.

[92]Ibid., pp. 324–338, 585–586; *Dora*, pp. 42–45.

[93]For elucidation of cases, see Margaret S. Mahler, Fred Pine, and Anni Bergman, *The Psychological Birth of the Human Infant: Symbiosis and Individuation* (New York: Basic Books, 1975), pp. 124–194; Ana-Maria Rizzuto, *The Birth of the Living God: A Psychoanalytic Study* (Chicago: The University of Chicago Press, Phoenix Books, 1979), pp. 93–173; for additional claims about therapeutic efficacy, see Heinz Kohut, "The Two Analyses of Mr. Z," *International Journal of Psycho-analysis* 60 (1979): 3–27; D. W. Winnicott, *Playing and Reality* (Harmondsworth, Middlesex, U.K.: Penguin Books, 1980/1971), pp. 24–29.

[94]Chadwick, p. 181. "tu autem, domine,…miserere mei secundum magnam misericordiam tuam propter nomen tuum et nequaquam deserens coepta tua consumma imperfecta mea" (O'Donnell, I:120).

[95]Ibid., pp. 181–182. "Hic est fructus confessionum mearum, non qualis fuerim sed qualis sim, ut hoc confitear non tantum coram te, secreta exultatione cum tremore et secreto maerore cum spe, sed etiam in auribus credentium filiorum hominum, et ego id ago factis et dictis, id ago sub alis tuis…parvulus sum, sed vivit semper pater meus et idoneus est mihi tutor meus" (O'Donnell, I:121).

[96]*Civilization and its Discontents*, pp. 19, 73–74.

[97]See note 7 above and *Gandhi's Truth: On the Origins of Militant Nonviolence* (New York and London: W. W. Norton & Company, 1969).

[98]Sudhir Kakar, *The Inner World: A Psycho-Analytic Study of Childhood and Society in India*, 2nd ed. (Delhi: Oxford University Press, 1981), pp. 160–181. My thanks to Dr. Kakar for encouragement to reread *Young Man Luther* before beginning the work that has led to this book (personal communication, spring 1988).

[99]Erik Erikson, *Childhood and Society*, 2nd ed. (New York and London: W. W. Norton & Company, 1963), esp. chaps. 2, 3, 4, 7.

[100]"Is the Oedipus Complex Universal?" in *Belief, Magic, and Anomie* (New York: Free Press, 1969), pp. 3–63.

[101]*Young Man Luther*, pp. 43 and 102.

[102]Kenneth Gergen, "Social Understanding and the Inscription of Self," in *Cultural Psychology: Essays on Comparative Human Development*, ed. James W. Stigler, Richard A. Shweder, and Gilbert Herdt (New York: Cambridge University Press, 1990), pp. 584–585.

[103]Richard A. Shweder, "Cultural Psychology—What Is It?" in *Cultural Psychology: Essays on Comparative Human Development*, ed. James W. Stigler, Richard A. Shweder, and Gilbert Herdt (New York: Cambridge University Press, 1990), p. 24.

[104]"Toward an Anthropology of Self and Feeling," in *Culture Theory: Essays on Mind, Self, and Emotion*, ed. Richard A. Shweder and Robert A. LeVine (Cambridge: Cambridge University Press, 1984), pp. 144–145.

[105]Richard A. Shweder, Manamohan Mahapatra, and Joan G. Miller, "Culture and Moral Development," in *The Emergence of Morality in Young Children*, ed. Jerome Kagan and Sharon Lamb (Chicago: University of Chicago Press, 1987), pp. 48–49.

[106]One useful resource for this project would be William S. Babcock, "Patterns of Roman Selfhood: Marcus Aurelius and Augustine of Hippo," *Perkins Journal* 29 (Winter 1976): 1–19.

[107]For comments on the temperament, see *AOH*, pp. 31–32, 203; Van der Meer, pp. 10, 196. See by contrast Miles, *Augustine on the Body*, pp. 6–7.

[108]On the notion that twentieth-century Euro-American psychology involves preferences regarding normality see, for example, Don S. Browning, *Religious Thought and the Modern Psychologies: A Critical Conversation in the Theology of Culture* (Philadelphia: Fortress Press, 1987).

[109]*Work of Culture*, xviii, 10–24, 51–68.

[110]Ricoeur, *Freud and Philosophy*, pp. 9–13.

Chapter 2: The Many and the One, Person and World

[1]See, for example, the Ten Commandments' injunction to have no other gods—only one! (Ex. 20:2–3, Deut. 5:6–7). Jn. 1:1–3 confirms the oneness of God and the Word, generally identified as Christ, and the belief that all things depend on God for their existence. See also among many others Jn. 17:3, 20–24, on the oneness of the Father and the Son and of the followers of Jesus on earth with both the Father and the Son.

[2]For examples of the changes of power during the first half of Augustine's life, see Neil B. McLynn, *Ambrose of Milan: Church and Court in a Christian Capital* (Berkeley: University of California Press, 1996), pp. 195–202, 223–232; also Sabine G. MacCormack, *Art and Ceremony in Late Antiquity* (Berkeley, Calif.: University of California Press, 1981), pp. 12–13, 99, 110–111.

[3]See F. Homes Dudden, *The Life and Times of St. Ambrose* (Oxford: Clarendon Press, 1935), II:414–421; Daniel H. Williams, *Ambrose of Milan and the End of the Nicene-Arian Conflicts* (Oxford: Clarendon Press, 1995), pp. 130–131.

[4]Dudden, *Life and Times of St. Ambrose*, I:79–80; Williams, *Ambrose*, pp. 130–131.

[5]Unrest to the south in North Africa was possible also. Michael Brett and Elizabeth Fentress, *The Berbers* (Oxford: Blackwell, 1996), pp. 70–79.

[6]See Brown, *WLA*, pp. 41, 122–124; MacCormack, *Art and Ceremony*, pp. 216–217, and plate 17.

[7]See Zygmunt Bauman, "Class, Social," in *The Social Science Encyclopedia*, 2nd ed., ed. Adam Kuper and Jessica Kuper (London: Routledge & Kegan Paul, 1996), p. 90. For a definition more closely tied to wealth than my own, see M. K. Hopkins, "Social Mobility in the Later Roman Empire: The Evidence of Ausonius," *Classical Quarterly* 11 (1961): 239.

[8]Hopkins, "Social Mobility," p. 240.

[9]For examples on wealth, see Augustine, *CA*, I.i.2, II.ii.3, II.ii.6; Gregory of Nyssa, *Life of Macrina*, 20, *FOC*, 58, *Saint Gregory of Nyssa: Ascetical Works*, pp. 177–178; wealth and family together are mentioned by Elizabeth A. Clark, "Friendship Between the Sexes: Classical Theory and Christian Practice," pp. 35–106, and Introduction to "The *Life of Olympias* and Sergia's *Narration Concerning St. Olympias*," pp. 107–126, in *Jerome, Chrysostom and Friends: Essays and Translations*, Studies in Women and Religion 2 (New York and Toronto: Edwin Mellen Press, 1979); Dudden, *Saint Ambrose*, I:22–56 (and especially the references); Anne Yarbrough, "Christianization in the Fourth Century: The Example of Roman Women," in *Studies in Early Christianity*, ed. Everett Ferguson, vol. 14, *Women in Early Christianity*, ed. with an Introduction by David M. Scholer (New York and London: Garland Publishing, 1993), pp. 320–321 and 324–327.

[10]R. A. Markus, "Paganism, Christianity and the Latin Classics in the Fourth Century," in *Latin Literature of the Fourth Century*, ed. J. W. Binns, Greek and Latin Studies: Classical Literature and Its Influence (London and Boston: Routledge and Kegan Paul, 1974), pp. 9, 13; Martial Douël, *L'Algérie romaine: Forums et basiliques* (Paris: Société d'Éditions Géographiques, Maritimes et Coloniales, 1930), pp. 114–117.

[11]Dudden, I:43; Augustine, *CA*, I.i.2.

[12]Hopkins, "Social Mobility," pp. 239–240, 242–245.

[13]Brown, *WLA*, pp. 26–28.

[14]Dudden, I:88–91.

[15]Dudden, I:98–101; Brown, *WLA*, p. 36.

[16]*Vita*, 1, p. 41; "de numero curialium parentibus honestis…" (p. 40).

[17]*S.*, 356.13; Brent D. Shaw, "The Family in Late Antiquity: The Experience of Augustine," *Past and Present* 115 (May 1987): 8–10.

[18]*S*, 356.4.

[19]Elizabeth A. Clark, "Theory and Practice in Late Ancient Asceticism: Jerome, Chrysostom, and Augustine," *Journal of Feminist Studies in Religion* 5 (Fall 1989): 39, 41–44.

[20]Shaw, "The Family," pp. 29–31.

[21]*Sol*, I.x.17, while this passage seems to speak of Augustine's earlier desire, he must have thought it would make sense to his intended audience; on education, see Elizabeth Clark, "Friendship," 71; also Brent D. Shaw, "The Age of Roman Girls at Marriage," *Journal of Roman Studies* 77 (1987): 37–39.

[22]Shaw, "The Family," pp. 23–24, 28, 31.

[23]Augustine, *Ep.*, 35.4.

[24]Augustine, *DBC*, 5.5; Peter Brown, *The Body and Society: Men, Women and Sexual Renunciation in Early Christianity*, Lectures on the History of Religions, N.S. 13 (New York: Columbia University Press, 1988), pp. 389–390; Yarbrough, "Christianization in the Fourth Century," pp. 326–327; Adolar Zumkeller, "Die geplante Eheschliessung Augustins und die Entlassung seiner Konkubine," in *Signum Pietatis: Festgabe für Cornelius Petrus Mayer*, ed. Adolar Zumkeller (Würzburg: Augustinus-Verlag, 1989), pp. 25–27.

[25]Robert A. Kaster, *Guardians of Language: The Grammarian and Society in Late Antiquity* (Berkeley: University of California Press, 1988), pp. 39–43, 51–52.

[26]*DUC*, vii.16; Brown, *WLA*, p. 32; Kaster, *Guardians*, pp. 104–10, 130–132, and, by contrast, pp. 123–125, 132–134.

[27]*Guardians of Language*, pp. 13–14.

[28]*AOH*, pp. 92-93.

[29]The relations of pagans and Christians during the fourth and fifth centuries, their mutual influence and their hostilities, are subjects of much discussion. See, among many others, J. W. Binns, ed., *Latin Literature of the Fourth Century*, Greek and Latin Studies: Classical Literature and Its Influence (London and Boston: Routledge and Kegan Paul, 1974); Charles Norris Cochrane, *Christianity and Classical Culture: A Study of Thought and Action from Augustus to Augustine* (London: Oxford University Press, 1940; paperback, 1957); Ramsay MacMullen, *Christianity and Paganism in the Fourth to Eighth Centuries* (New Haven and London: Yale University Press, 1997); Anne Yarbrough, "Christianization in the Fourth Century."

[30]W. H. C. Frend, *The Rise of Christianity* (Philadelphia, Pa.: Fortress, 1984), pp. 702–704; see *CTh*, XVI.x.12 for further evidence of the persistence of paganism.

[31]*DDC*, II.xix.29–xxiv.37; see also Frederic Van der Meer, *Augustine the Bishop: The Life and Work of a Father of the Church*, 2nd ed., trans. Brian Battershaw and G. R. Lamb (London: Sheed and Ward, 1978), pp. 56–75.

[32]Van der Meer, *Augustine the Bishop*, pp. 37–38.

[33]Jes P. Asmussen, ed. and trans., *Manichaean Literature: Representative Texts Chiefly from Middle Persian and Parthian Writings* (Delmar, N.Y.: Scholars' Facsimiles & Reprints, 1975), pp. 11-12, 39-40; Peter Brown, *WLA*, p. 164.

[34]See, inter alia, *Ep.*, 43 and 44, PL, 33, 159–180.

[35]For further information on the Donatist controversy, see Gerald Bonner, *St. Augustine of Hippo: Life and Controversies*, The Library of History and Doctrine (Philadelphia: Westminster Press, 1963); Peter Brown, "Religious Coercion in the Later Roman Empire: The Case of North Africa," *History* 48 (October 1963): 283–305; G. Finaert, "La législation impériale sur le Donatisme jusqu'en 400," *Traités anti-Donatistes*, vol. 1, *Bibliothèque Augustinienne, Oeuvres de saint Augustin* 28 (Paris: Desclée de Brouwer, 1963); W. H. C. Frend, *Donatist Church: A Movement of Protest in Roman North Africa* (Oxford: Oxford University Press, 1952); and Paul Monceaux, *Histoire littéraire de l'Afrique chrétienne depuis les origines jusqu'à l'invasion arabe*, vol. 4, *Le Donatisme* (Brussells: Culture et Civilisation, 1966; Paris: 1912); and vol. 7, *Saint Augustin et le donatisme* (Paris: Éditions Ernest Leroux, 1923). For Augustine's texts, some with extensive quotations from Donatist writers, see *Nicene and Post-Nicene Fathers of the Christian Church*, vol. 4 (Grand Rapids, Mich.: William B. Eerdmans Publishing Co., 1887 [1979]); and Jacques Paul Migne, ed., *PL*, vol. 33 (Paris, 1841).

[36]Despite insistence on broad similarities in the culture of late antiquity, regional variations in various aspects of life are often noted; see Suzanne Dixon, "Infirmitas Sexus: Womanly Weakness in Roman Law," *Tijdschrift voor Rectsgescheidenis* 52 (1984): 359; Yvette

Duval, "L'Inhumation privilégiée, pour quoi?" in *L'Inhumation privilégiée du IVe au VIIIe siècle en occident*, ed. Y. Duval and J.-Ch. Picard (Paris: De Boccard, 1986), p. 251; Paul-Albert Février, "Tombes privilégiées en Maurétanie et Numidie," in op. cit., p. 19; Kaster, *Guardians*, pp. 38–39.

[37]Noël Duval, "'L'Inhumation privilégiée' en Tunisie et en Tripolitaine," in *L'Inhumation privilégiée du IVe au VIIIe siècle en occident*, ed. Y. Duval and J.-Ch. Picard (Paris: De Boccard, 1986), p. 29.

[38]My translation, with help from Chadwick, p. 52, and Maria Boulding, trans., *The Confessions*, ed. John E. Rotelle, *The Works of Saint Augustine: A Translation for the 21st Century*, I/1 (Hyde Park, N.Y.: New City Press, 1997), p. 92. "seducebamur et seducebamus, falsi atque fallentes in variis cupiditatibus, et palam per doctrinas quas liberales vocant, occulte autem falso nomine religionis, hic superbi, ibi superstitiosi, ubique vani, hac popularis gloriae sectantes inanitatem, usque ad theatricos plausus et contentiosa carmina et agonem coronarum faenearum et spectaculorum nugas et intemperantiam libidinum, illac autem purgari nos ab istis sordibus expetentes, cum eis qui appellarentur electi et sancti afferremus escas de quibus nobis in officina aqualiculi sui fabricarent angelos et deos per quos liberaremur" (O'Donnell, I:33).

[39]*CTh*, XVI.v.3.

[40]First sentence, my translation; then Chadwick, pp. 104–105. "disponens ea inventa relinquere omnes vanarum cupiditatum spes inanes et insanias mendaces…non vacat legere… antemeridianis horis discipuli occupant: ceteris quid facimus? cur non id agimus? sed quando salutamus amicos maiores, quorum suffragiis opus habemus? quando praeparamus quod emant scholastici? quando reparamus nos ipsos relaxando animo ab intentione curarum?" (O'Donnell, I:68).

[41]Kaster, *Guardians of Language*, pp. 75, 112; Brown, *AOH*, pp. 115–116.

[42]Kenneth Gergen, "Social Understanding and the Inscription of Self," in *Cultural Psychology: Essays on Comparative Human Development*, eds. James W. Stigler, Richard A. Shweder, and Gilbert Herdt (New York: Cambridge University Press, 1990), pp. 585–586.

[43]George Herbert Mead, *On Social Psychology: Selected Papers*, ed. with an Introduction by Anselm Strauss (Chicago and London: University of Chicago Press, 1977), pp. 13, 15–18, 33.

[44]Chadwick, p. 61. "quoquoversum se verterit anima hominis, ad dolores figitur alibi praeterquam in te, tametsi figitur in pulchris extra et extra se. quae tamen nulla essent, nisi essent abs te. quae oriuntur et occidunt et oriendo quasi esse incipiunt, et crescunt ut perficiantur, et perfecta senescunt et intereunt: et non omnia senescunt, et omnia intereunt. Ergo cum oriuntur et tendunt esse, quo magis celeriter crescunt ut sint, eo magis festinant ut non sit: sic est modus eorum" (O'Donnell, I:38–39).

[45]Ibid., p. 62, except the last sentence. "laudet te ex illis anima mea, deus, creator omnium, sed non in eis figatur glutine amore per sensus corporis. eunt enim quo ibant, ut non sint, et conscindunt eam desideriis pestilentiosis, quoniam ipsa esse vult et requiescere amat in eis quae amat. in illis autem non est ubi, quia non stant: fugiunt…" (O'Donnell, I:38).

[46]Ibid., p. 63, with "let them be loved" substituted for "they are being loved." "si placent animae, in deo amentur, quia et ipsa mutabiles sunt et in illo fixae stabiliuntur: alioquin irent et perirent" (O'Donnell, I:40).

[47]Ibid., p. 63. "quidquid per illam sentis in parte est, et ignoras totum cuius hae partes sunt, et delectant te tamen. sed si ad totum comprehendendum esset idoneus sensus carnis tuae,…velles ut transiret quidquid existit in praesentia, ut magis tibi omnia placerent. nam et quod loquimur per eundem sensum carnis audis, et non vis utique stare syllabas sed transvolare, ut aliae veniant et totum audias. ita semper omnia, quibus unum aliquid constat (et non sunt omnia simul ea quibus constat)…sed longe his melior qui fecit omnia, et ipse est deus noster, et non discedit, quia nec succeditur ei" (O'Donnell, I:39–40).

[48]Ibid., p. 62. "et ibi est locus quietis imperturbabilis, ubi non deseritur amor si ipse non deserat" (O'Donnell, I:39).

[49]Ibid., p. 64. "beatam vitam quaeritis in regione mortis: non est illic" (O'Donnell, I:40).

[50]Ibid. "et descendit huc ipsa vita nostra, et tulit mortem nostram et occidit eam de abundantia viae suae…" (O'Donnell, I:40).

[51]Ibid., p. 61. "Deus virtutum, converte nos et ostende faciem tuam, et salvi erimus" (O'Donnell, I:38).

[52]Ibid., pp. 62–63. "fluxa tua reformabuntur et renovabuntur et constringentur ad te, et non te deponent quo descendunt, sed stabunt tecum et permanebunt ad semper stantem ac permanentem deum" (O'Donnell, I:39).

⁵³Ibid., p. 63. "non enim fecit atque abiit, sed ex illo in illo sunt. ecce ubi est…intimus cordi est, sed cor erravit ab eo. redite, praevaricatores, ad cor et inhaerete illi qui fecit vos" (O'Donnell, I:40).

⁵⁴Augustine's metaphors for this usually imply some notion of "sticking" to God, or, more elegantly, cleaving to God. John Burnaby highlights *"inhaerere," "haerere,"* and *"cohaerere" ("Amor Dei": A Study of the Religion of St. Augustine* [London: Hodder & Stoughton, 1938], p. 141.) Bernard McGinn adds *"adhaerere"* (*The Presence of God: A History of Western Mysticism,* vol. 1, *The Foundations of Mysticism* [New York: Crossroad, 1992], pp. 232, 253).

⁵⁵Browning, *Religious Thought and the Modern Psychologies,* pp. 224–225.

⁵⁶Heinz Kohut, "Introspection, Empathy, and the Semi-Circle of Mental Health," *International Journal of Psycho-analysis* 63 (1982): 400.

⁵⁷Heinz Kohut, "Forms and Transformations of Narcissism," in *SFS1:*429–430.

⁵⁸Sigmund Freud, *The Standard Edition of the Complete Psychological Works of Sigmund Freud,* trans. and ed. James Strachey, vol. 14, *On Narcissism: An Introduction* (London: Hogarth Press and the Institute of Psychoanalysis, 1957 [1914]), pp. 89, 93. On Kohut, see the following note.

⁵⁹Heinz Kohut, "The Psychoanalytic Treatment of Narcissistic Personality Disorders," in *SFS1:*477–478; Freud, *On Narcissism,* pp. 93–96.

⁶⁰Kohut, "Psychoanalytic Treatment," p. 489.

⁶¹Some good examples of empathic responses are found in Kohut, *ROS,* pp. 86–87; for the restorative process in psychoanalysis, see "Psychoanalytic Treatment," pp. 498–499.

⁶²Kohut, "Forms and Transformations," *SFS1:*433–434; Kohut, *AOS,* pp. 49–50.

⁶³See, for example, Kohut's comments on Miss F. in "Psychoanalytic Treatment," pp. 507–508.

⁶⁴Kohut, *ROS,* pp. 76, 274–275.

⁶⁵Heinz Kohut, "The Two Analyses of Mr. Z, "*International Journal of Psycho-analysis* 60 (1979): 14–15.

⁶⁶Kohut, *ROS,* pp. 125–128.

⁶⁷Kohut, "Forms and Transformations," pp. 438–441.

⁶⁸Kohut, *AOS,* pp. 55, 58–62.

⁶⁹Kohut, "Forms and Transformations," p. 437.

⁷⁰Kohut, *ROS,* pp. 187–188, n. 8, 190–191.

⁷¹Ibid., pp. 178–180.

⁷²Kohut, *AOS,* p. 67; idem, "Psychoanalytic Treatment," p. 487.

⁷³Ibid., pp. 198–199; idem, "Psychoanalytic Treatment," pp. 481, 487–491.

⁷⁴Kohut, "Remarks about the Formation of the Self, " *SFS2:*738.

⁷⁵Kohut, *AOS,* pp. 16–17.

⁷⁶Kohut, *ROS,* p. 137.

⁷⁷Kohut, "A Note on Female Sexuality," *SFS2:*788–789.

⁷⁸*Freud and Philosophy,* pp. 494–514.

⁷⁹Gananath Obeyesekere makes this connection explicit in *The Work of Culture: Symbolic Transformation in Psychoanalysis and Anthropology* (Chicago and London: The University of Chicago Press, 1990), pp. xviii–xix, 3, 17, 277–280.

⁸⁰Sigmund Freud, *Totem and Taboo,* trans. James Strachey (New York: W. W. Norton & Company, 1950 [1913]), pp. 147–155.

⁸¹See the description of the boy's second birth in Sudhir Kakar, *The Inner World: A Psycho-Analytic Study of Childhood and Society in India,* 2nd ed. (Delhi: Oxford University Press, 1981), pp. 127–128.

⁸²Shweder, "Cultural Psychology," p. 24.

⁸³Ricoeur, *Freud and Philosophy,* pp. 170–174.

⁸⁴Ibid., pp. 174–177, 521–524.

⁸⁵Chadwick, pp. 243–244. "me suscepit dextera tua in domino meo, mediatore filio hominis inter te unum et nos multos, in multis per multa, ut per eum apprehendam in quo et apprehensus sum, et a veteribus diebus conligar sequens unum, praeterita oblitus, non in ea quae futura et transitura sunt, sed in ea quae ante sunt non distentus sed extentus, non secundum distentionem sed secundum intentionem…" (O'Donnell, I:163).

Chapter 3: Early Childhood Grandiosity and Injury

[1]Mark Freeman, "History, Narrative, and Life-Span Developmental Knowledge," *Human Development* 27 (1984): 16.

[2]*Vita*, 26.

[3]James E. Dittes, "Continuities Between the Life and Thought of Augustine," *JSSR* 5 (October 1965): 133; Charles Kligerman, "A Psychoanalytic Study of the *Confessions* of St. Augustine," *The Hunger of the Heart: Reflections on the "Confessions" of Augustine*, in Donald Capps and James E. Dittes, eds., Society for the Scientific Study of Religion Monograph Series, no. 8 (West Layfayette, Ind.: Society for the Scientific Study of Religion, 1990), 98, 101, 104, 106; Phillip Woollcott, Jr., "Some Considerations of Creativity and Religious Experience in St. Augustine of Hippo," *JSSR* 5 (Spring 1966): 274, 275; cf. Goulven Madec, "Le neveu d'Augustin," *Revue des Études Augustiniennes* 39 (1993), p. 154; Brent D. Shaw, "The Family in Late Antiquity: The Experience of Augustine," *Past & Present* 115 (May 1987): 34.

[4]Robert A. Kaster, *Guardians of Language: The Grammarian and Society in Late Antiquity* (Berkeley: University of California Press, 1988), pp. 26–27.

[5]Sabine MacCormack, *The Shadows of Poetry: Vergil in the Mind of Augustine* (Berkeley: University of California Press, 1998), pp. xviii–xix, 3, 14, 48, 52, 89–90, 93–100.

[6]Henri-Irenée Marrou, *Saint Augustin et la fin de la culture antique* (Paris: Éditions de Boccard, 1938), pp. 28–30, 37.

[7]Margaret More O'Ferrall, "Monica, the Mother of Augustine: A Reconsideration," *Recherches Augustiniennes* 10 (1975): 38; A.-G. Hamman, *La vie quotidienne en Afrique du Nord au temps de saint Augustin*, nouvelle édition (Paris: Hachette, 1979, Préface 1985), pp. 88, 101.

[8]My translation. "parentes nostri ridebant tormenta quibus pueri a magistris affligebamur" (O'Donnell, I:8).

[9]James J. O'Donnell, *Augustine, Confessions*, vol. 2: *Commentary on Books 1–7* (Oxford: Clarendon Press, 1992), p. 61; see also Richard Saller, "Corporal Punishment, Authority, and Obedience in the Roman Household," in *Marriage, Divorce, and Children in Ancient Rome*, ed. Beryl Rawson (Oxford: Oxford University Press, 1991), p. 163; and Aimé Solignac, "L'Éducation à l'époque d'Augustin," in *Confessions, Bibliothèque Augustinienne, Oeuvres de saint Augustin*, vol. 13 (Paris: Desclée de Brouwer, 1962), p. 659.

[10]Shaw, "The Family," p. 31.

[11]Saller, "Corporal Punishment," p. 162.

[12]E.g., *CLP*, II.xcix.226; *In Johann.*, 7.11; see Shaw, "The Family," pp. 18–21, 23–24.

[13]Kaster, *Guardians of Language*, pp. 11, 20–24.

[14]*Vita*, 1.

[15]F. Homes Dudden, *The Life and Times of St. Ambrose* (Oxford: Clarendon Press, 1935), I:97–101; Shaw, "The Family," pp. 9–10.

[16]Chadwick, p. 13. "signabar iam signo crucis eius, et condiebar eius sale iam inde ab utero matris meae…" (O'Donnell, I:9).

[17]Ibid., p. 13, n. 19.

[18]My translation. "quasi necesse esset ut adhuc sordidarer si viverem, quia videlicet post lavacrum illud maior et periculosior in sordibus delictorum reatus foret" (O'Donnell, I:9).

[19]Chadwick, p. 13. "Audieram enim ego adhuc puer de vita aeterna promissa nobis per humilitatem domini dei nostri…vidisti, deus meus, quoniam custos meus iam eras, quo motu animi et qua fide baptismum Christi tui, dei et domine mei, flagitavi a pietate matris meae et matris omnium nostrum, ecclesiae tuae. et conturbata mater carnis meae, quoniam et sempiternam salutem meam carius parturiebat corde casto in fide tua, iam curaret festinabunda ut sacramentis salutaribus initiarer et abluerer, te, domine Iesu, confitens in remissionem peccatorum, nisi statim recreatus essem. dilata est itaque mundatio mea…" (O'Donnell, I:9).

[20]My translation. "ita iam credebam et illa et omnis domus, nisi pater solus, qui tamen non evicit in me ius maternae pietatis, quominus in Christum crederem, sicut ille nondum crediderat.…cui melior serviebat, quia et in hoc tibi utique id iubenti serviebat" (O'Donnell, I:9-10).

[21]Shaw, "The Family," 31; Kim Power, *Veiled Desire: Augustine on Women* (New York: Continuum, 1996), p. 210.

[22]Gal. 5:22.

[23]Chadwick, p. 20. "Quid autem mirem, quod in vanitates ita ferebar et a te, deus meus, ibam foras, quando mihi imitandi proponebantur homines qui aliqua facta sua non mala, si cum barbarismo aut soloecismo enuntiarent…" (O'Donnell, I:13).

[24]Ibid., p. 21. "magis timebam barbarismum facere quam cavebam, si facerem, non facientibus invidere. dico haec et confiteor tibi, deus meus, in quibus laudabar ab eis quibus placere tunc mihi erat honeste vivere" (O'Donnell, I:14).

[25]Paul Ricoeur, *Freud and Philosophy: An Essay on Interpretation*, trans. Denis Savage (New Haven and London: Yale University Press, 1970), pp. 171, 173.

[26]Sigmund Freud, *The Interpretation of Dreams*, trans. and ed. James Strachey (New York: Avon, Discus Books, 1965 [1900]), pp. 317–318, 342–343; *On Dreams*, trans. James Strachey (New York: W.W. Norton & Co., 1952 [1901]), pp. 49–50.

[27]Chadwick, pp. 6–7. "exceperunt ergo me consolationes lactis humani…tu etiam mihi dabas nolle amplius quam dabas, et nutrientibus me dare mihi velle quod eis dabas…nam tunc sugere noram et adquiescere delectationibus, flere autem offensiones carnis meae, nihil amplius" (O'Donnell, I:5).

[28]Shaw, "The Family," pp. 41–43.

[29]Chadwick, p. 6. "et susceperunt me consolationes miserationum tuarum, sicut audivi a parentibus carnis meae…" (O'Donnell, I:5).

[30]Ibid., p. 7. "Post et ridere coepi, dormiens primo, deinde vigilans. hoc enim de me mihi est indicatum…" (O'Donnell, I:5).

[31]Ibid., p. 10. "hanc ergo aetatem, domine, quam me vixisse non memini, de qua aliis credidi…" (O'Donnell, I:7).

[32]Heinz Kohut, *Self Psychology and the Humanities: Reflections on a New Psychoanalytic Approach*, ed. with an Introduction by Charles B. Strozier (New York and London: W. W. Norton & Co., 1985), p. 236.

[33]Margaret R. Miles treats the themes of book 1 both theologically and from a different psychological perspective than mine in this passage in her article, "Infancy, Parenting and Nourishment in Augustine's *Confessions*," *Journal of the American Academy of Religion* 50 (September 1982): 351–352, 355–358.

[34]Chadwick, pp. 6–7. "Sed tamen sine me loqui apud misericordiam tuam, me terram et cineram…ex te quippe bona omnia, deus, et ex deo meo salus mihi universa. quod animadverti postmodum, clamante te mihi per haec ipsa quae tribuis intus et foris" (O'Donnell, I:5).

[35]Ibid., p. 9. "ita inbecillitas membrorum infantilium innocens est, non animus infantium. vidi ego et expertus sum zelantem parvulum: nondum loquebatur et intuebatur pallidus amaro aspectu conlactaneum suum. quis hoc ignorat? expiare se dicunt ista matres atque nutrices nescio quibus remediis. nisi vero et ista innocentia est, in fonte lactis ubertim manante atque abundante opis egentissimum et illo adhuc uno alimento vitam ducentem consortem non pati. sed blande tolerantur haec, non quia nulla vel parva, sed quia aetatis accessu peritura sunt. quod licet probes, cum ferri aequo animo eadem ipsa non possunt quando in aliquo annosiore deprehenduntur" (O'Donnell, I:7).

[36]Miriam Elson, ed., *The Kohut Seminars on Self Psychology and Psychotherapy with Adolescents and Young Adults* (New York and London: W. W. Norton & Company, 1987), p. 56.

[37]The use of the word "object" offends people because it tends to denigrate their humanity. The justification for the term derives from Freud's effort to find a systematic and scientific analogy, such as physical attraction between physical objects, to elucidate the workings of the mind. Although this thinking allowed him to achieve sufficient distance from other conceptions of the mind to develop his psychology of the unconscious, the liabilities of his theoretical language entangle themselves with its benefits and carry over into writings, like Kohut's, which derived from Freud's.

[38]Elson, ed., *Kohut Seminars*, p. 41.

[39]Heinz Kohut and Ernest S. Wolf, "The Disorders of the Self and Their Treatment: An Outline," in *Essential Papers on Narcissism*, ed. Andrew P. Morrison (New York and London: New York University Press, 1986 [1978]), p. 177.

[40]*On Narcissism*, SE, 14:91.

[41]Kohut, "Forms and Transformations of Narcissism," *SFS1*:456–460.

[42]Sudhir Kakar, *The Inner World: A Psycho-Analytic Study of Childhood and Society in India*, 2nd ed. (Delhi: Oxford University Press, 1981), pp. 126–133.

[43]"The Vocabulary of Emotion: A Study of Javanese Socialization Processes," in *Culture and Personality: Contemporary Readings*, ed. Robert A. Levine (Chicago: Aldine Publishing Company, 1974), pp. 256–257.

[44]Chadwick, p. 19; my emphasis. "bonae spei puer apellabar" (O'Donnell, I:13).

[45]Ibid., p. 11. "ut in hoc saeculo florerem et excellerem linguosis artibus ad honorem hominum et falsas divitias famulantibus" (O'Donnell, I:8). The English editions evade the

word "famulantibus" (Pine-Coffin, pp. 29–30; Warner, p. 26; Watt, I:26–27), although Watt and Solignac include it in the Latin as does O'Donnell. Psychological interpretation need not suffer from its absence, but it seems to me crucial, if small, for theological understanding. Tréhorel's and Bouissou's translation includes the sense of *famulantibus*: "à briller dans ce monde, et à exceller dans les arts de la verbosité, servile accès aux honneurs des hommes et aux fausses richesses" (BA 13:299). Nonetheless, I think Augustine is saying that the arts of language were themselves *serving*, or as Tréhorel's and Bouissou's diction suggests, servile to, human honors and false riches.

⁴⁶My translation, because Chadwick's rendering (p. 19) of "deep psychological anxiety" for "disquieting enough to my soul" might seem to prejudice the interpretation. Chadwick's notes indicate Virgil's *Aeneid* 1.38 as the source for the speech. "Sine me, deus meus, dicere aliquid et de ingenio meo, munere tuo, in quibus a me deliramentis atterebatur. proponebatur enim mihi negotium, animae meae satis inquietum praemio laudis et dedecoris vel plagarum metu, ut dicerem verba Iunonis irascentis et dolentis quod non posset Italia Teucrorum avertere regem…" (O'Donnell, I:13).

⁴⁷Chadwick, p. 11. "et tamen, si segnis in discendo essem, vapulabam. laudabatur enim hoc a maioribus…" (O'Donnell, I:8).

⁴⁸Power, *Veiled Desire*, p. 78.

⁴⁹Chadwick, p. 11. "ridebantur a maioribus hominibus usque ad ipsis parentibus, qui mihi accidere mali nihil volebant, plagae meae, magnum tunc et grave malum meum" (O'Donnell, I:8).

⁵⁰Elson ed., *Kohut Seminars*, p. 71.

⁵¹Chadwick, p. 11. "multi ante nos vitam istam agentes praestruxerant aerumnosas vias, per quas transire cogebamur multiplicato labore et dolore filiis Adam" (O'Donnell, I:8).

⁵²Ibid., p. 21. "homo eloquentiae famam quaeritans ante hominem iudicem circumstante hominum multitudine inimicum suum odio immanissimo insectans vigilantissime cavet, ne per linguae errorem dicat, 'inter hominibus', et ne per mentis furorem hominem auferat ex hominibus, non cavet" (O'Donnell, I:14).

⁵³*Guardians of Language*, p. 50; p. 11 for the lower limit of children's age in the grammarian's school.

⁵⁴Chadwick notes, "The Latin is ambiguous and may mean 'restless urge for mimicry of comic scenes'" (p.22, n. 37).

⁵⁵Chadwick, pp. 21–22. "innumerabilibus mendaciis et paedagogum et magistros et parentes amore ludendi, studio spectandi nugatoria et imitandi ludicra inquietudine…furta etiam faciebam de cellario parentum et de mensa, vel gula imperitante vel ut haberem quod darem pueris ludum suum mihi quo pariter utique delectabantur tamen vendentibus. in quo etiam ludo fraudulentas victorias ipse vana excellentiae cupiditate victus saepe aucupabar. quid autem tam nolebam pati atque atrociter, si deprehenderem, arguebam, quam id quod aliis faciebam? et, si deprehensus arguerer, saevire magis quam ceder libebat" (O'Donnell, I:14–15).

⁵⁶Ibid., p. 22. "sentiebam meamque incolumitatem…" (O'Donnell, I:15).

⁵⁷See for instance "Thoughts on Narcissism and Narcissistic Rage," *SFS2*:657, n. 15, and "The Two Analyses of Mr. Z," *International Journal of Psycho-analysis* 60 (1979): 13–17; Kohut also comments on life-endangering physical expressions of grandiosity in *The Analysis of the Self: A Systematic Approach to the Psychoanalytic Treatment of Narcissistic Personality Disorders*, The Psychoanalytic Study of the Child 4 (New York: International Universities Press, 1971), p. 248, and "Forms and Transformations of Narcissism," pp. 443–444.

⁵⁸Chadwick, p. 22. "custodiebam interiore sensu integritatem sensuum meorum inque ipsis parvis parvarumque rerum cogitationibus vertitate delectabar…memoria vigebam, locutione instruebar, amicitia mulcebar, fugiebam dolorem, abiectionem, ignorantiam. quid in tali animante non mirabile atque laudabile?" (O'Donnell, I:15).

⁵⁹Chadwick, p.17. "nam et latina aliquando infans utique nulla noveram, et tamen advertendo didici sine ullo metu atque cruciatu, inter etiam blandimenta nutricum et ioca adridentium et laetitias adludentium. didici vero illa sine poenali onere urgentium, cum me urgeret cor meum ad parienda concepta sua, et qua non esset, nisi aliqua verba didicissem non a docentibus sed a loquentibus, in quorum et ego auribus parturiebam quid quid sentiebam. hinc satis elucet maiorem habere vim ad discenda ista liberam curiositatem quam meticulosam necessitatem. sed illius fluxum haec restringit legibus tuis, deus, legibus tuis a magistrorum ferulis usque ad temptationes martyrum, valentibus legibus tuis miscere salubres amaritudines revocantes nos ad te a iucunditate pestifera qua recessimus a te" (O'Donnell, I:12; variant reading of "et qua," O'Donnell, II: 82).

⁶⁰Clifford Geertz, "Religion as a Cultural System," in *The Interpretation of Cultures* (New York: Basic Books, 1973), p. 104.

⁶¹Don S. Browning, "The Psychoanalytic Interpretation of St. Augustine's *Confessions*: An Assessment and New Probe," in *Psychiatry and the Humanities*, vol. 2, *Psychoanalysis and Religion*, ed. Joseph H. Smith and Susan A. Handelman (assoc. ed.) (Baltimore and London: The Johns Hopkins University Press, 1990), pp. 148–149; Donald Capps, "Augustine's *Confessions*: The Scourge of Shame and the Silencing of Adeodatus," in *The Hunger of the Heart: Reflections on the "Confessions" of Augustine*, ed. Donald Capps and James E. Dittes, Society for the Scientific Study of Religion Monograph Series, no. 8 (West Lafayette, Ind.: Society for the Scientific Study of Religion, 1990), pp. 71–74; E. R. Dodds, "Augustine's Confessions: A Study of Spiritual Maladjustment," *The Hibbert Journal* 26 (1927–1928): 462; Leo C. Ferrari, "The Boyhood Beatings of Augustine," in *Hunger of the Heart*, ed. Capps and Dittes, pp. 55–67.

⁶²My translation. "ut dulcescas mihi super omnes seductiones quas sequebar…" (O'Donnell, I:12).

⁶³For similar ideas, see Donald Capps, "Parabolic Events in Augustine's Autobiography," *Theology Today* 40 (October 1983): 268.

⁶⁴Chadwick, p. 23. "augebuntur et perficientur quae dedisti mihi, et ero ipse tecum, quia et ut sim tu dedisti mihi" (O'Donnell, I:15).

⁶⁵Ibid., p. 12. "sed delectabat ludere et vindicabatur in nos ab eis qui talia utique agebant. sed maiorum nugae negotia vocantur, puerorum autem talia cum sint, puniuntur a maioribus, et nemo miseratur pueros vel illos vel utrosque. nisi vero approbat quisquam bonus rerum arbiter vapulasse me, quia ludebam pila puer et eo ludo impediebar quominus celeriter discerem litteras, quibus maior deformius luderem. aut aliud faciebat idem ipse a quo vapulabam, qui si in aliqua quaestiuncula a condoctore suo victus esset, magis bile atque invidia torqueretur quam ego, cum in certamine pilae a conlusore meo superabar?" (O'Donnell, I:8–9). On the amusements of adults as business, Chadwick cites Seneca in Lactantius and a similar sentiment expressed more generally by Plotinus (ibid., n. 17).

Chapter 4: Childhood, Ideals, and Disillusionment

¹Heinz Kohut, "The Psychoanalytic Treatment of Narcissistic Personality Disorders: Outline of a Systematic Approach," in *SFS1*, pp. 477–478.

²"Forms and Transformations of Narcissism," in *SFS1*, pp. 440–442.

³*AOH*, pp. 31–33; James E.Dittes, "Continuities Between the Life and Thought of Augustine," *JSSR* 5 (October 1965): 137; E. R. Dodds, "Augustine's Confessions: A Study of Spiritual Maladjustment," *The Hibbert Journal* 26 (1927–1928): 461, 464–465; Charles Kligerman, "A Psychoanalytic Study of the Confessions of St. Augustine," in *The Hunger of the Heart: Reflections on the "Confessions" of Augustine*, ed. Donald Capps and James E. Dittes, Society for the Scientific Study of Religion Monograph Series, no. 8 (West Layfayette, Ind.: Society for the Scientific Study of Religion, 1990), pp. 98, 104–105; Phillip Woollcott, Jr., "Some Considerations of Creativity and Religious Experience in St. Augustine of Hippo," *JSSR* 5 (Spring 1966): 276.

⁴Sigmund Freud, *Civilization and Its Discontents*, trans. and ed. James Strachey (New York: W. W. Norton & Company, 1961 [1930]), pp. 76–80; for a more sexually neutral description of the oedipal conflict see also *The Ego and the Id*, trans. Joan Riviere, rev. and ed. James Strachey (New York and London: W. W. Norton & Co., 1960 [1923]), pp. 19–27.

⁵Dittes, "Continuities," p. 133–134; Kligerman, "A Psychoanalytic Study," pp. 98–99, 101–104, 108; Woollcott, "Some Considerations," pp. 276–277.

⁶Andrès G. Niño, "Restoration of the Self: A Therapeutic Paradigm from Augustine's *Confessions*," *Psychotherapy* 27 (Spring 1990): 10.

⁷Chadwick, p. 26. "feriatus ab omni schola…" (O'Donnell, I:17).

⁸My translation. "monuerit cum sollicitudine ingenti, ne fornicarer maximeque ne adulterarem cuiusquam uxorem. qui mihi monitus muliebres videbantur, quibus obtemperare erubescerem" (O'Donnell, I:18).

⁹My translation. "cum dicitur, 'eamus, faciamus,' et pudet non esse impudentem" (O'Donnell, I:22).

¹⁰Robert A.Kaster, *Guardians of Language: The Grammarian and Society in Late Antiquity* (Berkeley: University of California Press, 1988), pp. 20–22.

¹¹Martial Douël, *L'Algérie romaine: Forums et basiliques: Timgad—Djemila—Khemissa—Madaure—Cherchell—Tipasa* (Paris: Société d'Éditions Géographiques, Maritimes et Coloniales, 1930), pp. 105–115; Paul MacKendrick, *The North African Stones Speak* (Chapel Hill, N.C.: University of North Carolina Press, 1980), pp. 253–255.

¹²Kaster, *Guardians of Language*, pp. 22–28.

¹³Brent D. Shaw, "The Family in Late Antiquity: The Experience of Augustine," *Past and Present* 115 (November 1987): 30.

¹⁴Brown, *AOH*, p. 248; A.-G.Hamman, *La vie quotidienne en Afrique du Nord au temps de saint Augustin*, nouvelle édition (Paris: Hachette, 1979 [Préface 1985]), pp. 95–97; Frederic Van der Meer, *Augustine the Bishop: The Life and Work of a Father of the Church*, 2nd ed., trans. Brian Battershaw and G. R. Lamb (London: Sheed and Ward, 1978), pp. 180–183.

¹⁵*Augustine the Bishop*, p. 181.

¹⁶Chadwick, p. 19. "nequam adulescentem proponentem sibi Iovem ad exemplum stupri…et vide quemadmodum se concitat ad libidinem quasi caelesti magisterio: …'qui templa caeli summo sonitu concutit./ego homuncio id non facerem? ego vero illud feci ac libens'" (O'Donnell, I:13). Chadwick identifies the play as *Eunuch* and the passages as 589–590. See also James J. O'Donnell, *Augustine: Confessions*, vol. 2: *Commentary on Books 1–7* (Oxford: Clarendon Press, 1992), p. 88.

¹⁷Ibid. "libenter haec didici, et eis delectabar miser, et ob hoc bonae spei puer appellabar" (O'Donnell, I:13).

¹⁸My translation. "vinum erroris quod in eis nobis propinabatur ab ebriis doctoribus, et nisi biberemus caedebamur, nec appellare ad aliquem iudicem sobrium licebat" (O'Donnell, I:13).

¹⁹Chadwick notes that Augustine's language toward the end of II.iv.9 is an "[e]cho of Sallust's language about Catiline. Augustine presents himself as a new Catiline" (*Conf.*, p. 29, n. 11).

²⁰Miriam Elson, ed., *The Kohut Seminars on Self Psychology and Psychotherapy with Adolescents and Young Adults* (New York and London: W. W. Norton & Company, 1987), p. 19; see also Freud, *On Narcissism*, *SE*, 14:82–83.

²¹My translation. "motu animi et…fide…ita iam credebam et illa et omnis domus, nisi pater solus, qui tamen non evicit in me ius maternae pietatis, quominus in Christum crederem, sicut ille nondum crediderat…(O'Donnell, I:9).

²²My translation. "nam illa satagebat ut tu mihi pater esses, deus meus, potius quam ille, et in hoc adiuvabas eam, ut superaret virum, cui melior…" The clause reads, "cui melior serviebat…" (O'Donnell, I:9–10). See Don S. Browning, "The Psychoanalytic Interpretation of St. Augustine's *Confessions*: An Assessment and New Probe," in *Psychiatry and the Humanities*, vol. 2, *Psychoanalysis and Religion*, ed. Joseph H. Smith and Susan A. Handelman (assoc. ed.) (Baltimore and London: Johns Hopkins University Press, 1990), p. 150; Kligerman, "A Psychoanalytic Study," pp. 8–99. Brown cites this passage as the sort by which Augustine "brought down on his own head the attentions of modern psychological observers" (*AOH*, p. 31); see also David Bakan, "Some Thoughts on Reading Augustine's *Confessions*," *JSSR* 5 (October 1965): 151.

²³Chadwick (trans.), *Conf.*, 14.

²⁴Augustine, *Confessions*, trans. with an Introduction and notes by Maria Boulding, ed. John E. Rotelle, *The Works of Saint Augustine: A Translation for the 21st Century*, vol. I/1 (Hyde Park, N.Y.: New City Press, 1997), p. 51.

²⁵O'Donnell gives several biblical references to God taking the place of another father in someone's life. His further comments on the tensions between Monica and Patricius are subtle and helpful (O'Donnell, II:69–70). For translations, see Chadwick, p. 14; Pine-Coffin, p. 32; Warner, p. 29; Watts, I:35. Tréhorel and Bouissou have "plutôt que" (BA, 13:305).

²⁶Paul Rigby, "Paul Ricoeur, Freudianism, and Augustine's Confessions," *Journal of the American Academy of Religion* 53 (Spring 1985): 100, could be seen as backing this reading.

²⁷My translation. "quanto ergo melius et cito sanarer et id ageretur mecum meorum meaque diligentia, ut recepta salus animae mea tuta esset tutela tua, qui dedisses eam" (O'Donnell, I:10). Allusion to Ps. 34:3.

²⁸My translation. "sed quot et quanti fluctus impendere temptationum post pueritiam videbantur, noverat eos iam illa mater et terram per eos, unde postea formarer, quam ipsam iam effigiem committere volebat" (O'Donnell, I:72). See also O'Donnell II:72.

²⁹O'Donnell II:72. Regarding "the image of God," see Gen. 1:27. The tone in the passage just cited from *Confessions* differs from a similar discussion in II.iii.8 in which Augustine tries to extrapolate his parents' reasons for raising him as they did. In II.iii.8 he adds to his speculations: "That at least is my conjecture as I try to recall the characters of my parents" (Chadwick, 28; "ita enim conicio, recolens ut possum mores parentum meorum" (O'Donnell, I:18). Did he and Monica discuss his early plea for baptism so that he could speak of her reasons without adding a reservation about "conjecture"?

244 Notes to pages 68–74

[30]Brown, *AOH*, pp. 106-107; Van der Meer, *Augustine the Bishop*, pp. 181–182.

[31]My translation. "illi…intuebantur…ad satiandas insatiabiles cupiditates copiosae inopiae et ignominiosae gloriae" (O'Donnell, I:10).

[32]My translation. "spes litterarum, quas ut nossem nimis volebat parens uterque, ille quia de te prope nihil cogitabat, de me autem inania, illa autem quia non solum nullo detrimento sed etiam nonnullo adiumento ad te adipiscendum futura existimabat usitata illa studia doctrinae" (O'Donnell, I:18).

[33]See Kohut on the "'telescoping' of genetically analogous experiences" (*ROS*, 14; *HDA*, p. 6; Elson (ed.), *Kohut Seminars*, pp. 235–236). Note that here "genetically" means "having to do with development," and does not refer to DNA, chromosomes, and the like.

[34]Kohut, "Thoughts on Narcissism and Narcissistic Rage," in *SFS2*:623–624.

[35]Elson, ed., *The Kohut Seminars*, pp. 12–13; "'On the Adolescent Process as a Transformation of the Self' by Ernest S. Wolf, John E. Gedo, and David M. Terman: Discussion," in *SFS2*, 660–662.

[36]Kohut, "Thoughts on Narcissism and Narcissistic Rage," *SFS2* 637–638.

[37]Lawrence J. Daly, "Psychohistory and St. Augustine's Conversion Process: An Historiographical Critique," *Augustinian Studies* (1978): 233–234, 243–252; idem, "St. Augustine's '*Confessions*' and Erik Erikson's '*Young Man Luther*': Conversion as 'Identity Crisis,'" *Augustiniana* 31 (1981):185–188, 193; Goulven Madec, "Le neveu d'Augustin," *Revue des Études Augustiniennes*, 39 (1993): 154; Cornelius Petrus Mayer, "Confessio—Der Weg des Christen aus der Verflochtenheit von Schuld und Schuldgefühlen bei Augustinus," in *Cassiciacum*, vol. 46, *Traditio Augustiniana: Studien über Augustinus und seine Rezeption*, ed. Adolar Zumkeller and Achim Krümmel (Würzburg: Augustinus-Verlag, 1994), citing Donald Capps and James Dittes, *Hunger of the Heart*.

[38]Heinz Kohut, *HDA*, pp. 5, 13–16.

[39]Browning, "The Psychoanalytic Interpretation of St. Augustine's *Confessions*," pp. 137, 138, 142, 146–147.

[40]Ibid., pp. 144, 150.

[41]Ibid., p. 138.

[42]"Is the Oedipus Complex Universal?" in *Belief, Magic, and Anomie* (New York: Free Press, 1969), pp. 15–32, 43–59.

[43]*The Inner World: A Psycho-Analytic Study of Childhood and Society in India*, 2nd ed. (Delhi: Oxford University Press, 1981), pp. 103–112, 126–139. For a different view, still arguing the variability of the oedipal conflict, see Gananath Obeyesekere, *The Work of Culture: Symbolic Transformation in Psychoanalysis and Anthropology* (Chicago and London: University of Chicago Press, 1990), pp. xx–xxi, and lecture 3.

[44]Hamman, *La vie quotidienne*, p. 101.

[45]Shaw, "The Family," p. 42.

[46]My translation, from Shaw, "The Family," p. 42.

[47]Hamman, *La vie quotidienne.*, pp. 100 ("La vie se passe hors de la maison"; my translation for this work) and 102. See also Shaw, "The Family," p. 43. Both refer to Augustine's *Tract. In Johann.*, 7.23.

[48]*Civilization and Its Discontents*, pp. 71–75.

[49]"The Family," p. 23.

[50]*La vie quotidienne*, p. 102: "Elle le surveille, l'accompagne, l'éduque." See also Shaw, "The Family," p. 42.

[51]*La vie quotidienne*, p. 103: "il reparaîtra dans la famille, quand la faim le tenaillera."

[52]Shaw, "The Family," pp. 30–31.

[53]Dittes, "Continuities," p. 134; Kligerman, "A Psychoanalytic Study," p. 104; Woollcott, "Some Considerations," p. 276.

[54]See also Kligerman, "A Psychoanalytic Study," pp. 101–102, 104.

[55]Paul Ricoeur, *Freud and Philosophy: An Essay on Interpretation*, trans. Denis Savage (New Haven and London: Yale University Press, 1970), pp. 171–172; Freud, *Leonardo Da Vinci and a Memory of His Childhood, SE*, 11:132, 136.

[56]Ibid., pp. 249–250, 523.

[57]Ibid., pp. 505, 509–514, 523–524.

[58]Dittes, "Continuities," p. 134; Kligerman, "A Psychoanalytic Study," p. 105; Paul Pruyser, "Psychological Examination: Augustine," *JSSR* 5 (Spring 1966): 285; Woollcott, "Some Considerations," p. 277.

[59]"Augustine and His Analysts: The Possibility of a Psychohistory," *Soundings* 61 (Summer 1978): 207–214; see also Diane Jonte-Pace, "Augustine on the Couch: Psychohistorical (Mis)readings of the *Confessions*," *Religion* 23 (1993): 76.

[60]*La vie quotidienne,* p. 101: "La nuit tombée, le plus tard possible, le mari retrouve son foyer. Là, son épouse mène une vie recluse, occupée à la vie du ménage et à l'éducation des enfants, entourée de domestiques. Frustrée, la mère porte son affection sur ses fils, au point de devenir abusive. Ce qui explique le comportement de Monique, la mère d'Augustin."

[61]Dittes, "Continuities," p. 137.

[62]He wrote a dialogue, *DM*, in which he and his son, Adeodatus, discuss the nature of teaching and learning. See chapter 7 below.

[63]*DBV*, I.6, II.12.

[64]Brown, *AOH*, p. 248.

[65]*SAE*, pp. 53–58; *SAC*, p. 115; *ACI*, p. 123.

[66]Brown, *AOH*, p. 172, n. 5, citing *Holmes-Laski Letters (I)*, ed. M. de W. Howe, 1953, p. 300. See also Jonte-Pace, "Augustine on the Couch," p. 73; Karl Joachim Weintraub, *The Value of the Individual: Self and Circumstance in Autobiography* (Chicago and London: University of Chicago Press, 1978), p. 383, n. 9.

[67]Donald Capps, "Parabolic Events in Augustine's Autobiography," *Theology Today* 40 (October 1983): 261.

[68]Chadwick, p. 31. "decerpta proieci…" (O'Donnell, I:20).

[69]Ibid., p. 33. "cur ergo eo me delectabat… ?" (O'Donnell, I:22).

[70]Ibid., p. 33. "risus erat quasi titillato corde, quod fallebamus eos qui haec a nobis fieri non putabant et vehementer nolebant" (O'Donnell, I:22).

[71]The parallel can be seen to be Adam tempted by Eve, perhaps because of Augustine's presentation of it in *DCD*, XIV.11–13. See Marjorie Suchocki, "The Symbolic Structure of Augustine's *Confessions*," *Journal of the American Academy of Religion* 50 (September 1982): 367–368; more generally on the biblical parallel, see Danuta Shanzer, "Pears before Swine: Augustine, *Confessions* 2.4.9," *Revue des Études Augustiniennes* 42 (1996): 44–48 and references.

[72]Genesis 3:4–5.

[73]*SAC*, p. 49.

[74]*DCD*, XIV.28; see also XIV.13. Indeed the language in *Conf.*, II.vi.14, foreshadows the language of *DCD*: "perverse te imitantur omnes qui longe se a te faciunt et extollunt se adversum te" (O'Donnell, I:21).

[75]*DCD*, XIX.24, 25.

[76]O'Donnell, II:141.

[77]Chadwick, p. 29. "turpis anima et dissiliens a firmamento tuo in exterminium" (O'Donnell, I:19).

[78]*Ad Simp.*, I.Q2.10, 12–18, 22.

[79]Gen. 3; Robert McMahon, *Augustine's Prayerful Ascent: An Essay of the Literary Form of the "Confessions"* (Athens, Ga., and London: University of Georgia Press, 1989), p. 54; Suchocki, "Symbolic Structure," pp. 367–368.

[80]See above, n. 9.

[81]Chadwick, p. 33. "et illud [consortium eorum cum quibus id feci] nihil est" (O'Donnell, I:22).

[82]Ibid., p. 32. "diligam te, domine, et gratias agam et confitear nomini tuo, quoniam tanta dimisisti mihi mala et nefaria opera mea. gratiae tuae deputo et misericordiae tuae quod peccata mea tanquam glaciem solvisti. gratiae tuae deputo et quaecumque non feci mala" (O'Donnell, I:21).

Chapter 5: Strengths of a Long Adolescence

[1]Chadwick, p. 35. "Veni Carthaginem, et circumstrepebat me undique sartago flagitiosorum amorum.…non bene valebat anima mea et ulcerosa proiciebat se foras, miserabiliter scalpi avida contactu sensibilium" (O'Donnell, I:23).

[2]Ibid. "Rapiebant me spectacula theatrica, plena imaginibus miseriarum mearum et fomitibus ignis mei" (O'Donnell, I:23).

[3]My translation. "et maior etiam eram in schola rhetoris, et gaudebam superbe et tumebam typho…" (O'Donnell, I:25).

[4]O'Donnell, II:164, for a discussion of what the "derogatory tone" of Augustine's phrase, "a certain Cicero": "In an address to God, the expression signifies the vanity of a fame like that of Cicero…"

[5]Chadwick, p. 39. "Inter hos ego inbecilla tunc aetate discebam libros eloquentiae, in qua eminere cupiebam…et usitato iam discendi ordine perveneram in librum cuiusdam Ciceronis…sed liber ille ipsius exhortationem continet ad philosophiam et vocatur 'Hortensius.' ille vero liber mutavit affectum meum, et ad te ipsum, domine, mutavit preces

meas, et vota ac desideria me fecit alia. Viluit mihi repente omnis vana spes,…et surgere coeperam ut ad te redirem" (O'Donnell, I:25).

[6]My translation. "Quomodo ardebam, deus meus, quomodo ardebam revolare a terrenis ad te, et nesciebam quid ageres mecum!…hoc tamen solo delectabur in illa exhortatione, quod non illam aut illam sectam, sed ipsam quaecumque esset sapientiam ut diligerem et quaererem et adsequerer et tenerem atque amplexarer fortiter…" (O'Donnell, I:25–26).

[7]Chadwick, p. 40. "Itaque incidi in homines superbe delirantes, carnales nimis et loquaces…" (O'Donnell, I:26).

[8]My translation, with help from Chadwick, p. 52, and trans. with Introduction and notes by Maria Boulding, *The Confessions*, ed. John E. Rotelle, The Works of Saint Augustine: A Translation for the 21st Century, vol. I/1 (Hyde Park, N.Y.: New City Press, 1997), p. 92. "seducebamur et seducebamus, falsi atque fallentes in variis cupiditatibus, et palam per doctrinas quas liberales vocant, occulte autem falso nomine religionis…" (O'Donnell, I:33).

[9]Chadwick, p. 73. "et ubi ego eram, quando te quaerebam? et tu eras ante me, ego autem et a me discesseram nec me inveniebam: quanto minus te!" (O'Donnell, 1:46).

[10]Ibid., p. 89. "itaque academicorum more, sicut existimantur, dubitans de omnibus atque inter omnia fluctuans, manichaeos quidem relinquendos esse decrevi…statuis ergo tamdiu esse catechumenus in catholica ecclesia mihi a parentibus commendata, donec aliquid certi eluceret quo cursum dirigerem" (O'Donnell, I:57).

[11]Ibid., p. 104. "Et ego maxime mirabar, satagens et recolens quam longum tempus esset ab undevicensimo anno aetatis meae, quo fervere coeperam studio sapientiae…et ecce iam tricenariam aetatem gerebam, in eodem luto haesitans aviditate fruendi praesentibus fugientibus et dissipantibus me…" (O'Donnell, I:68).

[12]Ibid., p. 127. "rapiebar ad te decore tuo moxque diripiebar abs te pondere meo, et ruebam in ista cum gemitu…" (O'Donnell, I:84).

[13]CA, II.ii.3, O'Meara, p. 67. "Tu me adolescentulum pauperem ad peregrina studia pergentem, et domo et sumptu, et, quod pius est, animo excepisti. Tu patre orbatum amicitia consolatus es, hortatione animasti, ope adjuvisti" (PL, 32:920). For other details about Augustine's age and the reckoning of age in late antiquity, see *Conf.*, III.iv.7; Brown, *AOH*, p. 39; O'Donnell, II:115; and Brent D. Shaw, "The Family in Late Antiquity: The Experience of Augustine," *Past and Present* 115 (May 1987):40–41.

[14]Ibid., I.i.2, O'Meara, p. 37. "si…conviviis quotidianis mensae opimae struerentur; quod cuique esset necesse, quod cujusque etiam deliciae sitirent indubitanter peteret, indubitanter hauriret, multa etiam non petentibus funderentur; resque ipsa familiaris diligenter a tuis fideliterque administrata, idoneam se tantis sumptibus paratamque praeberet; tu interea viveres in aedificiorum exquisitissimis molibus, in nitore balnearum, in tesseris quas honestas non respuit, in venatibus, in conviviis…quisquam tibi, Romaniane, beatae alterius vitae quisquam,…quaeso, mentionem facere auderet?" (PL, 32:906–907).

[15]F. Homes Dudden, *The Life and Times of Saint Ambrose* (Oxford: Clarendon Press, 1935), I:38–47; Ausonius, Epigram XLV, in *Ausonius*, vol. 2, trans. Hugh G. Evelyn White, Loeb Classical Library 115 (Cambridge: Harvard University Press, and London: William Heinemann Ltd, 1967/1921), 184–185; Brown, *WLA*, p. 40.

[16]Conf. IX.vi.14: "You [God] and no one else inspired us to educate him in your teaching" (Chadwick, p. 164); "quod enim et nutriebatur a nobis in disciplina tua, tu inspiraveras nobis, nullus alius" (O'Donnell, I:108). Chadwick adds a note: "The sentence is crucial evidence that Adeodatus was not brought up as a Manichee, and therefore that his mother was a Catholic girl" (p. 164, n. 17).

[17]Kim Power, *Veiled Desire: Augustine on Women* (New York: Continuum, 1996), p. 100; Shaw, "The Family," p. 45.

[18]My translation. "non ergo ad acuendam linguam referebam illum librum, neque mihi locutio sed quod loquebatur persuaserat" (O'Donnell, I:25).

[19]My translation. "et hoc solum me in tanta flagrantia refrangebat, quod nomen Christi non erat ibi, quoniam hoc nomen secundum misericordiam tuam, domine, hoc nomen salvatoris mei, filii tui, in ipso adhuc lacte matris tenerum cor meum pie biberat et alte retinebat, et quidquid sine hoc nomine fuisset, quamvis litteratum et expolitum et veridicum, non me totum rapiebat" (O'Donnell, I:26).

[20]On the problem of Manichaeism's appeal more generally, see Jes P. Asmussen, trans. and ed., *Manichaean Literature: Representative Texts Chiefly from Middle Persian and Parthian Writings*, Persian Heritage Series, no. 22, Ehsan Yar-Shater, gen. ed. (Delmar, N.Y.: Scholars' Facsimiles and Reprints, 1975), pp. 44, 46, 51.

[21]Asmussen, *Manichaean Literature*, pp. 15, 54; François Decret, *Essais sur l'Église manichéenne en Afrique du Nord et à Rome au temps de saint Augustin: Recueil d'études* (Rome: Institutum Patristicum Augustinianum, 1995), pp. 17–18.

[22]Asmussen, *Manichaean Literature*, p. 10.

[23]Decret, *Essais sur l'église manichéenne*, pp. 19–21, 93–98.

[24]Brown, *AOH*, pp. 47–53; Decret, *Essais*, p. 99, n. 178; Edmund Hill, *The Works of Saint Augustine: A Translation for the 21st Century: Sermons I (1–19) on the Old Testament*, trans. with notes by Edmund Hill, Introduction by Michele Pellegrino, ed. John E. Rotelle, *The Works of Saint Augustine: A Translation for the 21st Century* (Brooklyn, N.Y.: New City Press, 1990), I:305, n. 1.

[25]Brown, *AOH*, pp. 50–53, and 369.

[26]Chadwick, p. 69. "quas cum contulissem cum eis qui se dicebant vix eas magistris eruditissimis, non loquentibus tantum sed multa in pulvere depingentibus, intellexisse, nihil inde aliud mihi dicere potuerunt quam ego solus apud me ipsum legens cognoveram" (O'Donnell, I:43).

[27]Brown, *AOH*, p. 53.

[28]*CA*, II.ii.3.

[29]Chadwick, p. 67. "nullo conlaudatore mirabar" (O'Donnell, I:42).

[30]Brown, *AOH*, pp. 66–67.

[31]My translation. "insectabantur ignotorum verecundiam, quam proturbarent gratis inludendo atque inde pascendo malivolas laetitias suas" (O'Donnell, I:25).

[32]Chadwick, p. 80. "contra apud Carthaginem foeda est et intemperans licentia scholasticorum. inrumpunt impudenter et prope furiosa fronte perturbant ordinem quem quique discipulis ad proficiendum instituerit. multa iniuriosa faciunt mira hebetudine, et punienda legibus nisi consuetudo patrona sit…" (O'Donnell, I:51–52).

[33]Ibid., p. 81. "quos mores cum studerem meos esse nolui, eos cum docerem cogebar perpeti alienos" (O'Donnell, I:52).

[34]Brown, *AOH*, pp. 66–67, 70–71.

[35]*CLP*, III.xxv.30.

[36]Pierre Courcelle, *Recherches sur les Confessions de Saint Augustin* (Paris: Éditions de Boccard, 1950), pp. 86–87.

[37]*AOH*, p. 37, and Robert A. Kaster, *Guardians of Language: The Grammarian and Society in Late Antiquity* (Berkeley: University of California Press, 1988), pp. 26–27; see also M. K. Hopkins, "Social Mobility in the Later Roman Empire: The Evidence of Ausonius," *Classical Quarterly* 11 (1961): 239, 244–245.

[38]*DUC*, vii.16, Burleigh, pp. 303–304. "Nonne videmus quam pauci summam eloquentiam consequantur, cum per totum orbem rhetorum scholae adolescentium gregibus perstrepant?… Tullianis navandam operam…Haec appetunt omnes, quae majorum auctoriate firmata sunt. Eadem imperitorum turbae discere moliuntur, quae a paucis doctis discenda recepta sunt: assequuntur autem perpauci…" (*PL*, 42:76).

[39]Kaster, *Guardians*, p. 27, quoting Paulinus of Nola, *Carm.*, 24.481f., and Jerome, Letter 66.6.

[40]R. A. Markus, "Paganism, Christianity and the Latin Classics in the Fourth Century," in *Latin Literature of the Fourth Century*, ed. J. W. Binns, Greek and Latin Studies, Classical Literature and Its Influence (London and Boston: Routledge & Kegan Paul, 1974), p. 9.

[41]*CA*, II.ii.3.

[42]Power, *Veiled Desire*, pp. 94–95.

[43]Peter Brown, *The Body and Society: Men, Women and Sexual Renunciation in Early Christianity*, Lectures on the History of Religions, N.S. 13 (New York: Columbia University Press, 1988), p. 390.

[44]In fact, Power's term "common-law marriage" seems to get at the phenomenon reasonably well (*Veiled Desire*, p. 71), although the laws did mention it in writing (Aimé Solignac, "Augustin et la mère d'Adéodat," BA, 13:678–679). See also Brown, *AOH*, p. 62; idem, *Body and Society*, p. 393.

[45]Shaw, "The Family," pp. 12–14; see also Brown, *AOH*, p. 62; Suzanne Dixon, "*Infirmitas Sexus*: Womanly Weakness in Roman Law," *Tijdschrift Voor Rechtsgeschiedenis/Legal History Review* 52 (1984): 365, 369; Anne Yarbrough, "Christianization in the Fourth Century: The Example of Roman Women," in *Studies in Early Christianity*, ed. Everett Ferguson, 14: *Women in Early Christianity*, ed. with an Introduction by David M. Scholer (New York and London: Garland Publishing, 1993), p. 324 (reprinted from *Church History* 45 (1976): 149–165).

⁴⁶Arline Rousselle, *Porneia: On Desire and the Body in Antiquity*, trans. Felicia Pheasant (Oxford: Basil Blackwell, 1983), p. 80.

⁴⁷Shaw, "The Family in Late Antiquity," pp. 40–41.

⁴⁸Brown, *Body and Society*, pp. 389–390.

⁴⁹Dixon, "*Infirmitas Sexus*," 348, also 363 regarding women in Monica's position; Rousselle, *Porneia*, p. 100. Note, however, that both authors are writing primarily about earlier periods of Roman law. While the laws resulting from them seem to apply to later years as well, one should be careful to recall that laws changed over time and that regional variations occurred (Rousselle, *Porneia*, pp. 100–101).

⁵⁰*DO*, II.17.45.

⁵¹Brown, *AOH*, pp. 193–199; Dudden, *Saint Ambrose*, I:115–126.

⁵²Sandra Lee Dixon, "Faith Receiving Understanding: On the Proposition that Augustine's Mother Learned Something," paper presented to the Rocky Mountain-Great Plains Regional Meeting of the American Academy of Religion and Society of Biblical Literature, Denver, April 27, 1996; idem, "Monica and the Psychological Interpretation of Augustine's *Confessions*, 1996. See also O'Donnell, II:121; Power, *Veiled Desire*, pp. 87–89.

⁵³My translation. "quae me profectum atrociter planxit et usque ad mare secuta est. sed fefelli eam, violenter me tenentem ut aut revocaret aut mecum pergeret" (O'Donnell, I:52).

⁵⁴Chadwick, p. 80. "ista ducebant animum tunc meum" (O'Donnell, I:50).

⁵⁵Dudden, *Saint Ambrose*, I:2–21, 58–62.

⁵⁶*AOH*, p. 36.

⁵⁷Ibid., pp. 36–37, quoting *Conf.*, V.vi.11. "delectabar quidem motu affectuque disputantis et verbis congruentibus atque ad vestiendas sententias facile occurrentibus" (O'Donnell, I:50).

⁵⁸A. Solignac, "Doxographies et manuels dans la formation philosophique de saint Augustin," *Recherches Augustiniennes* 1 (1958): 115–137.

⁵⁹Gananath Obeyesekere, *Medusa's Hair: An Essay on Personal Symbols and Religious Experience* (Chicago and London: University of Chicago Press, 1981), pp. 184–192.

⁶⁰Charles Kligerman, "A Psychoanalytic Study of the Confessions of St. Augustine," Donald Capps and James E. Dittes, eds., *The Hunger of the Heart: Reflections on the "Confessions" of Augustine*, Society for the Scientific Study of Religion Monograph Series, no. 8 (West Lafayette, Ind.: Society for the Scientific Study of Religion, 1990), pp. 104–105; similar implication by Phillip Woollcott, Jr., "Some Considerations of Creativity and Religious Experience in St. Augustine of Hippo," *JSSR* 5 (Spring 1966): 277. Fredriksen first sharply protested this view of Augustine's departure from North Africa (Paula Fredriksen, "Augustine and his Analysts: The Possibility of a Psychohistory," *Soundings* 61 [Summer 1978]: 213).

⁶¹Richard A. Shweder and Nancy C. Much, "Determinations of Meaning: Discourse and Moral Socialization," in *Moral Development Through Social Interaction*, eds. William Kurtines and Jacob Gewirtz (New York: Wiley & Sons, 1987), pp. 200–202.

⁶²O'Donnell, II:307, quoting Camille Bennett, "The Conversion of Vergil: The Aeneid in Augustine's *Confessions*," *Revue des Études Augustiniennes* 34 (1988): 61.

⁶³Compare, for instance, *Conf.*, IV.8.13 with Cicero's *Laelius sive De Amicitia Dialogus*, ed. with an Introduction by H. E. Gould and J. L. Whiteley (London: Macmillan and New York: St. Martin's Press, 1968), 25.92, and Aristotle, *Nicomachean Ethics*, trans. with an Introduction and notes by Terence Irwin (Indianapolis, Ind.: Hackett Publishing, 1985), book 8, esp. 1156 b, 1166a–1167b, 1168b–1170b. A useful summary of the relationship of these two works appears in Brian Patrick McGuire, *Friendship & Community: The Monastic Experience 350–1250*, Cistercian Studies Series, 95 (Kalamazoo, Mich.: Cistercian Publications, 1988), pp. xxix–xxxvi.

⁶⁴Marie Aquinas McNamara, *Friendship in Saint Augustine*, Studia Friburgensia, ed. H. O. Luthi, n.s. 20 (Fribourg, Switzerland: The University Press, 1958), pp. vii–viii, 196–197; McGuire, *Friendship*, pp. 48–49; cf. *Conf.*, IV.iv.7.

⁶⁵Chadwick, pp. 60–61. "alia erant quae in eis amplius capiebant animum, conloqui et conridere et vicissim benivole obsequi, simul legere libros dulciloquos, simul nugari et simul honestari, dissentire interdum sine odio tamquam ipse homo secum atque ipsa rarissima dissensione condire consensiones plurimas, docere aliquid invicem aut discere ab invicem, desiderare absentes cum molestia, suscipere venientes cum laetitia: his atque huius modi signis a corde amantium et redamantium procedentibus per os, per linguam, per oculos et mille motus gratissimos, quasi fomitibus conflare animos et ex pluribus unum facere" (O'Donnell, I:38).

⁶⁶Chadwick, p. 145. "da mihi castitatem et continentiam, sed noli modo" (O'Donnell, I:96).

⁶⁷Kohut, "The Psychoanalytic Treatment of Narcissistic Personality Disorders," in *SFS1*:481.

⁶⁸Don S. Browning, "The Psychoanalytic Interpretation of St. Augustine's *Confessions*: An Assessment and New Probe," in *Psychiatry and the Humanities*, vol. 2, *Psychoanalysis and Religion*, ed. Joseph H. Smith, assoc. ed. Susan A. Handelman (Baltimore and London: Johns Hopkins University Press, 1990), pp. 153–154; Volney Gay, "Augustine: The Reader as Selfobject," in *The Hunger of the Heart: Reflections on the "Confessions" of Augustine*, Donald Capps and James E. Dittes, eds., Society for the Scientific Study of Religion Monograph Series, no. 8 (West Layfayette, Ind.: Society for the Scientific Study of Religion, 1990), p. 194.

⁶⁹Kohut, "Psychoanalytic Treatment," p. 489.

⁷⁰Kohut, *HDA*, pp. 194–197.

⁷¹Ibid., p. 77.

⁷²Chadwick, pp. 58–59. "miser enim eram et amiseram gaudium meum....et taedium vivendi erat in me gravissimum et moriendi metus....et eam repente consumpturam omnes homines putabam, quia illum potuit....mirabar enim ceteros mortales vivere, quia ille, quem quasi non moriturum dilexeram, mortuus erat, et me magis...vivere illo mortuo mirabar" (O'Donnell, I:37).

⁷³My translation. "et erat mihi *patria* supplicium et *paterna* domus mira infelicitas" (O'Donnell, I:36), my emphasis.

⁷⁴Eric J. Ziolkowski, "St. Augustine: Aeneas' Antitype, Monica's Boy," *Literature and Theology* 9 (March 1995): 8–13.

⁷⁵Luke 15:11–32. See Chadwick, *Confessions*, p. 20, n. 34, p. 34, n. 17; O'Donnell, II:95.

⁷⁶Chadwick, *Confessions*, p. 60, n. 16.

⁷⁷Plotinus, *Enn.*, I.6.8. Armstrong notes that the Odyssey formed Plotinus' thinking, or at least the expression of it: "Odysseus became in late antiquity, for Christians as well as pagans, the type of the soul journeying to its true home and overcoming all difficulties and temptations on the way" (p. 257, n. 1). The *Ennead* itself reads, "We shall put out to sea, as Odysseus did, from the witch Circe or Calypso—as the poet says (I think with a hidden meaning)—and was not content to stay though he had delights of the eyes and lived among much beauty of sense" (*Enn.*, 1.6.8, Armstrong, p. 257).

⁷⁸*DM*, xi.38, xiv.46.

⁷⁹I will take issue with this as a defining characteristic of symbols, but for now the tendency of symbols to return to the concrete should be noted, Paul Ricoeur, *Freud and Philosophy: An Essay on Interpretation*, trans. Denis Savage (New Haven and London: Yale University Press, 1970), p. 56.

⁸⁰Kligerman, "A Psychoanalytic Study," pp. 104–105; William B. Parsons, "St. Augustine: 'Common Man' or 'Intuitive Psychologist'?" *Journal of Psychohistory* 18 (Fall 1990): 158–159, 162–163.

⁸¹For another approach to nuances in the psychoanalytic reading, see Parsons, "St. Augustine," pp. 170, 173, 177–178.

⁸²Margaret More O'Ferrall, "Monica, the Mother of Augustine: A Reconsideration," *Recherches Augustiniennes* 10 (1975): 30–31, 33–35, 37; Power, *Veiled Desire*, p. 82.

⁸³Ambrose, Letter 41.12 (*PL*, 16:1116; *FOC*, 26:389, designated letter 62 in this edition); idem, *Contra Auxentium* (Letter 21, part 2), 2; 16.

⁸⁴*DDC*, IV.xxiv.53; see also Brown, *AOH*, p. 207, referring to Augustine's *Ep.*, 29.7.

⁸⁵*S*, XII.4.

⁸⁶My translation. "iusto dolorum flagello" (O'Donnell, I:52).

⁸⁷Emendation of Chadwick's rendering, 82. "reliquarium Evae, cum gemitu quaerens quod cum gemitu pepererat" (O'Donnell, I:52).

⁸⁸Kligerman, "A Psychoanalytic Study," p. 103; Parsons, "St. Augustine," p. 160.

⁸⁹Chadwick, p. 87, slightly emended. "veni Mediolanium ad Ambrosium episcopum..." (O'Donnell, I:56). This sentence probably owes its placement at the end of this chapter to chap. 7 of Brown, *AOH*, 72.

Chapter 6: Conversion at the Limits of the Self

¹Margaret R. Miles, *Augustine on the Body*, American Academy of Religion Dissertation Series, 31, series ed., H. Ganse Little, Jr. (Missoula, Mont.: Scholars Press, 1979), pp. 51, 84 on Neoplatonic ambivalence and pp. 67–68 on social achievement and sexuality.

²Chadwick, p. 106. "alternabant hi venti et impellebant huc atque illuc cor meum..." (O'Donnell, I:69).

³Chadwick, p. 110. "vae animae audaci quae speravit, si a te recessisset, se aliquid melius habituram! versa et reversa in tergum et in latera et in ventrem, et dura sunt omnia" (O'Donnell, I:72).

⁴Chadwick, p. 111. "clamabat violenter cor meum adversus omnia phantasmata mea, et hoc uno ictu conabar abigere circumvolantem turbam immunditiae ab acie mentis meae, et vix dimota in ictu oculi, ecce conglobata rursus aderat…" (O'Donnell, I:73).

⁵Henry Chadwick, "History and Symbolism in the Garden at Milan," in *From Augustine to Eriugena: Essays on Neoplatonism and Christianity in Honor of John O'Meara*, ed. F. X. Martin and J. A. Richmond (Washington, D.C.: Catholic University of America Press, 1991), pp. 42–45; Pierre Courcelle, *Recherches sur les Confessions de Saint Augustin* (Paris: Éditions de Boccard, 1950), pp. 188–202; idem, "Source chrétienne et allusions païennes de l'épisode du 'Tolle, Lege' (Saint Augustin, *Confessions*, VIII, 12, 29)," *Revue d'Histoire et de Philosophie Religieuses* 32 (1952): 171–200; Marjorie Suchocki, "The Symbolic Structure of Augustine's *Confessions*," *Journal of the American Academy of Religion* 50 (September 1982): 365–366.

⁶Chadwick, p. 87, emended. "et veni Medolianum ad Ambrosium episcopum…" (O'Donnell, I:56).

⁷Ibid., p. 88. My emphasis. "ille autem saluberrime docebat salutem. sed longe est a peccatoribus salus, qualis ego tunc aderam, et tamen propinquabam sensim et nesciens" (O'Donnell, I:57).

⁸Chadwick, p. 143. "quam legere coepit unus eorum et mirari et accendi, et inter legendum meditari…relicta militia saeculari servire tibi.…iratus sibi, coniecit oculos in amicum et ait illi, 'dic, quaeso te, omnibus istis laboribus nostris quo ambimus pervenire? quid quaerimus? cuius rei causa militamus? maiorne esse poterit spes nostra in palatio quam ut amici imperatoris simus? et ibi quid non fragile plenumque periculis? Et per quot pericula pervenitur ad grandius periculum? et quando istuc erit?" (O'Donnell, I:95).

⁹Chadwick, trans., *Confessions*, p. 143, n. 12.

¹⁰*Recherches*, p. 86: "un échange de politesses officielles…"

¹¹Ibid., p. 92: "l'évêque catholique de Milan, si occupé que fût-il, n'eût sans doute pas refusé au rhéteur officiel de sa ville quelque heures de conversation intime…"

¹²Courcelle notes that Augustine in fact would have spoken in favor of someone Ambrose opposed as late as January 1, 385 (*Recherches*, p. 94). On this opponent, the consul Bauto, see Neil B. McLynn, *Ambrose of Milan: Church and Court in a Christian Capital* (Berkeley: University of California Press, 1994), pp. 172, n. 56.

¹³Chadwick, p. 88. "suscepit me paterne…eum amare coepi, primo quidem non tamquam doctorem veri, quod in ecclesia tua prorsus desperabam, sed tamquam hominem benignum in me" (O'Donnell, I:56).

¹⁴Ibid. "studiose audiebam disputantem in populo, non intentione qua debui, sed quasi explorans eius facundiam, utrum conveniret famae suae an maior minorve proflueret quam praedicabatur, et verbis eius suspendebar intentus, rerum autem incuriosus et contemptor adstabam. et delectabar suavitate sermonis…" (O'Donnell, I:56).

¹⁵Ibid., p. 88. "veniebant in animum meum simul cum verbis quae diligebam res etiam quas neglegebam, neque enim ea dirimere poteram" (O'Donnell, I:57).

¹⁶Ibid. "maxime audito uno atque altero et saepius aenigmate soluto de scriptis veteribus, ubi, cum ad litteram acciperem, occidebar" (O'Donnell, I:57).

¹⁷*CA*, II.v.11, ACW, 12:76. "nec homini scientiam posse contingere earum duntaxat rerum, quae ad philosophiam pertinet;…tamen hominem posse esse sapientem, sapientisque totum munus… in conquisitione veri…Ex quo confici, ut nulli etiam rei sapiens assentiatur: erret enim necesse est, quod sapienti nefas est, si assentiatur rebus incertis" (*PL*, 32:924–925).

¹⁸*AOH*, p. 80.

¹⁹Brown, *AOH*, p. 82; Peter Brown, *The Body and Society: Men, Women, and Sexual Renunciation in Early Christianity*, Lectures on the History of Religions, N.S. 13 (New York: Columbia University Press, 1988), p. 342.

²⁰Courcelle, *Recherches*, pp. 86–87. Courcelle dates Monica's arrival in Milan in part by knowledge of when a voyage on the Mediterranean would have been possible. In addition, her presence at events of historical importance the next year helps define which spring would have been the time of her travel.

²¹McLynn, *Ambrose*, pp. 185–186, 191, n. 115; Gérard Nauroy, "Le fouet et le miel: Le combat d'Ambroise en 386 contre l'arianisme milanais," *Recherches Augustiniennes* 23 (1988): 4–6; Daniel H. Williams, *Ambrose of Milan and the End of the Nicene-Arian Conflicts* (Oxford: Clarendon Press, 1995), pp. 210–211.

[22]*CTh*, XVI.i.4; Nauroy, "Le fouet et le miel," p. 13.

[23]Chadwick, p. 165. "nos adhuc frigidi a calore spiritus tui excitabamur tamen civitate attonita atque turbata" (O'Donnell, I:109).

[24]Ambrose, Letter 20.4; Nauroy, "Le fouet et le miel," pp. 21, 77–79.

[25]Ambrose, Letter 20.19; *FOC*, 26:371–372. (I will give references in page numbers to the *FOC* edition of Ambrose's letters in addition to the number of the letter and the paragraph because the numbering of the letters in the *FOC* edition does not follow that in *PL* nor are paragraph numbers given.)

[26]Ibid., 20.5; *FOC*, 26:366–367.

[27]Ibid., 20.11; *FOC*, 26:368.

[28]Williams, *Ambrose*, p. 215; Letter 20.13; *FOC*, 26:368.

[29]Ambrose, Letter 20.22; *FOC*, 26:373; McLynn, *Ambrose of Milan*, p. 193, n. 124.

[30]Ambrose, Letter 20.22–23; McLynn, *Ambrose of Milan*, p. 194.

[31]Ambrose, *Contra Auxentium*, 30 (*NPNF*,10:435; Letter 21.2.30 in *PL* 16:1016).

[32]Ambrose, Letter 20.24, *FOC*, 26:374; McLynn, *Ambrose*, p. 195.

[33]Ambrose, Letter, 20.27, *FOC*, 26:375; "Si vobis jusserit Ambrosius, vinctum me tradetis" (*PL* 16:1002).

[34]Chadwick, p. 165. "excubabat pia plebs in ecclesia, mori parata cum episcopo suo, servo tuo. ibi mater mea, ancilla tua, solicitudinis et vigiliarum primas tenens, orationibus vivebat" (O'Donnell, I:109).

[35]Letter 20.7, *FOC* 26:367. "Palatina omnia officia, hoc est, memoriales, agentes in rebus, apparitores diversorum comitum temperare a processu jubentur, specie qua seditioni interesse prohibebantur: honoratis multa minabantur gravissima, nisi basilicam traderent" (*PL* 16:996).

[36]Letter 22.13, *FOC*, 26:380–381.

[37]Chadwick, pp. 165–166. "illius inimicae animus etsi ad credendi sanitatem non applicatus, a persequendi tamen furore compressus est" (O'Donnell, I:109). Williams accepts Augustine's view (*Ambrose*, p. 221). McLynn sees the checking of the persecution more in the popular support for Ambrose than in the miracles attributed to the martyrs' relics (*Ambrose*, p. 215). Moreover, he disputes the amount of power available to Justina (pp. 171–172).

[38]Clifford Geertz, "Ritual and Social Change: A Javanese Example," in *The Interpretation of Cultures* (New York: Basic Books, 1973), pp. 142–144; Peter Gay, *Freud for Historians* (New York and Oxford: Oxford University Press, 1985), pp. 171–180; Gananath Obeyesekere, *Medusa's Hair: An Essay on Personal Symbols and Religious Experience* (Chicago and London: University of Chicago Press, 1981), pp. 114–115.

[39]Chadwick, p. 123. "Et inde admonitus redire ad memet ipsum, …intravi et vidi qualicumque oculo animae meae supra eundem oculum animae meae, supra mentem meam, lucem incommutabilem, non hanc vulgarem et conspicuam omni carni, nec quasi ex eodem genere grandior erat… non hoc illa erat sed aliud, aliud valde ab istis omnibus…superior, quia ipsa fecit me, et ego inferior, quia factus ab ea. qui novit veritatem, novit eam, et qui novit eam, novit aeternitatem; caritas novit eam. o aeterna veritas et vera caritas et cara aeternitas, tu es deus meus…et cum te primum cognovi, tu adsumpsisti me ut viderem esse quod viderem, et nondum me esse qui viderem" (O'Donnell, I: 81–82).

[40]*SAE*, pp. 46, 48.

[41]Chadwick, p. 127, except last sentence; also substituting "fleshly" for "sexual" to modify "habit." Augustine's word "carnalis" certainly includes the notion of sexual habit, but has wider application, that I believe Augustine wanted to include here. See Paula Fredriksen, "Augustine and His Analysts: The Possibility of a Psychohistory," *Soundings* 61 (1978): 209. "mirabar quod iam te amabam, non pro te phantasma, et non stabam frui deo meo, sed rapiebar ad te decore tuo moxque diripiebar abs te pondere meo, et ruebam in ista cum gemitu; et pondus hoc consuetudo carnalis. sed mecum erat memoria tui, neque ullo modo dubitatem esse cui cohaererem, sed nondum me esse qui cohaererem…" (O'Donnell, I:84).

[42]Chadwick, p. 139. "sed ubi mihi homo tuus Simplicianus de Victorino ista narravit, exarsi ad imitandum: ad hoc enim et ille narraverat" (O'Donnell, I:92).

[43]Matthew 19:21. W. H. C. Frend, *The Rise of Christianity* (Philadelphia, Pa.: Fortress, 1984), p. 422; Athanasius, *Vita S. Antonii (Life of Saint Anthony)*.

[44]Chadwick, p. 153. "non in comessationibus et ebrietatibus, non in cubilibus et impudicitiis, non in contentione et aemulatione, sed induite dominum Ieusum Christum et carnis providentiam ne feceritis in concupiscentiis" (O'Donnell, I:101).

[45]Ibid., p. 153. "infirmum autem in fide recipite" (O'Donnell, I:102).

⁴⁶Ibid., p. 106. "praesidatus" (O'Donnell, I:69).

⁴⁷Brent D. Shaw, "The Age of Roman Girls at Marriage: Some Reconsiderations," *Journal of Roman Studies* 77 (1987): 33, 42–44.

⁴⁸Anne Yarbrough, "Christianization in the Fourth Century: The Example of Roman Women," in *Women in Early Christianity*, ed. with an Introduction by David M. Scholer, *Studies in Early Christianity*, vol. 14, ed. Everett Ferguson (New York and London: Garland Publishing, 1993), pp. 326–327.

⁴⁹Chadwick, p. 107. "me iam coniugatum baptismus salutaris ablueret…" (O'Donnell, I:70).

⁵⁰Aimé Solignac, "Augustin et la mère d'Adéodat," BA, 13:679; Adolar Zumkeller, "Die geplante Eheschliessung Augustins und die Entlassung seiner Konkubine: Kulturgeschichtlicher und rechtlicher Hintergrund von conf. 6, 23, 25," in *Signum Pietatis: Festgabe für Cornelius Petrus Mayer*, ed. Adolar Zumkeller (Würzburg: Augustinus-Verlag, 1989), p. 26. Power seems to disagree about the legal proscription, but does not undertake an argument to make this particular point. *Veiled Desire: Augustine on Women* (New York: Continuum, 1996), p. 96.

⁵¹James E. Dittes, "Continuities Between the Life and Thought of Augustine," *JSSR* 5 (October 1965): 133; Paul Pruyser, "Psychological Examination: Augustine," in *The Hunger of the Heart: Reflections on the "Confessions" of Augustine*, ed. Donald Capps and James E. Dittes (West Lafayette, Ind.: Society for the Scientific Study of Religion, 1990), p. 36.

⁵²Brent D. Shaw, "The Family in Late Antiquity: The Experience of Augustine," *Past and Present* 115 (May 1987): 34; Power, *Veiled Desire*, p. 27.

⁵³Shaw, "The Family," pp. 32–33; Power, *Veiled Desire*, p. 26 (although Power seems to miss Suzanne Dixon's point in "Infirmitas Sexus" (p. 348) that freedom from tutelage for women was standard after about 300 C.E.).

⁵⁴My translation. "Et instabatur impigre ut ducerem uxorem" (O'Donnell, I:70).

⁵⁵*Sol.*, I.x.17; see Power, *Veiled Desire*, pp. 98, 101.

⁵⁶My translation. "quia ea placebat, exspectabatur" (O'Donnell, I:70).

⁵⁷"comme elle plaisait, on attendait" (BA, 13:567).

⁵⁸O'Donnell, II:377.

⁵⁹Chadwick, p. 109. "impedimento coniugii…" (O'Donnell, I:71).

⁶⁰Power, *Veiled Desire*, pp. 96, 106.

⁶¹*Gandhi's Truth: On the Origins of Militant Nonviolence* (New York and London: W. W. Norton & Company, 1969), Part 3, chap. 1, "A Personal Word."

⁶²Adapted from Chadwick, p. 109. "ego infelix nec feminae imitator, dilationis impatiens, tamquam post biennium accepturus eam quam petebam, quia non amator coniugii sed libidinis servus eram, procuravi aliam, non utique coniugem, quo tamquam sustentaretur et perduceretur vel integer vel auctior morbus animae meae satellitio perdurantis consuetudinis…" (O'Donnell, I:71).

⁶³My translation; see also Chadwick, p. 109. "cor, ubi adhaerebat, concisum et vulneratum mihi erat et trahebat sanguinem… nec sanabatur vulnus illud meum quod prioris praecisione factum erat, sed post fervorem doloremque acerrimum putrescebat…" (O'Donnell, I:71). See Fredriksen, "Augustine and His Analysts," p. 211, for an opinion like my own.

⁶⁴Power, *Veiled Desire*, p. 74.

⁶⁵Chadwick, p. 109. "in Africam redierat, vovens tibi alium se virum nescituram… nec feminae imitator…" (O'Donnell, I:71).

⁶⁶Geertz, "Ritual and Social Change," pp. 142–144; Gay, *Freud for Historians*, pp. 171–180.

⁶⁷Sigmund Freud, *The Origin and Development of Psychoanalysis*, Introduction by Eliseo Vivas (Washington, D.C.: Regnery Gateway, 1965/1910), pp. 59–69 (reprinted from *SE*, vol. 11, *Five Lectures on Psychoanalysis*); Gananath Obeyesekere, *The Work of Culture: Symbolic Transformation in Psychoanalysis and Anthropology* (Chicago and London: University of Chicago Press, 1990), pp. 20–24.

⁶⁸Power, *Veiled Desire*, pp. 99–104.

⁶⁹*Enn.* 1.8.4, *Plotinus I: Porphyry on the Life of Plotinus and the Order of His Books, Enneads I.1–9*, trans. A. H. Armstrong, Loeb Classical Library, vol. 440 (Cambridge: Harvard University Press, 1989), p. 287. For Ambrose, see, for example, *De bono mortis*, iii.11–12, FOC, vol. 65, pp. 78–79.

⁷⁰*Enn.*, 1.8.4, Loeb, I:287.

⁷¹Ibid., 1.8.7, Loeb, I:299.

⁷²See O'Connell, *SAE*, pp. 9–10 on the *Enneads* Augustine would have read.

[73]*Enn.*, 1.6.8, Loeb, I:255, 257, 259.

[74]Ibid., 1.6.9, Loeb I:259; quotes from Plato's *Phaedrus* 252D7 and 254B7.

[75]Ibid., Loeb I:261.

[76]Or intensified it (Miles, *Augustine on the Body*, p. 58).

[77]Ambrose, *De bono mortis*, 6.24, *FOC*, 65:88–89. "His ergo anima quae cupit evolare, deponitur. Sed tu obluctare quasi bonus miles Christi Jesu, et inferiora despiciens, terrena obliviscens, ad coelestia et aeterna contende. Attolle animam tuam, ne eam illiciat esca laqueorum. Voluptates saeculi, escae quaedam sunt; et quod pejus est, escae malorum, escae tentationum. Dum voluptatem quaeris, laqueos incurris. Oculos enim meretricis, laqueus amatoris est…Laqueus est aliena possessio plena amoenitatis. Omne iter istius vitae plenum laqueorum est" (*PL*, 14:551–552).

[78]Ibid., 12.55, *FOC*, 65:110; "Sequimur te, Domine Jesu: sed ut sequamur accersi, quia sine te nullus ascendit. Tu enim via es, veritas, vita, possibilitas, fides, praemium" (*PL*, 14:565).

[79]Ibid., *FOC*, 65:112; "Festinemus ergo ad vitam…Ibi ergo quaeramus eum, ubi quaesivit Joannes, et invenit. Ille eum in principio (Joan. I,1) quaesivit, et invenit viventem apud viventem, Filium apud Patrem" (*PL*, 14:566–567).

[80]Plotinus, *Enn.*, 1.6.8, Loeb I:259.

[81]Étienne Gilson, *The Christian Philosophy of Saint Augustine*, trans. L. E. M. Lynch (New York: Random House, 1960), p. 3; O'Connell, *SAE*, p. 205.

[82]Michael P. McHugh, "Introduction," *Jacob and the Happy Life*, Fathers of the Church, vol. 65 (Washington, D.C.: Catholic University of America Press, 1972), p. 117, n. 3.

[83]*De Jacob et beata vita*, I.i.1, *FOC*, 65:119. "Necessarius ad disciplinam bonus omnibus sermo, plenus prudentiae; et mens rationi intenta praecurrit virtutibus, passiones coercet. Docibilis enim virtus. Denique studio et discendo acquiritur, dissimulando amittitur" (*PL*, 14:597–598).

[84]Ibid., I.i.2, *FOC*, 65:120. "Quis enim tantus, ut corporalem motum possit auferre…" (*PL*, 14: 599).

[85]Ibid., I.i.4, *FOC*, 65:121–122. "Potest igitur mens sobria impressiones refrenare ac reprimere quamvis gravium passionum, et fervorem omnem cupiditatis flagrantissimae refrigerarer, derivare alio motus, et rectae rationis tractatione despuere passiones. Etenim Deus hominem constitueret, et in eo mores sensusque plantaret, tunc motibus ejus imposuit regale mentis imperium; ut omnes sensus motusque hominis, ejus vigore ac potestate regerentur" (*PL*, 14:600).

[86]Ibid., I.iii.9.

[87]Ibid., I.iii.10, *FOC*, 65:125. "Non est quod cuiquam nostram ascribamus aerumnam, nisi nostrae voluntati. Nemo tenetur ad culpam, nisi voluntate propria deflexerit. Non habent crimen quae inseruntur reluctantibus: voluntaria tantum commissa sequitur delictorum invidia, quod in alios derivemus" (*PL*, 14:602).

[88]Ibid., I.iv.16, *FOC*, 65:130. "Quod enim conturbamur, fragilitatis est: quod evadimus, Christi" (*PL*, 14:606).

[89]Ibid., I.vii.28, *FOC*, 65:137. "Ergo causa bene vivendi, non delectatio corporalis, sed mentis prudentia est…" (*PL*, 14:610).

[90]Ibid., I.vii.30, *FOC*, 65:138. "Nihil itaque aliud quaerit perfectus ille, nisi solum et praeclarum bonum. Unde et dicit: Unam petii a Domino, hanc requiram: ut inhabitem in domo Domini omnes dies vitae meae, et videam delectationem Domini (*Psal.* xxvi, 4)" (*PL*, 14:610).

[91]Ibid., I.vii.31, *FOC*, 65:139. "Hujus igitur propositi vir nec dispendiis minuitur, nec adversis frangitur, nec repagulis inhibetur, nec suorum amissionibus moestificatur.… . Qui autem contristatur his, non secundum Deum contristatur. Quod autem non secundum Deum, hoc plenum stultitiae. A perfecto igitur abest hujus mundi tristitia quae non secundum Deum, et omnis sollicitudo corporalis aerumnae" (*PL*, 14:611).

[92]Chadwick, pp. 133–134. "mihi autem displicebat quod agebam in saeculo et oneri mihi erat valde, non iam inflammantibus cupiditatibus, ut solebant, spe honoris et pecuniae ad tolerandam illam servitutem tam gravem. iam enim me illa non delectabant prae dulcedine tua et decore domus tuae, quam dilexi…et inveneram iam bonam margaritam, et venditis omnibus quae haberem emenda erat, et dubitabam" (O'Donnell, I:88–89).

[93]For a similar view of the length of Augustine's conversion, see O'Connell, *SAE*, p. 58; Solignac, "Introduction aux Confessions," BA, 13:163. For a theoretical social scientific account of conversion as an extended process more generally, see Lewis R. Rambo, *Understanding Religious Conversion* (New Haven, Conn.: Yale University Press, 1993).

[94]Shweder, "Cultural Psychology—What Is It?", p. 2.

[95]Ibid., p. 23.

[96]My translation. "neque ullo modo dubitabam esse cui cohaererem, sed nondum me esse qui cohaererem…" (O'Donnell, I:84). See *SAC*, pp. 1–3, and BA, 13:616–617, n. 1.

[97]Chadwick, p. 145. "iniquitatem…sed dissimulabam et cohibebam et obliviscebar" (O'Donnell, I:96).

[98]My translation. "ibi tot pueri et puellae, ibi iuventus multa et omnis aetas, et graves viduae et virgines anus, et in omnibus ipsa continentia nequaquam sterilis, sed fecunda mater filiorum gaudiorum de marito te, domine. et inridebat me inrisione hortatoria, quasi diceret, 'tu non poteris quod isti, quod istae? an vero isti et istae in se ipsis possunt ac non in domino deo suo? dominus deus eorum me dedit eis. quid in te stas et non stas? proice te in eum! noli metuere. non se subtrahet ut cadas: proice te securus! excipiet et sanabit te.' et erubescebam nimis, quia illarum nugarum murmura adhuc audiebam, et cunctabundus pendebam. et rursus illa, quasi diceret, 'obsurdesce adversus immunda illa membra tua super terram, ut mortificentur. narrant tibi delectationes, sed non sicut lex domini dei tui.' ista controversia in corde meo non nisi de me ipso adversus me ipsum" (O'Donnell, I:100).

[99]William James, *The Varieties of Religious Experience: A Study in Human Nature*, with an Introduction by Reinhold Niebuhr (New York: Macmillan, Collier Books and London: Collier Macmillan Publishers, 1961/[1902]), p. 165.

[100]Ibid., pp. 163–167.

[101]Ibid., pp. 174–176.

[102]Chadwick, p. 152, slightly altered. "Ubi vero a fundo arcano alta consideratio traxit et congessit totam miseriam meam in conspectu cordis mei, oborta est procella ingens ferens ingentem imbrem lacrimarum. et ut totum effunderem cum vocibus suis, surrexi ab Alypio… ego sub quadam fici arbore stravi me nescio quomodo, et dimisi habenas lacrimis… et non quidem his verbis, sed in hac sententia multa dixi tibi: 'et tu, domine, usquequo? usquequo, domine, irasceris in finem? ne memor fueris iniquitatum nostrarum antiquarum.' sentiebam enim eis me teneri. iactabam voces miserabiles: 'Quamdiu, quamdiu "cras et cras"? quare non modo? quare non hac hora finis turpitudinis meae?'" (O'Donnell, I:101).

[103]Ibid., Chadwick, p. 153, emended. "'tolle lege, tolle lege'…nihil aliud interpretans divinitus mihi iuberi nisi ut aperirem codicem et legerem quod primum caput invenissem… 'non in comessationibus et ebrietatibus, non in cubilibus et impudicitiis, non in contentione et aemulatione, sed induite dominum Iesum Christum et carnis providentiam ne feceritis in concupiscentiis'" (O'Donnell, I:101).

[104]Chadwick, p. 133. "de mea vero temporali vita nutabant omnia et mundandum erat cor a fermento veteri. et placebat via ipse salvator, et ire per eius angustias adhuc pigebat" (O'Donnell, I:88).

[105]*AOS*, p. 177, n. 8.

[106]Ricoeur talks about this type of analysis as analogical, the only kind of analysis of historical figures that he sees as defensible. Paul Ricoeur, *Freud and Philosophy: An Essay on Interpretation*, trans. Denis Savage (New Haven and London: Yale University Press, 1970), pp. 171–172.

[107]*AOS*, p. 177.

[108]John E. Gedo and Arnold Goldberg, *Models of the Mind: A Psychoanalytic Theory* (Chicago and London: University of Chicago Press, 1973), p. 65.

[109]*AOS*, p. 184.

[110]*ROS*, p. 213.

[111]Ibid., p. 205.

[112]Ibid., p. 213.

[113]Chadwick, p. 92. "ad quaerendum intentus et ad disserendum inquietus erat animus meus…" (O'Donnell, I:59).

[114]My translation. "Inhiabam honoribus, lucris, coniugio…quam ergo miser eram, et quomodo egisti ut sentirem miseriam meam die illo quo, cum pararem recitare imperatori laudes, quibus plura mentirer et mentienti faveretur ab scientibus…neque enim eo me praeponere illi debebam, quo doctior eram, quoniam non inde gaudebam, sed placere inde quaerebam hominibus, non ut eos docerem sed tantum ut placerem" (O'Donnell, I:62–63).

[115]My translation. "et certe ille laetabatur, ego anxius eram, securus ille, ego trepidus. et si quisquam percontaretur me utrum mallem exultare an metuere, responderem, 'exultare' rursus si interrogaret utrum me talem mallem qualis ille, an qualis ego tunc essem, me ipsum curis timoribusque confectum eligerem, sed perversitate—numquid veritate?" (O'Donnell, I:63).

[116]My translation. "et ille ipsa nocte digesturus erat ebrietatem suam, ego cum mea dormieram et surrexeram et dormiturus et surrecturus eram, vide quot dies!…nimirum quippe

ille felicior erat, non tantum quod hilaritate perfundebatur, cum ego curis eviscerarer, verum etiam quod ille bene optando adquisiverat vinum, ego mentiendo quaerebam typhum" (O'Donnell, I:63).

[117]Williams, *Ambrose*, p. 113.

[118]Chadwick, p. 92. "ipsumque Ambrosium felicem quendam hominem secundum saeculum opinabar, quem sic tantae potestates honorarent; caelibatus tantum eius mihi laboriosus videbatur" (O'Donnell, I:59).

[119]*De bono mortis*, 3.12, FOC, 65:78–79. "Multas igitur occupationes nobis corporis huius necessitas gignit, atque usus invehit, quibus impeditur animae vigor, ac revocatur intentio…. ipsa vita in luto. Nulla firmitudo sententiae, nulla constantia" (*PL*, 14:545–546).

[120]Ibid., 9.41, FOC, 65:100. "anima quae adhaeret illi invisibili bono Deo, atque immortali, et ipsa corporea haec fugit, et terrena, et mortalia derelinquit, fitque illius similis quod desiderat, in quo vivit et pascitur…" (*PL*, 14:559).

[121]Brown, *AOH*, pp. 92–93, 102; O'Donnell, II:414–416.

[122]*CA*, II.ii.5; *ACW* 12:69. "Et quoniam nondum aderat ea flamma, quae summa nos arreptura erat; illamque lenta aestuabamus, arbitrabamur vel esse maximam. Cum ecce tibi libri quidam pleni… ubi illi flammulae instillarunt pretiosissimi unguenti guttas paucissimas; incredibile, Romaniane, incredibile… incredibile incendium concitarunt" (*PL* 32:921).

[123]*De Jacob*, 1.4.16, FOC, 65:130. "Quod enim conturbamur, fragilitatis est: quod evadimus, Christi" (*PL*, 14:606).

[124]Ibid., 1.6.25, FOC, 65:135. "Sed vereris dubios vitae anfractus, et adversarii insidias, cum habeas auxilium Dei, habeas tantam ejus dignationem…Et Filius mortis acerbitatem sentire non potuit. Quod in Patre fuit, nihil sibi ipse reliquit: totum pro te obtulit: quod in plenitudine divinitatis, nihil ipse amisit, et te redemit" (*PL*, 14:608).

[125]Heinz Kohut, "Thoughts on Narcissism and Narcissistic Rage," in *SFS2*:623.

[126]Chadwick, pp. 90–91. "ei cum indicassem non me quidem iam esse manichaeum, sed neque catholicum christianum, non quasi inopinatum aliquid audierit, exilivit laetitia… feretro cogitationis offerebat ut diceres filio viduae, 'iuvenis, tibi dico, surge'…placidissime et pectore pleno fiduciae respondit mihi credere se in Christo quod priusquam de hac vita emigraret me visura esset fidelem catholicum" (O'Donnell, I:58).

[127]*Sol.*, II.xiv.26.

[128]Chadwick, p. 92. "saepe erumperet, cum me videret, in eius praedicationem gratulans mihi, quod talem matrem haberem…" (O'Donnell, I:59).

[129]My translation, adapted from Chadwick, p. 107. "quo me iam coniugatum baptismus salutaris ablueret…" (O'Donnell, I:70).

[130]Sandra Lee Dixon, "Faith Receiving Understanding: On the Proposition that Augustine's Mother Learned Something," paper presented to the Rocky Mountain-Great Plains Regional Meeting of the American Academy of Religion and Society of Biblical Literature, Denver, Col., April 27, 1996; Sandra Lee Dixon, "Monica and the Psychological Interpretation of Augustine's *Confessions*," 1996; Power, *Veiled Desire*, pp. 87–88.

[131]Power, *Veiled Desire*, pp. 98, 102.

[132]My translation. "desperabam de inventione veri" (O'Donnell, I:58).

[133]My translation. "avulsa a latere meo tamquam impedimento coniugii cum qua cubare solitus eram, cor, ubi adhaerebat, concisum et vulneratum mihi erat et trahebat sanguinem…post fervorem dolermque acerrimum putrescebat, et quasi frigidius sed desperatius dolebat" (O'Donnell, I:71). A. Solignac refers to these passages as support for the idea that Augustine felt a real love ("un réel amour") for his concubine ("Augustin et la mère d'Adéodat," BA., 13:679).

[134]*AOS*, p. 149; Kohut, *ROS*, p. 110; Kohut, *HDA*, pp. 17–18; 193–194.

[135]"A Note on Female Sexuality," in *SFS2*:789.

[136]Power, *Veiled Desire*, p. 99.

[137]*DBC*, V.5.

[138]Zumkeller, "Die geplante Eheschliessung Augustins," p. 33, quoting approvingly A. Maxsein in Aurelius Augustinus, *Das Gut der Ehe* (Würzburg, 1949), p. 52; see also Power, *Veiled Desire*, pp. 105–107.

[139]Chadwick, p. 98. "saepe advertebam in his quomodo mihi esset, et inveniebam male mihi esse et dolebam et conduplicabam ipsum male et, si quid adrisisset prosperum, taedebat apprehendere, quia paene priusquam teneretur avolabat." "Congemescebamus in his qui simul amice vivebamus…" (O'Donnell, I:63–64).

[140]Slightly revised from Chadwick, pp. 88–89. "nec tamen iam ideo mihi catholicam viam tenendam esse, quia et ipsa poterat habere doctos adsertores suos, qui copiose et non

absurde obiecta refellerent, nec ideo iam damnandum illud quod tenebam quia defensionis partes aequabantur. ita enim catholica non mihi victa videbatur, ut nondum etiam victrix appareret.

"Tum vero fortiter intendi animum, si quo modo possem certis aliquibus documentis manichaeos convincere falsitatis…itaque academicorum more, sicut existimantur, dubitans de omnibus et inter omnia fluctuans, manichaeos quidem reliquendos esse decrevi… quibus tamen philosophis, quod sine salutari nomine Christi essent, curationem languoris animae meae committere omnino recusabam" (O'Donnell, I:57).

[141]Chadwick, p. 92. "Nec iam ingemescebam orando ut subvenires mihi, sed ad quaerendum intentus et ad disserendum inquietus erat animus meus…" (O'Donnell, I:59).

[142]Chadwick, p. 93. "et eum quidem in populo verbum veritatis recte tractantem omni die dominico audiebam…tamen gaudens erubui non me tot annos adversus catholicam fidem, sed contra carnalium cogitationum figmenta latrasse" (O'Donnell, I:60).

[143]Chadwick, p. 94. "tanto igitur acrior cura rodebat intima mea, quid certi retinerem, quanto me magis pudebat tam diu inlusum et deceptum promissione certorum puerili errore et animositate tam multa incerta quasi certa garrisse…etsi nondum compertam vera docentem, non tamen ea docentem quae graviter accusabam. itaque confundebar et convertebar…" (O'Donnell, I:60–61).

[144]Chadwick, p. 146. "surgunt indocti et caelum rapiunt, et nos cum doctrinis nostris sine corde, ecce ubi volutamur in carne et sanguine!…" (O'Donnell, I:96).

[145]Margaret R. Miles, "Infancy, Parenting, and Nourishment in Augustine's *Confessions*," *Journal of the American Academy of Religion* 50 (September 1982): 355.

[146]My translation. "mater filiorum gaudiorum de marito te, domine…quid in te stas et non stas? proice te in eum! noli metuere. non se subtrahet ut cadas: 'proice te securus! excipiet et sanabit te.' et erubescebam nimis…" (O'Donnell, I:100).

[147]Miles, "Infancy, Parenting, and Nourishment," pp. 358–361.

[148]My translation. "ut venirem neque dubitarem, et extendens ad me suscipiendum et amplectendum pias manus plenas gregibus bonorum exemplorum…" (O'Donnell, I:100).

[149]Chadwick, p. 93. "aestus autem illi mei otiosum eum valde cui refunderentur requirebant nec umquam inveniebant" (O'Donnell, I:60).

[150]Ibid., pp. 144–145. "tu autem, Domine, inter verba eius retorquebas me ad me ipsem, auferens me a dorso meo, ubi me posueram dum nollem me attendere, et constituebas me ante faciem meam, ut viderem quam turpis essem, quam distortus et sordidus, maculosus et ulcerosus. et videbam et horrebam, et quo a me fugerem non erat. sed si conabar avertere a me aspectum, narrabat ille quod narrabat, et tu me rursus opponebas mihi et impingebas me in oculos meos, ut invenirem iniquitatem meam et odissem. noveram eam, sed dissimulabam et cohibebam et obliviscebar.

"Tunc vero quanto ardentius amabam illos de quibus audiebam salubres affectus, quod se totos tibi sanandos dederunt, tanto exsecrabilius me comparatum eis oderam…" (O'Donnell, I:95–96).

Chapter 7: Christian Life up to 397 C.E.

[1]E.g., Brown comments on Paulinus of Nola (*AOH*, p. 144), and Elizabeth Clark writes of well-to-do women surrounding Jerome (*Jerome, Chrysostom, and Friends: Essays and Translations*, Studies in Women and Religion 2 [New York and Toronto: Edwin Mellen Press, 1979], pp. 44–45, 76).

[2]Pierre Courcelle, *Recherches sur les "Confessions" de saint Augustin* (Paris: Éditions de Boccard, 1950), pp. 7–12; O'Donnell, I:xx–xxxii; Robert J. O'Connell, "The Visage of Philosophy at Cassiciacum," *Augustinian Studies* 25 (1994): 65–67; A. Solignac, "Introduction aux Confessions," BA, 13:55–84, 158–163.

[3]*CA*, III.xxix.43.

[4]*DBV*, 1.4; see O'Connell, "Visage of Philosophy," pp. 69–75, for more instances discovered through a careful reading in cultural terms.

[5]On the date, see O'Donnell, III:104.

[6]Chadwick, p. 175. "quod erat tempori congruum…" (O'Donnell, I:116).

[7]After the death of the emperor Maximus (*CLP*, III.xxv.30), who died in the summer of 388; see also Courcelle, *Recherches*, p. 232.

[8]Brown, *AOH*, p. 140 and n. 6 re: Alypius, p. 201 re: Alypius and Evodius.

[9]Compare *DME*, 33.70.

[10]Herbert T. Weiskotten, *Sancti Augustini Vita Scripta a Possidio Epicopo*, ed. and trans. with an Introduction and notes by Herbert T. Weiskotten (Princeton: Princeton University Press, 1919), p. 147, n. 1.

[11]Ibid., p. 149, n. 4.

[12]Brown, *AOH*, p. 138, quoting Augustine's *S*, 355.2.

[13]*Vita*, 3.

[14]Brown intimates such a possibility (*AOH*, p. 137).

[15]Brown, *AOH*, pp. 138–139; Henry Chadwick, "On Re-reading the *Confessions*," in *Saint Augustine the Bishop*, ed. Fannie LeMoine and Christopher Kleinhenz (New York and London: Garland Publishing, 1994), p. 139.

[16]Paulinus of Milan, *Vita Ambrosii*, in *Paulin de Milan et la "Vita Ambrosii": Aspects de la religion sous le Bas-Empire*, trans. and ed. Émilien Lamirande (Paris: Desclée and Montréal: Bellarmin, 1983), 6–9; Neil B. McLynn, *Ambrose of Milan: Church and Court in a Christian Capital* (Berkeley: University of California Press, 1994), pp. 1–12; for comments on the literary figure of the unwilling clerical draftee, see Daniel H. Williams, *Ambrose of Milan and the End of the Nicene-Arian Conflicts* (Oxford: Clarendon Press, 1995), pp. 113–115. For the nearly successful forced recruitment of another well-known man as a priest, see Augustine, *Ep.*, 125 and 126.

[17]*Vita*, 5; see Brown, *AOH*, pp. 139–140; Frederic Van der Meer, *Augustine the Bishop: The Life and Work of a Father of the Church*, 2nd ed., trans. B. Battershaw and G. R. Lamb (London: Sheed and Ward, 1978), pp. 6–7.

[18]*Ep.*, 21.

[19]Augustine, *Retractations*, trans. Mary Inez Bogan, *Fathers of the Church*, vol. 60 (Washington, D.C.: Catholic University of America Press, 1968), I.16 (xvii in *PL*), p. 74 and n. 1; *Retractationes, PL*, 32:612.

[20]*Vita*, 8; Brown, *AOH*, pp. 140, 203–204; Van der Meer holds that the consecration was irregular (*Augustine the Bishop*, p. 9), while Weiskotten argues for a nuance of interpretation that would make it "entirely lawful" (*Vita*, p. 153, n. 3).

[21]Van der Meer's *Augustine the Bishop* is a vivid source of information on Augustine's ecclesiastical work.

[22]O'Connell, "Visage of Philosophy," p. 68.

[23]*CA*, III.xx.43.

[24]*DBV*, 4.27.

[25]*DO*, II.v.16; see O'Connell, "Visage of Philosophy," p. 73.

[26]*Sol.*, I.ii.7, I.xv.27, II.xviii.32.

[27]Ibid., I.xiii.22, Burleigh, p. 37. "ego autem solam propter se amo sapientiam..." (*PL*, 32:881).

[28]Although he does in *DBV*, 4.34; see O'Connell, "Visage of Philosophy," p. 74. See, inter alia, Wisd. 1:6, 6:13–27, 7:7, 15, 22, 25—8:1, 10:1–3, 10:18–21; I Cor. 1:18–30.

[29]O'Connell, *SAE*, pp. 52–57.

[30]*Sol.*, I.vi.12.

[31]Ibid., II.xix.33—II.xx.34.

[32]See 1 Cor. 13:13; Robert J. O'Connell, *ACI*, p. 26.

[33]*Sol.*, I.i.2–3, Burleigh, p. 24. Citing 1 Cor. 15:54. "pater veritatis, pater sapientiae, pater verae summaeque vitae, pater beatitudinis, pater boni et pulchri, pater intelligibilis lucis... a quo averti, cadere; in quem converti, resurgere...Deus cui nos fides excitat, spes erigit, charitas jungit...Deus per quem mors absorbetur in victoriam" (*PL*, 32:870).

[34]*SAE*, pp. 66–73.

[35]*CA*, I.i.3–4, *ACW*, 12:38-39. The gender of philosophy is clear in the Latin throughout the passage: "in philosophiae gremium confugere...Ipsa me nunc...nutrit ac fovet...Ipsa enim docet, et vere docet nihil omnino colendum esse, totumque contemni oportere, quidquid mortalibus oculis cernitur, quidquid ullus sensus attingit...Philosophia est enim, a cujus uberibus se nulla aetas queretur excludi..."(*PL*, 32:907).

[36]Ibid., II.ii.6 My translation: "ad ejus pulchritudinem blandus amator et sanctus, mirans, anhelans, aestuans advolaret" (*PL*, 32:922); O'Connell, *SAE*, pp. 71–72.

[37]*Sol.*, I.ii.7.

[38]*Sol.*, I.xiii.22–23, Burleigh, p. 37. "Nunc illud quaerimus, qualis sit amator sapientiae, quam castissimo conspectu atue amplexu, nullo interposito velamento quasi nudam videre ac tenere desideras, qualem se illa non sinit, nisi paucissimis et electissimis amatoribus suis. An vero si alicujus pulchrae feminae amore flagrares, jure se tibi non daret, si aliud abs te quidquam praeter se amari comperisset; sapientiae se tibi castissima pulchritudo, nisi solam

arseris, demonstrabit? A…Quem modum autem potest habere illius pulchritudinis amor, in qua non invideo caeteris, sed etiam plurimos quaero qui mecum appetant, mecum inhient, mecum teneant, mecumque perfruantur; tanto mihi amiciores futuri, quanto erit nobis amata communior. R. Prorsus tales esse amatores sapientiae decet. Tales quaerit illa cujus vere casta est, et sine ulla contaminatione conjunctio" (PL, 32:881).

[39]*SAC*, pp. 57, 72–73

[40]*Sol.*, I.xiv.25, I.xv.27.

[41]Ibid., I.xv.30.

[42]*CA*, I.i.1. My translation: "hominem sibi aptum…virtus…posset auferre, ut ab ea sibi auferri neminem patitur jam tibi profecto injecisset manum, suique juris te esse proclamans, et in bonorum certissimorum possessionem traducens, ne prosperis quidem casibus servire permitteret" (PL, 32:905).

[43]Ibid. My translation. "divinum animum mortalibus inhaerentem, nequaquam sapientiae portus accipiat, ubi neque adversante fortunae flatu, neque secundante moveatur; nisi eo illum fortuna ipsa, vel secunda, vel quasi adversa perducat: nihil pro te nobis aliud quam vota restant, quibus ab illo cui haec curae sunt Deo, si possumus, impetremus ut te tibi reddat; ita enim facile reddet et nobis; sinatque mentem illam tuam, quae respirationem jamdiu parturit, aliquando in auras verae libertatis emergere" (PL, 32:905).

[44]*Enn.*, VI.5.7, p. 341; O'Connell, *SAE*, pp. 62–63.

[45]My translation. "Cumque ad eum finem sermo perduceretur, ut carnalium sensuum delectatio quantalibet, in quantalibet luce corporea, prae illius vitae iucunditate non comparatione sed ne commemoratione quidem digna videretur, erigentes nos ardentiore affectu in idipsum, perambulavimus gradatim cuncta corporalia et ipsum caelum, unde sol et luna et stellae lucent super terram. et adhuc ascendebamus interius cogitando et loquendo et mirando opera tua. et venimus in mentes nostras et transcendimus eas, ut attingeremus regionem ubertatis indificientis, ubi pascis Israhel in aeternum veritate pabulo, et ibi vita sapientia est, per quam fiunt omnia ista…et dum loquimur et inhiamus illi, attingimus eam modice toto ictu cordis. et suspiravimus et reliquimus ibi religatas primitias spiritus et remeavimus ad strepitum oris nostri…" (O'Donnell, I:113). See the excellent notes on translation in BA, 14:550–555; also Bernard McGinn on *toto ictu cordis* (*The Presence of God: A History of Western Mysticism*, vol. 1, *The Foundations of Mysticism* (New York: Crossroad, 1992), pp. 234–235).

[46]Augustine's use of Rom. 8:23 is his own reinterpretation of that text (Aimé Solignac, "Primitiae spiritus," BA, 14:552–555); also *The Confessions*, trans. with an Introduction and notes by Maria Boulding, The Works of Saint Augustine: A Translation for the 21st Century, I/1, ed. John E. Rotelle (Hyde Park, N.Y.: New City Press, 1997), p. 228, n. 102. Paul Henry notes nearly a dozen biblical allusions in the Ostia vision passages. *The Path to Transcendence: From Philosophy to Mysticism in St. Augustine*, trans. with an Introduction by Francis F. Burch, The Pittsburgh Theological Monograph Series, no. 37 (Pittsburgh, Penn.: The Pickwick Press, 1981), p. 29.

[47]Augustine uses several related words to talk about adhering to God. They include "*inhaerere*," "*haerere*," "*cohaerere*," and "*adhaerere*," and appear in translation as words like "cling to," "cleave to," "adhere to," and even "stick to." See comments in John Burnaby, "*Amor Dei*": *A Study of the Religion of St. Augustine* (London: Hodder & Stoughton, 1938), pp. 61–62; McGinn, *Presence of God*, I:253; Oliver O'Donovan, *The Problem of Self-Love in St. Augustine* (New Haven and London: Yale University Press, 1980), pp. 21–22.

[48]*DME*, 6.10. My translation: "Deus igitur restat, quem si sequimur, bene: se assequimur, non tantum bene, sed etiam beate vivimus" (PL, 32:1315).

[49]Ibid., 7.11. My translation. "avertit sese: intueri non potest, palpitat, aestuat, inhiat amore, reverberatur luce veritatis, et ad familiaritatem tenebrarum suarum, non electione, sed fatigatione convertitur" (PL, 32:1315).

[50] Ibid., "opacitas"

[51]Ibid., 7.12. My emphasis, *NPNF* 4:44. "nequaquam intelligere poterimus, nisi ab humanis et proximis incipientes, verae religionis fide, praeceptisque servatis, non deseruerimus viam quam nobis Deus…munivit" (PL, 32:1315–1316).

[52]Ibid., 8.13, cf. *NPNF* 4:45. Matt. 22:37 (Latin in note 56 below); Rom. 8:28: "diligentibus Deum omnia procedunt [sunergei…] in bonum" (in italics in the original; PL, 32:1316).

[53]Ibid., 9.14, quoting Deut. 6:5 for the first great commandment.

[54]*DME*, 11.18, *NPNF*, 4:46. My emphasis. "Secutio igitur Dei, beatitatis appetitus est: consecutio autem, ipsa beatitas. At eum sequimur diligendo, consequimur vero, non cum hoc omnino efficimur quod est ipse, sed ei proximi, eumque mirifico et intelligibili modo

contigentes, ejusque veritate et sanctitate penitus illustrati atque comprehensi. Ille namque ipsum lumen est; nobis autem ab eodem illuminari licet" (*PL,* 32:1319).

[55]*DBV,* 2.11, 2.12, 3.21, 4.34–35.

[56]*DME,* 11.18, *NPNF,* 4:46. "*Maximum* ergo quod ad beatam vitam ducit, *primumque mandatum est, Diliges Dominum Deum tuum ex toto corde tuo et anima et mente...quis...nihil nobis aliud esse optimum, ad quod adipiscendum postpositis caeteris festinare oporteat, quam Deum?" (*PL,* 32:1319).

[57]Ibid., 13.22, *NPNF,* 4:48. "charitate...qua sola efficitur ut a Deo non avertamur, eique potius quam huic mundo conformemur..."(*PL,* 32:1321).

[58]Ibid., 13.23, *NPNF,* 4:48, quoting Romans 5:5. "charitas Dei diffusa est in cordibus nostris per Spiritum sanctum qui datus est nobis" (*PL,* 32:1321; in italics in the original).

[59]Ibid., 26.49, *NPNF,* 4:55. "Diliges proximum tuum tanquam teipsum (Matt. xxii, 39)" (*PL,* 32:1331; in italics in original).

[60]Ibid., 26.49. My translation. "Quod ergo agis tecum, id agendum cum proximo est; hoc est, ut ipse etiam perfecto amore diligat Deum. Non enim cum diligis tanquam teipsum, si non ad id bonum ad quod ipse tendis, adducere satagis. Illud est enim unum bonum, quod omnibus tecum tendentibus non fit angustum. Ex hoc praecepto nascuntur officia societatis humanae..." (*PL,* 32:1331–1332).

[61]*Sol.,* I.xiii.22–23; see also O'Connell, *SAE,* pp. 52–58.

[62]*DME,* 26.50, *NPNF,* 4:55, quoting Rom. 13:10. "Accipe etiam quid Paulus dicat: 'Dilectio,' inquit, 'proximi, malum non operatur' (Rom. 13, 10)... 'Scimus quoniam diligentibus Deum omnia procedunt in bonum' (Ibid., viii, 28)" (*PL,* 32:1332; quotations from scripture in italics in the original).

[63]Ibid., 33.70.

[64]Ibid., 33.71, *NPNF,* 4:61. "meminerunt enim quantopere Scripturis omnibus commendata sit charitas; meminerunt, 'Omnia munda mundi' (Tit. 1, 15);... Itaque non rejicendis generibus ciborum quasi pollutis, sed concupiscentiae perdomandae, et dilectioni fratrum retinendae invigilat omnis industria" (*PL,* 32:1340; quotation from scripture in italics in the original).

[65]Ibid., 33.73. My translation. "Charitas praecipue custoditur; charitati victus, charitati sermo, charitati habitus, charitati vultus aptatur; coitur in unam conspiraturque charitatem: hanc violare tanquam Deum nefas ducitur" (*PL,* 32:1341).

[66]E.g., Augustine, *On Baptism, Against the Donatists* (*De Baptismo contra Donatistas*), VII.xlix.97; *NPNF,* 4:511; *PL,* 43:240; Rémi Crespin, *Ministère et sainteté: Pastorale du clergé et solution de la crise donatiste dans la vie et la doctrine de saint Augustin* (Paris: Études Augustiniennes, 1965), p. 137.

[67]*Retractations,* I.8.1.

[68]*DLA,* I.ii.4.

[69]The philosophical topics include lust and its power to divert the soul (*DLA,* I.viii.18, I.x.20—xii.24); three levels of life (vegetable, animal, human) as found in Aristotle (*DLA,* I.viii.18), cf. Aristotle, *Nicomachean Ethics,* trans. with an Introduction and notes by Terence Irwin (Indianapolis, Ind.: Hackett Publishing, 1985), 1097b–1098a; the importance of order and therefore justice in the soul (*DLA,* I.vii.16–xiii.27); and the four classical virtues (*DLA,* I.xiii.27); and others.

[70]*Retractations,* I.8.1.

[71]*DLA,* II.viii.22–24.

[72]Ibid., II.xiii.35—II.xvii.45.

[73]Ibid., II.xvi.41—xvii.45.

[74]Ibid., II.xvi.43.

[75]As Étienne Gilson claimed and many scholars agree, Augustine saw his writings throughout his life as a Christian philosophy. *The Christian Philosophy of Saint Augustine,* trans. L. E. M. Lynch (New York: Random House, 1960), p. 37; Robert A. Markus, "Augustine. Biographical Introduction: Christianity and Philosophy," in *Cambridge History of Later Greek and Early Medieval Philosophy,* ed. A. H. Armstrong (Cambridge: Cambridge University Press, 1967), pp. 352–353; O'Connell, *SAE,* pp. 4–5; James Wetzel, *Augustine and the Limits of Virtue* (Cambridge: Cambridge University Press, 1992), p. 10.

[76]Augustine later affirms this principle in *DDC,* IV.iv.6, viii.22—xiii.29, xix.38, xxii.51, xxv.55.

[77]*DUC,* 3.5.

[78]Ibid., 6.13, 7.17.

[79]Ibid., 7.14, 7.17, 8.20.

[80]*Acts or Disputations Against Fortunatus, the Manichaean*, 32, *NPNF*, 4:123. "Deus omnipotens, inviolabilis, incommutabilis, cui nocerit nihil possit, quare huc animam ad miserias, ad errorem, ad ista quae patimur, misit?" (*PL*, 42:128). The question is echoed in various terms at 7, 25, 30, 33.

[81]Ibid., 15, 20; see also *DLA*, I.i.1.

[82]See also Franois Decret, "L'utilisation des Épîtres de Paul chez les Manichéens d'Afrique," in *Essais sur l'Église manichéenne en Afrique du Nord et à Rome au temps de saint Augustin: Recueil d'études* (Rome: Institutum Patristicum Augustinianum, 1995 [1989]), pp. 55, 76–79.

[83]*Acts or Disputations* 11, *NPNF*, 4:115, slightly amended. "aliud esse Deum, aliud animam. Deum esse inviolabilem, incorruptibilem, et impenetrabilem, et incoinquinabilem, et qui ex nulla parte corrumpi possit, et cui nulla ex parte noceri potest. Animam vero videmus et peccatricem esse, et in aerumna versari, et veritatem quaerere, et liberatore indigere. Haec mutatio animae ostendit mihi quod anima non sit Deus" (*PL*, 42:116).

[84]Ibid., 22, quotation from *NPNF*, 4:121. "Postquam autem ipse libera voluntate peccavit, nos in necessitatem praecipitati sumus, qui abejus stirpe descendimus…Hodie namque in nostris actionibus antequam consuetudine aliqua implicemur, liberum habemus arbitrium faciendi aliquid, vel non faciendi. Cum autem ista libertate fecerimus aliquid, et facti ipsius tenuerit animam perniciosa dulcedo et voluptas, eadem ipsa sua consuetudine sic implicatur, ut postea vincere non possit, quod sibi ipsa peccando fabricata est" (*PL*, 42:124).

[85]Ibid., quoting Gal. 5:13 and Rom. 8:2, respectively. Citation from Augustine is from *NPNF* 4:122. "Cum autem gratia Dei amorem nobis divinum inspiraverit, et nos suae voluntati subditos fecerit, quibus dictum est, 'Vos in libertatem vocati estis' (Gal. 5, 13); et 'Gratia Dei liberavit me a lege peccati et mortis' (Rom. 8, 2)" (*PL*, 42:125; citations from scripture in italics in the original).

[86]Paula Fredriksen Landes, Introduction, in *Augustine on Romans: Propositions from the Epistle to the Romans, Unfinished Commentary on the Epistle to the Romans*, Society of Biblical Literature, Texts and Translations, no. 23, Early Christian Literature Series, no. 6 (Chico, Calif: Scholars Press, 1982), p. ix; *Retractationes* 1.23 (22).1.

[87]E.g., *Inch. Ex.*, 11–12.

[88]*Inch. Ex.*, 3. For extensive treatment of the interaction between Virgil's texts and Augustine's thinking see Sabine MacCormack, *The Shadows of Poetry: Virgil in the Mind of Augustine* (Berkeley: University of California Press, 1998).

[89]*Propp.*, prefatory remarks of Augustine, Landes, p. 3. "operum legis et gratiae" (Landes, p. 2).

[90]Ibid., 13–18, Landes, p. 5. "sollicite satis legenda sunt, ut neque lex ab apostolo improbata videatur neque homini arbitrium liberum sit ablatum…" (Landes, p. 4).

[91]Ibid. "Itaque quattuor istos gradus hominis distinguamus: ante legem, sub lege, sub gratia, in pace. Ante lege sequimur concupiscentiam carnis, sub lege trahimur ab ea, sub gratia nec sequimur eam nec trahimur ab ea, in pace nulla est concupiscentia carnis" (Landes, p. 4).

[92]*Nicomachean Ethics*, 1103a–1105b.

[93]*Propp.*, 13–18, Landes, p. 7. "iacens, cum se quisque cognoverit per seipsum surgere non valere, imploret liberatoris auxilium. Venit ergo gratia, quae donet peccata praeterita et conantem adiuvet et tribuat caritatem iustitiae et auferat metum. Quod cum fit, tametsi desideria quaedam carnis, dum in hac vita sumus, adversus spiritum nostrum pugnant, ut eum ducant in peccatum, non tamen his desideriis consentiens spiritus, quoniam est fixus in gratia et caritate dei, desinit peccare. Non enim in ipso desiderio pravo, sed in nostra consensione peccamus" (Landes, p. 6).

[94]Ibid., 13–18, 51.

[95]Rom. 9:13–18. Words in quotation marks appear in italics without quotation marks in the Douay Bible. The citations in order are to Mal. 1:2–3, Ex. 33:19, and Ex. 9:16, respectively.

[96]*Propp.*, 61–62.

[97]Ibid., 60, Landes, p. 33, with some minor adjustments. "Quia nisi quisque credat in eum et in accipiendi voluntate permaneat, non accipit donum dei, id est spiritum sanctum, per quem diffusa caritate bonum possit operari. Non ergo elegit deus opera cuiusquam in praescientia, quae ipse daturus est, sed fidem elegit in praescientia, ut quem sibi crediturum esse praescivit ipsum elegerit, cui spiritum sanctum daret, ut bona operando etiam aeternam vitam consequeretur.… Quod ergo credimus, nostrum est, quod autem bonum operamur, illius qui credentibus in se dat spiritum sanctum" (Landes, p. 32).

⁹⁸*Inch. Ex.*, 9.

⁹⁹Ibid., 8, Landes, p. 63. "Gratia est ergo a deo patre et domino Iesu Christo, qua nobis peccata remittuntur, quibus adversabamur deo, pax vero ipsa, qua reconciliamur deo. Cum enim per gratiam remissis peccatis absumptae fuerint inimicitiae, restat ut pace adhaereamus illi, a quo nos sola peccata dirimebant…" (Landes, p. 62).

¹⁰⁰Ibid., 10, Landes, pp. 63, 65. "Porro iustitiae divinae tanta constantia est, ut cum poena spiritualis et sempiterna poenitenti fuerit relaxata, pressurae tamen cruciatusque corporales, quibus etiam martyres exercitatos novimus, postremo mors ipsa, quam peccando meruit nostra natura, nulli relaxetur. Quod enim etiam iusti homines et pii tamen exsolvunt ista supplicia, de iusto dei iudicio venire credendum est. Ipsa est quae in sacris scripturis etiam disciplina nominatur, quam nemo iustorum effugere sinitur. Neminem quippe excepit, cum diceret: 'Quem enim diligit deus, corripit, flagellat autem omnem filium quem recipit'" (Landes, pp. 62, 64; quotation from Hebrews is in italics in the original).

¹⁰¹Ibid., p. 65. "Nam et ipsam pacem cum promitteret dominus, ait: 'Haec dixi, ut in me pacem habeatis, in mundo autem pressuram'" (Landes, p. 64; the quotation from John is in italics in the original).

¹⁰²Ibid. "tribulationes et molestiae…bonos et iustos…ab omni labe penitus purgant. Pax enim perfecta etiam corporis suo tempore roborabitur, si nunc pacem, quam dominus per fidem dare dignatus est, inconcusse spiritus noster atque incommutabiliter teneat" (Landes, p. 64).

¹⁰³Geoffrey Grimshaw Willis, *Saint Augustine and the Donatist Controversy* (London: S. P. C. K., 1950), pp. 172–173; see also Burnaby, *"Amor Dei,"* p. 55; Van der Meer, p. 127.

¹⁰⁴*Inch. Ex.*, 15, p. 75. "Ipsa denique catholicae ecclesiae tam insignis auctoritas, quae in eodem dono spiritus sancti omnium sanctorum mater toto fecunda orbe diffunditur, cui umquam haeretico vel scismatico spem liberationis, si se corrigat, amputavit? Nonne omnes ad ubera sua, quae superbo fastidio reliquerunt, cum lacrimis revocat?" (Landes, p. 74). PCPD, ll. 270–274, 287–291.

¹⁰⁵*Inch. Ex.*, 15; Landes, p. 75. "alii sacramenta eius exsufflent et baptizatos in nomine patris et filii et spiritus sancti denuo baptizare non dubitent" (Landes, p. 74).

¹⁰⁶Brown, *AOH*, pp. 214, 221, 224–225, 237–238; Robert A. Markus, *Saeculum: History and Society in the Theology of St. Augustine* (Cambridge: Cambridge University Press, 1970), pp. 30–33, 36–37. F. Edward Cranz disagrees about the influence of Augustine's ecclesiastical role on his thought, although perhaps only with regard to the topic of Augustine's views of society ("The Development of Augustine's Ideas on Society," pp. 382–383).

¹⁰⁷*DBV*, 1.5, *FOC*, 5:49. "Quid enim solidum tenui, cui adhuc de anima quaestio nutat et fluctuat? Quare obsecro te per virtutem tuam, per humanitatem, per animarum inter se vinculum atque commercium, ut dexteram porrigas. Hoc autem est, ut me ames, et a me vicissim te amari credas charumque haberi…Quid autem agam, quove modo ad istum portum necessarios meos congregem ut cognoscas, et ex eo animum meum (neque enim alia signa invenio quibus me ostendam) ut plenius intelligas, initium disputationum mearum, quod mihi videtur religiosius evasisse, atque tuo titulo dignius, ad te scribendum putavi, et ipso tuo nomine dedicandum" (*PL*, 32:962).

¹⁰⁸On the baths as a setting for discussion and intellectual interchange see A. G. Hamman, *La vie quotidienne en Afrique du Nord au temps de saint Augustin*, nouvelle éd. (Paris: Hachette, 1985 [1979]), pp. 39–40.

¹⁰⁹*DBV*, 1.6, *FOC*, 5:50. "Idibus novembris mihi natalis dies erat…omnes qui simul non modo illo die, sed quotidie convivabamur, in balneas ad consedendum vocavi;…Erant autem, non enim vereor eos singulari benignitati tuae notos interim nominibus facere, in primis nostra mater, cujus meriti credo esse omne quod vivo; Navigius frater meus, Trygetius et Licentius, cives et discipuli mei…nec Lastidianum et Rusticum consobrinos meos, quamvis nullum vel grammaticum passi sint, deesse volui, ipsumque eorum sensum communem, ad rem quam moliebar, necessarium putavi. Erat etiam nobiscum aetate minimus omnium, sed cujus ingenium, si amore non fallor, magnum quiddam pollicetur, Adeodatus filius meus" (*PL*, 32:962).

¹¹⁰Robert A. Kaster, *Guardians of Language: The Grammarian and Society in Late Antiquity* (Berkeley: University of California Press, 1988), p. 23.

¹¹¹*DBV*, 4.36, *FOC*, 5:84. "Quam vellem, inquit Trygetius, hoc modo nos quotidie pasceres. Modus, inquam, ille ubique servandus est, ubique amandus, si vobis cordi est ad Deum reditus noster" (*PL* 32:976).

¹¹²*DO*, I.iii.6; *Sol.* I.xiv.25.

[113]Chadwick, pp. 160–161. "Quas tibi, deus meus, voces dedi, cum legerem psalmos David, cantica fidelia, sonos pietatis excludentes turgidum spiritum,…et quomodo in te inflammabar ex eis et accendebar eos recitare, si possem, toto orbi terrarum adversus typhum generis humani!…quam vehementi et acri dolore indignabar manichaeis et miserabar eos rursus, quod illa sacramenta, illa medicamenta nescirent et insani essent adversus antidotum quo sani esse potuissent! vellem ut alicubi iuxta essent tunc et, me nesciente quod ibi essent, intuerentur faciem meam et audirent voces meas quando legi quartum psalmum in illo tunc otio. quid de me fecerit ille psalmus…

"Inhorrui timendo ibidemque inferbui sperando et exultando in tua misericordia, pater. et haec omnia exibant per oculos et vocem meam, cum conversus ad nos spiritus tuus bonus ait nobis, "filii hominum, quousque graves corde? ut quid diligitis vanitatem et quaeritis mendacium?" (O'Donnell, I:106). Hjalmar Sundén has already interpreted this passage in its context in Augustine's life through a theory of role-taking. "Augustine at Cassiciacum: Hearing the Words of Another," in *The Hunger of the Heart: Reflections on the Confessions of Augustine*, ed. Donald Capps and James E. Dittes, Society for the Scientific Study of Religion Monograph Series, no. 8 (West Lafayette, Ind.: Society for the Scientific Study of Religion, 1990), pp. 289–301; see also William S. Babcock, "Patterns of Roman Selfhood: Marcus Aurelius and Augustine of Hippo" *Perkins Journal* 29 (Winter 1976): 5.

[114]*DO*, I.x.29, *FOC*, 5:266–267. "Et ambobus: Itane agitis, inquam?…si videretis, vel tam lippientibus oculis quam ego, in quibus periculis jaceamus, cujus morbi dementiam risus iste indicet! O, si videretis! Quam cito, quam statim, quantoque productius eum verteretis in fletus…" (*PL*, 32:991).

[115]*DO*, I.x.30. My translation. "lacrymae mihi modum imposuerunt…" (*PL*, 32:991).

[116]Ibid., *FOC*, 5:268. "vos…tamen et in philosophiam, et in eam vitam quam me tandem occupasse laetor, aemulationis labificae atque inanis jactantiae ultimam, sed nocentiorem caeteris omnibus pestem introducere ac proseminare conamini…" (*PL*, 32:992).

[117]James E. Dittes, "Continuities Between the Life and Thought of Augustine," *JSSR* 5 (October 1965): 138; for an earlier discussion of how to move beyond the reductionistic interpretation of the conversion, see William B. Parsons, "St. Augustine: 'Common Man' or 'Intuitive Psychologist'?" *Journal of Psychohistory* 18 (Fall 1990): 171, 174–178.

[118]McGinn, *Presence of God*, pp. 318, 322, 324.

[119]My translation. "regionem ubertatis indeficientis, ubi pascis Israhel in aeternum…" (O'Donnell, I:113).

[120]My translation. "erigentes nos ardentiore affectu in idipsum…" (O'Donnell, I:113).

[121]Chadwick, p. 172, emended slightly. "loquatur ipse solus non per ea sed per se ipsum, ut audiamus verbum eius, non per linguam carnis neque per vocem angeli nec per sonitum nubis nec per aenigma similitudinis, sed ipsum quem in his amamus, ipsum sine his audiamus…" (O'Donnell, I:114).

[122]Henry, *Path*, pp. 40, 95; O'Donnell, III:128.

[123]Ibid., pp. 27–28.

[124]*Enn.*, V.1.6.

[125]O'Connell, *SAC*, p. 115.

[126]Chadwick, p. 172. "extendimus nos et rapida cogitatione attingimus aeternam sapientiam super omnia manentem…" (O'Donnell, I:114).

[127]"Forms and Transformations of Narcissism," *SFS1*: 454–455.

[128]Ibid., p. 456.

[129]*Vita*, XXXVI.

[130]Kohut speaks of "expansion of the self, late in life, when the finiteness of individual existence is acknowledged" ("Forms and Transformations," *SFS1*:456).

[131]*DME*, 31.65; *NPNF*, 4:59. "quidquid est, praestantius est rebus humanis" (*PL*, 32:1337).

[132]Chadwick, p. 172. "si continuetur hoc et subtrahantur aliae visiones longe imparis generis…" (O'Donnell, I:114). See Babcock, "Patterns of Roman Selfhood," p. 10.

[133]Paul Ricoeur, *Freud and Philosophy: An Essay on Interpretation*, trans. Denis Savage (New Haven and London: Yale University Press, 1970), pp. 515, 539–543.

[134]For a more skeptical view of the details of early Christian texts about women, see Elizabeth A. Clark, "Holy Women, Holy Words: Early Christian Women, Social History, and the 'Linguistic Turn,'" *Journal of Early Christian Studies* 6 (1998): 419–422.

[135]O'Connell, *SAC*, p. 119.

[136]My revision of Chadwick's translation, pp. 174–175. Major revisions appear in the second paragraph, especially the first and third sentences of the English. "ergo die nono

aegritudinis suae, quinquagesimo et sexto anno aetatis suae, tricesimo et tertio aetatis meae, anima illa religiosa et pia corpore soluta est.

"...audito autem quid ageretur, convenerunt multi fratres ac religiosae feminae et... ego in parte, ubi decenter poteram, cum eis qui me non deserendum esse censebant, quod erat tempori congruum disputabam eoque fomento veritatis mitigabam cruciatum tibi notum, illis ignorantibus et intente audientibus et sine sensu doloris me esse arbitrantibus" (O'Donnell, I:116).

[137]Chadwick, p. 175. "et quia mihi vehementer displicebat tantum in me posse haec humana, quae ordine debito et sorte conditionis nostrae accidere necesse est, alio dolore dolebam dolorem et duplici tristitia macerabar" (O'Donnell, I:116).

[138]Ambrose, *Jacob and the Happy Life*, trans. Michael P. McHugh, *Fathers of the Church*, vol. 65 (Washington, D.C.: Catholic University of America Press, 1972), p. 139 (*PL*, 14: 611; see chap. 6, p. 117 for full text); *Enn.*, I.4.4; Wetzel, *Augustine and the Limits of Virtue*, p. 102.

[139]Chadwick, p. 174, emended slightly. "tum vero ubi efflavit extremum, puer Adeodatus exclamavit in planctu atque ab omnibus nobis cohercitus tacuit. hoc modo etiam meum quiddam puerile, quod labebatur in fletus, iuvenali voce cordis cohercebatur et tacebat. neque enim decere arbitrabamur funus illud questibus lacrimosis gemitibusque celebrare, quia his plerumque solet deplorari quaedam miseria morientium aut quasi omnimoda extinctio. et illa nec misere moriebatur nec omino moriebatur. hoc documentis morum eius et fide non ficta rationibusque certis tenebamus" (O'Donnell, I:115).

[140]Chadwick, p. 175. "Cohibito ergo a fletu illo puero, psalterium arripuit Evodius et cantare coepit psalmum. cui respondebamus omnis domus, 'misericordiam et iudicium cantabo tibi, domine'" (O'Donnell, I:116).

[141]Psalm 100 in the Douay (101, RSV): 3–4.

[142]"Augustine's *Confessions*: The Scourge of Shame and the Silencing of Adeodatus," in *Hunger of the Heart Reflections on the Confessions of Augustine*, ed. Donald Capps and James E. Dittes, Society for the Scientific Study of Religion Monograph Series, no. 8 (West Lafayette, Ind.: Society for the Scientific Study of Religion, 1990), pp. 85–86, 88–92.

[143]Chadwick, p. 176, emended slightly. "si peccatum invenerit, flevisse me matrem exigua parte horae, matrem oculis meis interim mortuam quae me multos annos fleverat ut oculis tuis viverem, non inrideat sed potius, si est grandi caritate, pro peccatis meis fleat ipse ad te, patrem omnium fratrum Christi tui.

"Ego autem, iam sanato corde ab illo vulnere in quo poterat redargui carnalis affectus..." (O'Donnell, I:117).

[144]*Jacob and the Happy Life*, I.vii.31.

[145]My translation with first four words from Chadwick, p. 176. "mentesque fessas allevet/ luctuque solvat anxios" (O'Donnell, I:117).

[146]Chadwick, p. 176. "Atque inde paulatim reducebam in pristinum sensum ancillam tuam conversationemque eius piam in te et sancte in nos blandam atque morigeram, qua subito destitutus sum, et libuit flere in conspectu tuo et de illa et pro illa, de me et pro me. et dimisi lacrimas quas continebam, ut effluerent quantum vellent, substernens eas cordi meo. et requievit in eis, quoniam ibi erant aures tuae, non cuiusquam hominis superbe interpretantis ploratum meum" (O'Donnell, p. 117).

[147]Ibid., pp. 174–175, adjusted. "Quid...nisi ex consuetudine simul vivendi, dulcissima et carissima, repente dirupta vulnus recens? gratulabar quidem testimonio eius, quod in ea ipsa ultima aegritudine obsequiis meis interblandiens apellabat me pium et commemorabat grandi dilectionis affectu numquam se audisse ex ore meo iaculatum in se durum aut contumeliosum sonum...quoniam itaque deserebar tam magno eius solacio, sauciabatur anima et quasi dilaniabatur vita, quae una facta erat ex mea et illius" (O'Donnell, I:115–116).

[148]Ibid., p. 59, n. 14: "Ovid, *Tristia*, 4.4.72; Aristotle in Diogenes Laertius, 6.1.20."

[149]"cruciatum immanem" (O'Donnell, I:36).

[150]Chadwick, p. 59. "eam repente consumpturam omnes homines putabam, quia illum potuit...et me magis, quia ille alter eram, vivere illo mortuo mirabar" (O'Donnell, I:37).

[151]Ibid., p. 56. "mecum puer creverat et pariter in scholam ieramus pariterque luseramus. sed nondum erat sic amicus, quamquam ne tunc quidem sic, uti est vera amicitia, quia non est vera nisi cum eam agglutinas inter haerentes tibi caritate diffusa in cordibus nostris per spiritum sanctum, qui datus est nobis. sed tamen dulcis erat nimis, cocta fervore parilium studiorum" (O'Donnell, I:35).

[152]Ibid.

[153]Ibid., I:115.

[154]My translation. "attingimus eam modice toto ictu cordis" (O'Donnell, I:113).

[155]Chadwick, p. 172. "sicut nunc extendimus nos et rapida cogitatione attingimus aeternam sapientiam super omnia manentem…" (O'Donnell, I:114).

[156]My thanks to Gregory Allen Robbins for conversations about the interpretation of Monica's death as the death of a friend in comparison to the death of the friend in book 4 of the *Confessions*. As at so many other times, Greg's acuity of thought and diction helped me come to understand part of the *Confessions*. O'Donnell comments on the two deaths on pp. 137–138 of volume 3 of his edition of the *Confessions*.

[157]See McGinn, *Presence of God*, pp. 234–235, on Augustine's notion of knowledge in his mysticism.

[158]On the loss close in time of lover and mother, see Kim Power, *Veiled Desire: Augustine on Women* (New York: Continuum, 1996), pp. 101–103.

[159]But see Power, *Veiled Desire*, p. 103.

[160]"cubare solitus eram" and "consuetudinis" (O'Donnell, I:71).

[161]"ex consuetudine simul vivendi" (O'Donnell, I:115).

[162]Ibid., II:385.

[163]Margaret R. Miles, *Desire and Delight: A New Reading of Augustine's Confessions* (New York: Crossroad, 1992), p. 84.

[164]*DME*, 30.62–63. My translation. "Merito, Ecclesia catholica, mater Christianorum verissima, non solum ipsum Deum, cujus adeptio vita est beatissima, purissime atque castissime colendum praedicas…sed etiam proximi dilectionem atque charitatem ita complecteris…

"Tu pueriliter pueros, fortiter juvenes, quiete senes, prout cujusque non corporis tantum, sed et animi aetas est, exerces ac doces…Quibus honor debeatur, quibus affectus, quibus reverentia, quibus timor, quibus consolatio, quibus admonitio, quibus cohortatio, quibus disciplina, quibus objurgatio, quibus supplicium, sedulo doces…" (*PL*, 32:1336–1337).

[165]*AOH*, chap. 15.

[166]Chadwick, p. 164. "ingenio preveniebat multos graves et doctos viros…horrori mihi erat illud ingenium" (O'Donnell, I:108).

[167]Heinz Kohut, "Introspection, Empathy and the Semi-Circle of Mental Health," *International Journal of Psycho-analysis* 63 (1982): 404–405; *ROS*, p. 234.

[168]4.7, Burleigh, p. 74; "Acutissime omnino…" (*PL*, 32:1198).

[169]Ibid., 5.11, Burleigh, p. 77; "Bene attendisti" (*PL*, 32:1201).

[170]Ibid., 8.24, Burleigh, p. 86; "Bene te quidem hoc modo adversus illum esses paratus…" (*PL*, 32:1209).

[171]Ibid., 8.21, Burleigh, p. 85; "Perge potius ut coepisti: nam nunquam ego contemnenda putem quae tu dicenda vel agenda putaveris" (*PL*, 32:1207).

[172]Erikson's cogwheeling of the generations can in such instances take on the form described by Kohut's self psychology. Erik H. Erikson, *Insight and Responsibility: Lectures on the Ethical Implications of Psychoanalytic Insight* (New York and London: W. W. Norton & Company, 1964), p. 114, for the word "cogwheeling"; pp. 96, 130, 133 for the idea.

[173]*DM*, 5.14, Burleigh, p. 79; "Acute quidem falleris, sed ut falli desinas, acutius attende quod dicam, si tamen id dicere, ut volo, valuero: nam verbis de verbis agere tam implicatum est, quam digitos digitis inserere et confricare; ubi vix dignoscitur, nisi ab eo qui id agit, qui digiti pruriant, et qui auxilientur prurientibus. *Ad[eodatus]*. En toto animo adsum, nam ista haec similitudo me intentissimum fecit" (*PL*, 32:1202). See also 9.28.

[174]Ibid., 14.46, Burleigh, p. 101. "Verumtamen huic orationi tuae, qua perpetua usus es, ob hoc habeo maxime gratiam, quod omnia quae contradicere paratus eram, praeoccupavit atque dissolvit; nihilque omnino abs te derelictum est, quod me dubium faciebat, de quo non ita mihi responderet secretum illud oraculum, ut tuis verbis assereretur" (*PL*, 32:1220).

[175]John J. O'Meara, "The Historicity of the Early Dialogues of Saint Augustine," *Vigiliae Christianae* 5 (July 1951): 171–172.

[176]*DM*, 3.5, Burleigh, p. 72. "Miror te nescire, vel potius simulare nescientem, responsione mea fieri quod vis omnino non posse; siquidem semocinamur, ubi non possumus reponere nisi verbis. Tu autem res quaeris eas quae, quodlibet sint, verba certe non sunt, quas tamen ex me tu quoque verbis quaeris. Prior itaque tu sine verbis quaere, ut ego deinde ista conditione respondeam. *Aug[ustine]*. Jure agis, fateor: sed…" (*PL*, 32:1197).

[177]*CA*, I.ii.6–3.7, I.iv.11, II.7.16–17; *DBV*, 2.14–15, 3.19; *DO*, I.iii.8, I.iv.11, I.x.28, II.ii.4.

[178]*DM*, 14.45–46, Burleigh, p. 100. "At istas omnes disciplinas quas se docere profitetur, ipsiusque virtutis atque sapientiae, cum verbis explicaverint; tum illi qui discipuli vocantur,

utrum vera dicta sint, apud semetipsos considerant, interiorem scilicet illam veritatem pro viribus intuentes. Tunc ergo discunt...
"Sed de tota utilitate verborum, quae si bene consideretur non parva est, alias, si Deus siverit, requiremus. Nunc enim ne plus eis quam oportet tribueremus... ; ut jam non crederemus tantum, sed etiam intelligere inciperemus quam vere scriptum sit auctoritate divina, ne nobis quemquam magistrum dicamus in terris, quod unus omnium magister in coelis sit (Matt. 23, 8–10). Quid sit autem in coelis, docebit ipse a quo etiam per homines signi admonemur et foris, ut ad eum intro conversi erudiamur: quem diligere ac nosse beata vita est, quam se omnes clamant quaerere, pauci autem sunt qui eam vere se invenisse laetentur. Sed jam mihi dicas velim, quid de hoc toto meo sermone sentias" (*PL*, 32:1219–1220).

[179]7.11. My translation. "intueri non potest...ad familiaritatem tenebrarum suarum, non electione, sed fatigatione convertitur" (*PL*, 32:1315).

[180]26.48, *NPNF*, 4:55. "nullus certior gradus ad amorem Dei" (*PL*, 32:1331).

[181]J. Patout Burns, *The Development of Augustine's Doctrine of Operative Grace* (Paris: Études Augustiniennes, 1980), pp. 45–48. His diminished conception of the power of the human will and the heightened evaluation of the need for God's grace expounded in *Ad Simp.* is also crucial. See Paula Fredriksen, "Paul and Augustine: Conversion Narratives, Orthodox Traditions, and the Retrospective Self," *Journal of Theological Studies*, NS 37 (April 1986): 22–24, 27–28.

[182]Kohut, "Thoughts on Narcissism and Narcissistic Rage," SFS2:638–640, 649–650.

[183]Volney Gay, "The Reader as Selfobject," *JSSR* 25 (March 1986): 65.

Chapter 8: Augustine and *Confessions*, Books 10–13

[1]Paula Fredriksen, "Beyond the Body/Soul Dichotomy: Augustine on Paul against the Manichees and the Pelagians," *Recherches Augustiniennes* 22 (1988): 104–105; Diane Jonte-Pace, "Augustine on the Couch: Psychohistorical (Mis)readings of the Confessions," *Religion* 23 (1993): 72.

[2]E.g., *DUC*, i.1.

[3]*Ad Simp.*, Preface. "pater Simpliciane" (*PL*, 40:102).

[4]Pierre Courcelle, *Recherches sur les Confessions de saint Augustin* (Paris: Éditions de Boccard, 1950), pp. 29–31. Courcelle cites Paulinus' letter number 3 (*Corpus Scriptorum Ecclesiasticorum Latinorum*, 29:16) and Augustine's *Ep.*, 27 (see *PL*, 33:107–111).

[5]Brown, *AOH*, p. 162.

[6]Ibid., p. 262.

[7]Fredriksen, "Beyond the Body/Soul Dichotomy," p. 103.

[8]Robert McMahon, *Augustine's Prayerful Ascent: An Essay on the Literary Form of the "Confessions"* (Athens, Ga. and London: University of Georgia Press, 1989), p. 41.

[9]McMahon, *Augustine's Prayerful Ascent*, pp. xi, 1–2, 26; Henri-Irenée Marrou, *Saint Augustin et la fin de la culture antique* (Paris: Éditions de Boccard, 1938), pp. 63–64, and *Saint Augustin et la fin de la culture antique*, with "Retractatio" (Paris: Éditions de Boccard, 1949), pp. 670–672, where Marrou rejects his earlier judgment and puts Augustine's style of composition in its rhetorical context.

[10]For Christian views of penance, see Cornelius Petrus Mayer, "Confessio—Der Weg des Christen aus der Verflochtenheit von Schuld und Schuldgefühlen bei Augustinus," in *Cassiciacum*, vol. 46, *Traditio Augustiniana: Studien über Augustinus und seine Rezeption*, ed. Adolar Zumkeller and Achim Krümmel (Würzburg: Augustinus-Verlag, 1994), pp. 7–10.

[11]8.21, Burleigh, p. 85. "Dabis igitur veniam, si praeludo tecum non ludendi gratia, sed exercendi vires et mentis aciem, quibus regionis illius, ubi beata vita est, calorem ac lucem non modo sustinere, verum etiam amare possimus" (*PL*, 32:1207).

[12]*SAC*, p. 16.

[13]Karl Joachim Weintraub, *The Value of the Individual: Self and Circumstance in Autobiography* (Chicago and London: The University of Chicago Press, 1978), p. 39.

[14]See Paul Ricoeur, *Time and Narrative, Volume 1*, trans. Kathleen McLaughlin and David Pellauer (Chicago and London: The University of Chicago Press, 1984), pp. 5–30, for a thorough discussion of book 11 on time.

[15]Weintraub, *Value of the Individual*, pp. 40–41.

[16]See Albert C. Outler, "Introduction," in *Augustine: Confessions and Enchiridion*, trans. and ed. by Albert C. Outler, Library of Christian Classics, vol. 7. (Philadelphia: Westminster Press, 1955), pp. 19–20.

[17]Weintraub, *The Value of the Individual*, pp. 45–46.

[18]Margaret More O'Ferrall, "Monica, the Mother of Augustine: A Reconsideration," *Recherches Augustiniennes* 10(1975): 28–30; McMahon, *Augustine's Prayerful Ascent*, pp. 119, 135–136; Kim Power, *Veiled Desire: Augustine on Women* (New York: Continuum, 1996), p. 73; see also Brown, *AOH*, pp. 168–169; O'Connell, *SAC*, pp. 113–114.

[19]Courcelle, *Recherches*, p. 193; Jn. 1:48.

[20]See, for example, Marjorie Suchocki, "The Symbolic Structure of Augustine's *Confessions*," *Journal of the American Academy of Religion* 50 (September 1982): 366, 371.

[21]Paula Fredriksen, "Paul and Augustine: Conversion Narratives, Orthodox Traditions, and the Retrospective Self," *Journal of Theological Studies* 37 (April 1986): 5–6.

[22]Brown, *AOH*, pp. 159–161, 177–178; Weintraub, *The Value of the Individual*, pp. 1, 17.

[23]*DDC*, III.xii.18–xvi.24.

[24]II.xviii.28, Robertson, p. 54. "imo vero quisquis bonus verusque christianus est, Domini sui esse intelligat, ubicumque invenerit veritatem…" (*PL*, 34:49).

[25]*Ad Simp.*, 1.Q1.5, p. 378, quoting Rom 7:11 ("Peccatum enim…occasione accepta per mandatum, fefellit me, et per illud occidit"; *PL*, 40:104); 1.Q1.7, Burleigh, p. 379, quoting Romans 7:14 ("Scimus enim…quia lex spiritualis est; ego autem carnalis sum"; *PL*, 40:105); 1.Q1.8, Burleigh, p. 380, quoting Rom. 7:15 ("Non enim quod volo, hoc ago; sed quod odi, illud facio"; *PL*, 40:106). All Latin in italics in the original.

[26]Ibid., 1.Q1.4, 5, 9.

[27]Ibid., 1.Q1.10, Burleigh, p. 380. "assiduitate voluptatis"; "frequentati peccati" (*PL*, 40:106).

[28]Ibid., 1.Q1.7, Burleigh, p. 379. "pretium mortiferae voluptatis amplectitur dulcedinem illam qua fallitur, et delectatur etiam contra legem facere, cum tanto magis libet, quanto minus licet. Qua suavitate frui non potest quasi pretio conditionis suae, nisi cogatur tanquam emptum mancipium servire libidini. Sentit enim se servum dominantis cupiditatis, qui prohibetur, et se recte prohiberi cognoscit, et tamen facit" (*PL*, 40:105).

[29]Ibid., 1.Q1.9, Burleigh, p. 380. "Si autem quod nolo, hoc facio; consentio legi, quoniam bona est…Vincitur enim nondum per gratiam liberatus, quamvis jam per legem et noverit se male facere, et nolit" (*PL*, 40:106). Quotation from scripture in italics in the original.

[30]Ibid., 1.Q1.13, Burleigh, pp. 381–382, quoting Romans 7:22–23. "'Condelector enim,' inquit, 'legi Dei secundum interiorem hominem'…'Video autem,' inquit, 'legem aliam in membris meis, repugnantem legi mentis meae, et captivantem me sub lege peccati, quae est in membris meis.'…Per quod fit etiam saepe ut invicte delectet quod non licet" (*PL*, 40:107). Quotation from the Bible in italics in the original.

[31]Ibid., 1.Q1.14, quoting Rom. 7:24–25, Douay. "quis me liberavit de corpore mortis hujus? Gratia Dei per Jesum Christum Dominum nostrum" (*PL*, 40:108). Quotation from the Bible in italics in the original.

[32]Ibid., 1.Q1.15, Burleigh, p. 383. "Porro qui acceperunt legem, praevaricant eam, nisi per gratiam consequantur posse quod jubet. Ita fit ut non dominetur eis qui jam sub gratia sunt, implentibus eam per charitatem, qui erant sub ejus timore damnati" (*PL*, 40:108).

[33]Ibid., 1.Q2.2, Burleigh, p. 386. "Et primo intentionem Apostoli, quae per totam Epistolam viget, tenebo, quam consulam. Haec est autem, ut de operum meritis nemo glorietur, de quibus audebant Israelitae gloriari…Non enim intelligebant, quia eo ipso quo gratia est evangelica, operibus non debetur: 'alioquin gratia jam non est gratia' (Rom. xi, 6)…non se quisquis arbitretur ideo percepisse gratiam, quia bene operatus est; sed bene operari non posse, nisi per fidem perceperit gratiam. Incipit autem homo percipere gratiam, ex quo incipit Deo credere, vel interna vel externa admonitione motus ad fidem" (*PL*, 40:111). Quotation from scripture in italics in the original.

[34]Ibid., 1.Q2.4, Burleigh, pp. 388–389. "Et major serviet minori"; "Jacob dilexi, Esau autem odio habui…" (*PL*, 40:113). Quotation from scripture in italics in the original.

[35]Rom. 9:15, referring to Ex. 33:19, Douay.

[36]*Ad Simp.*, 1.Q2.14, Burleigh, p. 396. "quis enim dicat modum quo ei persuaderetur ut crederet, etiam Omnipotenti defuisse?" (*PL*, 40:119).

[37]Ibid., 1.Q2.15, also quoting Rom. 9:16; Burleigh, p. 396. "cum ipse subjungat Apostolus, 'Dicit enim Scriptura Pharaoni, Quia ad hoc te excitavi, ut ostendam in te potentiam meam, et ut annuntietur nomen meum in universa terra?' Hoc autem subjecit Apostolus documentum, quo probaret quod supra dixerat, 'Igitur non volentis neque currentis, sed miserentis est Dei.'" (*PL*, 40:119–120); scripture quotations are in italics in the original.

[38]Ibid., I.Q2.16, Burleigh, p. 397. "credatur…esse alicujus occultae atque ab humano modulo investigabilis aequitatis…" (*PL*, 40:120). Fredriksen, "Beyond the Body/Soul Dichotomy," p. 94–98.

[39]Ibid., 1.Q2.18, Burleigh, p. 400. "Est autem peccatum hominis inordinatio atque perversitas; id est, a praestantiore Conditore aversio, et ad condita inferiora conversio…Sed dilexit in eo non culpam quam delebat, sed gratiam quam donabat. Nam et Christus pro impiis mortuus est (Rom. v 6): non tamen ut impii permanerent, sed ut justificati ab impietate converterentur, credentes in eum qui justificat impium (Id., iv 5); odit enim Deus impietatem. Itaque in aliis eam punit per damnationem, in aliis adimit per justificationem, quemadmodum ipse judicat esse faciendum illis judiciis inscrutabilibus" (*PL*, 40:122–123).

[40]Ibid., 1.Q2.22, Burleigh, p. 406. "Sed cum hoc statuero, ita me ridebit ille qui infirma mundi elegit ut confundat fortia, et stulta mundi ut confundat sapientes (1 Cor. 1, 27), ut cum intuens et pudore correctus, ego irrideam multos prae quibusdam peccatoribus castiores, et prae quibusdam piscatores oratores" (*PL*, 40:128).

[41]William James, *The Varieties of Religious Experience: A Study in Human Nature*, with an Introduction by Reinhold Niebuhr (New York: Macmillan, Collier Books, and London: Collier Macmillan Publishers, 1961 [1902]), pp. 299–301.

[42]My thanks go to William B. Parsons, without whose comments over the years this whole line of discussion would probably have escaped me entirely. His article on Augustine's mysticism, and more writings on relevant topics, are eagerly anticipated.

[43]My translation. "Magna vis est memoriae, nescio quid horrendum, deus meus, profunda et infinita multiplicitas. et hoc anima est, et hoc ego ipse sum. quid ergo sum, deus meus? quae natura sum? varia, multimoda vita et immensa vehementer" (O'Donnell, I:129).

[44]My translation. "transibo ergo et memoriam, ut attingam eum qui separavit me a quadrupedibus et a volatilibus caeli sapientiorem me fecit. transibo et memoriam, ut ubi te inveniam, vere bone, secura suavitas, ut ubi te inveniam?" (O'Donnell, I:129). For reference to Job, see Chadwick, p. 195.

[45]Chadwick, pp. 200–201. "tu dedisti hanc dignationem memoriae meae, ut maneas in ea, sed in qua eius parte maneas, hoc considero. transcendi enim partes eius quas habent et bestiae cum te recordarer, quia non ibi te inveniebam inter imagines rerum corporalium, et veni ad partes eius ubi commendavi affectiones animi mei, nec illic inveni te. et intravi ad ipsius animi mei sedem, quae illi est in memoria mea, quoniam sui quoque meminit animus, nec ibi tu eras, quia sicut non es imago corporalis ne affectio viventis, qualis est cum laetamur, contristamur, cupimus, metuimus, meminimus, obliviscimur et quidquid huius modi est, ita nec ipse animus es, quia dominus deus animi tu es. et commutantur haec omnia, tu autem incommutabilis manes super omnia et dignatus es habitare in memoria mea, ex quo te didici" (O'Donnell, I:133–134).

[46]Ibid., p. 201. "et nusquam locus, et recedimus et accedimus, et nusquam locus. veritas, ubique praesides omnibus consulentibus te simulque repondes omnibus etiam diversa consulentibus" (O'Donnell, I:134).

[47]Ibid., p. 201. "sero te amavi, pulchritudo tam antiqua et tam nova, sero te amavi! et ecce intus eras et ego foris, et ibi te quaerebam, et in ista formosa quae fecisti deformis inruebam. mecum eras, et tecum non eram. ea me tenebant longe a te, quae si in te non essent, non essent. vocasti et clamasti et rupisti surditatem meam; coruscasti, splenduisti, et fugasti caecitatem meam; fragasti, et duxi spiritum et anhelo tibi; gustavi et esurio et sitio; tetigisti me, et exarsi in pacem tuam" (O'Donnell, I:134).

[48]Margaret R. Miles, *Desire and Delight: A New Reading of Augustine's Confessions* (New York: Crossroad, 1992), p. 97.

[49]O'Connell notes, "lightest of the four elements, a preponderance of 'fire' in anything forces it to seek its natural place 'on high'" (*SAC*, p. 57).

[50]Chadwick, p. 202. "per continentiam quippe conligimur et redigimur in unum, a quo in multa defluximus…o amor, qui semper ardes et numquam extingueris, caritas, deus meus, accende me! continentiam iubes: da quod iubes et iube quod vis" (O'Donnell, I:135).

[51]1 Jn. 2:16; see also O'Connell, *SAE*, p. 174.

[52]Chadwick, p. 220. "pro nobis tibi victor et victima…" (O'Donnell, I:146).

[53]Ibid. "ille tuus unicus, in quo sunt omnes thesauri sapientiae et scientiae absconditi, redemit me sanguine suo…et laudant dominum qui requirunt eum" (O'Donnell, I:147).

[54]Brown, *AOH*, pp. 165–167.

[55]Ibid., p. 221, slightly amended. "affectum meum excito in te, et eorum qui haec legunt, ut dicamus omnes, 'magnus dominus et laudabilis valde.'…nam et oramus, et tamen veritas ait, 'novit pater vester quid vobis opus sit, priusquam petatis ab eo.' affectum ergo nostrum patefacimus in te confitendo tibi miserias nostras et misericordas tuas super nos…quoniam vocasti nos, ut simus pauperes spiritu et mites et lugentes et esurientes ac sitientes iustitiam et misericordes et municordes et pacifici" (O'Donnell, I:148).

[56]Ibid., p. 224. "Ecce sunt caelum et terra! clamant quod facta sint; mutantur enim atque variantur" (O'Donnell, I:150).

[57]See O'Donnell, II:394–395; Plotinus, *Enn.*, V.3.15.

[58]Chadwick, p. 225. "ergo dixisti et facta sunt atque in verbo tuo fecisti ea" (O'Donnell, I:150).

[59]Ibid. "Sed quomodo dixisti? Numquid illo modo quo facta est vox de nube dicens, 'hic est filius meus dilectus'? illa enim vox acta atque transacta est, coepta et finita. sonuerunt syllabae atque transierunt, secunda post primam, tertia post secundum atque inde ex ordine, donec ultima post ceteras silentiumque post ultimam" (O'Donnell, I:150).

[60]Quoting Jn. 1:1–3 (Douay).

[61]See also O'Donnell, III:266, 268.

[62]Chadwick, p. 227, adapted. "quia et per creaturam mutabilem cum admonemur, ad veritatem stabilem ducimur, ubi vere discimus, cum stamus et audimus eum et gaudio gaudemus propter vocem sponsi, reddentes nos unde sumus. et ideo principium, quia, nisi maneret cum erraremus, non esset quo rediremus. cum autem redimus ab errore, cognoscendo utique redimus; ut autem cognoscamus, docet nos, quia principium est et loquitur nobis" (O'Donnell, I:151–152).

[63]Ibid., p. 228. "et conantur aeterna sapere, sed adhuc in praeteritis et futuris rerum motibus cor eorum volitat et adhuc vanum est. quis tenebit illud et figet illud, ut paululum stet, et paululum rapiat splendorem semper stantis aeternitatis..." (O'Donnell, I:152–153).

[64]Ibid., p. 244. "at ego in tempora dissilui quorum ordinem nescio, et tumultuosis varietatibus dilaniantur cogitationes meae, intima viscera animae meae, donec in te confluam purgatus et liquidus igne amoris tui.

"Et stabo atque solidabor in te, in forma mea, veritate tua..." (O'Donnell, I:163).

[65]*AOH*, p. 164; see also p. 177.

[66]Chadwick, p. 246. "caelum caeli domino..." (O'Donnell, I:165).

[67]Ibid. "ubi est caelum caeli, domine, de quo audivimus in voce psalmi..." (O'Donnell, I:165).

[68]Ibid., p. 255. "priore quippe omnium creata est sapientia..." (O'Donnell, I:171).

[69]Ibid. "sapientia...plane coaeterna et aequalis...profecto sapientia quae creata est, intellectualis natura scilicet, quae contemplatione luminis lumen est..." (O'Donnell, I:171).

[70]Ibid., p. 256. "ergo quia prior omnium creata est quaedam sapientia quae creata est, mens rationalis et intellectualis castae civitatis tuae, matris nostrae, quae sursum est et libera est et aeterna in caelis (quibus caelis, nisi qui te laudant caeli caelorum, quia hoc est et caelum caeli domino?)" (O'Donnell, I:171). Psalm 115:16 (English) is Psalm 113:16 in the Douay.

[71]O'Donnell, III:319; see Plotinus, *Enn.*, V.3.11–12.

[72]McMahon, *Augustine's Prayerful Ascent*, p. xviii, quoting Kenneth Burke, *The Rhetoric of Religion: Studies in Logology* (Berkeley: University of California Press, 1970), p. 156.

[73]McMahon, p. xviii.

[74]Chadwick, p. 273. "Invoco te, deus meus, misericordia mea, qui fecisti me et oblitum tui non oblitus es. invoco te in animam meam, quam preparas a capiendum te ex desiderio quod inspirasti ei...priusquam invocarem praevenisti et institisti crebrescens multimodis vocibus, ut audirem de longinquo et converterer et vocantem me invocarem te. tu enim, domine, delevisti omnia mala merita mea, ne retribueres manibus meis, in quibus a te defeci, et praevenisti omnia bona merita mea, ut retribueres manibus tuis, quibus me fecisti, quia et priusquam essem tu eras, ne eram cui praestares ut essem, et tamen ecce sum ex bonitate tua praeveniente totum hoc quod me fecisti et unde me fecisti. neque enim eguisti me aut ego tale bonum sum quo tu adiuveris, dominus meus et deus meus, non ut tibi sic serviam quasi ne fatigeris in agendo, aut ne minor sit potestas tua carens obsequio meo" (O'Donnell, I:184). See also XIII.iv.5 and xi.12.

[75]Ibid., p. 276. "superferebatur super aquas." "et multa diximus de caelo caeli et de terra invisibili et incomposita et de abysso tenebrosa... et tenebam iam patrem in dei nomine, qui fecit haec, et filium in principii nomine, in quo fecit haec, et trinitatem credens deum meum, sicut credebam, quaerebam in eloquiis sanctis eius, et ecce spiritus tuus superferebatur super aquas. ecce trinitas deus meus, pater et filius et spiritus sanctus, creator universae creaturae" (O'Donnell, I:185–186).

[76]Ibid., p. 278, slightly adjusted. "pondus meum amor meus; eo feror, quocumque feror. dono tuo accendimur et sursum ferimur; inardescimus et imus" (O'Donnell, I:187).

[77]First three sentences, my translation; then Chadwick, p. 278. "in dono tuo requiescimus: ibi te fruimur. requies nostra locus noster. amor illuc attolli nos et spiritus tuus bonus exaltat humilitatem nostram de portis mortis" (O'Donnell, I:187).

[78]Chadwick, p. 278. "corpus pondere suo nititur ad locum suum. pondus non ad ima tanta est, sed ad locum suum. ignis sursum tendit, deorsum lapis..." (O'Donnell, I:187).

[79]O'Connell, *SAC*, p. 57.

[80]Adjusted from Chadwick, p. 278, my emphasis. "igne tuo, igne tuo bono inardescimus et imus, quoniam sursum imus ad pacem Hierusalem..." (O'Donnell, I:187).

[81]McMahon, *Augustine's Prayerful Ascent*, p. 13.

[82]Ibid., pp. 26–30.

[83]Chadwick, p. 285. "diligens proximum in subsidiis necessitatum carnalium... quoniam ex nostra infirmitate compatimur ad subveniendum indigentibus similiter opitulantes, quemadmodum nobis vellemus opem ferri, si eodem modo indigeremus..." (O'Donnell, I:191).

[84]Ibid., p. 285. "erumpat temporanea lux nostra, et de ista inferiore fruge actionis in delicias contemplationis verbum vitae superius obtinentes appareamus sicut luminaria in mundo, cohaerentes firmamento scripturae tuae. ibi enim nobiscum disputas, ut dividamus inter intellegibilia et sensibilia tamquam inter diem et noctem vel inter animas alias intellegibilibus, alias sensibilibus deditas, ut iam non tu solus in abdito diiudicationis, sicut antequam fieret firmamentum, dividas inter lucem et tenebras, sed etiam spiritales tui in eodem firmamento positi atque distincti manifestata per orbem gratia tua luceant super terram et dividant inter diem et noctem et significent tempora..." (O'Donnell, I:192).

[85]Ibid., pp. 290–291. "Operentur ergo iam in terra ministri tui... et sint forma fidelibus vivendo coram eis et excitando ad imitationem. sic enim non tantum ad audiendum sed etiam ad faciendum audiunt..." (O'Donnell, I:195).

[86]Ibid., p. 291. "'quaerite deum et vivet anima vestra, ut producat terra animam viventem; nolite conformari huic saeculo, continete vos ab eo.' evitando vivit anima, quae appetendo moritur. continete vos ab immani feritate superbiae, ab inerti voluptate luxuriae, et a fallaci nomine scientiae, ut sint bestiae mansuetae et pecora edomita et innoxii serpentes. motus enim animae sunt isti in allegoria..." (O'Donnell, I:195).

[87]Ibid., p. 292, quoting Rom. 12:2. "reformamini...in novitate mentis vestrae ad probandum vos quae sit voluntas dei..." (O'Donnell, I:196).

[88]Ibid. "et doces eum iam capacem videre trinitatem unitatis vel unitatem trinitatis" (O'Donnell, I:196).

[89]Mayer, "Confessio," p. 9.

[90]Chadwick, p. 294. "iudicat etiam spiritalis approbando quod rectum, improbando autem quod perperam invenerit in operibus moribusque fidelium, elemosynis tamquam terra fructifera et de anima viva mansuefactis affectionibus, in castitate, in ieiuniis, in cogitationibus piis de his quae per sensum corporis percipiuntur. de his enim iudicare nunc dicitur, in quibus et potestatem corrigendi habet" (O'Donnell, I:198).

[91]McMahon, *Augustine's Prayerful Ascent*, pp. 118–119, 147.

[92]Chadwick, pp. 303–304. "(quoniam super nos erant peccata nostra et in profundum tenebrosum abieramus abs te, et spiritus tuus bonus superferebatur ad subveniendum nobis in tempore opportuno), et iustificasti impios et distinxisti eos ab iniquis et solidasti auctoritatem libri tui inter superiores, qui tibi dociles essent, et inferiores, qui ei suberentur, et congregasti societatem infidelium in unam conspirationem, ut apparerent studia fidelium, ut tibi opera misericordiae parerent, distribuentes etiam pauperibus terrenas facultates ad adquirenda caelestia...haec omnia videmus et bona sunt valde, quoniam tu ea vides in nobis, qui spiritum quo ea videremus et in eis te amaremus dedisti nobis.

"Domine deus, pacem da nobis (omnia enim praestitisti nobis), pacem quietis, pacem sabbati, pacem sine vespera..." (O'Donnell, I:204). Note that the punctuation (e.g., parentheses) is the choice of the editor of the text and was not inserted by Augustine.

[93]Ibid., pp. 304–305. "et nos alio tempore moti sumus ad bene faciendum, posteaquam concepit de spiritu tuo cor nostrum; priore autem tempore ad male faciendum movebamur deserentes te: tu vero, deus une bone, numquam cessasti bene facere. et sunt quaedam bona opera nostra ex munere quidem tuo, sed non sempiterna: post illa nos requieturos in tua grandi sanctificatione speramus...et hoc intellegere quis hominum dabit homini? quis angelus angelo? quis angelus homini? a te petatur, in te quaeratur, ad te pulsetur: sic, sic accipietur, sic invenietur, sic aperietur" (O'Donnell, I:205).

[94]*Ad Simp.*, 1Q2.18, Burleigh, p. 401, quoting Rom. 9:20. "subauditur, 'Tu quis es, qui repondeas Deo?' ut recurrente sententia ad verba superiore iste sit sensus: si volens Deus ostendere iram, attulit vasa irae; tu quis es, qui repondeas Deo?" (*PL*, 40:123). Quotation from scripture in italics in the original.

[95]Chadwick, p. 12. "aut aliud faciebat idem ipse a quo vapulabam, qui si in aliqua quaestiuncula a condoctore suo victus esset, magis bile atque invidia torqueretur quam ego, cum in certamine pilae a conlusore meo superabar?" (O'Donnell, I:9).

[96]See note 40 above.

[97]*Ad Simp.*, 1Q2.16, Rom. 11:33; Burleigh, p. 398. "Inscrutabilia enim sunt judicia ejus, et investigabiles viae ipsius (Rom. xi, 33)" (*PL*, 40:121).

[98]See John Burnaby, *"Amor Dei": A Study of the Religion of St. Augustine* (London: Hodder & Stoughton, 1938), pp. 198–199, responding to an argument he takes from Augustine's *Ennarationes in Psalmos.*

[99]See note 43 above.

[100]See note 44 above.

[101]See note 45 above.

[102]Chadwick, p. 221. "domine, cum tua sit aeternitas…'magnus dominus et laudabilis valde'" (O'Donnell, I:148).

[103]See note 70 above.

[104]Chadwick, p. 256, slightly adjusted. "inest ei tamen ipsa mutabilitas, unde tenebresceret et frigesceret nisi amore grandi tibi cohaerens tamquam semper meridies luceret et ferveret ex te" (O'Donnell, I:172).

[105]Ibid. "o domus luminosa et speciosa, dilexi decorem tuum et locum habitationis gloriae domini mei, fabricatoris et possessoris tui! tibi suspiret peregrinatio mea, et dico ei qui fecit te ut possideat et me in te, quia fecit me" (O'Donnell, I:172).

[106]Ibid., p. 257, slightly revised. "Hierusalem patriam meam, Hierusalem matrem meam, teque super eam regnatorem, inlustratorem, patrem, tutorem, maritum, castas et fortes delicias et solidum gaudium et omnia bona ineffabilia, simul omnia, quia unum summum et verum bonum" (O'Donnell, I:172).

[107]See chap. 4 above, pp. 71–75.

[108]Chadwick, p. 257. "conligas totum quod sum a dispersione et deformitate hac et conformes atque confirmes in aeternum, deus meus, misericordia mea" (O'Donnell, I:172).

[109]Ibid. "et non avertar donec in eius pacem, matris carissimae, ubi sunt primitiae spiritus mei, unde ista mihi certa sunt, conligas totum quod sum…" (O'Donnell, I:172).

[110]See note 74 above.

[111]See note 84 above.

[112]Chadwick, p. 284. "idem namque illis finis est temporalis et terrenae felicitatis, propter quam faciunt omnia, quamvis innumerabili varietate curarum fluctuent" (O'Donnell, I:191).

[113]See note 92 above.

[114]See note 93 above.

Chapter 9: Reflections on Hearing Music in Life

[1]Margaret R. Miles, *Desire and Delight: A New Reading of Augustine's Confessions* (New York: Crossroad, 1992), pp. 12–13.

[2]Paul Ricoeur, "The Model of the Text: Meaningful Action Considered as a Text," in *Interpretive Social Science: A Reader*, ed. Paul Rabinow and William M. Sullivan (Berkeley: University of California Press, 1979), pp. 100–101.

[3]Porphyry, *On the Life of Plotinus and the Order of His Books*, 1, in *Plotinus*, vol. 1: *Porphyry on the Life of Plotinus and the Order of His Books, Enneads I.1–9*, trans. and ed. A. H. Armstrong, Loeb Classical Library, vol. 440 (Cambridge: Harvard University Press, 1989), p. 3.

[4]Don S. Browning, "The Psychoanalytic Interpretation of St. Augustine's *Confessions*: An Assessment and New Probe," in *Psychiatry and the Humanities*, vol. 2, *Psychoanalysis and Religion*, ed. Joseph H. Smith, associate editor Susan A. Handelman (Baltimore and London: The Johns Hopkins University Press, 1990), pp. 138, 154–155. Rambo raises this question for conversion more generally. Lewis R. Rambo, *Understanding Religious Conversion* (New Haven and London: Yale University Press, 1993), pp. 156–157.

[5]Don S. Browning, *Religious Thought and the Modern Psychologies: A Critical Conversation in the Theology of Culture* (Philadelphia: Fortress Press, 1987), pp. 8, 10–14, 69–71, 157–159, 182–185, 226–230.

[6]In the midst of a discussion of psychological consequences of conversion, Rambo notes as a consequence of Augustine's conversion the gift of the *Confessions* to future generations (*Understanding Religious Conversion*, pp. 158–159).

[7]Stanza 2, ll. 3, 4, *PL*, 43:25. Several stanzas of the song, the "Psalmus contra partem Donati," appear in Frederic Van der Meer, *Augustine the Bishop: The Life and Work of a Father of the Church*, 2nd ed., trans. Brian Battershaw and G. R. Lamb (London: Sheed and Ward, 1978), pp. 105–109, with the Latin in notes 129, 130, 132, 133, 136 on pp. 608–609.

⁸*CLP*, II.xiv.31-32, *NPNF* 4: 536. "'Vere viperae facti sunt, qui insontibus populis mortes morsibus vomuerunt.'…Recita illa ipsa tibi et a nobis in vos…Ecce idipsum vipereum est, non habere in ore firmamentum veritatis, sed venenum maledictionis, sicut scriptum est, 'Venenum aspidum sub labiis eorum'" (*PL*, 43:267). Augustine quotes Psalm 14:5 as found in the Septuagint. Material in single quotation marks is in italics in the original. See also *CLP*, II.xlix.114.

⁹Ibid., III.xxvii.32. My translation. "Libet autem intueri quam garrulus ea proposuerit, quasi facillime convulsurus et eversurus" (*PL*, 43:363).

¹⁰For fuller treatment of the cultural and psychological currents in Augustine's arguments for coercing the Donatists, see Sandra Lee Dixon, "The Many Layers of Meaning in Moral Arguments: A Self Psychological Case Study of Augustine's Arguments for Coercion," Ph.D. diss., University of Chicago, 1993.

¹¹*DDC*, I.iv.4, trans. D. W. Robertson, The Library of Liberal Arts (Indianapolis: Bobbs-Merrill Educational Publishing, 1958), pp. 9–10; "Frui enim est amore alicui rei inhaerere propter seipsam. Uti autem, quod in usum venerit ad id quod amas obtinendum referre, si tamen amandata est…Quomodo ergo, si essemus peregrini, qui beate vivere nisi in patria non possemus, eaque peregrinatione utique miseri et miseriam finire cupientes in patriam redire vellemus, opus esset vel terrestribus vel marinis vehiculis quibus utendum esset ut ad patriam, qua fruendum erat, pervenire valeremus; quod si amoenitates itineris, et ipsa gestatio vehiculorum nos delectaret, et conversi ad fruendum his quibus uti debuimus, nollemus cito viam finire, et perversi suavitate implicati alienaremur a patria, cujus suavitas faceret beatos: sic in hujus mortalitatis vita peregrinantes a Domino (2 Cor. V, 6), si redire in patriam volumus, ubi beati esse possimus, utendum est hoc mundo, non fruendum; ut invisibilia Dei, per ea quae facta sunt, intellecta conspiciantur (Rom. 1, 20), hoc est, ut de corporalibus temporalibusque rebus aeterna et spiritualia capiamus" (*PL*, 34:20–21).

¹²Volney Gay, "Augustine: The Reader as Selfobject," *JSSR* 25 (March 1986): 65; see also Don S. Browning, "The Psychoanalytic Interpretation of St. Augustine's *Confessions*," p. 142.

¹³*CLP*, III.x.11, III.xvii.20.

¹⁴PCPD, stanza 21, ll. 4–28; *PL*, 43:31–32.

¹⁵*AOH*, p. 177; Brown also claims, "The writing of the *Confessions* was an act of therapy" (p. 165).

¹⁶Miles helpfully expands the notion of *therapeia* (Margaret R. Miles, "Infancy, Parenting, and Nourishment in Augustine's *Confessions*," *Journal of the American Academy of Religion* 50 [September 1982]: 351). See also Andrés G. Niño, "Restoration of the Self: A Therapeutic Paradigm from Augustine's *Confessions*," *Psychotherapy* 27 (Spring 1990): 9; William B. Parsons, "St. Augustine: 'Common Man' or 'Intuitive Psychologist'?" *Journal of Psychohistory* 18 (Fall 1990): 156, 170–171; cf. Browning, "Psychoanalytic Interpretation of St. Augustine's *Confessions*," pp. 139–142; Donald Capps, "Augustine as Narcissist: Some Comments on Paul Rigby's 'Paul Ricoeur, Freudianism and Augustine's *Confessions*,'" *Journal of the American Academy of Religion* 53 (Spring 1985): 124; Paul Rigby, "Paul Ricoeur, Freudianism, and Augustine's *Confessions*," *Journal of the American Academy of Religion* 53 (Spring 1985): 93; Phillip Woollcott, Jr., "Some Considerations of Creativity and Religious Experience in St. Augustine of Hippo," *JSSR* 5 (Spring 1966): 283.

¹⁷*DDC*, I.xxvii.28., Robertson, p. 23; "qui rerum integer aestimator est…ne aut diligat quod non est diligendum, aut non diligat quod est diligendum…" (*PL*, 34:29).

¹⁸Ibid., I.xxii.21, Robertson, p. 19. "Sic enim eum diligens tanquam seipsum, totam dilectionem sui et illius refert in illam dilectionem Dei, quae nullum a se rivulum duci extra patitur, cujus derivatione minuatur…" (*PL*, 34:27).

¹⁹For similar ideas and statements, see Erik H. Erikson, *Childhood and Society*, 2nd ed. (New York and London: W. W. Norton & Company, 1963), pp. 256–258; idem, *Insight and Responsibility: Lectures on the Ethical Implications of Psychoanalytic Insight* (New York and London: W. W. Norton & Company, 1964), pp. 114–122, 152–157; idem, *Young Man Luther: A Study in Psychoanalysis and History* (New York: W. W. Norton & Company, The Norton Library, 1962), pp. 60, 69–70.

Index